Get **more** out of libraries

THE TATTERED REMNANTS

THE TATTERED REMNANTS

Eric Burgoyne

The Book Guild Ltd
Sussex, England

First published in Great Britain in 2002 by
The Book Guild Ltd
25 High Street,
Lewes, East Sussex
BN7 2LU

Typesetting in Times by
Keyboard Services, Luton, Bedfordshire

Printed in Great Britain by
Antony Rowe Ltd, Chippenham, Wiltshire

A catalogue record for this book is available from
The British Library

ISBN 1 85776 666 0

*Dedicated to
the Men
of the
British Sumatra Battalion*

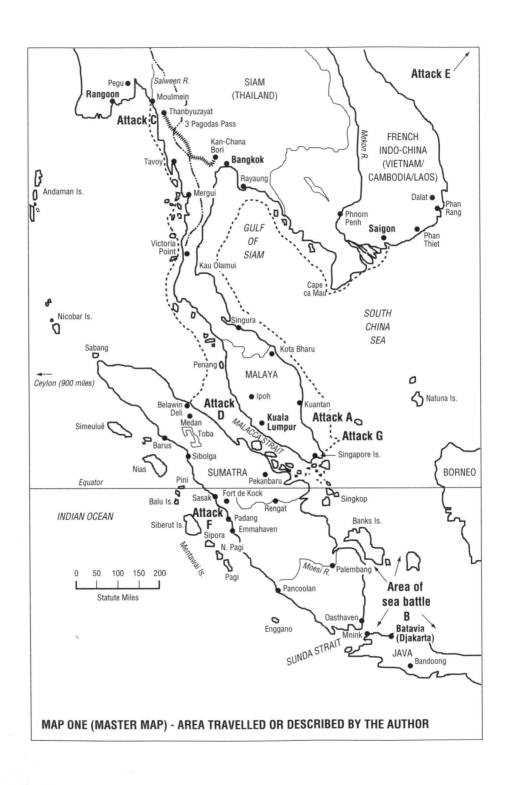

MAP ONE (MASTER MAP) - AREA TRAVELLED OR DESCRIBED BY THE AUTHOR

MAP ONE (MASTER MAP)

Legend: Japanese Air Force attack 'A' Naval battle 'B'
Attacks on POW vessels 'C' to 'G'

x-x-x- Author's sea journeys after capture*

A 10 Dec 1941 British Navy 'Force Z' – battleship *Prince of Wales*, battle-cruiser *Repulse* & escorts off Xuantan, East Malaya
The capital ships and some escorts sunk

B Feb 1942 Allied navies – 'Battle of the Java Sea'

C Mar 1943 Some survivors from 'B' – Off cruisers HMAS *Perth*; USS *Houston* & Dutch vessels – also troops stationed in Java – en route to Burma–Siam Railway. Attacked (POW transport vessel unknown) bombed near Rangoon   – 60 killed

D 26 Jan 1944 *Harikiki Maru* (ex van Waerwijk) 3,800 tons sunk by British submarine HMS *Truculent*. 724 POWs aboard
– 178 drowned

E 12 Sep 1944 *Kachidoki Maru* (10,500 tons) carrying 900 British POWs
Rakuyo Maru (9,500 tons) – 600 British plus 718 Australian
Sunk by US submarine pack. Total aboard 2,218
– 1,433 drowned

F 18 Sep 1944 *Junyo Maru* (5,500 ton freighter) carrying 1,750 POWs of mixed European nationalities, 600 Ambonese, 5,500 Javanese. Sunk by British submarine HMS *Tradewind*.
Total aboard 7,850   – 6,962 drowned

G 17 Jan 1945 See Chapter 37 for details.

Notes: Mention is made of the above in the text at the appropriate dates and further details are given in Appendix IV (Vessels). There were many other attacks on/sinkings of vessels carrying far-east POWs, some details of which are fully recorded within the Corgi publication *The Knights of Bushido* by Lord Russell of Liverpool, CBE, MC, 1960 and reprints through to 1967, first published in Cassell edition, 1958.

*Maps TWO (see over) and THREE (Chapter 8) plot his attempted escape routes.

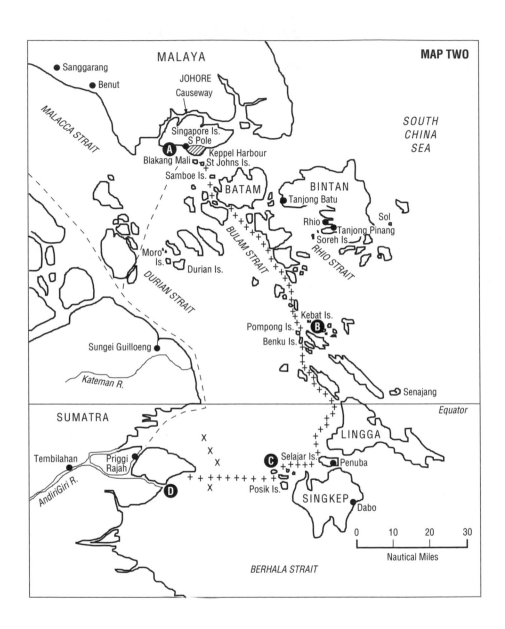

MAP TWO:

CONTENTS

PART THREE

PART FOUR

PART FIVE

PART SIX

APPENDICES

ACKNOWLEDGEMENTS

With grateful thanks to my son-in-law Denis Drinan for all his efforts to ensure that my much revised and amended typescript was expertly formatted and computerised; to my family, for their understanding of my obsession to get this account of a unique body of men completed before I 'drop off my perch'.

Also a thank-you to Janice Mullin, Emma Cummings and Peter Kent of the Photographic and Archive department of the Imperial War Museum for their help in identifying and validating items for copyright consent.

Photographs taken along the 'Organisation' escape route were rare and are now hard to come by. So, a special thank you to Stanley Saddington (one of the few of us still soldiering on) for permission to portray three from a batch which he took and successfully concealed throughout his captivity.

FOREWORD

'In my opinion the palm for enterprise at Singapore's Dunkirk goes to the small parties and even individuals who set out at short notice, with no preparation, in anything they could lay their hands on...'

Lieutenant Commander Geoffrey Brooke RN, author of *Singapore's Dunkirk* and a key co-ordinator along the 'Organisation' escape route

'This is a story of brutality told in a direct fashion that gains in impact throughout its unvarnished style. Eric Burgoyne does us a service in reminding us just how thin is the skin of civilisation.'

Richard Page, MP

PADANG – WEST SUMATRA

15 April 1942. DIRECTIVE:

From General Commanding Japanese Army HQ, SUMATRA
To Captain R A MORLEY, Commandant British POW Camp,
PADANG

You are required to supply 20 officers and 480 men to travel north for work on Railway construction. Your selection must be ready by the end of the month in order that the interpreter and my Staff Officers can discuss it with you.

9 May 1942 (Padang). The draft has been selected and the Movement Order issued.

I was standing on parade in front of 479 men with a remit to introduce myself and to straighten them out as necessary. Most of the men were ragged and bootless, many were dispirited and sullen and among those were a scattering of hard cases and troublemakers that Captain Morley had decided to offload on us. Around 300 of them were comprised of officerless Royal Navy and RAF personnel and 110 Royal Artillerymen of 30 Heavy Ack Ack unit; the remainder were men from about 20 other Army units; plus two Royal Marines and a merchant sea-man.

AND THIS IS WHAT I SAID TO THEM...

...I am Eric Burgoyne of the Royal Corps of Signals! We are

now the newly formed and self-styled British Sumatra Battalion and I consider it a great honour to have been appointed as your Battalion Sergeant Major! You will all have heard that we are going north from here today and to an unknown final destination at which we will be doing railway construction work which the Japanese Emperor has called 'the noble project of railway building'. He has also said that we are the tattered remnants of a degenerate nation. Now tattered we may be, but...

And now I must leave the rest of this story until I have related how those 500 officers and men – who left Singapore as escapees or evacuees during February 1942 – came to be standing on that parade ground as POWs two months later.

(*Note:* full details of the make-up of the British Sumatra Battalion are shown in the appendices.)

PART ONE

1

SINGAPORE – SURRENDER AND ESCAPE

20.30 hours Sunday 15 February 1942 – Singapore

I came out of 55 Brigade HQ, started up my motorcycle and drove south in the general direction of the harbour. Anywhere there would do me as long as I could get to the waterside and then – God willing – find something to float me away from this shattered island and the shame of our defeat.

It was around 20.00 hours when I took down the message that we had surrendered to General Yamashita at the Ford depot close to where we were making our last stand. There had been earlier negotiations with the threat that the McRitchie reservoir would be poisoned unless we submitted and I had asked permission to attempt an escape with anyone else who wanted to accompany me. I had been very blunt about my feelings and had told our brigadier – a one-armed veteran of the 1914–18 war – 'there is no way that I will accept being herded into captivity without first attempting to escape!' I was well and truly 'steamed up' by the bungling, lack of discipline – and even anarchy – that had been signalled through our office over the past week or two and felt a deep sense of frustration that we hadn't resisted longer.

As it turned out I needn't have been so outspoken because he said that I not only had his blessing, but he wished that he could be allowed to go too. I had been surprised enough to discover earlier that no-one else wanted to 'have a go', and even more so when it was known that the Japanese would not be occupying the city area until the next morning. That meant that even though I might fail to get away, there would be ample time left in which to rejoin our unit.

* * *

3

So there I was, alone, winding my way between craters, debris and bodies in the muggy heat of an equatorial night and with the black-out still in force. I had only the occasional glimpse of dim light to aid my progress; but the city wasn't dark! I was heading towards a distant and confusing glare coming from buildings burning un-attended by the fire brigade. Here and there I had to bounce over hoses abandoned for lack of water and dodge round fallen masonry and wrecked vehicles. The devastation was total; and after a while I could no longer be sure that I was going in the right direction.

It was just as well that I had to stop and ask the way, because I was within a few yards of a tangle of telephone wires and a toppled pole; and, amid them, there was the body of a despatch rider. He had been tripped by the wire and thrown headfirst into a wall; and it had happened so recently that the front wheel was still spinning round.

I moved on with far greater caution after that and as a result became far more aware of what was going on around me.

There were shadowy figures flitting in and out of doorways, who I guessed were mainly of civilians gathering their families and pos-sessions together (perhaps hiding them) against the uncertainties of the following day. Presumably the Chinese amongst them would be fully aware of what might be in store for *them*! Only a few hours separated them from Japanese divisions that had fought, vandalised, pillaged and raped their way through two vicious campaigns in Manchuria and whose attitude to all Chinese was, 'If you don't like the look of any of them, shoot them'!

There were also bewildered and exhausted soldiers to dodge and plenty of drunken and riotous looters creating havoc and terrorising the locals as they smashed their way into offices and shops.

Unfortunately every army has an element of scum that readily surfaces when out of reach of discipline. During the final week of combat I received reports that suspected deserters were causing trouble in the city. Some of the earlier culprits had been rounded up by the military police but more recently they had been seen roaming in gangs and, for the most part, unchecked. However, far worse than those were some well-armed and organised groups of thugs that had forced their way onto ships reserved solely for the evacuation of vulnerable citizens (civilian and services families) and nurses in charge of the wounded. To their shame the Australians were responsible for the most violent of those outrages. They shot and killed the official 'Dockmaster' for attempting to restrain them; and similar though lesser violations followed before the last evacuation vessel got away.

I was soon driving through the more dingy south-west quarter of the city. Acrid smoke was drifting into the area from blazing oil-storage tanks and go-downs (warehouses), most of which were sited on the waterfront and nearby islands. Despite the cease-fire there were still bursts of small arms fire, the racket of ammunition exploding and – strangely – the occasional thump of a heavy gun.

And so I rode on; and then – reaching the waterside – I ran into an area of darkness and quiet where I stopped, dismounted and began my search for a boat.

2

THE FIRST LINK IN MY GOLDEN CHAIN

22.30 hours

When I was a lad my elder brothers were so convinced that I was lucky that they said, 'Eric, if you ever fell down a sewer you would be bound to surface with a gold chain round your neck!' I have no recollection of ever being *that* lucky then, but I would soon be catching up with a combination of fate, calculated chance-taking – and luck – that would see me safely through the next three-and-a-half years!

I had only walked about a hundred yards along the quayside before seeing four men crouching below and pulling at the gunwale of a sampan that had drifted in and jammed under the harbour wall.* That was my first bit of luck, because they had just happened upon it without having any prior intention to escape. So, all I had to do was assert rank and my ability to handle a boat, and then to organise things for the 'off'.

What a relief it was to have found a boat instead of having to steal one. That would have definitely involved confrontation and might have alerted some of the undesirables that I had seen earlier; but I did have other problems though.

While preparing to leave HQ my intentions were to travel light, alone, and to live off the land in the same manner as most of the Japanese army had done when dashing south through Malaya. So apart from what I was wearing and my weapons – a .38 revolver and a few hand grenades – I had packed only what extra food, clothes and personal items that could be contained either within my side-pack and pockets or added to my webbing equipment; but now I had others who were totally unprepared to think about.

---

*We were by the dockside within Keppel Harbour but I didn't know it at the time!

A quick examination of the sampan had shown that the total contents were some short lengths of rope, a battered baling tin and two long sweeps which – thank God – were safely housed inboard. Our priorities were for a lot more rations than I had packed, some water containers and any bits of timber that might be used for seating and serve as a temporary rudder. The four men didn't know me from Adam! So, in order to gain their trust, I sent two of them off to make a half-an-hour search further up the harbour side while the other two were kept where they could keep an eye on the sampan – *and me* – while we searched nearby. They were told to keep a low profile and I promised them that I would not cast off until all five of us were together again.

Although we did our best to keep quiet, the distant searchers were heard and they returned with six well-equipped and genuine escapers in tow who had asked to join us.

I was only too glad to have the extra manpower of men like that and gladly welcomed them aboard. Then, having stowed our gear and the gleanings from the dockside, we were about to cast off when two more escapers appeared above us and asked if they could come.

I went up to question them and discovered that they were army Pay Corps lieutenants carrying satchels which – they said – contained packs of high-value notes; but they could give me no convincing story of how they had come by them. After some discussion I agreed to have them aboard but only on the three conditions that they would forget rank, accept me as leader and – most importantly – say nothing to the others about the money. They agreed! So, on they came and we once again prepared to leave.

The sampan was about 18 feet long, $4\frac{1}{2}$ feet wide and it had an unladen freeboard of about 2 feet. Despite the considerable laden weight it was to prove quite stable – even when anyone moved about – provided that they kept to the middle and ducked between positions. As for stowage, there was nothing more than a few square feet of decked-over strutting at each end.

It was fortunate that only a few weeks earlier when sailing up to Singapore I had watched how the boatmen handled their craft. Most of them had a crew of two, one of whom stood in the middle pulling on and rotating two sweeps in front of his chest, while the other used a third sweep to steer and assist progress from the rear. Well, I had a 'make-do' piece of timber for our rudder, so my only concern was how best to use our two lengthy and heavy sweeps for rowing 'western style'.

Even a skilled local boatman would have found it impossible to go both fast and far with our load aboard using his method, so the question was, 'how must we row?' I decided that two men would have to kneel at each sweep facing each other while one pushed and the other pulled and – at each stroke – one sweep must be passed over the other. A further problem was that most of the crew had no more experience of boating than an occasional trip round a boating pool with their girlfriend; and none of them had done any sailing.

There were some open recesses and pegs along the gunwale which would later have to be adapted for use by both methods but, as a temporary measure, we lashed across the pegs with the bits of rope and tied the loose ends to the sweeps to contain them and to prevent their loss overboard. Then the oarsmen took station kneeling on whatever padding they could contrive and we were ready for 'the off'!

However, the sampan had other ideas. As soon as we started to pull, it dipped sideways at the stern as if anchored – *which it was in fact*, and in a gruesome way! A taut rope led downward from the sternpost and when I tugged it, the body of a Sikh broke clear from within the staging and floated towards me. Perhaps *he* had been shot while stealing the sampan? We would never know, of course, but – for whatever reason – he hadn't been long in the water, because his turban was still in place.

I unravelled the rope and we at last made headway – albeit erratically. Many 'crabs' were caught and explicit oaths exchanged when knuckles crashed together; and, despite heaving on the rudder, I was finding it impossible to steer a straight course. In the end – crazy as it may seem – I had to stop there in the middle of the harbour to conduct a 'tutorial'. After that it was 'in, pull, out and back' for the next hour or so until they finally got the hang of it.

We knew that the mouth of the harbour was mined because the pilot had had to dodge some mines when we brought 18 Div in. However, in our wooden and shallow-draft vessel that was the least thing for any of us to worry about. My chief concern was that we must land somewhere soon to have it decked over with camouflage, the sweeps adapted and get disguises for myself and the oarsmen; and it was while I was thinking about that that I realised that my oil-filled army compass must have slipped from its webbing pouch when I leant out to free up the stern.

My intention had been to go west from the harbour, head directly for Sumatra and then 'hedge-hop' south along its vast coastline – hiding during daylight – down to Java. However, one of the crew was adamant that we could more quickly turn south if we set off east. So, once clear of the harbour we got moving that way between Singapore and Pulau Brani; and, fortunately, he was correct.*

We were now rowing steadily along and constantly aware of the inferno to port which was releasing thick black smoke across the strait, enshrouding us and blotting out an otherwise clear sky. We neither met anyone nor heard anything, other than the continuing sound of explosions in the city. There was plenty of time for talking and thinking, though, and mostly it was about our hopes and – of course – the fate of the thousands of our men still left on the island who would be shortly rounded up and put into POW camps.

I was also thinking of my alleged luck and the number 13! Having been born on the thirteenth of August I had always defied superstition and considered the number lucky. Well, I had suddenly realised that we had a crew of 13 – three shifts of oarsmen – which could allow plenty of rest from aching knees and blistering hands. However, it was going to be more about my experience of 'mucking about in boats' that was going to help me now; and that began when I was a nine-year-old living in Hackney.

We were a family of seven and until 1926, we five children had rarely enjoyed any holidays other than one day excursions to Southend. Then my grandfather retired to nearby Thorpe Bay and became friendly with the three Bryant brothers who each ran day-tripping yachts; and that was when our *real* holidays began. Throughout three long summer holidays my two brothers and I were allowed aboard to 'crew'. I only rarely took the helm but learnt

* When I was able to look at an atlas three weeks later I could see that the western route would have confined us close to Singapore and on the only (and busy) shipping lane that the Japanese must use for taking troops and materials through the Malacca Strait to Burma.

9

quite a lot about sailing. Then – about a year later – when my mother was ill, I was sent to live with my grandmother in Kidlington, near Oxford, to attend the village school. During three terms I made full use of the family 'right' to fish and go boating on the river Cherwell. Later still, when I was about 15 years old, I cycled over to Windsor to join an older cousin and live on his boat while we rowed up to Oxford. He was an expert oarsman having won several 'firsts' in prestigious events on the Thames and it was he who taught me the most about handling boats, including the tricky business of rowing a skiff.

Well those were my useful bits of experience, and now for my bit of luck!

Only nine weeks before Singapore fell, 18 Div was aboard British troopships anchored off Nova Scotia. We had arrived there after dusk and during the night we were covertly trans-shipped to two United States troopships – the *Mount Vernon* and *West Point* – which were converted cruise liners. Everything had to be 'hush hush' because the US – although supposed to be entirely neutral – was helping us make a quick turn round of our diminishing merchant fleet.

I was on the *Mount Vernon* and, apart from inheriting their crew, we had a few American citizens aboard, one of whom was a young astronomer. It was said that he was off on a spy mission, which was no doubt true because I was ordered to give him a crash course on Morse code signalling. He was very friendly, and in return he taught me how to recognise stars and how to use them for navigation. What luck that was! How could I have known then that I was learning a skill that would be vital for our escape only nine weeks later now that my compass was lost.

3

THE SECOND GOLDEN LINK

Monday 16 February

At about 2 a.m. there were flickers of light to starboard and turning towards them I saw the outline of St Johns Island. We landed, tied up alongside a roughly fashioned slipway and walked up to discover that we were bang in the middle of a leper colony.

Most of the patients were awake and sitting on ringside seats from which – for many weeks – they had watched the comings, goings, bombings and other happenings in Singapore and on the waters around them. This night was special, of course. It was the final act; and they were watching the death throes of their city, the end of one form of Imperial rule and the advent – with all the uncertainties – of another.

My first thoughts were 'God help you' and 'Who will provide you with food and medicine now?' Many of them couldn't even rise to return our greeting.

None of us could speak more than a few words of Malay but their superintendent – a missionary, I believe – spoke passable English and, once told our needs, he took over. We knew that a canopy was standard on most sampans and he said that he had both the craftsmen and the materials available to fit one and to modify the rowing position – and that there would be no charge.

Most of the materials had been deposited on St Johns as the flotsam and jetsam from crippled and sunken evacuation boats (many of which had been targeted before they had left Singapore harbour), and we were given another sweep, some canvas and a lifeboat flagmast from the accumulated wreckage.

There was surely nowhere else where we could have got better, quicker and more willing help than there; and moreover, in the middle of the night. It was more than a matter of luck, it was a miracle that within three hours of our arrival, we were ready to leave having been fed, given the 'leftovers', all the utensils used, two large water containers, dry rations (rice and dahl) and the sarongs and coolie-style hats that we needed for our disguise.

It was about two hours before dawn when we said our farewells, leaving most of the lepers still sitting above resuming their vigil. All of us had plenty to reflect on – they, far more than us, having watched the 'contest' from the start.

They would have been astounded by the Japanese blitzkrieg tactics which within three days of their seventh of December attack on Pearl Harbour saw them securing a foothold in north Malaya and sinking the battleship *Prince of Wales* and the cruiser *Repulse*.

They would have seen those vessels sail proudly in to port and then, barely one week later, heard that they had gone north from the Naval Base to be annihilated off east Malaya in a massive and unopposed aerial torpedo attack. What an ill-conceived sacrifice that was! They were sent up there with an inadequate escort and virtually no air cover, just 'to show the flag'! Then (as if that hadn't been enough attrition) one week later, our regular divisions were forced into making a staged retreat from Kuala Lumpur down to a new defence line in Johore. Allied planes were few and mainly outdated, and the overworked pilots that survived the often suicidal combat were soon being evacuated. They were sent 300 miles south to defend oilfields at Palembang (Sumatra) – the prime target of the Japanese campaign! (By comparison with their need for fuel, Singapore was only a necessary side-issue.)

Most readers will already know that the land-based 15-inch naval guns were traversed to fire from south Singapore right across the island and onto Jahore – the bombardment commenced when the last of our troops had retreated across the Causeway. However, few readers will know that General Yamashita's divisions took so much punishment that they were on the point of withdrawing to regroup when the guns ceased firing, some from lack of ammunition and others due to over-heating.

I know how terrifying it is to be on the wrong end of 15-inch shell fire. In September 1940 I was with an army Signals unit attached to Royal Marine Commando signalmen aboard the battle-ship *Barham*. We were 'control' for British and Free French commando signal detachments on three accompanying troopships and had trained for a night assault (via the Thies Peninsula) into the rear of Dakar, Senegal – a Vichy-French stronghold! However, all secrecy had already been compromised ten days earlier when – prior to flying out to join us – General de Gaulle, at a banquet in England, had openly toasted to what he called 'the success of the Dakar incident'! Because of that bit of crass stupidity the *Barham*, the *Resolution*, their escorts and the troopships could all have been sunk. In the event, the Vichy-French – forewarned – engaged us with submarine and surface vessels, planes, shore batteries and with the formidable assistance of their battleship *Richelieu*. The latter was grounded in the harbour but brought all her guns to bear.

We managed to withdraw the troopships unscathed but then, had to 'slug it out' in a naval battle during which the *Resolution* took two torpedoes and the *Barham* was forced to heave-to, rig a tow and pull her clear. While all that was going on '15 inch expresses' from the *Richelieu* were whizzing past us.

What a fiasco that was – just like the *Prince of Wales* incident – and now we were right in the middle of another unnecessary sacrifice.*

It was because of our commitments at home and in the Middle East that support for us was little and came too late.

For instance, it was *already* too late when 18 Div arrived to be bombed at the dockside. We had been sent on from India in the 'Yankee' vessels to reinforce more recent untrained and unbloodied arrivals committed to the same lost cause. We were hastened out of the dock gates in our deck slippers without vehicles or heavy equipment – much of which had already been smashed or sunk within other vessels – and marched over the Causeway to support our Australian, British and Indian troops with their steady retreat.

During the two weeks that followed until the surrender, the lepers

*Message from Rear-Admiral Cunningham to commander *Resolution*: 'Hard luck old man! I see that you have been hit for six! Better innings next time!' The *Resolution* was patched up in Freetown harbour, taken to the US and overhauled. The *Barham* was eventually attacked in the Mediterranean and sunk by a German submarine with the loss of 962 officers and men.

on St Johns would have seen unopposed formations of 27, 54 and once, 81 Japanese planes drift over the island and pattern-bomb it with high-fragmentation bombs. The attrition – particularly among the civilians in the city – was only exceeded by the numbers of 'essential' civilian, Army and RAF evacuees who could have survived if they had been sent away earlier.

Having been thrown back off the mainland and before the Japanese invaded, 55 Brigade were regrouping in woodland north of Sembawang when we were infiltrated by three kamikaze soldiers. They lashed themselves to the upper branches of trees and stayed put until detected and shot. It was calculated suicide, but they had scored two for one for their emperor before we got them; and, in their philosophy, the odds were totally acceptable.

It was not a happy thought, therefore, that some of their equally dedicated compatriots would soon be out and looking for us. We had no illusions about the sadistic capabilities of their army. They had overrun the Indian Military hospital and massacred everyone including the surgeons while operating. My view of them – fuelled by the avid reading of comics in my youth – was that they were skilled in, and ready to use, all forms of torture. That – for most of them – was true and, coupled with their fanatical belief in a god emperor and their militaristic cult, it made for a very nasty enemy.

The fact that they were also brave, adaptable, highly mobile, equipped with some weapons that were superior to ours and had outmanoeuvred us was also beyond question.

06.30 hours 16 February

It was no use dwelling on such things any longer. Dawn was coming up and we had to think of today.

All gloom was dispelled when I decided to don my sarong. I must leave you to imagine the jokes and amorous advances that were directed my way. Once the crew had settled down and I put on the coolie hat, I would have passed for the real thing at more than just a casual glance, except, that is, for my lily white arms. They stood out like beacons because, being red-haired and freckled, I took great care to keep out of the sun. However, someone came up with the bright idea of covering my arms with a filthy mixture of mud and heaven knows what else, which they scooped up from the bilge.

We had kept close to land on the starboard to begin with, but it began to slant away to the south and then – easing round a head-land – we were soon into open water. I decided to keep going that way and when the first island showed up, to hide there and move on again after dark.

Everything was serene out there with no sound from any direction and with no other craft in sight. We were naturally keeping a good lookout towards Singapore and couldn't believe our luck that nothing was moving in that direction either.

Although that seemed rather strange at the time, I now know that the Japanese had not only been exhausted but also celebrating their victory.

I was now steering south-west heading for Samboe Island. We were still well within the focus of anyone using binoculars from east Singapore so, before visibility improved, I had replaced the four oarsmen with just the one, dressed as I was and using the sweeps in 'eastern mode'.

This period of inaction and calm couldn't be expected to last much longer – nor did it! While still looking that way, we saw an aeroplane making height above Kallang civilian airport. It circled and then moved off over Keppel Harbour to make a sweep over the strait and the islands off east Sumatra. There was some firing, probably on some of the smaller pre-surrender evacuation craft that had been wrecked on exposed sandbanks and were now sitting targets for follow-through attacks. Within about half an hour the pilot had changed course, drifted across the strait and returned to home.

We were greatly relieved that he had come no nearer to us and I took the calculated risk of reverting to Western mode and upping the stroke.

The pilot must have been assigned a regular patrol because, about one hour later, he came up again and – taking far less interest in the west – criss-crossed the waters we had travelled the previous night (to the west of St Johns), to search inlets that by now were out of our sight. It was a sector by sector search and before he came our way we were in eastern mode again – which was just as well!

When he reappeared it became obvious that we were the next in line for a 'look-see' when the plane dropped low over the water and came up astern.

It didn't take a lot of imagination to sense the gun-sights boring into my back. I felt the sweat oozing from my body as I continued waggling the sweep. It was our disguise that must have saved us from attack. Most of what the pilot might otherwise have seen – the other 11 men under the canopy – was in deep shadow. Imagine our relief, when – without making a second pass – he went back to Kallang again.

Two hours later when we were within 200 yards of Samboe Island, up he popped once more and without any preliminaries, came hounding down behind us again and seemed even more menacing than before. He reached us just as we hit the shore and we two – shaking like jellies – jumped out as casually as possible in the circumstances, while the others remained concealed. He swept up and over us and then disappeared behind some trees.

We then moved very fast indeed! Everyone else jumped out and helped to heave the sampan up the beach and out of sight.

We had to be lucky that there was no backup by the assault craft that had been used for the invasion of Singapore. They had been moved into the Malacca strait in preparation for the invasion of Sumatra. Nevertheless, it had all been rather hairy; so we kept everyone out of sight for the rest of the day.

It was time for taking stock before we moved on that night. We had enough food to keep us going for three or four nights of strenuous rowing. Water wasn't going to be much of a problem – except that it would always have to be boiled. We also had the prospect of collecting rain now that the pre-monsoon showers had set in. I had discounted all ideas of stealing food unless desperation drove us to such ends. Stealing would rebound on us in animosity – and the certainty that some who were robbed would have embraced the new 'era of Co-Prosperity' and, would inform the Japanese. That proved to be a wise decision because, unknown to us at the time, the 'long knives' were already out against Europeans within some factions along our intended route.

All in all night travel would be our ally. We need only approach the locals when it suited us, we could always row with a team of

16

four, and avoid the certainty of dehydration and sunburn that would arise from being in the open at the equator all day.

Hygiene was next on my list and in particular the matter of what one of my companions called 'testing our dropping gear'. Well no-one had boarded with a 12-pack of Bronco but we had soap and an ocean of water.

Then there were the strengths and weaknesses of the crew to consider. These had mostly been self-evident already, and the men had responded to our circumstances well. The only thing that bugged me was the two lieutenants. They were – and they still remain – an enigma to me. During the only private discussion that I can remember having with them on the subject, they said that 'their' money was given them with the order to get it off the island out of reach of the Japanese. This may have been how it was; but I remain convinced that they had an eye to personal gain without any question of accountability later. Whatever the truth may have been, I set great store on protocol, so I made sure that they were perceived as having some influence in the decisions that I made despite their being unconvincing and totally devoid of initiative. So much for that!

It was nearly sunset – time to leave – and I had already marked the east–west line by the sun. During the day we had seen the faint outline of an island about 12 miles off to the south-west; so, as soon as the stars appeared, I made a projection and off we went. It was a clear night, making it simple to stay on course, but I realised that cloudy nights would give me problems.

We arrived at about 05.00 hours. Seven hours of steady rowing was enough for one night so we went ashore, recced and holed up for the day.

We went through the same routine the following night but went further. Arriving at about 05.00 hours, we spotted a fisherman about a hundred yards off – shrouded in the pre-dawn gloom and moving out for an early start. As he left he hailed us. I waved back in distant salutation while replying with a lot of gobbledegook that must have sounded to him like a constipated Chinaman trying to lay an egg. We had no wish to make contact, so as soon as he had moved well away, I changed course, making for the other side of the island, found good cover and checked around. Our recce party went back to the other side and returned to report that the boatman had stopped to fish for a while and then moved right off and out of sight behind an islet. So, we stayed, ate, slept and lounged around for the rest of the day.

Perhaps this is the right time to dispel the romantic idea that a typical tropical island is one solely of swaying palm trees, an abundance of luscious fruit, golden beaches and beautiful sunsets. We soon discovered that the most predictable things were hosts of insects that had been created to bite, nip, or otherwise torment all visitors; and they worked in shifts! Mosquitoes and unidentifiable torturers had the monopoly after dark. Sandflies were active – as were enormous ants – all day; and most of them were after a ration of blood; but there *were* beautiful sunsets!

4

HEADING FOR DANGER AND A VERY LUCKY THIRD LINK

It was the eighteenth of February and we were still resting up ready for the next night's journey. All had gone well during the day. There had been no alarms but there had been time to regret having missed the opportunity to buy some of that lone fisherman's catch. I had hand grenades and we had seen some sizeable fish close inshore, but fishing by that method would be a last option. We had been very lucky so far; everything had remained tranquil and we wished it to stay that way. However, tomorrow was going to bring a surprise or two and there was a momentum afoot which was going to draw us into great danger. Fortunately, I suppose, the days of the transistor radio were yet to come, so we were spared all news of the ongoing mayhem along the Singapore–Java shipping lane. It transpired that during the previous two weeks the Japanese had had total domination – by sea and air – over the whole of our escape route and were currently securing all the territory as well. We all knew that movement on these waters had been dangerous for the past month or two and that the hazards had been increasing by the day until the climax on the night of the fourteenth/fifteenth when the last of the official evacuation boats had left to run the gauntlet down through the straits. So sufficient unto the day just to know that we were nightly rowing through bits of wreckage that had housed so many hopeful escapers, who had been variously bombed, blitzed, chased and bayoneted.

We had christened our sampan *Arse End Charlie* since we were one of the last boats of any description out of Singapore and certainly the very last of any that were rowed out. Our late departure had been helpful in some respects since nothing like us would have been expected to be moving down that way so late in the day.

19

Because of that, we had also been spared having to witness the sight of those larger boats being smashed to pieces and the resultant human carnage, not to mention the agonising decisions that would have had to be made about how many people we could save before leaving the rest to drown.

(03.00 on the 19th)

We had started our night journey just before midnight and had reckoned that a general south of west course should fetch us up among a group of small islands somewhere around dawn, where we might surprise another lone fisherman before moving into cover. It must have been around 03.00 hours when we ran up close to a small islet. Reckoning that it was too early to stop there and that in any case it would not afford us much cover, we decided to move on. Feeling quite safe, I suppose we had made more noise than usual, and I was startled when hailed in English by two men stranded beside a holed and oarless dinghy. As I recall, they were RAF ground staff who – after having been bombed off an evacuation launch – had swum to this place and stayed there for three days without food and with just one bottle of water between them.

They were lucky to have heard us because no-one else would be following us! It turned out that we were beyond the eastern limit of an official escape and rescue body known as 'the Organisation', which had been set up a few months earlier *in expectation of* the fall of Singapore. It was now funding and provisioning local headmen to search out, direct and give succour to all escapers – and survivors from attacks – who were expected to arrive on their shores cold, starving and, in so many cases, badly injured.

It would have been invaluable for chancers like us to have known that. I knew our brigadier well enough to know that if he had been told about it, he would have told me. Even though it might have been restricted information prior to surrender, he wouldn't have retained it on the 'old boy network' after that. As it turned out I probably wouldn't have gone that way anyway, but it would have been nice to have the option!

Our two castaways had started off that way, and at one stage they had sailed through the aftermath and carnage of an attack and sinking of a large evacuation vessel which had had civilians and nurses tending wounded men aboard. They were still on the jump about what they had seen.

So, we now had a complement of 15 aboard – including the two wolfing down some of our cold rations on the hoof.

There was one more surprise in store for us that night and in one respect it was a welcome one. Finding a likely island in time, we had grounded, come ashore and even started to unload, before we discovered a small boat drawn in under a tangle of foliage within about 20 feet of our own; and shortly after that we saw the owners.

They were two unprepossessing characters who looked both villainous and furtive, and it was obvious that they would have slipped away if they could have got to their boat unnoticed. They had been fishing and had taken a good catch. We had surprised *them* as they were finishing a meal; and they *us*, because their fire had been raked out for grilling! Even if we had known about the helpful natives mentioned above, there were all the signs that these two were not members of the Salvation Army. We could sense their hostility despite our offer to buy the rest of their catch.

Perhaps it was our strength and the sight of my revolver that persuaded them to part up, because we didn't menace them in any way. However, we were bloody hungry and they would have soon realised that we were in no mood to be refused.

They were quite obviously eager to leave and hasten off to announce our presence to all. So, I acted out a little drama of enquiring the way to Java and made as though to resurrect the embers for cooking our fish. With that, they took themselves off and headed in the direction that they had pointed out to me. That made us all the more suspicious that they were well outside the rescue and goodwill category! As soon as they were out of sight, we broke camp, went aboard and made for an island that *was* along our intended route; and, once there, prepared our most satisfying meal since leaving the leper colony.

By blotting out thoughts of danger and of our hand-to-mouth existence there were times when you could be persuaded that our life was idyllic. And this was one of them. Our stomachs were full and we had been under no great threat since the first night, so lying there in the shade, and although being a bit scruffy and unshaven, I for one felt perfectly at ease. After all, we were young, fit and

21

mostly sufficiently adventurous to make joking comparisons with our scouting days. Despite my overall responsibilities it did not take too much to make me contented. My pipe, matches and several ounces of a mixture of St Bruno Flake and Rough Cut took care of that. If I had any worry at all it was the suspicion that we had been carried by the tide a few miles further south than I would have wished during the last day or two. Our enforced night travel had also caused some navigational problems. There had been times when I had a stiff neck and nearly went boss-eyed in my endeavour to track across from one guiding star to another and then lock onto it before the previous one became obscured. Although I was occasionally relieved, the overall responsibility was mine; and it was a very wearing experience.

On the night of the nineteenth we set off on what turned out to be two totally uneventful days except for an increasing awareness of our hunger, and by the evening of the twentieth we had used up all that remained of our reserves. So, by the following evening we would either have to find more food or start fishing with grenades – or so we thought! But it didn't turn out to be quite as bad as that because our next island provided us with some fruit and a fair selection of shellfish which just about satisfied the pangs. I discovered then – and was glad to use the knowledge later – that by smoking my pipe I could forget about hunger to some extent, and there was a bonus too: the mosquitoes didn't seem to fancy the smell of tobacco. Apart from that I had a normal young man's healthy appetite and never did develop into what I called a 'fag for breakfast wallah'.

The following day we hunted for shellfish and one of our number found a palm cabbage which not only held some good drinking water within it but also proved to be quite palatable. So once again no grenades were used, but we were getting increasingly hungry. It was with great relief that just before dawn on the twenty-second we came in close to a large island with all the sounds and signs of habitation about it.

Pulling into the shelter of a small inlet, we landed to recce while taking great care to stay under cover. Nothing was found in one direction; but setting off the other way we soon arrived at the edge of sparse scrub; and then, looking through some trees, we were surprised to see a post displaying a foreign flag; and close to that, there was a huddle of shacks. It was quite reassuring to discover that the flag was not of the dreaded Japanese 'fried egg' variety and we guessed that it must be Dutch. Then we surprised one of the inhabitants. He confirmed that it was a Dutch island and helped us to bring the sampan round closer to the huts. Dawn was just about breaking as we beached it some 30 yards below them. They were a dilapidated cluster of three comprising a watermen's café, a barber's shop and a store full of fishing gear. Although this seemed to be the main beaching point, no other boats were there. That suited our purpose well because all we wanted was a quick meal, a chance to clean ourselves and shave, and to buy some provisions; and all those things appeared to be available there without the hindrance of any distractions.

The various proprietors began to arrive and coffee was provided for all. A meal of rice and fish was ordered and while it was being prepared some of us booked into the barber's chair. More inhabitants were arriving from across a *padang* (Malay for a common field) to the rear and one of them was sent back to fetch the 'boss'. He appeared within minutes and – to our surprise – he was an immaculately dressed Dutch *Controleur*; and then, almost immediately after that, our idyllic world started to collapse about us!

5

THE LINK THAT NEARLY SNAPPED

No proper introductions had been made and we hadn't had time to find out where we were, when one of the locals drew our attention to the bow waves of three motorised craft approaching from about a mile off to the north; and if any of us needed confirmation that they carried Japanese, it soon came with the arrival of mortars.

Within moments I decided to leave the sampan – which was totally exposed to their fire – and cut and run for it in the hope of picking up another. An immediate vote was taken which resulted in four others agreeing to accompany me. The others wished to stay with the *Controleur*, who had persuaded them – and himself – that he would be able to safely surrender them under the protection of his flag.

It was only then that I thought of the officers' money – and found that they hadn't had the wit to bring their satchels ashore. So, dashing down to the sampan, I came back with them and more or less demanded some of the money to aid our escape.

There was barely enough time to register the looks of astonishment on seeing that hoard before I was up and running in pursuit of the other four.

We had about 300 yards of fairly open land to cross before we could reach the protection of trees. Although the mortaring had ceased as the landing craft neared, an aeroplane could be seen hounding in for a low-level attack. It was then – while I was shouting to warn the others – that I caught sight of the closest of them haring along with one side of his face as bald as a badger's arse and the other bearded and covered with soap. Despite our laughter, we still managed the last stretch at a speed that would have delighted my school sportsmaster. Thankfully, we were soon into cover and all firing ceased. None of the Japanese landing party were following us, so, after slowing down, we finally stopped on meeting an ancient Chinese couple.

They were quite agitated and it didn't need me to tell them the Nipponese had arrived. After all, they could have hardly escaped the sight or knowledge of the destruction that followed the Japanese naval blockade; and now, their worst enemy was right in amongst them!

Unfortunately we had little time for consolation. I was soon urgently miming our need for food, drawing the outline of a boat in the dust and showing them our money.

Despite their own worries, their help for us was immediate. We were beckoned along the path to their dilapidated dwelling and the old lady fetched us out two rusty and unlabelled tins. The old man then took us up a side-path and along some faint tracks leading down to the shoreline, and finally up again into a well hidden clearing which contained a hut and a pool. Then, with two sweeps of a hand to show that he would be back during the evening of the next day, he was off!

It was an ideal hideout. Even the most diligent search wouldn't have discovered it except by chance. However, there we would have to stay for at least 36 hours, far from being optimistic, up the creek without a paddle and starving. It did nothing to improve our mood either when, after contemplating the fate of the others, we heard shots from the direction of the *padang*. Then, just to make matters worse, we had to retreat into the hut due to a torrent of rain like stair-rods that lasted well into the night.

We stayed huddled together for hours while being invaded by mosquitoes, sleeping fitfully and, – of course – talking of the day's events and our prospects for further escape. We were bloody ravenous by then and it didn't do to think too much about the meal that was being prepared for us when the Japanese arrived.

They had captured our only tin-opener, so we had to chance making a noise when bashing into the tins. We were into pineapple, and the reward of about eight small chunks each!

It was a nasty experience sitting there and speculating on whether we had heard the others being executed or not. I thought so (although it has never been fully confirmed) and was also sure that if we had been overtaken while still at sea, that we would have been shot without mercy.

We reckoned that we had already rowed about 90 miles and it

baffled me that the others had been so easily persuaded to surrender after coping so well for several nights. It was agreed that we must be on a fairly large island to have warranted a resident *Controleur* and a permanent flag; also, that he must have been forewarned to have dressed so appropriately early in the morning.* We didn't talk of surrender at all! Instead we had decided that if the Chinese didn't find us a sampan when promised, we would have to steal one – and food – and then chance a crossing of what we guessed to be about 35 miles to east Sumatra. That would have to be attempted sometime anyway, but I preferred that it should be done at a time of my choosing and not under duress.

None of us were 'gung-ho' characters, so I ruled for our safety that we must make do without a fire, smoking or going down to the shore to look for shellfish. It was fortunate that we had remained spooked by the closeness of the Japanese because around mid-morning we heard one of the landing craft starting up. Within a matter of minutes it was clear of the inlet and moving through a channel between our 'hide' and a sandbank. It passed within a few yards of us with two crew aboard who were chatting and laughing as if they were out on a jaunt. They probably were, because it was not long before they returned and stayed put for the rest of the day; and that was reassuring in a peculiar way. It would appear that either they didn't know – or perhaps, didn't care – that we had taken to our heels before they had landed. Nevertheless we were not about to chance anything so we stayed put and tried our luck at fishing in the pool. The pounding rain had stirred it up and excited some tiny fish into darting about hunting for food. They were inquisitive and voracious little beggars, reminding me of the wrasse that used to steal my bait when I fished off Southend pier.

We rigged up lines from the repair kit in our army 'hussifs' and in less than an hour we had garnered the lot. It would be wrong to claim that we caught them! They committed hara-kiri by frantically throwing themselves at an unidentified cocktail of wriggly things that we found at the edge of the pool; and, within a few minutes they were cleaned, gutted and eaten raw.

The rest of the day seemed endless and the second night of waiting even worse – if that were possible. At around five o'clock, when it was still quite dark, we were startled by the sound of two Malays

*I have since guessed that we were on one of the southern islands in the Bulan Strait.

26

calling quietly from the shore. Then the old Chinese man – who was already waiting hidden nearby – stepped forward with gifts of food wrapped in leaves. They had obviously needed to be secretive but it did nothing for our nerves – or pride – to admit that had they been Japanese, we would have already been dead. They were very brave to have put their own lives on the line, particularly the old man, who later refused any reward.

We went down to the shore and, despite the half-light, it was easy to see that we were not being offered the pick of the fleet. It was another sampan, without seating or canopy. However, it was furnished with three sweeps, the bilge was dry and, there was an unexpected bonus of a scrap of canvas – albeit there was nothing on which it could be rigged.

I had been given 2,200 dollars and my first offer was 1,000. We haggled up to 1,300, at which figure the old man gave me the nod. There would have been no point in bargaining further. The Malays had the advantage anyway! I paid them but with the warning that they must not go flashing the notes around. I did that by pointing to the serial numbers, holding one close to my face; then, looking away and saying 'Nippon'. I screwed it up and rubbed it in the dirt. I was pleased with that bit of mime! The old man got the message straight away and – as far as I could see – made the Malays understand it also, because they mimed back their belief that the rest of our party had been shot and, if that were so, the Japanese would be holding notes with numbers sequential to ours.

The Malays then left us but the old man stayed for a bit. He was delighted when he saw us sampling some of the food. For his own safety we didn't say anything of our further plans for escape. We didn't 'talk' much anyway!

How could we have properly thanked a stranger who – although he couldn't speak our language – had put his own life in danger to save ours and, moreover, without any wish for reward? I never saw him again but I have never forgotten our debt to him and his wife. My hope is that they have been (as I believe that they would have wished) and remain happily reunited with their ancestors!

As soon as he left we rowed across the channel, pulled the sampan beneath a fringe of shrubbery and camouflaged the gaps. There wasn't much cover over there – in fact far less than we had thought –

27

and we had to make do for ourselves by kicking out scrapes; and once it was light we had to lie in them for the rest of the day. We even had to relieve ourselves in that position. It was a terrible but necessary experience! We were in the only position where we were able to look north into the inlet to see what the Japanese were up to, as well as south beyond a headland to get a bearing on a likely refuge for the following day.

We had food and also plenty of water – the night of continuous rain had taken care of that – and thank heavens, I had a camouflaged gas-cape to share around for protection from the sun. It was suffocating but at least we didn't fry.

Around mid-morning a boatman came out to fish and he stayed opposite us for a couple of hours. I had been worried that our sampan might be visible at the waterline but, if it had been, he would surely have come over to investigate. We couldn't have done anything about it anyway. It was reassuring though because, shortly after he left, one of the landing craft went by and – as on the previous day – returned to base without making a search.

We had gambled correctly! The Japanese wouldn't be expecting to find five idiots still close to their base after having 48 hours' start!

From then on everything went to plan – except our continuing discomfort.

It was about 9 o'clock and quite dark when we uncovered the sampan and muffled the oars. I did the first bit of rowing. Slowness didn't matter but stealth was essential and I knew that I not only could, but *must*, do the job on my own.

My feeling was that since I had got us into this mess, I should get us out beyond the headland and into deeper water before handing over to the others. We had ten less crew aboard, of course, and no cladding, but we would need a lot more food before we could do heavy rowing again. The lack of a canopy would in fact prove to be a blessing in many ways. It would lessen the weight, give us an almost invisible silhouette and, if it rained, we would welcome a few showers to keep us cool.

6

THE CHAIN BEGINS TO HANG TOGETHER AGAIN

Just before dawn on the twenty-fifth things began to pick up again. It all started when – shortly after landing – we ran smack into the middle of three Malays. There now seemed to be more people about on the islands as we moved further south, so I suppose a few encounters were going to be inevitable. This meeting turned out to be a very welcome and essential one for us. We had known that we would soon have to find some food, or starve; and they had got it in great variety. They had arrived in some kind of trading craft, were open for barter or purchase and, better still, they were not too frightened by the sight of high-value notes. Once we had taken the precaution of hiding both of our boats they became quite relaxed in their manner. Reassuring as that undoubtedly was, I posted a lookout and made sure that none of the men left our sight. We did excellent trade there as well as getting some useful small change. Among our treasures we now had tea, packs of rice, beans, spices and some kind of sweetened and compressed rice cake. We had also bought some fresh fish, which the Malays helped us to prepare, and once the meal was ready, we gathered round the fire.

It is quite remarkable what can be conveyed by sign language if you really put your mind to it! They managed to tell us that they had seen many others like us over the past few weeks and some of those quite recently. When they left we went down to the shore with them and they pointed out where we should make for. Predictably, that was to the west. There was something about the encounter that had left us so relaxed that we decided to just stay where we were for the rest of the day. I still kept a lookout posted but we smoked, slept, fed, drank tea and even bathed. We felt the strength coming back into our bodies to such an extent that we were forced to acknowledge how exhausted and tensed up we had been before. Most of that could have been put down to hunger, I suppose.

We were away again at nightfall, taking with us the added luxury of a cooked meal. It turned out to be another of those nights when I had to chase the stars round the heavens as they ducked in and out of heavy cloud. There was also a bit of rain, which we just had to sit through and rather enjoyed. It did, however, make me think a bit more about our abandoned canopy and native attire. My big worry was that the men we had left behind might not have had either the time or the presence of mind to dash back to the sampan to collect the clothing and hide it; otherwise, if there had been any mercy going when they were caught, the discovery of those disguises would have been more than enough to tip the balance against them.

We hid up as usual before a dawn that was to herald three days and nights of eventful and even bizarre happenings. During the first night we were hailed by six British servicemen – all gunners, I believe – who had run ashore after hitting a reef, and then lost their oars during the scramble that ensued. Their boat had been saved and it did not appear to be a write-off, but with the loss of their oars they appeared to have lost heart, since no repairs had been attempted. I discovered that it leaked a bit but it seemed to me that if a day or two had been spent on caulking it with bits of cloth, it could have been coaxed into use again. They had been stuck there for several days but had fortunately had sufficient rations until the previous evening. What did seem to have got at them more than anything else was that another boatload of escapees had passed by two days earlier and had allegedly taken no notice of their calls for help. I found it hard to believe that anyone would have ignored an SOS from comrades, even if they had been loaded down to water level, and prefer to think that they were most likely to have been mistaken for Japanese. After all, it would have been all too easy for us to have also sheered off had we not been near enough to recognise that we were being hailed in English.

Well, we spent a day there, and having more than doubled our complement we had used up the better part of all our reserves of food. During that day – and while a good lookout was posted – I chanced a search for the oars along the shoreline and was lucky to find not only them, but also some other useful bits of timber in places that would have been inaccessible to anyone searching from onshore. They were going to be invaluable, because with the oars, the extra crewmen and the use of our bit of canvas we made quicker and far less exhausting progress later.

The next morning presented us with a far more bizarre situation than any of us could have imagined. We had beached before dawn on a small island and some of the crew had gone off on a cautious recce. They were soon back with us again to report having heard furtive rustlings and – they thought – the voices of Australians. Everyone kept very quiet while I went off with a second party. There *were* Aussies there, and we walked right into them; had they been armed, we could have been well into a shoot-out before any questions had been asked. They had no shelter despite having been there a long time. They also had no boat! What they did have, however, was an abundance of chickens scampering about all over the place, which they kept referring to as 'chooks'. (The men had apparently got there from off a bombed ship that had been sunk nearby.) The most remarkable thing was that they were quite adamant in their intention to stay there come what may! It appeared to me that they were living for the day. This really baffled me and there was nothing that I said could persuade them to face the fact that when all the chickens had been eaten they would starve; and also, but for the rapidly advancing monsoon season, they might die of thirst first. It was a pint-sized claustrophobic little island containing just one small brackish pool and insufficient foliage to protect them from rain.

We were made very welcome and we scarcely had to do more than reach out our hands, either for a meal or for reserves to take along with us when we left that evening. Just before we pushed off I offered to ferry some of them to a larger island where they might be able to find a boat and then stage the others over to join them. It was 'no thank you', and the same when I made a final offer to do the staging myself. So, we left them with their chooks!

There have been many times over the past 50 years when I have tried to read some rationality into the behaviour of those men. They seemed so relaxed about the whole affair and if they did have some hidden scheme for escape they must have been damn good actors.

That day we had rigged the bit of canvas on a very makeshift mast. It was a small apology for a jib; and our rope – contrived from the lanyards of two or three jack-knives – allowed very little scope for positioning it to catch the wind. The mast was jammed into timbers placed across the thwarts and lashed into position with army webbing. It was obvious that anything other than a mild wind would make it thresh about like a dervish. However, beggars couldn't be choosers!

And so we were off again following the usual routine, but with a lot more 'engine-power'. We made good progress despite the difficulties of lowering clouds and squalls of rain, and a tide that was nudging us south. I had suspected *that* for the past few days but it was now quite apparent; and despite having the extra elbow power to hold off against it, it would have been silly to waste energy by fighting it. We were still gaining to the west although more gradually now, it would appear. The sail must have given us some help and would probably become much more useful when we got used to it; but with all aids combined, nothing stopped us being tugged onto the windward shore of an island. I had to face the fact that we were being carried along rather than navigated. It was no longer possible to make the usual professional arrival by gliding in and backing the sweeps. This time we were thrust onto the shore in a very undignified manner. Despite all that, we could not have made much noise, so our next bit of adventure was as much of a surprise to us in some ways as our encounter with the Aussies the day before had been.

Going cautiously ashore, we found that the island was reasonably 'open'. We discovered a path leading back to another bit of the shoreline, and then another which led us up to a small tower-like building that resembled a truncated lighthouse. There was nobody about either when we entered or as we made our way inside and quietly climbed up a winding stairway. The building was no more than 20 feet high and we soon got to the top. Then we came up against another door; and that one was closed. Hearing movement inside, I got someone to stand by with a grenade. I was about to challenge, when we heard the unmistakable sound of a baby crying. The door had been partly jammed and as I pushed it I heard agitated chattering and cries of fear. Once inside, I could just make out the dim outline of a family of Malays crouched in the far corner of what might be described as the lantern room. They were all quite terrified; and it took a lot of reassurance to get them settled down. Perhaps it had been just our sudden arrival that had scared them.

In order to further placate them we went outside, built a fire and brewed up a cup of tea. This reassured the father because he plucked up the courage to come down and visit us. I greeted him with an offer of a bit of my tobacco, which he rolled between leaves and lit with a brand from the fire. St Bruno Flake is a bit too strong for most tastes and I had never before seen it rolled and smoked as a cigarette. I still laugh at the memory of how he choked and coughed while doing his best to pretend that he was both delighted and thankful for my kindness; but the joke was really on me, since I then had to accept one of his thick, green and very old cheroots in return. When I lit that up, it spluttered and sparked in my mouth like a firecracker. Those introductions then thankfully behind us, I asked him the direction of (and distance to) Sumatra. That did not evoke any response. He must have known the answers, but probably only knew Sumatra by another name.

So, when we left that night we just headed for a large island that was not too far off and in the general direction of where we would wish to come ashore the following morning. It was raining a bit and there was a wind gusting about. I suppose any local boatman would have readily recognised that to be a warning of really bad weather ahead, and stayed put. For my part, the wind appeared to be a god-send because we were soon being pulled along by the sail without too much effort being required from the men working the oars and sweeps. There must have been a good tide running because we came up to the island much more quickly than we expected. It then started to rain more heavily and it soon became quite impossible to navigate by the stars any more. They were fast disappearing from our patch of the sky and no others were coming into view beyond. We were moving parallel to a long stretch of coastline which – so far as I could see at that time – offered no outlet to open water. A bit further on we saw the contours open up to reveal white water whipping up from the rocks of what later turned out to be the division between two islands, and we were being pulled along on a fast tide and right in towards it. I had no intention of going that way voluntarily.

In the other direction there was a much shorter coastline – probably only a mile in length – but to get round it meant rowing against the tide. The sail was taken down and then we turned and commenced to row back that way. We just pulled and pulled for about an hour but I doubt that we gained any more than 200 yards. Then, as the wind increased and the rain got heavier – and we just got weaker – I realised that we were losing the fight entirely. It started to pelt with rain, then to thunder and lighten and, finally, an even stronger wind began whipping up the waves and threatening to swamp us. I had no alternative but to surrender to the storm.

So, as we managed to turn again, the oars were brought inboard and I gave the order for everyone to crouch down as we started to race back along our tracks in the grip of the tide and the wind. I stayed at the stern, grasping the sweep in an endeavour to steer us away from the threatening gap. It was quite useless though! We were thrust right into the chaos of rocks and water; and once there, there was nothing much that I could do about it. Large rocks were being uncovered within inches of our gunwale, only to disappear again when the turbulent waves rose to thrust us upwards, past and – sometimes – over them. To this day I find it impossible to understand how it was that we went in one side of the gap, hurtled out the other; and then onwards over the edge of the reef without even scratching the sampan. I can only clearly remember poling away from the rocks on the starboard side while others of the crew thrust away to port as each menacing rock revealed itself. If ever there was a time for believing that my brothers were right about that golden chain, that was it. But the danger did not finish there by any means. We had taken on so much water that but for the fact that we now had the temporary protection of a lee shore, we would soon have sunk. We started to wallow in the troughs of the waves and I knew that we must turn and – with the wind behind us – set the sail and head out to sea; and, moreover, while bailing for our lives. Everybody – except those who were being seasick – used everything including their hands to scoop the water out. Most of it had been coming in over the gunwale. We had not been holed, and, as I suspected it would, the intake eased as we headed off and out again. Then, with the lee tide now helping us along, I just followed its track.

I have many times since that day watched canoeists shooting rapids and seemingly totally in control of the situation as they turned away from boulders; while I can only claim to have acted by instinct born of a mixture of fright and good luck. To start with, I had only held on to the sweep for the simple reason that I didn't want to lose it, and only later came the realisation that I could also use it to good effect.

I wish I could say that there was anything more in it than that, but there wasn't! We raced on while the thunder, lightning and rain

34

continued. It was many hours before the storm abated, the sea calmed, and we began to row again. It was still dark when a wispy white mist started to creep across the water to develop, thicken and finally enshroud us. Unable to see much more than a yard or two ahead of us and absolutely nothing above, we then drifted along like some disembodied Ophelia on her way downstream.

There was still the lightest of breezes coming from behind us, which occasionally flapped our little sail; and it was that noise that made my disorientated brain unscramble and remember that we had approached – and come through that gap – on precisely the same course as that which we had started on the previous evening, and therefore we were still heading in the same direction. That knowledge came to me just in time to answer various comments made by men rowing, such as 'How does the sergeant know where we are going? And why should we keep on rowing when we could be going round in circles in this bloody mist?' How nice it was to be able to say, 'Just keep at it, I know where we are, and I always have been heading a bit south of west.'

All things come to an end somewhere or somehow. For us it came when we nearly bumped into some tall poles and rickety steps that supported a small hut. What a journey that had been! We had covered at least 35 miles with the minimum of effort, while traversing a main shipping lane; and while in the protection of the mist, we had heard the thumping beat of a large vessel as it moved in a northerly direction behind us. The whole experience seemed like a miracle to me, knowing that the aftermath of the terrible storm had turned out to be our salvation by both speeding and hiding us while we crossed that wide expanse of hostile water. And from what I was to hear before long, that unseen vessel had more than likely been a Japanese destroyer.

We moored the sampan and then went up the steps to investigate. It was quite roomy up there, and after ferreting around we discovered a small pack of rice near a raised stone hearth, lit a fire, and stripped off our sodden clothes. We didn't find anything large to cook in, but improvised with mess tins. As each tinful came off, the contents were devoured, and then back it went on the fire again until we were all comfortably replete, and sleepy.

It was now an hour or two past dawn but the mist still enclosed us. We lay there and speculated on the reason for this strange structure being – as we thought – well out to sea. We had some vague knowledge of what a *pagar* (fishing trap) looked like but this was not enclosed, and we had not found any nets or baskets lying about. Then looking in the direction from which we had come, I saw the vague outline of the tops of masts, and rigging come into focus; and then, as the mist rolled back a bit further, the ghostly shape of a Chinese junk was revealed. It was about half a mile off from us. I told everyone to keep out of sight and then called for a volunteer to row over there with me. We each had a grenade and I had my revolver as we descended into the mist. I left a corporal in charge and told him that if he heard shots they were to keep out of sight until some native boatman arrived; and then get him to take them west to Sumatra.

Sunday 1 March

So off we went. There was going to be more than a fifty-fifty chance that the junk would be crewed entirely by Chinese and not one that had been commandeered by the Japanese. Fortunately for us, that is precisely how things turned out. We came alongside and we were invited aboard. It was as simple as that; but what a revelation for us to see the inside of the vessel. It had a deep and capacious hold. The timbers were as sturdy as a battleship; and I remember thinking that our two grenades wouldn't have done much damage if we had had to lob them in there. We moved along the edge of the hold to a small well-deck from which we ascended to the level of the crew's living quarters, which were simply but tastefully appointed. Then, after exchanging a few bows and smiles, I tried to convey our wish to be taken to Australia, having by then been convinced that the junk could have taken us safely through any weather to any place in the world. If they understood me there was certainly no interest shown in the proposition. So, having failed in that bid, I went over to a large binnacle that housed a very ornate compass, intending to confirm west – our way to Sumatra. It was a beautifully fashioned instrument and I doubt that I will ever have the pleasure of seeing one quite like it again. However, for our purpose, it might just as well have been faced with the mysteries of the Rosetta stone, since all directions were marked with symbols of birds and animals, among which I can particularly remember seeing a cockerel and a bear.

It wasn't in my nature to give up without a struggle, so I then began to mime while pointing and saying 'Sumatra'. I was talking to a sparsely bearded and very old granddad who I at first thought to be quite intelligent until he started pointing straight down through the bottom of the boat. This was too much for me, and mentally saying you silly old beggar – or words to that effect – I started off once again on my special form of sign language. We carried on in this way, capering about and gesticulating, until one of the crew called me to the side and pointed across the water in the direction of the pagar, and there beyond it we could see a vast coastline gradually coming into view. It seemed to stretch endlessly in both directions and I had to admit that I should have realised that the old chap had been telling me that we were already there; as it turned out, he was the skipper. Before we left he treated us to a lovely cup of tea.

That wasn't to be the end of surprises for us that day. We had got no more than half way back to the fishing trap when a racing yacht appeared from round a headland and bore down on us. It came at such a lick that we had barely time to tie up before he swept up alongside us. The sole occupant was a young, well-dressed and highly educated man – more Indian than Malayan in appearance – who spoke excellent English. And from that moment until we got ashore it can quite fairly be said that he took us over. It was only then that I had proof that there was an organised escape route. With that came the realisation that chance alone had brought us to within five miles of the first main staging post of its route; and also that, but for being hurled along by that storm, we could have finished up miles away and perhaps well outside the limits of his search. My motive – or, one might say fixation – in easing down south as much as west, had been mainly dictated by the natural instinct to combine distance with direction while getting away from the Japanese. But it had been recently revealed that we had been running into just as much danger as any that we had left behind. So, given the knowledge I now had, would I have changed course? I had only had a vague recollection from my school days of being told that much of the north-eastern coastline of Sumatra was unexplored or, at best, undeveloped and inhospitable. That has since turned out to be true, but then mostly only of the section that I had chosen to avoid. Hundreds of other evacuees and escapees had either opted to land along that unwelcoming stretch of coast, or had been forced onto it by enemy attack. They had been mostly the ones who had left Singapore well before the surrender, or those who later got there quickly by means of small motorised craft. There they had either had to stay and hope to be rescued, or attempt to hack their way inland and discover someone who could put them onto tracks leading to the west coast. There was a group of about a hundred artillerymen who took that last option but those who survived paid a great price in morale and fitness. So, all in all, I must have added at least three more golden links to my chain within the past 48 hours of choice and chance.

Our rescuer decided to take three of us along in his yacht and asked me to get the rest to follow along his track. This arrangement worried me a great deal at first because I had seen how quickly he could crack along. It was obvious that he was soon going to leave the others well behind and later go completely out of sight of them. But, as I have already said, he was doing the organising now and I was just beginning to enjoy an overwhelming sense of relief that I could at last – for the time being at least – just sit back and enjoy the rare luxury of having no responsibilities. He convinced the others that he knew those waters like the back of his hand and that all they had to do was to stay in sight over the first few miles and then keep heading down that way until he returned again to guide them in. It was intended that I should be hastened in first to see someone else in the 'Organisation' who would soon be leaving to go up-river with another boat-load of escapees on what he described as the last run before the escape route was shut down. So, our sampan had been very aptly named *Arse End Charlie* because there was now only going to be one or two local boatmen left to look out for any stragglers. And, in the event, no others followed us into what turned out to be the mouth of the Andiri Giri River.

The quickest way to acquaint you with the details of the Organisation is by the following direct quote from the dust cover of *The Escape From Singapore*, by Richard Gough, which reads as follows:

This book tells the story of an attempt by a small secret unit to organise an evacuation of troops from the island (Singapore) and how this became an official escape route which saved thousands of lives. A veteran of Dunkirk, Colonel Alan Warren, Royal Marines, was the head of a small unit under the War

Office and he anticipated soldiers would try to escape rather than face capture. His unit stocked desert islands with supplies and made an arrangement with the Dutch to move escapers across Sumatra to the port of Padang. This book is their story, and that of thousands of escapers and survivors that took part in the last minute rush to escape.

Well, I am sure that that puts the whole thing in a nutshell and it will avoid the repetition of any of his story and the unpardonable temptation to steal any of his thunder. The work that they did and the bravery of their undertakings deserve all the publicity that can be given to them; and I, with all my comrades who used that route regardless of how, from where, or why, gratefully salute them. I would add further while on the subject of escape, that in order to get into context what was going on in Singapore just before it fell, it is necessary to hear part of the last despatch sent by General Wavell after his own official evacuation to take up more useful service elsewhere: '...also, just before cessation of hostilities opportunity must be given to any determined bodies of men or individuals to escape by any means possible'. And now my question about that is – and always has been – 'Why in God's name were none of us lesser mortals acquainted with either the contents of that message or of the founding and availability of that escape route?' It is also ironic to think that one of my sections may have taken down the coded copy of it that must have surely been sent out to all brigadiers. None of it need have been published abroad if the generals had thought that it might inspire troops to desert. My own firm conviction is that those few deserting rats that did scuttle off before the surrender would have done so anyway. Surely all that would have been necessary and morally correct at that time was that officers could not only say – as my Brigadier did – 'Yes you have my blessing!' *and then also say*, 'Make for island X, and there you will find supplies, and guides to point you further down an organised escape route'. Instead of that, I had had to rely on chance, chance and still more chance.

Just how many people were there who did not have my luck and perished, when they could at the very least have been given the chance to be saved?

7

IN AND OUT OF PRIGGI RAJAH

It cannot have been more than an hour after transferring to the yacht before we slid in alongside a ramshackle jetty. We debarked before an equally dilapidated hut. Behind that there was a 20-foot high mound which enclosed most of the small fishing village of Priggi Rajah. There was no sign of a boat. The yachtsman told me that it must have gone back up-river already and in that case we should find a message nailed to a support post in the centre of the hut. I sent someone off to check that while the rest of us waited at the jetty.

Priggi Rajah was at the delivery end of a long chain of places that had been put at the disposal of the Organisation by co-operating headsmen; and it owed its importance not only to the fact that it was the first reporting and marshalling point but also that it received us in and onto Dutch East Indies territory. The yachtsman reported in to a waiting colleague and after introducing me he departed to lead in the rest of the party. Tea was brewed up and I sat down to give an account of our escape and journey, which at its beginning was typical of that made by the few other individuals who had made it out in a variety of small rowing craft. But there the similarity ended because, according to him, nobody else had rowed all the way down. He told me that some of the others had, as I had, lost and gathered in other personnel, but each of them eventually had to be rescued themselves and brought on down by larger vessels – both motorised and in sail.

I went on to describe the Dutch island, the loss of the officers and men there, and our subsequent adventures; and when I told him of the small islet swarming with chickens it raised a lot of interest, because he thought the Aussies there might yet be located by one of the few local boatmen who were still aiding him. However, he didn't have any better ideas than I had about why they had elected to stay there. I told him of our recent adventures in the storm and he marvelled at our survival because inland it had caused damage and flooding right along the river, which – by comparison with the open sea – was obviously far more protected. I also said that the wind and tide had helped us to cover what I estimated would have otherwise taken four or five nights of normal running; but that I had no idea whence we had started. None of this helped him very much; and his own suggestion that I might already have been at the mouth of the estuary couldn't possibly have been right. He then casually informed me that throughout the previous day – dawn to dusk – there had been two Japanese destroyers anchored at the point from which we had just entered.

When the others arrived, we were shown what rations were available and then left to prepare our own meal. The amenities consisted of just two chairs and a very uninviting earth floor on which to sleep – no more! The previous party had left us very little to eat so our stolen rice came in handy. I went over to read the message on the pole for myself, and found that a certain Sergeant Harry Pearce of 30 Heavy Ack Ack had asked us to wait in the hut until he came back with the river boat next morning. Below that he had appended the very significant message, that it was almost certainly going to be his last trip. This set me thinking about the risks that those men of the Organisation were taking on our behalf. The message, left in an unattended hut, could have been seen by any Japanese foraging party who could then have waited for his return.

The yachtsman and his companion had by now disappeared back to their own secret lairs, having first warned us that we should not involve any of the village people in our affairs, since the less they knew about us the safer they would be if the Japanese did arrive. All that they had left behind with us for company was a mighty army of mosquitoes. They came winging in to us off the nearby mangrove swamps as dusk approached.

We were all exhausted and craving sleep but none of the others heeded my warning that they must stay awake unless they had adequate protective clothing.

I had too many memories of my previous service in Sierra Leone – the 'White Man's Grave' – to offer myself up to their attack.

Despite having individual mosquito nets and specially designed clothing there the whole of the Royal Marine Commando were designated sick within four months and sent home. We were in a tented camp at the foot of Mount Auriol and close to the Kissy swampland in Freetown. The area around the city had a population suffering from 65 per cent VD, malaria and blackwater fever and 90 per cent humidity. The poor old 1st/5th Essex regiment was already well into a maximum 12-month tour of duty when we arrived and they remained there for many months after we left. Many of them died there and the cemeteries were full of the casualties from previous regiments. The place was a 'pest-hole', and Priggi Rajah was obviously another!

The embers of our fire were still glowing outside the hut. I converted it into a smudge fire, covered my face with a spare pair of pants, lit up my pipe and stuck it though the 'exit' hole; and then I went up the embankment in the hope that I might attract someone's attention within the village. I knew that it was against the rules but I was desperate for relief from the constant stinging.

There was a huge water supply tank up there. I remained beside it for several minutes looking down on the large assemblage of huts. It was an eerie experience. No lights showed, no dogs barked and nobody answered my calls. Perhaps it was just as well that they didn't because I must have looked like a member of the Ku Klux Klan!

Despite the countless horrible nights I would suffer later that one stands out above all others. I had had to be awake and on the alert for over 48 hours. So, with the arrival of dawn, I went into the hut, told the corporal to let me know when the boat arrived and then crashed out to enjoy three hours of sleep.

It was about ten o'clock when I was shaken awake and told that Harry had just arrived, having taken everyone by surprise. He had throttled back the engine, and then drifted silently down and round a bend of the river. He had come down in a clapped out old steamboat with an empty barge-like raft in tow. After a brief introduction he went into the hut to remove the notice from the pole while I checked over the site to ensure that nothing else was left behind to compromise the village – or the Organisation for that matter. Harry told me that he would probably be back again the next day but that we had had to clear up in case not. We then picked up our gear and went aboard, leaving *Arse End Charlie* as the only witness to our departure, having never – even once – seen any occupant from the village. On climbing into the raft, I covered myself up from the burning heat of the sun and then fell asleep again, lulled by the *chug chug* of the old engine beating its way back upstream. I didn't wake up again until we had pulled into the bank to pick up more logs to fire its boiler.

8

ACROSS SUMATRA TO PADANG

2 to 12 March 1942

(see MAP THREE at the end of this chapter)

By the time the re-fuelling had been completed I was well awake
and starting to catch up on Harry's account of those who had used
the Organisation route before us.

Even before Singapore fell, evacuees had been moving down this
escape route after being bombed off boats bound either for Australia
or through the Java Straits and on to India. This influx had put a
great burden not only on our organisers, but also on the Dutch
Controleurs and the resources of the civilian population along the
route. The demand for medical facilities, housing, transport and food
became increasingly difficult to supply; and by the time the main
flow of services evacuees and escapees started coming in, the whole
situation had become quite chaotic. Even by the eighteenth of
February – only three days after the fall of Singapore – there had
been hundreds of troops moving through Priggi Rajah and up to
Rengat, which was a large town about a hundred miles up-river; and
every day had seen more and more of them piling in. These new
arrivals compounded the problem for the organisers and a further
and even direr situation developed when some of the servicemen
started helping themselves to food without paying. Some even went
further than that and looted the property of the same civilians
who had helped them. Many others sold their arms in order to get
money for food. All this served to turn what had been a sympathetic, willing – but also overstretched – population into a largely
non-co-operative, and even openly hostile, community. In effect, it
was the Singapore Syndrome all over again in that a few deserters

and other rabble started to adopt an 'every man for himself and the devil take the last' attitude. In the context of this situation it cannot be said too often that the officers of the Organisation – and the men they had singled out to help them – were deserving of far more acclaim and recognition than most of them received after the war – posthumously or otherwise. The Dutch were quite rightly outraged by what they saw and they made the valid point that their *Controleurs* had been ordered to stay at *their* posts and officially hand over the various islands and towns to the Japanese – and this they were already starting to do – whereas some of the senior British and Australian officers and NCOs were just chasing through regardless of the indiscipline they were leaving behind them. This situation inevitably became counter-reactive to the extent that many of the lower ranks were then able – either with real or imagined grievances – to say that 'so and so who should have stayed to look after us had just cleared off and left us stranded'. This became a situation that was ripe for anarchy and on certain occasions and in certain places it became just that.

Once again, the behaviour of a few disaffected people had caused problems and – on occasions even chaos too – for the many, services and civilians alike. These few refused to accept the 'last in, last out' rule and the selfish and outrageous actions that they indulged in once again resulted in a large degree of *non*-co-operation of the Dutch forces and civilians when they ultimately arrived at Padang hoping to pick up an evacuation boat. All this had started to happen three weeks before my party had chanced upon the route. Well before we arrived, the Dutch had found it necessary to disarm all 'other ranks', since many weapons were getting to the locals who had already sided with Dr Sukharno (the Nationalist leader), who they ultimately assisted to escape from arrest.

Meanwhile, our leading craft – the *Joan* – had been slogging its way upstream against a strong current and a mass of debris that was being constantly swept down from upper levels of the Andiri Giri. Harry had been telling the lads that it had all started after our sea-storm chased across and hit the mainland, and then continuous heavy monsoon rain had flowed down, heightening the bankside levels and picking up loose material as it went by. He said that we would be doing a run of about 40 miles up to the small township of Tambila-han, where we would then have to wait our turn until the last of the men ahead of us had been moved on to the next staging post.

We didn't have much farther to go up that winding and tempestuous stretch of water – but far enough for me to see crocodiles sunning themselves on mudbanks and the rather eerie sight of brilliantly coloured but totally songless birds flitting from tree to tree ahead of us to watch our progress up the river. They reminded me of porpoises leaping before the prow of a ship.

Harry said that he would be leaving Tambilahan soon and he would follow us within a day or two after leaving the place to function on its own as a 'last hope' holding-point for any other escapees who might yet find their own way up and along the route.

As last of the 'last in, last out' groups, we were going to find that at each further stage – Rengat, Ayer Molak and Sawahalunto – that although there were still bottlenecks, the worst of the awkward squads had moved on ahead of us. During the earlier stages of the evacuation the Organisation had itself coped with the feeding of everyone heading for Padang but by now they had left just a few volunteers like Harry to run the river craft. The Dutch army and civilians were doing the rest.

Our next stop – the last one for the *Joan* – would be at Rengat, which was a large township and the last navigable point of the river for sea-going vessels. Some of the intake there had either been too impatient to wait for ongoing transport or had caused disruption by jumping the queue. Among the former were groups that had decided to footslog onwards up a riverside path leading to Ayer Molak. It would have been better if they had waited because the Dutch did eventually bring lorries and buses up to move everyone on. Others had decided to do a four-day trek in temperatures of over 100 degrees through a gloomy rain forest within which everyone sweated while being pestered by the attention of flies and mosquitoes. One of the parties that followed that route was a group of sailors among which were many survivors from HMS *Jarak*, *Scorpion*, *Dragonfly* and *Grasshopper*. They eventually caught up with the others at Basra – a riverside township – from whence they were all moved on in transport to Taluk.

However, that final move was delayed by the torrential monsoon downpours that had at first flooded many roads and tracks and then swept on to smash and sweep away bridges. No doubt it was a lot of the debris from that damage that we had been running through recently. Those Navy lads had an equally torrid time, and they too didn't gain much distance on the rest of us.

Perhaps we should have kept *Arse End Charlie* as our logo because we seemed fated to continue making journeys in the aftermath of chaos!

We were eventually taken up to Ayer Molak on small river craft and stayed there for a few days in the care of a smartly dressed Cub Scout group housed in an abandoned factory which had processed rubber. They and their families did a great job of feeding and caring for us despite their own diminished resources.

While waiting there we heard plenty more about the work of the Organisation and other heroes who by their voluntary efforts rescued and cared for hundreds of civilians and servicemen who would otherwise have perished on the way down from Singapore. The Organisation was fast being wound down, leaving Harry – who was now billeted with us – plenty of time to fill in the details about such people as Colonel Coates (later Sir Arthur Coates) of the Australian Army Medical Corps. He was an eminent surgeon who with a few of his dedicated assistants had volunteered to stay on the route in order to perform essential operations and give other vital medical care to many evacuees who would otherwise have died. His team had at first had to work in primitive and frustrating conditions. Many of the surgical instruments had to be improvised. Some amputations were done with the use of butchers' knives and choppers. During the early days of evacuation he had been given very little accommodation or assistance from the Dutch authorities. They had had to be constantly cajoled into providing suitable transport for stretcher cases that needed to be moved down to Padang in order to make way for the continuing influx of other wounded civilians and servicemen that Harry had been ferrying up from the carnage out at sea. Arthur Coates had worked himself into a state of near total exhaustion but despite urgings from his senior officers he had refused to leave his patients in order to go down to Padang for a rest; and when he did finally get there he arrived in the company of the last of his patients. Once there, he was given the chance to be evacuated but he still elected to stay behind to use his great surgical skills where he quite correctly anticipated that they would be most needed. He was a very dedicated and brave man.

I came to know a lot more about the Colonel during the next three and a half years. Thankfully he was not alone in such selflessness. There were many others who had either worked or would be working with the same amount of dedication and loyalty, thank God. We needed them.

Modest Harry Pearce was one of that number himself. He had experienced similar conditions while aiding in the evacuation of Dunkirk and more recently while getting out of Singapore. On repatriation he was awarded a well-merited BEM for the work he did as a prisoner-of-war from May to December 1943; but I find it quite strange that his citation failed to mention the work he did for the Organisation.

Other memorable contributors to their work were Captain Dudley Apthorp, Royal Norfolks; MSM McLaren, RASC; and Lance Corporal J. E. (Nobby) Clarke (also of the Norfolk Regiment), all of whom are notable for the fact that having got to Priggi Rajah with their own escape parties, they then went back out to sea to seek out and bring in stranded civilians and servicemen who would otherwise have perished. Two other men who must be remembered were Leading Seaman Puncheon and Able Seaman R. McCaffery, who remained to the end with Sergeant Pearce to man the escape boats on the Andiri Giri River.

Most of them became my comrades later and I feel privileged to have shared the company of such men, whose earlier feats have been more fully described in Richard Gough's book *The Escape from Singapore* and another, entitled *Singapore's Dunkirk*, by Geoffrey Brooke.

And now, on with my story again! We were waiting our turn to be moved on to Sawahalunto in Dutch army and commandeered lorries; and for the organisation of that, we had to rely on the mood of a vociferous and gung-ho Dutch officer. He was renowned for his brave actions when fighting the Japanese in a retreat from the northern port of Medan against well-seasoned troops (released from Singapore) right down to his final position just north of the Dutch barrack-township of Fort-de-Kok. He was a giant of a man and quite scathing of what he saw as our scant contribution to the war effort both in Malaya and here in Sumatra, where we were – he said – only getting in his way. I suppose the last part of that was fair comment. However, all of us still in Ayer Molak – including himself – knew nothing of the fact that Colonel Warren had offered to form a volunteer guerrilla force from among the British and Australian servicemen still left in Padang. This had been turned down by the Dutch authorities on the grounds that it would have been an unnec-

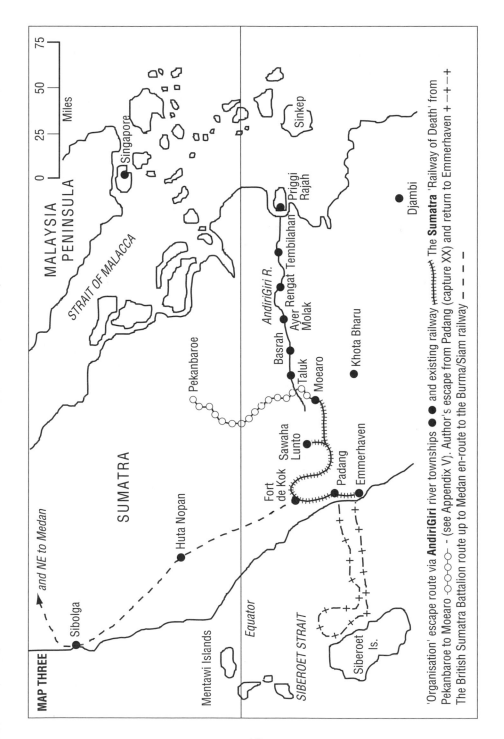

MAP THREE

Miles
0   25   50   75

MALAYSIA PENINSULA

STRAIT OF MALACCA

Singapore

Sinkep

and NE to Medan

Sibolga

Equator

Mentawi Islands

SUMATRA

Huta Nopan

Pekanbaroe

AndiriGiri R.

Priggi Rajah

Djambi

Ayer Rengat Tembilahan
Molak
Basrah
Taluk
Moearo

Khota Bharu

Fort de Kok
Sawaha Lunto

Padang
Emmerhaven

Siberoet Is.

SIBEROET STRAIT

'Organisation' escape route via **AndiriGiri** river townships ● and existing railway ┼┼┼┼┼┼┼ The **Sumatra** 'Railway of Death' from Pekanbaroe to Moearo ‑o‑o‑o‑o‑ ‑ ‑ (see Appendix V). Author's escape from Padang (capture XX) and return to Emmerhaven + ‑ + ‑ + The British Sumatra Battalion route up to Medan en‑route to the Burma/Siam railway ‑ ‑ ‑ ‑

49

essary sacrifice of the lives of men who would have to face an increasingly hostile and subversive native population as well as some very dangerous wild animals.

Long after the event, I was told that the details of that discussion had remained with a few 'need to know' officers within the Padang hierarchy. However, despite his ignorance of events, I am sure that our irascible Dutch officer did his best for us under very difficult circumstances. He was, after all, still engaged in a situation where the maintenance of supplies to his army was of prime importance. Whenever a truck became available for our use he had it brought up under guard not only against the above dangers, but also the possibility that some remaining malcontents might attempt a hijack in order to jump the queue. If any of them had tried that I am sure that he would have shot them; and had that been done they would not have got any posthumous sympathy from me despite the fact that our little group was going to be last anyway, except for Harry Pearce and his fraternity of boatmen.

When our turn came we made a very bumpy, steep and blazing hot journey over the mountain to Sawahalunto; and we were all very glad that we had not attempted the 160 mile route on foot. Having reached the railhead there was the inevitable overnight wait for train space. We were given a meal and then lodged in an empty tobacco warehouse.

The following day – Thursday the twelfth of March – was no doubt memorable to the Dutch because we were to be the last trickle from the flood of Allied evacuees that had passed that way. For our part, before leaving, we got the very unwelcome news that the last official evacuations from nearby Emmerhaven had taken place on the eleventh and that no more ships were expected.

We were entrained in open-sided passenger carriages hauled by a steam train which relied on a ratchet and pinion mechanism similar to that used on Snowdon. We just sat back and enjoyed the scenic ride as it chuntered down over a 60-mile loop of winding track and then onwards to Padang.

During the previous three or four weeks the local population had seen the daily spectacle of a motley crowd of foreigners passing through. Among the watchers on that final day I saw an elderly and unkempt ginger-bearded Dutchman standing beside the track with his Sumatran wife and seven children. Three of the children – although dark-skinned – had bright ginger hair. I remember hoping that when the Japanese arrived – which was inevitable – they would just leave this family to continue their lives in peace. The Dutch had always been very relaxed about mixed marriages and that old boy, who had quite obviously gone native many years before I saw him, seemed to be both happy and harmless.

By the greatest of coincidences I saw them all lined up there again four weeks later. So, he had at least kept his family together that long. By then, in common with the other families around them they were waving miniature Nippon flags. He was displaying himself so openly that he at least must have been convinced that he was going to be left there undisturbed. I hope that it did turn out that way!

9

PADANG – AND THEN, WHERE NEXT?

As far as I can tell, no other party came into Padang later than mine and by then at least 1,500 people – civilian and servicemen – had been evacuated by the Royal and the merchant navies; and remaining was a mixed group of wounded and late arrivals who it seemed were never going to be able to get away.

There were about 1,100 servicemen left – 400 Australian and 700 British – housed in two complexes which had been vacated by Malay and Chinese children. The officers, the wounded and a few British civilians were outhoused elsewhere in the town. Things were pretty well organised by the time we arrived but they had been quite chaotic until Colonel Warren appointed Sergeant Major Roadnight to ensure – at the insistence of the Dutch authorities – that all servicemen must be under curfew from dusk to dawn.

Once again the majority had had to suffer due to the actions of a minority of men who had been out in the town looting under cover of darkness. Although this restraint was by no means totally effective, most of the men were reasonable in their behaviour and Roadnight was a sufficiently forceful character to command the assistance and respect of most NCOs. The exceptions to this – even among some of the more senior NCOs – were those who saw fit to retain their ranks while sinking into the cosy obscurity of being just one of the boys – and there will certainly be more said about that later!

I was given the simple task of supervising the issue of breakfast and the cleaning of an area in which about a hundred of us slept. The rest of the day was mine! Having said my farewells to the crew of the sampan *Arse End Charlie*, they went off to join others of the same rank or unit as themselves. That was that, and typical of those hectic days of brief encounters.

When weapons were being handed in, I had parted with my grenades but retained my revolver since I had every intention of getting out and away again before the Japanese moved down from the north. I told CSM Roadnight that and he made no objections; but the sly old devil didn't tell me that he intended to do the same himself. The great thing is that he succeeded. He was rescued while out in the Indian Ocean and later joined the Chindits under the command of Michael Calvert.

However, I soon found other dedicated escapers and eight of us pooled our resources. Two of them had already accompanied me on a walk round the small harbour while we noted down likely vessels to escape in. We had been told that each evening the Dutch put a chain across the entrance to Padang harbour; and that machine-gun posts had been installed to deter anyone from trying to break out. It was frustrating to find vessels that could have taken several hundred people to safety but not one Dutchman who was prepared to take a chance and release one to us. The fact of the matter was that the Dutch had long past made plans to hand us all over within the terms of their own surrender. They had then more recently firmed up on that, with the further agreement to transfer all the dockyard installations at Emmerhaven intact for immediate use again by the Japanese. Emmerhaven was their naval port! It was a few miles south of Padang and we had been warned against going there. The warning was given because – it was said – that we would need to have an escort to guard us against attack by some of the local populace: but the more likely reason would have been their determination that we should not get near any of their naval vessels.

Time was getting so short now. In effect Padang was about to be declared an open town and we were intended to be little more than pawns to be used in a transfer deal. Knowing that, it became even more important to keep up with our search: and we did find two very likely-looking diesel-powered motor launches. They were both in trim condition and in the process of being stocked up for an ocean-going journey but they were both well attended by armed British navy personnel who made it quite clear that we were not welcome there. Barrels of extra diesel oil had been lashed to the deck of one of them in preparation for a journey that had all the hallmarks of 'top brass'.

So we turned our attention to some smaller and more tatty boats lying alongside the harbour wall and then went back to the school

53

to see if anyone else would be interested in joining us, but nobody was.

We eight were all latecomers into Padang and all had retained the impetus for further escape. The first to arrive there had been three members of the Fortress HQ Royal Engineers and they had teamed up with Private Ingham of the RASC. Then I had arrived; and shortly after that, Harry Pearce came in bringing with him two naval men who had been doing evacuation work with him. The REs were led by Sergeant Stracchino – Stracc to most of us – and his unit companions were Lance Corporal A. K. Armstrong and Sapper Harry Adrian; all of them were 'regulars'. Stracc was a tough and resourceful character who was (and always remained) very much his own man. Nevertheless, despite his independence, he still retained all the loyalties expected of a man of his rank. During the fighting in Malaya he, his two companions and many others had been captured by the Japanese and linked by ball and chain before being marched down the peninsula. Stracc had managed to free himself and the other two. He then led them across to the west coast, where he stole a small boat, brought them on down to Sumatra and then, mercifully, into Harry Pearce's care.

Harry Pearce and his companions had come into Padang last and with little done in preparation for a further escape. Having also done a recce of the harbour with the navy lads, they came back to tell the rest of us that they had only seen craft which had either no canvas aboard or were too closely attended by their owners.

It hadn't surprised me to find that we three sergeants had all hidden our revolvers when weapons were being called in. We were all like-minded and Harry Pearce spoke for all when he said, 'There is no way that any cheese-eating yaffler is going to have my revolver when I am on the point of making another escape.' Stracc and Co had already got some very useful escape items, which included a school atlas, some binoculars, medicines, barbers' equipment, a variety of small tools and enough food to meet their own needs for a week.

I still had all of my equipment intact, and the remainder of the wad of Malay dollars, and had been given an army issue compass – so I was well prepared!

It was the fifteenth of March now and rumours were already about that the Japanese would be in amongst us within two days, so we made our final plans. Harry Pearce was set on buying some canvas in case we might yet steal one of the unequipped craft mentioned earlier. He wanted enough of it for a local tailor to make clothing for some of his mates who had been stranded on the east coast in little more than their underpants. So I gave the two Harrys (Pearce and Adrian) enough money for that and – if possible – to buy extra tinned food. They came back with tinned food but no canvas, but a tailor had run up a few pairs of shorts from second-hand curtain material.

We did our final rounds of the harbour on the morning of the sixteenth. Then, on coming back to the school for a midday meal, we found a message from Colonel Warren telling us that the Japanese were expected to arrive that evening, that anyone who was determined to escape would have to do so by 19.00 hours, and that those who were staying must sign their names by 18.30 hours.

So that was that! And with the exception of the escape option, it was going to be Singapore all over again!

Rumours were rife. It was said that Colonel Warren had provisioned a small vessel for a few lucky men of the Organisation who had won their places on an escape party by the turn of a card. That was one of the many rumours flying about that turned out to be true, and I say good luck to them – and CSM Roadnight – because, but for men like them, many of those that were being left to wait in the school would never have lived to get that far.

Colonel Warren – who could so easily have left on one of the launches – subsequently made the brave decision to stay and get as good a deal as possible from the Japanese for the men who would be remaining in Padang.

Well, the time had come for leaving; and having abandoned all hope of stealing one of the smaller boats from the harbour, we went out of the school, down to the coast and started walking north in the hope that we might find one there.

10

INDIA? CEYLON? HERE WE COME! WE HOPE!

20.00 hours 16 March

On the face of it, it might appear to have been a crazy idea to go north. After all, the Japanese would soon be on their way down from that direction, and moreover, coming along the coastal road leading south from Fort-de-Kok. However, we had reasoned that provided that we kept parallel to them and on the beach itself, that would be safer than going south from Padang into what was fast becoming Nationalist territory.

We were quite prepared to live on our wits (in much the same way as we had done when coming out of Singapore) by hedge-hopping up the west coast and then striking out towards India via the Andaman Islands. No-one had told us that the coastline would get less and less hospitable as we went north, or that it would finally get quite dangerous if we ever reached the territory of the warlike Achinese tribe in the north-west. So, it is just as well that we didn't get that far north.

It wasn't long before we came to a fishing kampong. Scattered along the beach were crude log-boats, called *koleks*, fitted with outriggers and used for night in-shore fishing. Unfortunately – for him at least – one of the fishermen was busy loading his craft with nets when we arrived; and that was going to be the last that he was ever going to see of it again. We made the instant decision to take it and head for an island about five miles off which we had spotted during one of our recces. Our plan was to paddle out there and lie up for 24 hours while the Japanese were coming down from Fort-de-Kok, and then drop back onto the coast the following evening. We took the view that a bird in the hand etc. ... and that this boat was better than none at all. There was no time for further discussion anyway, because we could now hear the Japanese lorries swishing past us as they paralleled the coastal trees barely 200 yards away.

Having waved our revolvers at the fisherman, the poor devil had no option but to throw his nets out onto the beach again. However, unknown to the others, I had slipped him some of my dollars. I doubt that what I gave him would have covered all of his losses. It must have been enough to appease him, though, because instead of dashing off to raise a hullabaloo in the village, he not only stayed with us to help with the launch but also called over two more boatmen to assist with our preparations.

The next part of our operation could well have been scripted 'Comic Cuts'.

We floated the boat in the shallows, put our possessions into the 'sharp end', and then six of us piled in after them. It was so cramped in there that we had to sit with knees up and backsides slotted into each other like a row of peas in a pod. Then the paddles were held at the ready while the other two men gave us a push before jumping in themselves. Stracc had taken command and he had told us that we would have to time things just right. We had to meet the first roller and then strike out fast to get beyond it to avoid being dragged back by the undertow.

Everything went well until a bung came out of the bottom of the boat and a fountain of water shot up. We were then literally picked up by the next roller and unceremoniously dumped back on the beach in a tangled heap of kit and bodies.

Thankfully the fishermen had stayed to watch the fun, and they helped us to re-tamp the plughole and to repair an outrigger that had been torn from its housing.

(Jerome K Jerome could have made a meal out of that incident in a special publication entitled *Eight Men in a Log-boat! And not to mention the Bunghole!*)

And all the time those lorries had been passing behind us on the way down to Padang!

The repairs were completed in about half an hour. We piled in again and made our second bid for freedom; but even that effort was not all plain sailing. We had to paddle furiously and then only just topped the second roller to get clear and away. With great relief we heard the diminishing sound of the waves pounding the beach behind us. It was quite remarkable that such a crude and overloaded craft had stayed stable in such turbulent water.

We reached the island in about three hours and were fortunate to make a landfall. The compass had kept us on a recollected direction – not a setting. Moonlight and a certain amount of luck did the rest!

The *kolek* was pulled clear of the tidemark and then we went inshore to light a fire where it wouldn't be seen from the mainland. Although the Japanese would be unlikely to come our way until they had consolidated their positions within Padang and Emmerhaven, we weren't going to take any chances!

It was too dark to look for fresh water and, wishing to conserve our supplies, we decided to milk some coconuts; but that wasn't going to be easy! There were none on the ground and none of us were able to shin up 20 branchless feet of tree-trunk, so we had to chop one down. Then, while Harry Adrian was preparing a meal, I went off to double-check that the *kolek* was safely beached.

It was okay, and I had just started back when I heard rustling in some thick undergrowth. I looked to my left and my hair shot up like a bottlebrush with the discovery that I was within a few yards of a dragon-like creature. I don't know how many seconds it was that I stood there taking in the scene before the realisation came that all it was doing was licking out the remains of some food from a tin which one of us had tossed aside. It was so engrossed in its beachcombing activities that it hadn't noticed me so far – but I had no intention of staying close to see if it might turn its attention on me next. So, drawing my revolver, I backed off very slowly, and as I took aim the horrible thought came to me that 0.38 rounds would just bounce off that horny hide. So I shouted out 'shoo!' – and how ridiculous that must have sounded! But it did the trick, because it turned slowly away and then went crashing off through the undergrowth.

When I got back and told the others that I had seen a 7-foot dragon, it was a case of 'pull the other leg, it's got bells on it' from most of them, who were convinced that I had seen nothing more than a large lizard. However, I have since discovered that I had – at the very least – seen a second cousin to a Komodo dragon, or perhaps the real McCoy! The species was first found on the island of that name to the east of Sumatra within the area now known as Indonesia. It can weigh up to 300 pounds and grow to 10 feet in length, and although it feeds largely on eggs and small mammals, it has also been known to eat the occasional wild pig and small deer. So, I have to be thankful that *my one*, whatever it was, had never developed a liking for 'long pig'.

It has always intrigued me how such an animal could have got onto such a small and isolated island in the first place. Had it perhaps been the latest of a line of thousands of generations going back to the time when the island had formed part of a large land mass? Having no ready answer to that question myself I must leave it to the experts to sort out.

I was the fidgety one in our party. Having wakened early the next morning, I just had to go down to check if the *kolek* was still safely aground. It was barely dawn and a thick misty haze hung about the surface of the water. While standing at the shoreline I became vaguely aware of thuds at first, and then voices as well, coming from a short distance out to sea. My immediate thoughts were that either the fishermen had come out in force to retrieve the *kolek*, or – far worse – that the Japanese had already commenced a search for missing vessels.

I went back to alert the others. We struck camp and went back to the beach with the intention of either camouflaging the *kolek* or working it round to the other side of the island before the mist cleared. There had been a bit of squally rain about but it had now eased enough for us to see the misty outline of a largish boat yawing around with its sails flapping.* The boom was swinging from side to side and the boat seemingly out of control. And then we heard some good old Anglo-Saxon language from out there and one of our number was equally poetic with the remark, 'Well I'm buggered! This is our next boat delivered to us by a lot of landlubbers!'

We grabbed our kits, scrambled into the *kolek* and quickly paddled out to join them. We were almost upon them before we were noticed and the reception we got was far from friendly at first. We were told that they only had enough food for their own needs and therefore they couldn't allow us aboard. The conversation had begun in a gentlemanly manner as we argued our case with the four resident officers; but having heard their rejection, we were in no mood to be abandoned to the mercies of the sea – or of the Japanese – in our tiny craft while this large sea-going vessel was on hand. So we had to set about trying to convince them that *they* needed *our* help.

*The *Bintang Dua* (Malay: *Two Stars*).

It was Sergeant Stracchino who – as it were – fired the first shot by saying, 'None of you can bloody well sail and at least three of us can.' That remark was a bit of an understatement in his case, because he went on to inform them that he had served as a deck-hand on a trawler operating in the North Sea, so, unless they wanted to stay there all day in full view of the Japanese, they had better move over and let him do the sailing for them.

I told them that we were reasonably self-sufficient and that we would willingly pool our food with them. Quite apart from that, it was plain that we three sergeants were armed because our revolvers were by now holstered and clipped to our webbing belts. Although there was no overt threat implied in that, I have often wondered since what we might have done if they had still refused to take us aboard. Would we have forced our way on? I really think that we would have! In the event, it was just as well that we were ultimately invited aboard because nobody else on there had any weapons and we soon found out that some of the men were not only stowaways but real troublemakers.

As the great bard Willie Spokeshave would have it, 'Misery acquaints a man with strange bed-fellows' – and dangerous ones sometimes!

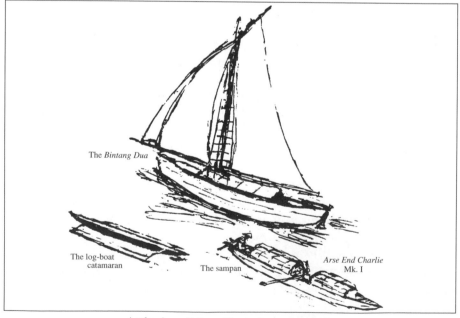

The *Bintang Dua*

The log-boat catamaran

The sampan

Arse End Charlie Mk. I

Author's *well-found* fleet of escape vessels

11

OFF TO SIBERUT ON THE *BINTANG DUA*

One of the officers aboard was Lieutenant Harold Dicker (now major, retired) of 30 Heavy Ack Ack. It was only quite recently (after a lapse of 45 years) that I discovered his address, visited him, and obtained his permission to quote the following passage from his narrative of the event:

> In the quest for water it was decided to sail to Siberut, at the southern end of the island of that name which lies about 60 miles to the west of Sumatra. Whilst on this course we were hailed by the occupants of a dugout canoe who came paddling furiously towards us. Sunburnt and bearded, a more villainous lot of pirates I have never seen but we eventually realised that their shouting was in English, so we took them aboard. They turned out to be sergeants Burgoyne, Pearce and Stracchino, plus four others. Each of the sergeants was armed, and that was the total of the armaments of the ship's company.
>
> Sergeant Pearce had been the engineer of the launch *Joan* previously mentioned, but had somehow missed being evacuated from Padang. Of the others sergeant Stracchino, a sapper, was a truly remarkable man who could turn his hand to almost anything. What was more important – he had spent time in sailing vessels, and was in fact, worth more than the rest of us put together.

Well I cannot find too much wrong with that except that he has left out the details of our altercation before they let us come aboard and that, but for their floundering around in a state of total disarray, we would never have had time to get launched and go out to join them.

It didn't take long for Stracc to sort us out in watches, to put the

61

kolek in tow and get under way. Once we had settled down we were told how the others had managed to slip out of Padang harbour. That part of our saga has been documented in a book entitled *The British Sumatra Battalion*, written by Ann Apthorp (the widow of another of the other officers aboard), to which both Harold Dicker and I contributed a large part of the narrative. It also contains several of my sketches.

So, with Ann's permission (this time), I will tell as much of that account as is necessary to connect the details of their escape up to the time when we joined them. Their complement had been largely formed from two or three parties that had – as we had – been ferreting around within the harbour looking for a likely vessel. Lieutenant Dicker's party had earlier discovered what appeared to be a well-found motor vessel but it later turned out to have a sabotaged engine. This had happened during the early part of the evening of surrender, so they were beginning to get desperate when they happened upon a smaller party led by Captain Apthorp aboard the *Bintang Dua*.

Fortunately for Lieutenant Dicker, there had been some delay in trying to get it rigged and under way and he had arrived just as a helpful but nervous Dutch policeman named van Dyl was urging them to leave.

The two parties joined forces, and were still trying to sort out a tangled heap of rigging and canvas when they saw the lights of trucks and guessed that they could only be loaded with Japanese coming down from Fort-de-Kok. They posed a more dangerous threat to them than they had been to us because their route would soon be taking them along a stretch of the road close to – and within sight of – the harbour. So they cut the mooring rope, shipped the rudder and then just drifted out of control into the darker areas of the harbour. It was during that frantic effort to get away from the moorings that the stowaways had managed to slip aboard. They were later to become much more than a pain in the neck by deriding the officers, criticising the rest of us and doing sweet Fanny Adams themselves unless threatened into action by Stracc.

Four of the malcontents were Australian. There was also an alleged Australian officer (Lieutenant Tranter) aboard and a British officer (Captain Purvis) of 30 Heavy Ack Ack who, although junior to Captain Apthorp, was the only person with any real knowledge of sailing, and had somehow managed to stir some willing but inexperienced men into getting a bit of canvas rigged and to flounder their way out of the river and into the sea.

During the late evening and early morning they got the mainsail rigged but then – having become broached-to – the whole lot came down again and they nearly capsized.

By the time they reached the islet – and heaven alone knows how they managed that – it had been ten hours from when they left the harbour wall some eight miles away, whereas we had only taken three hours to cover five miles before having a meal and a good sleep!

There will be times when I will later deny the existence of a God, but right at that moment I was convinced that nothing short of a miracle of Divine intervention could have brought us together within 200 yards of each other and needing each other's help.

The *Bintang Dua* looked very much as depicted in the sketch. She was about 35 feet long and her hold was covered by an ark-like roof. There were small 'decks' fore and aft; on the former was the cooking hearth – a slab of stone mounted at waist level – and on the latter, the tiller and a compass. We had a complement of 27 men, most of whom had recently got to Padang by a variety of routes after starting out from Singapore at varying dates. Captain Purvis and Lieutenant Dicker had left there in a *tonkan* (the *Hock Siew*) equivalent in size to a junk. It was carrying 130 officers and men of 30 Battery, the 3rd Heavy Ack Ack Regiment, but only the above two officers had set out on this second escape.

By contrast, Captain Apthorp's departure had been a far more spontaneous affair, which started when he swam out into Singapore harbour on the night of capitulation to bring in a small boat which was then used to stage the build-up of a large group that eventually hijacked the junk *Hiap Hin*. It was sailed down through the Rhiouw archipelago and they were fortunate enough to be directed to one of the food dumps that had been left by the Organisation. They rescued a large number of stranded evacuees and arrived at the Andiri Giri river with a mixed and greatly expanded complement of 217. Captain Apthorp had only a few 'unit' ties with them and once they reached Padang they all went their various ways.

There were seven dedicated troublemakers with us and they continued to sit about doing nothing other than complain. I have no idea what units they belonged to.

So that was what we looked like when Stracc got the vessel under way and he soon demonstrated that as a sailor he was in a class of his own. He had the tackle and sails sorted out very quickly and by dusk we must have made about 40 miles to the west despite having to tack into a crosswind. By then we all needed a rest, so a sea anchor was rigged, a watch set and the rest of us crawled into the hold and onto our various bits of makeshift bedding. Next day – the eighteenth – we continued west until land was sighted and, after turning south-south-west for a few miles, we once again anchored for the night. On the twentieth we sailed on south along the coast of Siberut and by the afternoon we had anchored in the capital and port of that name.

It had become quite obvious to all of us that much of the canvas that we were carrying was in need of repair, and even if that were to be done it would hardly be likely to live through anything other than the friendliest of winds. There was a small reserve of canvas stowed in the forrard locker but it was even more threadbare than that in use. We went ashore to seek repairs, food and water; and – most important of all – some large containers in which to store water. The locals were mainly Indonesians and they gave us a very friendly reception. There were also some from the Mentawi tribe, who, apart from being quite primitive, were unfriendly and remained aloof.

The local craftsmen soon set about repairing the tears in the sails, but the patching that they did seemed far from convincing to me. The finished job reminded me of that biblical warning that one should never mix old wine with new. There were no large water receptacles available, so we had to make do with large bamboo with the inner sections punched out. We also took on a good supply of coconuts which – together with the prospect of rain ahead – seemed adequate provision in the way of liquids, even if we were to make a direct run across to India or Ceylon.

It is surprising what can be gleaned from a school atlas. We had certainly put our one to good use already and it became even more useful to us as we started to plan ahead. We found that we would be moving into a bad period of monsoon weather and that it could last for many weeks. That prospect seemed to be both good and bad news because while we were not going to lack for water, it looked as though we might be in for some very severe storms. The worst discovery was that the prevailing winds would be mainly northeasterlies. That would have favoured a run south down the whole length of the western coasts of Sumatra and Java before striking out for Australia, except that we knew that the Japanese had that route pretty well sewn up.

After much consideration the vote was that we should make the north-westerly haul along the west coasts of the Nicobar and Andaman islands – and then perhaps keep going towards the north-west of Burma, with the option of striking west to India if circum-stances should dictate later. That latter option would have had to depend mainly on the state of the boat and the weather. However, despite the hazards of a direct ocean journey, there was a lot to commend it, since we were by no means sure if the above islands were occupied by the Japanese or not.

We had arrived in Siberut to find that another escape vessel – a *prahu* – had come in ahead of us. It had tied up the day before with 11 men aboard who had sailed over from Sungei Penang – a small fishing kampong a few miles south of Padang. They had had trouble getting over to Siberut as the craft was flat-bottomed and, true to its reputation, despite being fitted with outriggers, this had caused it to drift off course. They too had had to make do with threadbare canvas, and all these problems had combined to cause major damage when they ran into bad weather.

Although much of their repair work had been done before we met, they were of the opinion that our vessel looked far more seaworthy and asked if they could join with us. We took a vote and found that the majority were against it on the grounds that we were cramped enough as it was. That was certainly true; but the most compelling reason for our refusal was that we saw them as a rather menacing lot of individuals, to the extent that I had put the word round that we had a machine-gun aboard. The full story of their tragic bid to escape has been told by one of their number – Sergeant D. Gavin of the East Surreys – in his book *Quiet Jungle, Angry Sea.*

We left on the twenty-first sailing north into the wind, and by dint of considerable tacking made some headway during the next two days while always keeping the island in view on the port side. Despite our slow progress we really had no alternative but to con-tinue in that direction up to the Mentawi Straits at the northern tip of Siberut Island. To have gone south from the port and then come up the opposite (western) coast would have trebled the distance, albeit it would certainly have given us the protection of a lee shore.

On the afternoon of the twenty-third disaster struck!

Sergeant Stracchino was on watch as helmsman. We had a look-out forrard and soundings were being taken at regular intervals because the wind had been taking us in towards shallows. Nevertheless everything seemed to be going well and we were in any case only drifting along until Stracc suddenly shouted out, 'What's that ahead?' and was told, 'It's only a patch of brown water.'

With that, Stracc hitched the tiller, leapt forward, jumped partway up the mast and then shouted, 'It's bloody rocks, you silly sod!' By then it was far too late to turn and ease away from the danger. Even with the helm hard over, the forward momentum made us just drift slowly into that so-called 'brown water', which was in fact sea wrack waving above a slightly submerged coral encrusted reef. We tried to pole away from the danger – but it was all too late! We just bumped and scraped our way along the top of the reef, tearing the rudder from its mounting and bending the pintles as it came away.

Sergeant Wringe of the East Indian Corps of Clerks was the first to react. He went over the side and just managed to rescue the rudder before it could drift out of reach. He was quickly followed by others – including myself – who jumped barefooted out into the shoulder-deep water in an attempt to push the boat into a slightly deeper channel on the starboard side. It was all to no avail and a very painful business too, because the sharp coral lacerated our feet and left deep cuts for the salt water to work on. To make matters worse, we found that the seams had been sprung, then water began to seep steadily into the hold; but strangely enough though, that turned out to be a bit of a godsend because the more the boat filled, the more it settled, until it became completely grounded, and with that, all the wearing and scraping noises ceased.

It soon began to look as though our bid for escape had ended. The water kept coming in until it levelled with the sea outside. However, there was just a hope that we might be able to get some help from ashore. We still had the *kolek* in tow and there was a rather battered but seaworthy dinghy lashed to the decking. So it was decided to send a few men ashore while the rest got on with the damage-control work.

At about that time the *prahu* that we had seen in Siberut went sailing by a few hundred yards to seaward of us. We were seen by its crew, but according to Sergeant Gavin's account, there wasn't much that they could have done about it and that they thought we were managing all right! – or words to that effect. To that version of the event I would prefer to say no more than that our earlier decision not to take them aboard had caused a fair amount of acrimony on both sides.

We were about to lower the dinghy, when two outrigger canoes were seen coming out to us. They were manned by Mentawi tribesmen and they took our kit and all but four of us ashore. It was just as well that they were in charge because they had to do quite a bit of manoeuvring before we could get in close to their kampong. It was almost dark when we arrived and we were soon surrounded by most of the community.

They crowded round us in an inquisitive and aggressive manner, making it quite obvious that they expected to be given some of our possessions for services rendered. I am sure that they would have helped themselves but for the fact that two of us were armed. There was only one official among them – a Sumatran. He had apparently been left there by the Dutch in the hope that he might keep them in order. It was a vain hope because they had already realised that their colonial masters were not going to come back and were paying scant attention to any of his orders. He looked harassed and scared and we thought that he should have long ago made himself scarce. However, he did eventually succeed in stopping their pestering and then offered us accommodation in a small stone building near the sea-shore.

He went off to fetch some palm-oil lamps and then took us into a store-cum-gaol comprising one large and two small rooms – the latter having low stone platforms along their walls.

After dumping most of our kit we left a guard at the doorway – which couldn't be locked – and then came out to meet the Mentawis again to start negotiations for some food. We had a few guilders between us but the tribesmen seemed far more interested in doing barter – that is, if they had to – and thievery, if they thought they could get away with it. Lieutenant Dicker has described them well as sullen-looking tattooed men wearing a bun tied at the nape of their necks and sporting a red and white flower over the left ear; and also, that the only woman in evidence was an old crone who went through our belongings and appropriated everything that she fancied – toothpaste in particular! I must thank him for that description because I cannot remember very much about that evening – or the next day, for that matter – because I was beginning to feel unwell and thought that I was in for a bout of malaria.

By the following morning I had become quite groggy, so the others told me that they were going to leave me while they went out with some Mentawis to help with salvaging the boat.

That idea didn't appeal to me very much because when we first met them I had noticed that the tribesmen carried bows and arrows; and now, some of them were assembled at the doorway with their weapons and they looked quite villainous to me. I was feverish at the time and might well have imagined more threat than actually existed. However, I can remember saying to someone, 'Make sure that you come back for me,' and I asked them to stack all their kit where I could see it within our inner room. I then told the agent to let it be known that I had a loaded revolver and would shoot anyone who tried to enter while the rest of the party was away.

I had realised by then that I hadn't got malaria but some other kind of fever which appeared to be far worse. Although I had got the 'shakes' and my forehead was hot, those symptoms were not followed by a sweating and the further bout of shakes that one gets with an attack of malaria until the fever breaks. Instead of that, I could feel that my temperature was just going up and up.

I was nearly delirious by the time the others got back. The four who had stayed out on the boat overnight had done a great salvage job. They had managed to patch up the seams and bale out the boat until it had been sufficiently lightened to float it off the reef. It had then been brought into a sheltered inlet. Stracc was one of the four. He had a thermometer and discovered that I was running a temperature of close on 105 degrees. I could hardly believe that since I remembered having been told that 108 was the absolute limit. My temperature seemed to be on the way down now, so I should already have been dead before they came back! However, I now know that I must have been suffering from dengue fever, which causes the temperature to shoot up to alarming heights for a few hours followed by recovery within two days; and so it turned out for me. By the following afternoon – while the others were busy careening and caulking the boat – I felt well enough to get up and go out for a short walk along the seashore.

I hadn't gone far before I saw a family of wild pigs down by the sea lapping at the salt water in what appeared to be isolated contentment – until one of them suddenly contorted and crashed to the ground with an arrow through its body. The rest of them turned and ran up from the beach, squealing as they made for cover. Very few of them made it, though. They were confronted by a group of Mentawi hunters who, having netted the scrub, were waiting above the beach to slaughter them. My belief is that the arrow was just a bit of 'theatricals' in order to show that they could have picked me off as well.

Later that day I was told that the awkward squad had stolen the dinghy and cleared off. I had thought that we were a few short! Probably because of my illness, everyone had thought that I had been given the news earlier – not that it mattered much to me really. I saw it as a very welcome fait accompli.

I went off to join the others still working on the boat and took with me two bearers carrying a squealing pig strapped to a board, and some chickens. The chickens were housed in the hold within a makeshift run and the pig was put in a pen which – for him – was ominously close to the galley.

We were all busy about our various tasks when someone shouted out that the mutineers had come back and that they were about to come aboard, having announced that they wished to rejoin us now that our craft had been made serviceable again. They found themselves facing three loaded revolvers while Captain Purvis took a vote on the matter. The judgement was that they should be given a quarter of our provisions before being sent packing. The final scene of the event was recorded by Captain Apthorp, who wrote, '... Stracchino, fingering his revolver, looking grim and not disposed to argue, they tumbled back into their boat. Stores were divided and handed over; then to our surprise – and quite unconcerned – they hoisted sail and passed out of sight behind a mangrove swamp bordering the water's edge'.

Captain Apthorp, Stracc and Sergeant Wringe had all worked heroically when stranded out on the reef. The Captain was one of those dogged characters who, when given a job to do stuck with it unremittingly until it was completed. He had done most of the caulking by the time the others came out to help; and the two sergeants had gone overboard time and time again to straighten the pintles ready for the rudder to be re-set; and to do the first part of that, Stracc had had to work for long stretches under the water holding his breath.

By the morning of the twenty-sixth of March the last of the provisioning and all of our kit had been put aboard and stowed. So off we went north into the wind and made little headway as we slowly tacked our way towards the Mentawi Straits. After three days we came to a complete standstill in a flat calm. The sun – which had been beating down fiercely during the first few days – became even more intense as the wind stilled and the sails ceased to flap. It was so calm that the water became like a mirror and we were able to look 30 or 40 feet down to a seabed decked in a multi-coloured scattering of kelp, coral and marine life. It was unimaginably calm. I can remember someone laying a cigarette paper down on the deck and even that didn't stir.

This unscheduled stop proved to be the greatest test of our temperaments and our resolve. Some of the ship's company had voted to sail back southwards three days earlier, and it has to be admitted that had we done so, we would have had the direct assistance of a two-day breeze coming from the north-east. However, we still had a majority who were voting for continuing rather than running back down the coastline for 80 miles; and then what? The answer to that had to be the proverbial lemon! After all we were by now nearly up to the northernmost point of the main island and would be needing just a few hours of moderate wind to ease us clear and away into the Indian Ocean. So we went to sleep that night with our spirits high and praying for just one small 'assist' from the weather to get us on our way.

By the following morning it seemed that our prayers had been answered as we felt a light though sluggish response on the helm, but by midday the breeze had abated and we once more lay motionless in a flat calm.

It was then that we noticed what appeared to be a medium-sized merchant vessel coming through the strait towards us. Once we were sighted, it turned to close to a distance of about half a mile before starting to circle us. Meanwhile we were all straining to pick out some distinguishing markings or an ensign flying. Our hopes rose with the thought that a Japanese vessel would surely have been flying the 'fried egg'. Unfortunately our bid for freedom was ended by a burst of machine-gun fire across our bow.

The steamer lowered a launch. It came towards us with uniformed

70

and armed men aboard, and while it closed on us we held a very quick council of war. We soon decided to ditch our revolvers, knowing that the Japanese never stopped to ask questions before shooting anyone carrying arms. Having done that, we were surprised to find that the launch was crewed by five or six Indonesian sailors of the Konniglyke Marine (Royal Netherlands Navy). They came alongside and passed up a message which read: 'Please send over your Commander unarmed'.

We watched Captains Apthorp and Purvis go off, and it wasn't long before the rest of us were ordered across onto what turned out to be the SS *Bangui*, a 600-ton vessel (with passenger accommodation) which in peacetime had mainly been used for servicing lighthouses.

Two of the sailors had been left on the *Bintang Dua* with the outrigger attached. A tow was put out from the *Banggai* and then we steamed off in line.

12

CATCH 22! – 'WE'RE BRITISH, YOU KNOW!'

When our two officers came aboard they were amazed at being confronted by the same Menheer Willem van Dyl (Dutch Commissioner of Police) who had assisted them two weeks previously with getting the *Bintang Dua* safely out of Padang harbour.

This time he was to become their very reluctant and apologetic gaoler-cum-interrogator. When the rest of us had been transferred we were brought to join them in the passenger saloon.

He told us that the owners had reported their loss to the Japanese and he had been sent out with an armed detachment of his native policemen to find us and bring us back. The skipper had sailed to Siberu harbour first; and, finding that we had gone north, he went south and then up the west coast of the island in the hope that it would give us time to get away. However, once we had been sighted, he then had no option but to arrest us because he couldn't trust all of his crew to keep that knowledge from the Japanese.

Van Dyl and the skipper were now doing their best to make amends! To start with, he left us alone to concoct the hopefully convincing story that we had all been evacuated from Singapore before it fell; and we came up with an agreed tale that we had been despatched to Java as a cadre of officers, RAs, REs, Signals, RASC and drivers to build up a unit to carry on the fight there; – and it would further our case if we said that the '*glorious*' Japanese air force had attacked and sunk our vessel near Priggi Rajah, forcing us to seek a replacement on the west coast.

Willem must have known that the capture of the *Banggai* would be next on our agenda but he still left us on our own. He even allowed us to get some fresh air outside the saloon and to wander round the deck. We noted the sentry and machine-gun positions then returned to the saloon to concoct a plan. It was decided that we would go out again but singing together this time; and then – on an agreed word – jump the nearest guard. It was 'Roy of the Rovers' stuff but nevertheless feasible. Most of us were for it, but only if Willem would co-operate, so we called him in. After all, he had helped before, so why not give him a chance to escape too!

He went off and consulted with the skipper, who agreed but pointed out that he would need to get back to Siberu to refuel, and while there, leave any non-cooperating crew or policemen behind.

That seemed to be that but then – and heavens only knows why he left it so late – Willem told us that all of their families were being held hostage against their return.

A meal was brought in and once again we were left alone!

We put the matter to the vote and our decision was almost unanimous. We would surrender ourselves into the captivity of the Japanese! *After all, we were British, you know!* We just couldn't contemplate theoretically signing the death warrants for dozens of innocent civilians just to save our own skins.

We had been thoroughly downcast when first picked up but by now we felt totally frustrated as well by the decision that we had been forced to make. To compound our frustration, it had been taken at a time when a light wind that had been blowing for an hour or so had developed into a strong wind. If only it had started up a few hours earlier we would have been to hell and away over the horizon in the *Bintang Dua* and free from complicated decision making.

The wind then increased to such an extent that the two men left on the *Bintang Dua* had to cut the outrigger adrift as it started to fill with water; and then we had to divert and tow her back into Siberu, where we anchored for the night.

The next day (the thirty-first of March) we headed back to Sumatra. It was the first of April of all days when we steamed into Emmerhaven and were taken ashore to meet our real captors.

None of us knew what to expect. There were some of us who thought that we would just be searched and then put in with the POWs who had stayed in Padang; but I was one of the pessimists who expected summary treatment from the outset. So – for me at least – it came as quite an anticlimax when we were in fact taken in buses to the Japanese HQ, rather casually searched, and then, as the others had predicted, we were taken under escort to what had been the local Dutch barracks. There had been a lot of shouting but no violence on the way. Once there, we were handed over to other guards, who led us without any fuss over to the corner of the parade ground and left us to our own devices.

Apparently nothing much had happened while we had been away other than that the Navy and Air Force officers had been taken back to Singapore.

What was evident – and quite natural, I suppose – was that the men had split into cliques within cliques, the first being of the three service groupings and the second of the various mates within them. However, what was markedly lacking in many of those divisions was any sense of common cause or discipline; and for the fragmented individuals who were not of any common group, it seemed to be a case of every man for himself and the devil take the last. That was even more evident later when a meal was served up without any visible attempt to ensure fair rationing. There was fighting and doubling-up which the few responsible NCOs set at the ration points were finding almost impossible to control.

As soon as the meal was over, our party was ordered to parade again. We were then harangued by a Japanese NCO. After that, an interpreter told us that Japanese HQ had now reasoned that we were dangerous men who might corrupt the others; so, they had decided that we must be segregated. After that – and much to our surprise – van Dyl appeared again, looking rather dejected and bewildered. He arrived in the company of a Japanese officer and a different escort. It would appear that he had been elected chief dogsbody for ensuring that their orders were carried out.

The Japanese then took us out of the camp again; the officer led in his staff car with the escort. The rest of us followed on by bus.

Under any other circumstances it would have been an interesting and scenic journey up into the hills north of Padang. However, after winding our way up on a good metalled road for about an hour, we had just rounded a sharp bend when the escort signalled us to halt by a bridge. It spanned a torrent fed by a waterfall that cascaded and thundered down from the hills above. We were ordered out of the bus and told to stand over on the far side against a parapet.

There wasn't one person amongst us who didn't then think, 'Oh what a lovely line-up for a firing squad!' We could have been shot, our bodies pushed over the top and the sound would have been

74

masked by the noise from the torrent below. I will always remember those few moments watching the water pounding round a group of exposed rocks before racing down to the valley below; and, at the same time, debating with Stracc and Harry Adrian the chances of surviving a dive over the parapet into a rock-free patch of water.

We had just decided that anything would be better than standing there passively while waiting to be shot, when to our obvious relief, the Japanese officer took a camera from his pocket and started taking snaps of the waterfall. What an anticlimax it was to realise that far from being murderous, the officer had been thoughtful enough to give us a chance to stretch our legs. And, we got a further surprise when he came to us and then, in good English, said, 'Don't be tempted to try and escape because you wouldn't get very far. There are man-eating tigers in these hills as well as some very unfriendly natives!'

With that, we went off again and after winding our way up to Fort-de-Kok, we were de-bussed, marched over to a nearby bungalow and told to sit on the lawn. Shortly after that the Japanese came back with a German in tow who told us that he was there to act as interpreter.

Captain Apthorp tried – but without much success – to convey the details of our cover story. The German did not appear to know much Japanese. His English was also inadequate, so nobody got very far! Things went on quite aimlessly for some time until the Japanese – having got nowhere – didn't appear to know what to do next. Captain Apthorp then interrupted the proceedings with the request that we might have some food; and that settled the matter for the time being. We were then taken off to the nearby barracks and given a good meal prepared by a group of Dutch POWs. After eating that, our officers were taken off one way (and we another) to some furnished buildings where were left to sleep for the night. It was all rather strange because we were once again left to our own devices, but this time without any apparent restriction on our movements. We tested this out and found that there was no guard outside and that we were able to wander in and out of adjacent buildings at will.

The following day brought us more pleasant surprises. The Dutch continued to feed us with tasty and well-cooked meals; and, although we were supposed to have no verbal contact with them, there wasn't anyone about to stop us doing so, as far as we could see. We had been housed in part of what had been their HQ complex and was now largely occupied by a Japanese transport unit. There was a theoretical 'no go' assemblage of buildings between us which were abandoned Dutch army food and clothing stores.

Having been fed and counted, we were again left unguarded; so we went off, entered the buildings and helped ourselves to just anything that took our fancy. And a lot of it did!

We found a lot of tins that had been opened on spec by the Japanese, sampled, and then discarded for various reasons. Outside there were several large tins which had contained butter. These had been emptied because the Japanese – out of their ignorance – had thought that they were axle grease. The place was an absolute goldmine! Its treasures were there to sample or loot at will.

When we went into the clothing store it was the same. We just took our time kitting ourselves out with items of Dutch uniform in the knowledge that we could reject anything that didn't fit or take our fancy. There were also piles of neatly stacked accessories such as haversacks, mess tins and water bottles. Taking a large haversack, I stuffed it with Dutch uniform and toilet requisites. I also carted off a Dutch army hat, a small folding camp bed and a big pile of tinned food – the latter in the expectation that someone would soon arrive to lock the food store; but I needn't have worried because it remained open throughout our stay.

That was the good side of events. The bad side was a further series of interrogations, some buffeting and haranguing, and a far from pleasant session of intimidation. There was nothing very physical about our earlier encounter but it had left us fearing for the future.

The Japanese had had time to digest our story about being officially evacuated, and while they had seemed to be satisfied that a cadre should have officers and men representative of varying units and skills, the sticking point for them was that we had declared two of our number to be drivers. They simply did not – or would not – understand Captain Apthorp's explanation that such men were essential to a unit in order to ensure its mobility. That doubt – and for no good reason that we could see – made them waver between acceptance and the out-and-out rejection of our story, in the belief that the drivers were some kind of sinister super-specialists.

We had made the fatal error of not taking the Japanese too seriously during the first couple of days, and when asked to number off we had counted through to ten and then followed on with jack, king, queen, no trumps, etc., which after the second or third day brought a questioning response from the guard of 'No trumska?' It was just a bit of fun at first but once they had 'cottoned on', the man who declared no trumps was given a thump in the ribs with a rifle butt. Another comic when asked to declare his peacetime occupation had put himself down as a milestone counter. Later, when asked to explain further, it was fortunate that the German was still with us, because we passed the man off as a surveyor, although the Japanese did not appear to be very happy about that either.

All of this was, of course, rather childish but it did serve to work off some of the frustrations of having been captured. We were lucky that the Japanese did not have a good interpreter with them at that time because I am quite sure that none of them were blessed with any sense of humour.

Once again there was a deterioration in the attitude of the Japanese. It started with a lot more abuse and buffeting and then the insistence that we must bow every time we saw a Japanese officer, no matter how distant he might be.

A day or two after that they introduced a 9 a.m. *tenko* (parade) for our NCOs and other ranks only. This took us by surprise because we had had our usual *tenko* alongside the Dutch an hour earlier and in a different part of the camp.

We were brought before the Japanese Commandant by an escort of armed NCOs. He had us lined up in single file and spaced well apart. Then he started waving a bit of paper at us and shouting – in Japanese, of course! If we had had more experience of the Japanese at that time we would have known that it was always bad news when there was no interpreter around. We were assailed with a vicious staccato of unintelligible words that were spat out rather than spoken in a high-pitched voice that eventually became a scream. Then came a pause in which we were supposedly expected to show some kind of penitent reaction. It was then I realised that he was manic or stupid – or both – to expect that we should know what the fuss was about. It seemed that the bit of paper had something to do with our interrogation, but if that were so, we had no means of knowing what part of it had particularly displeased him, or why.

So, we just stood there and stared at him blankly while waiting to see what would happen next. And we didn't have to wait long!

Drawing his sword, he advanced on us and, wielding it above the first man, he brought it swishing downwards and sideways, skimming his head and then away above his shoulder in a deft parabola that swept upwards and just past the head of the next man in line. It was terrifying. Each of us got the treatment in turn, some in silence and others to the accompaniment of a triumphant shriek. There was just nothing that any of us could do about it other than stand stock still and pray that he wasn't going to go completely berserk and decapitate one of us. Believe me, I was not thinking of much else at the time. However, he eventually got to the end of the line – and with nobody's severed head twitching on the ground. I think that he had hoped that one of us would have broken file and made a run for it. That would have given him all the excuse he needed for executing him for trying to escape. Alternatively – and we were never going to know the answer – he might just have been amusing himself at our expense. Whatever the reason may have been, he went through the same ritual for the next two days until (as we liked to think) he gave us best, having by then been impressed by our unflinching behaviour.

Throughout those three days we were still given the freedom of the manor and we were still stealing tins of food to supplement the already excellent meals that the Dutch were cooking for us. We had also started to investigate more distant buildings within the 'no go' area, having discovered that it was patrolled only twice daily and in a very casual fashion.

We had noticed a large stone building, which was locked until Stracc got to work on it. It had a small entrance area with a large inner room which led to a smaller room that was securely locked. Several of us had been slipping into the large room to look at a shelved display of ancient Dutch and native military artefacts. There was nothing in there worth liberating but it was an interesting place to wander round in.

I was in there and – as I thought – on my own on the second day of the sword-wielding saga when I heard a noise in the inner room. The door had been unlocked, so I went in and discovered Lieutenant Dicker, Stracc and Private Ingham examining a collection of antique pistols, swords and native weapons. After looking round for a bit, I wandered back out again without having noticed that Stracc had taken a wooden box from one of the shelves. There were cartridges inside it and an old but well-preserved shotgun which he started to fiddle about with and then load, all unknown to me.

So without any warning I was startled by the sound of a loud bang, which was then followed by the rapid retreat of the others. I tailed on behind them and we all dashed outside. Once in the open we slowed to a casual saunter and assumed an air of innocence.

We had covered about 20 yards when an investigating guard appeared round the corner of a distant building and saw what appeared to be four innocent POWs taking a gentle stroll just beyond the 'no go' perimeter. He routed around for a bit but made no challenge and finally went off again without checking any of the buildings – thank God, because when we scuttled out, we left a very strong smell of burnt cordite behind us.

The outcome of that was an order issued by the Commandant that *POWs should not make any noises that might frighten his soldiers!* Had the Japanese got a sense of humour after all?

Having posed that question, there was soon every indication that the answer was '*No*', because the day after our final assignation with the manic sword-wielder all of us – officers and men – were called out on parade before a gathering of senior Japanese officers and NCOs without knowing why. A table and a chair were then brought out and set before them.

Shortly after that we saw a fat, very senior and drunk Japanese officer come waddling unsteadily out of the HQ building. He was so short that his sword trailed on the ground, leaving a cloud of dust in his wake. We were given the order '*kiotski*' (attention), and with the realisation that he was 'number one top brass' we didn't wait to be invited to bow *him* onto the stage.

Once the formalities were over he reached into a pocket, produced the inevitable piece of paper and then, moving over to the chair, he attempted to mount it in order to get up onto the table. He scrabbled around for a bit before realising that his legs were too short and that he was too pissed to even climb onto the chair. By then, his face – which had already been flushed with drinking – was taking on the complexion of an apoplectic gargoyle; and our faces were also going red with our efforts to keep from laughing.

He finally managed to hoick his knees up onto the seat; but the next move up to the tabletop proved to be beyond him. He stayed there floundering around on his elbows with his nose pressed down firmly on the table. Finally – and without one smile from his entourage – two Japanese officers came forward and literally propelled him upwards by his elbows and the seat of his trousers. Once there he scrambled to his feet and stood swaying and peering at the bit of paper that had miraculously remained grasped in his hand.

That was not the last of the entertainment by any means! He then went into overdrive pounding his feet on the tabletop and delivering his message in such a mounting frenzy of oratory that two of his attendants closed on him from behind to assume a catching position in case he should fall off.

All good things have to come to an end, unfortunately. He finished the speech and was helped down; and then the interpreter came over and handed us a translation.

There was one copy only, and when my turn came to read it I did so slowly before handing it back to the officers. I never had any occasion (or necessity) to read it again. The words were burnt into my brain and they have stayed in my memory ever since.

No wonder there had been all that palaver! The edict had come direct from the Japanese High Command and with the blessing of their top-hatted fart of a god-emperor; and essentially, in these words:

You men are the tattered remnants of a degenerate nation! The Japanese Emperor has seen fit to spare your lives for work on the noble project of railway building! Thousands of you will die and leave your bones to bleach on the lines!

So it would appear that our concocted story had bought us just enough time to save ourselves from summary execution but I was in no mood to see it in that light at the time; quite the opposite, in fact! They had instilled in me such a feeling of hatred for the whole bloody lot of them due to their arrogant posturing and their promise to work us to death that the feeling remained with me (and in a peculiar way also served to sustain me) through the following three and a half years.

It was as well to know from the start where we stood with our Japanese captors. They were highly strung, cruel, manic and Jekyll and Hyde characters to a man. We were to be treated as *romushas* – lesser people – which would place us at the bottom of the pecking order. Rated just above us were the Koreans – a subject race. Many of them would later be our guards, and find pleasure in taking their feelings out on us. At the top of the roost were the millions who saw themselves as equals to the Japanese within the so-called *Co*-Prosperity Sphere. The fact that they were deluded often worked in our favour later, thank God.

It was the eighteenth of April and I was sitting in the train on the way back to Padang loaded with valuable loot, thinking of these things (and also, being scarcely able to believe that so much had happened in the two months since I had escaped from Singapore). My attention was taken by the locals standing at the trackside and waving those 'flaming arsehole' flags. Among them once again was the ginger-bearded Dutchman and his native family. So at least something was still well with the world.

On arrival at Padang station we were marched across the town and taken into the barracks to rejoin the POWs that we had met briefly two weeks before.

PART TWO

13

COME AND JOIN US – IN AT THE DEEP END!

18 April 1942 – Padang

We were lodged within a small open-fronted room in the corner of the parade ground, which much to the annoyance of those already there had been cleared for us by a detachment of high-handed and heavy-booted Japanese sentries.

It was fortunate for us that we had been put together because the whole atmosphere of the place had deteriorated during our absence. Any discipline that might have been in evidence when we came through a fortnight previously was by now virtually non-existent. A small group of NCOs had been striving to keep some sort of order but they had been gradually losing ground to factions that had decided that a 'soldiers' army' would serve them best. Men had already begun to thieve from one another and they had been raiding the ration store. So for the benefit of the few the majority were being made to go hungry. A POW guard of NCOs and men had been put on the store but that arrangement soon became useless once the villains got in on the act and by bribery and bullying managed to subvert the so-called 'trusties'. After that things had got into such a state of disorder that the guard had to be replaced by an all-officer detail.

Such behaviour was quite alien to our party. We had developed such a good level of comradeship and trust that no-one had ever thought it necessary to keep an eye on our kit. Now we had to ensure that someone was around to guard it. This was very restrictive and it involved a lot of manoeuvring to keep the area in view at *tenko* and meal times.

There was now such a distinct sense of unease throughout the ranks of the more responsible officers and men that it was easy to see that any further lapses from decent communal behaviour might result in a state of anarchy; and then (with no semblance of organisation in place) it would present an open invitation to the Japanese to get in amongst us to divide, dictate and punish at will.

There were those – and they were the hard cases – who were either so basically vicious or out-and-out thick that they thought such a situation would benefit them. It might well have done so in the short run, but they were all incapable of thinking ahead to a time when they might become like the very people they had been abusing – in other words, the weak and the sick – and then, where would *they* find comfort and support?

On the other end of the scale there were those whose condition was largely due to the privations that they suffered while on the escape route. Many of them had commenced POW life in a kitless and exhausted condition. Others had found POW life in general more than enough to cope with without the further problem of intimidation by thugs.

Between those extremes were many men who – although difficult if not openly surly, for lack of direction and discipline – were still hoping for some form of leadership around which they could rally for their own safety and for the wellbeing of the whole. Fortunately that middle ground also contained large groupings of Royal Navy and RAF personnel who, despite having had their officers withdrawn, had still maintained a fair degree of cohesion, comradeship and discipline. So, there was something to build on there. If only those officers had been retained someone might have emerged of senior rank and competence to the Army officer that was in post – and in confusion! – now.

The officer in question was Captain R. Morley of 30 Heavy Ack Ack. He had come out from Singapore on the night of surrender under the command of his CO, Major Rowley-Conway, in a junk named the *Hock Siew*. It was a well-organised evacuation of virtually the whole of 30 HAA battery which included Captain Purvis and Lieutenant Dicker, my erstwhile companions on the *Bintang Dua*. Their journey (which had started well) had later developed into a bit of a shambles due to bad seamanship and (as I recall) a certain amount of insubordination of the men and a degree of bickering among the officers. Their CO had eventually gone his own way and he had arrived in Padang early enough to get away with a group of high-rankers which included members of the SOE and

86

of Colonel Warren's Organisation. Their vessel the *Sederhana Djohannis* was a well-found ketch provisioned and crewed by a number of men who knew their job. They were one of only two groups that avoided destruction or capture and got safely over to Ceylon; and incidentally, history has revealed that we were perhaps lucky to have been captured because patrolling the Indian Ocean at that time between our intended destination was a flotilla of Japanese vessels (which included battleships and an aircraft carrier) intent on shooting up every Allied vessel in sight and blitzing Colombo. They intercepted one escape vessel and destroyed another.

However, getting back to the calamities that befell the *Hock Siew* and the disarray within 30 Heavy AA Battery, their craft was finally beached. Then, after being ferried on up a less hospitable river than the Andiri Giri, they had to make an arduous and lengthy trek through malarial swampland. By the time they had picked up the trail that led to the Sawahalunto railhead the officers and men had – to say the least of it – found cause for dispute, the finer points of which were never fully revealed to me. Nevertheless, quite a lot of it can be imagined in what happened next.

Captain Morley was soon given the chance to offload the greater part of his overall command of about 700 men. The Japanese ordered that a party of 20 officers and 480 men were to be selected by him preparatory to being sent north towards some Shangri-La where we would start on that 'noble project of railway building'. All we knew about it to begin with was that we would be entrained for the short trip to the railhead at Fort-de-Kok. A day or two later we found that the officers selected to go into the unknown, had decided to call us 'The British Sumatra Battalion'. It would be marched down to Padang station under Japanese escort while the officers, the sick and the little heavy kit that anybody had would be taken down there in a lorry led by a Japanese staff car, which in the event once again saw Menheer Willem van Dyl on parade and one of its occupants.

It was quite consistent with normal army practice that when an officer got the chance to make a posting he would automatically take the opportunity to 'biff' any of his trouble-makers over to the receiving unit with as glowing a report as possible about their virtues – if any! So, it must have come as an overwhelming shock to Lieutenant Dicker when he was hit with what I can only describe as a double-double whammy.

Virtually all of the *Bintang Dua* party including Lieutenant Dicker had been selected. That was no surprise since it was 'last in and first out' in part of Morley's reasoning; but he then discovered that practically the whole of 30 HAA (110 men) would be going with him. He was the only – and their most junior – officer selected. He had also been landed with a complaining senior NCO who was alleging that he had been badly served by his officers on the way over from Singapore and had therefore decided to sink into the anonymity of being just 'one of the boys'. (For the record, neither the lieutenant nor I ever found out whether the alleged injustice was real or just perceived by the man. One thing is sure about him, though, and that is that he did such a good job travelling incognito that I cannot even recall what he looked like.) That wasn't the end of things for Lieutenant Dicker because when the time came to parade ready for departure only one of the other officers of 30 HAA had the decency to come across and bid him good luck. He found himself standing among what he himself has described as 'a bunch of misfits', who as far as he could see had been biffed off by Morley because their faces didn't fit.

I agree with his assessment, and made this further comment when writing to Ann Apthorp – our new CO's widow – in the following passage of her book *The British Sumatra Battalion*:

> Several of the officers had no experience whatsoever, having been given rank when they came under the aegis of the Army – (for their protection mainly) – straight from civilian employment in Malaya in such occupations as rubber planter, tin miner, forestry commission, etc. One was even the public hangman!

The most astounding thing to me at the time was that Lieutenant Dicker knew practically nothing about the men of 30 HAA, having only been posted into the battery just before the surrender of Singapore and, moreover, into an outstationed unit. So, what on earth had caused Morley to abdicate his most essential duty of seeing that his battery stayed under *his* command and not with one junior officer? My best guess in answer to that has always been that Harold Dicker came up through the ranks. He is far too loyal a man to have said such a thing about his own senior officer and particularly so, perhaps, because when he came out of captivity he still had to complete his army career. Don't get me wrong, he was a loyal man anyway and he proved it as a POW by the support he gave to his CO, Captain Apthorp, when most of his other colleagues were giving little or none.

Well, so much for that bit of the preamble to the move! I was also right in the thick of things. It was only two days before 'the off' when Captain Apthorp came to me and said, 'I would like you to accept acting promotion to BSM (Battalion Sergeant-major) and take not only charge of the men, but also "straighten out" the rogues among them!' I asked him why he had selected me, a junior to many of the other senior NCOs, and he said, 'I like the way you have conducted yourself since you joined us on the *Bintang Dua* and also what I have heard about your leadership when rowing down from Singapore.' I had to be proud of that and I thanked him; but first asked to have a day to think about it and, more importantly, to find out why those others had not been approached, or indeed, if they had been and he hadn't told me! He agreed to that and off I went to search them out. In the event it turned out to be an easier task than I had at first thought, despite the fact that the barracks was a bit of a rabbit warren.

The CO had thought that the naval petty officers and the RAF NCOs would wish to identify with their men now that they were without their officers; and so it turned out. There were still some good sergeants within the 30 HAA battery despite their disarray. They were of the same mind as the Navy and RAF NCOs being all quite happy that I should accept the job. So in a matter of one or two hours I had already dealt with the NCOs representative of about 270 of the 480 men. Harry Pearce and Stracc were well known to me already. Harry was from 30 HAA anyway; and, as I have said earlier, Stracc – a regular and both older and senior to me – was very much his own man but nevertheless willing to co-operate in any way that I might wish; and he did, even to the extent of using his eyes and ears later to warn of an intended threat on my life. There was then a miscellaneous assortment of other sergeants attached to small unit groupings and others, like Sergeant Tim Healy and our two very senior mechanised sergeant-majors who had already been earmarked for other appointments. In fact, there were some very loyal and reliable men among them all, but I came away satisfied that they didn't want the responsibility for one reason or another and, more importantly for me, were satisfied that I should accept it.

89

So, it was back to the CO again, but I still had one further request to make: and that was that after I had paraded the Battalion ready for our departure and he had addressed them, I then wanted to use that golden opportunity when all of them were assembled, to have my say in giving the villains a bollocking and the others a sense of purpose and hope for the future.

Those preliminaries had been very worthwhile because they had not only given me a much clearer insight into the problems that would be ahead of us all but I had also discovered that I was known as 'that crazy sergeant who had rowed all the way down from Singapore'. I wasn't going to be coy about that exaggerated accolade because I would be needing all the clout that I could attract when I stood before the 480 men the following morning. It was a daunting prospect for me, and having got the CO's permission to have my say, I then went away to write, rehearse and commit to memory what had to be said. I was well aware of the fact that a supposedly 'off-the-cuff' delivery would hit the target much better than something read from a prepared speech.

14

OFF TO THE VALLEY OF DEATH WENT THE 500

9 May 1942 – Padang

The draft had been selected, the Movement Order issued, and I was at last standing before the parade of 479 men.

Captain Apthorp had introduced himself with the announcement that he had been appointed as their CO and that from henceforth we would be known as the newly formed and named British Sumatra Battalion. He told them how we would be travelling, about the arrangements made to get the sick men down to Padang railway station and as much as he knew – which was very little – about our ultimate destination; and then, having introduced me, he said, 'And now the BSM wishes to address you before we move off!'

It was now my turn, and I went in head first with ... 'I consider it an honour to have been appointed BSM to the British Sumatra Battalion. There are things that some of you may not wish to hear from me, so I'll get them out of the way first, and if when I have finished the cap fits, be man enough to wear it! I have been asked to straighten out the few villains amongst you and that I intend to do. I know them and the rest of you do too! So there will be no need to name names. I am talking of those men – and some of them to their shame are NCOs – who have been stealing rations, fighting and, even worse, doubling up in the food queues to get second helpings, with the result that some of you have had to go without.

'Well I will now make you a few promises! The first is that I will never expect nor accept one grain more of rice in my meals than the next man. The second is that if I catch anybody doubling up in future, they will be made to go without any food for the next twenty-four hours. Such men are despicable and those who are NCOs have forfeited any right to retain their rank.

'I want you to remember that you are still servicemen within the three armed forces, and that means that you are still under services discipline; and that is what I intend to reimpose; and don't confuse discipline with bullshit! There is no place for that here. It will be a shared discipline to ensure an equal chance of survival for all of us.

'You will all know that I was one of a party of men who visited this camp briefly a few weeks ago before being taken off to Fort-de-Kok; but you will not know that while we were up there we had to listen to a manic speech from a senior Japanese officer in which we were told "You are the tattered remnants of a degenerate nation". Well, there is no doubt that most of you are tattered. There is no shame to be found in that, but rather a sense of pride in how most of you have managed to cope with your present situation. Many of you that stand before me bootless and nearly naked do so only as a result of the sacrifices that you made in rescuing and helping others on the way down from Singapore. As for degenerate, I have already dealt with the few who deserve that description.

'And now all that remains to be said by me is the request that when I march you away from here that you will leave the camp with your heads held high whistling the tune and singing the words of *Colonel Bogey* just to show those bastards that you are disciplined and above all, that you are British and proud of it!'

Off we then went amid farewells from the 200 or so men left behind, and the last they ever heard of us was the gradually diminishing sound of the words 'Bollocks, and the same to you! Bollocks, they make a damn fine stew!...' and so it went on all the way down to the station.

We had made a good start, and if only Captain Morley had had the decency and foresight to leave us with more officers that had identity with the men, we might have fared better. However, youth being what it is, there would have been few men among us who didn't consider that they in particular were going to dodge the flak; but I was already a bit worried about those who thought that their salvation was no further away than a couple of Yankee battleships and an aircraft carrier. It was going to be a long war, and I had said so, and the sooner the over-optimistic men among us woke up to that fact, the better it would be for their chances of survival.

I was particularly worried about one lad who had stopped me when on my rounds the previous day to tell me that he couldn't eat rice; and my reply had been, 'Well, in that case you're already dead!' It was a harsh thing to say I know, but if he got the message behind it, it would have hardened his resolve and that was what was intended.

I am an old man now and as I type these words the memory of those events haunt me. I can see the faces of those men and I weep with the knowledge that so many of them (buoyant and hopeful as they were then) were sacrificed on the altar of inhumanity and deprivation.

That is why I hated our captors then, I still do – and always will – for the manner in which they planned and carried out such human destruction.

We arrived in Fort-de-Kok during the late afternoon. After being herded into the chapel of a convent, we were given a meal of rice and chopped vegetables which had been prepared for us by the same group of Dutch POWs who had fed our *Bintang Dua* fraternity so well.

The men then settled down for the night. Space was so limited that hardly anyone was able to lie down other than some Navy lads who had got in first to occupy the space around the altar. Some of them had even cleared the altar of ornaments to create two bed spaces. Those men were perhaps the most ill-equipped of the lot, so it didn't surprise me to find that the altar cloths had been used as blankets. When Private R.A.S. Pagani – a Catholic – came to me and complained about the outrage the following morning, I took the pragmatic view that Christ would have wished them to have warmth and comfort during the night. However, someone else had alerted the guards and they came wading in with boot, rifle butt and anything else that was handy until everything had been set to rights again. That was another lesson learnt. The Japanese revered temples but didn't give a toss for our comfort.

Despite that little rumpus, I found that the same group of men had safely liberated vestments and other bits of clothing; and by then the realisation of our plight was such that my only thoughts were good luck to them, even though some of the nuns might – as it were – be feeling the draught in a day or two.

There would be no more comfortable train journeys for us! We were at the terminus and the buzz word that morning was 'Medan',

93

which Stracc's atlas revealed to be several hundred kilometres to the north on the Malacca Strait. The abacus was very much in evidence at that morning *tenko* and so was a mixture of foreign words that only we POWs and the Japanese could ever hope to understand. It was a lingua franca that took on board English, Dutch, Malay and Japanese in an agglomeration of words and phrases that were used freely by all of us. We soldiers were *heitai* (Japanese), second helpings of food were leggy (*laigi*, Malay), plenty was *takusan* (Japanese) – a word which we rarely had cause to use when talking about food, of course – and the Japanese had the strange habit of suffixing our words, mainly by the use of '*ka*'. So when they were inclined to be less than manic we were informed that something we had done was 'no good-ka'. If anything really upset them we were assailed with 'buggero (*bakkaro* to them, I believe) and *kunero*'. Although I am told that the Japanese have no swear words in their language and that *buggero* and *kunero* mean little more than silly fellow, they were spat out with such venom that we had always thought that they had adopted our language – and I won't elaborate on that any further while the vicar is around.

There were dozens of words like that that were commonly used; and anyone given authority like myself had to take them on board quickly if they were Japanese words, or receive a bash round the ear. We were only just being introduced to the Japanese drill and numbering at this time and needed to know that *kiotski* meant attention, or there would be another bash. You learnt very quickly when under such sympathetic tuition!

We were well into a period of hot and oppressively humid weather, so before we paraded, I had checked out how many water containers were available. It was only then that I fully realised the extent of our deprivation. Little more than a fifth of the men still possessed an issue water bottle. Other than those, there was a scattering of containers – none of them large – such as discarded wine bottles and tins, many of which were without corks or lids. That was bad enough but the situation for food containers I already knew to be worse, having seen the receptacles used for our meal the previous evening. We were far worse off for 'issue' mess tins and the alternatives used had surprised me. It had not been so apparent when the men had been queuing down in Padang, but crammed together in that chapel I had seen the whole lot within the compass of a few feet. Some men had received their rice in straw hats and many of them in leaves, others had had to wait for a mate to finish his meal – which had to be gobbled down – before they could get the use of his container, or else use it together, which of course was courting trouble if one of them had diarrhoea. There were also coconut shells, sections of bamboo and God knows what else in use.

I was a realist if nothing else and had quickly decided that we had to become scavengers to survive and that the only time that I would intervene with any thievery would be if any of the men stole from another of our Battalion. And I told them that!

Lieutenant Dicker called them 'Appy's Locusts' – Appy being the nickname for our CO, Captain Apthorp, when he wasn't around to hear us use it.

Having given the warning that we must both share and conserve water while on the move and that we should each take a supply of leaves (other than prickly pear leaves, which make your eyes water), we were counted into lorries in batches of 30 and away we all went like bats out of hell.

The Japanese drivers were modern Jehus to a man and I am sure that much of their recklessness came from the worry that if they had slowed down one of us might have jumped out of the back. So they crashed their way through and up to top gear and then hurtled along over bumps and ruts regardless of any damage that might have been done to the vehicle and – of course – were unconcerned about our comfort. The only times that we slowed down were when we had to weave our way through villages. Even then they went dangerously fast, which resulted in near misses of inhabitants, animals and even buildings. Here and there we had brief glimpses of children waving miniature Japanese flags as we dashed through.

In normal circumstances the journey would have been very interesting. It was quite scenic in parts. We saw mountains east and west of us for most of the day, and many of the valleys that we were running through had streams and vegetation reminiscent of the more remote areas of Wales. However, this was not an outing, it was an endurance test! We had had a sweaty, dusty and uncomfortable ride. The equatorial heat was almost unbearable under the canvas hoods and we had had to change positions constantly to get to the tailboard and gulp in some fresh air.

Towards the evening we ran into the small township of Huta Nopan, having only stopped once for a short time to relieve ourselves. We had gone the whole day without food and with just a few sips of water.

Our billet was a small disused school building and there at last we were given a meal of rice and sardines. (Each lorry had a guard-cum-co-driver who was in charge of rations supplied from the Fort-de-Kok store.) Everyone was learning fast on this enforced survival course, so once again anything that was moveable and of use – particularly for eating or drinking from – was purloined. For instance, when we arrived every room was fitted out with conical metal lamp-shades, and when we left, a lonely pile of light bulbs. Locusts! Gleaners! Call us what you like! A rose by any other name etc. That was us!

The next day started much as the day before. The Japanese drivers were still hell-bent on self-destruction. When we started climbing up into the mountains, they showed off by sliding the lorries round hairpin bends while the wheels on the precipice side were spinning to get a grip. Those of us who wanted to relieve themselves had to work their way to the tailboard and then, 'hang on to all that makes life happy' with one hand and the metal frame to the canvas hood with the other. It was inevitable that some men couldn't hold out until evening to 'test their dropping gear' and when that happened it was dangerous for them and revolting for the rest of us.

Despite all those aggravations we could not help but enjoy the scenery, which during the morning offered us a 'diet' of hills, mountains and scatterings of tangled and colourful jungle. In the early afternoon we ran down to a valley, then through the seaside town of Sibolga before turning east and driving on and up towards the market town of Tarutung, where we were going to stay the night. There had been one unscheduled stop on the way because an incline had forced the drivers to slow right down. So out we had to get for a *tenko* to check if anyone had jumped from the back of a lorry.

There were then two more unscheduled stops. The first because a lorry broke down and eventually had to be abandoned, resulting in a redistribution of bodies and a protracted *tenko* during which the guard's abacus worked overtime. However, like the computers of today it kept on feeding back the information that the last idiot had put into it. It was exasperating for me, because I was keeping a tally and getting the same answer each time; but it was no good telling the Japanese that.

The final stop was for another breakdown. It was well into the afternoon by then and with the imminence of sudden nightfall, the Japanese – very fortunately – let two of our RASC lads swap places and do the repairs, because the rest of us were soon leaving behind one hell of a tropical storm.

It was almost dark when we ran into Tarutung. The lorries were driven away and we were corralled in the open, on the market square and within a tall wire fence. The only thing going for us was that the storm in all its vivid violence crashed and lightened around us but left us dry.

This was the first time in our journey that I was able to test the organisation that we had set up, and the conditions could scarcely have been more severe.

The Japanese had as usual turned on their screaming and kicking act to persuade us 500 animals into occupying an area in which there was insufficient space to lie down. My first question to the leading manic bastard among them was 'Where do we go for a *benjo*?' (the wee housie). The reply was an interrogative '*Benjo-ka*?' followed by a string of *buggeros* and *kuneros* as he led me over to the perimeter, pointed to the ground and said, '*Orral haita benjo*', which freely translated meant all men will crap here! After that, he hissed out the further single word '*masu*', which we lesser beings heard as *meshi* (food) – and off he went out of the compound.

I asked the various group NCOs to get the men to stand firm while I marked out the areas that would have to be used. Everyone was then told to 'work from' the fence inwards – if you get my meaning – in order to avoid treading in their own ordure, and that the rest of the perimeter would have to be left accessible to be peed through.

The only light we had came from a few faint flares sited outside the wire. The officers occupied the only corner that allowed any privacy (but very scant) alongside two sides of a brick hut. I told them where Tim Healy and I would be and that some kind of food would be supplied in due course.

It eventually arrived in the form of 2,500 miniature loaves (5 per man, and by volume the size of a small Hovis loaf). The baker knew his job all right and he could also count. They were delivered freshly baked and in flour sacks. I knew there were 2,500 there because in the immortal words of Brian Hanrahan – when our planes flew off to bomb the Falklands – some of the group sergeants, officers and I counted them all out and counted them all back again into the sacks before distributing them. I would like to be able to say that everything went smoothly from then on, but it didn't! I had watchers in the queues who knew who most of the villains were but we still ran short by ten loaves after setting aside 100 for the men who were still stranded with the lorry. Nevertheless, with no nominal roll, the poor light and little space, I considered that to be something of a minor miracle. The only reason why I have given this account in such detail is that the servers and a few of the officers in the corner had to go one short and some officers then started 'nannying' about it.

Colonel Coates – the eminent Australian surgeon – was among the 20 officers. Heaven knows what he made of their debutante wittering, or said, for that matter! 'Whingeing Pommies' comes readily to mind, and perhaps with a few ripe antipodean oaths thrown in for good measure! I was more than pleased with having achieved the improbable that day and had high hopes of doing the impossible in the days ahead. The men on the repaired lorry came in at around midnight *expecting* that their food would have been saved for them. It had! And that was good too.

What was not good was that the Japanese made us depart from the compound leaving the disgusting mess to be cleared up by the locals. However, it wouldn't have done the starry-eyed fanatics among them any harm to realise that the '*Co*' in Co-Prosperity meant that they only ranked with dogsbodies and shit-shovellers in the Japanese philosophy. And, if they had needed any more proof of that, they were soon going to witness young college students being driven up to do railway extension work as slaves (*romushas*) on the Pekanbaroe Railway system who were going to be worked without shelter and then abandoned to die without food or care; and – God help them! – that was where the lads that we had left in Padang would also finish up, albeit within a more cohesive group similar to our own.

15

THE LAST LAP – AND THEN INTO MEDAN

We had managed to avoid too much confrontation during our last halt other than the habitual buffetings and screaming. We were lucky, though, because Captain Apthorp told me later that some of the men had grabbed money from local traders without handing over the items that they had offered to sell. That was despicable and inexcusable; but typically there was no-one willing to name names because of their very real fear of retribution from our villains if they had. There was, for instance, a Scottish gang whose modus operandi was to isolate their victim in the dark and then put the heed (head) in if there was any resistance. Thankfully it never got much beyond a mob beating-up because one of that gang of despicable vermin was known to carry a razor. He had learnt his trade as a Glaswegian razor-slasher; and while in the Army just prior to the fall of Singapore, he had slashed – without murdering the man – the throat of one of his NCOs. I came very near to becoming the victim of that loathsome man ... but more of that later.

12 May

This day was going to be our last and equally uncomfortable journey on the lorries but it was marked by views of even more breathtaking scenery than before.

We started off by heading further up into the mountains and as we switchbacked along the winding dirt roads, the inland waters and islands of Lake Toba came into view. To begin with there were just glimpses of it through the trees as we paralleled the southern shore; but around midday – when we swung north-west – the vast expanse of it was revealed.

We then kept running close to the eastern shore for about 40 miles before stopping at the small lakeside village of Prapat for a meal. Everything was so idyllic and peaceful there that it was hard to believe that there had been recent heavy fighting over the area. Indeed, we had seen only a few military vehicles along the whole of the route from Fort-de-Kok. Very few were wrecked, so it would seem that the advance units of the Japanese – as in Malaya – had travelled light and side-stepped to get behind the opposition and isolate it from its lines of supply. There must have been a few units of the Japanese army still deployed along the Medan–Padang route somewhere, if only to act as a 'presence' in order to keep the road open and, of course, to contain the militant Achinese tribesmen over to the west and north-west of the lake.

It was going to be a long time before any Allied threat – other than the occasional submarine or reconnaissance plane – put in an appearance, so there was no need for too much presence at that time, I suppose; and since their administration ratio to fighting men was about 4 to 100, such numbers could be kept well out of sight. The Japanese were pastmasters at living off the land, travelling unencumbered and making everyone else work for them – or else! When it came to feeding their troops, and the occasional group of POWs in transit like us, they deployed field kitchens which were more often than not manned by Japanese cooks and – if necessary – augmented by locally hired or press-ganged labour. The equipment was crude, but adequate for preparing their basic rice diet; and it consisted of little more than two or three *kwalis* (large woks), some wooden tubs, and locally salvaged oil drums and petrol tins in which to boil and dispense water and soup. The hearths were constructed of clay and boulders and the fuel was gathered locally. As for the food – apart from the inevitable sacks of rice and tins of soya sauce, most of the ingredients were either looted or bought at a non-negotiable price. Anything more permanent was housed under simple structures made of bamboo, attap and rattan, and the supplies were kept moving with captured Dutch army vehicles (like those we were travelling in) and for the most part maintained by Dutch POWs. The whole set-up was a model of simplicity, mobility and frugality.

After our meal we went up and away from the lakeside, and then by mid-afternoon we were back down on a metalled road which ran north, traversing tracts of agricultural land, many of which were paddy fields. By late afternoon we entered and then ran through the city of Medan.

There was plenty of evidence of fighting along that last stretch because it was in the area in which the Japanese had landed, launched their first attacks and then made their breakthrough to the south. The convoy kept going for about another 12 miles north of the city until around nightfall, when we reached the port of Belawin Deli. Then, after the usual palaver of being counted and re-counted, we were marched off into Uni Kampong – a camp previously used for housing dock workers which was now an internment camp for Dutch civilians. We were dumped there, in the open, within an enclosure of barbed wire that seperated us from the Dutch; and – no thanks to the Japanese! – we just got lucky with the weather once again.

They usually didn't give a toss for our well-being but I believe their intention this time had been to provide us with just one meal from the Dutch kitchens before marching us back into Belawin Deli to board one of the ships that we had seen in the harbour. However, the Japanese had the British Army beaten into a cocked hat for farting about when a draft was being organised; and on this occasion, they excelled themselves. We went through a three-day saga of *tenkos*, marching out and marching back in again, hysterical screaming and use of the boot.

I was ordered to take a detail to the cookhouse to pick up a meal. By the time we came back the Dutch were busy passing gifts of clothing, food and money through the unguarded sections of the wire. Knowing our 'locusts', it came as no surprise to me to hear that some of the more adventurous of them had breached the defences and got into the Dutch quarters to do a bit of private trading. The Dutch were appalled by our general state of deprivation and ill health and did their level best to help us. But once again, some of our villains helped themselves. Many extras such as soap and other toiletries were spared from their small reserves. I was given office materials and stationery such as pencils, rubbers, paper etc., and even some carbon paper, which Tim later used on a battered old typewriter. Heaven alone knows where he got the typewriter from! Although the ribbon soon wore out, the carbon paper served us well for at least two years. He used to type through a sandwich of paper and carbon.

Many food containers were also gifted – or acquired – and I got

Stracc to get his RE lads to make up rice and soup scoops from wood, discarded food tins amd wire. Fortunately for the Battalion, he also had the foresight to bundle up spare lengths of wire because we hardly ever saw any more of suitable gauge later. A strange thing about the Japanese, was that they had the obsession that wire 'meant' wireless aerials, whatever the gauge. As for paper, that 'meant' secret messages. The outcome being that we were only allowed five official users of paper – the CO, the adjutant, a pay NCO, Tim and myself; and at various stages in our POW life all five of us had armbands covered in Japanese writing which presumably said so.

On the third day we were paraded and ready to leave with gunner Kerr on a stretcher at the rear of the column when it became obvious (even to the Japanese) that he was in such a bad shape that he would have to be left in the care of the civilians. Colonel Coates had declared that he would be unlikely to recover so it was nice to know that he would be well cared for. We were now 499 strong and that number caused all kinds of troubles for the 'abacus wizards'.

I know that I should only remember the sixteenth of May for the reason that it would be our last day on Sumatra soil; but usually, the main thing that comes to mind is of my first sight of the white chamber pot. It was delightful, hygienic and unadorned, and it was bouncing along on the backside of one of the men as we marched into the docks. I doubt that it had been gifted to him and I never did find out whether it was full or empty when he had 'lifted' it. It was a robust and simply crafted child-sized potty which lasted for at least two years as one of the finest food receptacles in the Battalion. It was cherished by the owner, and for me it acted as a sort of reassuring talisman every time that I saw it leaving camp with a working-party and coming back unscathed.

It took about two hours for the Japanese to orchestrate the *tenko* and manhandle us aboard the *England Maru*. Menheer Hess – a Japanese-speaking interpreter from the Dutch encampment – had come with us to the docks. He was a rather over-officious man albeit he had the very difficult job of trying to serve two masters. It was obvious that, in the interest of his own safety, he had to please the Japanese on far more occasions than he did us when trying to balance their orders against our requests. Many of the Battalion members hated the sight of him but they were soon going to wish that he could have accompanied us to make up the 500 again and to sort out some of the problems on our way up to Burma; because that was where we were off to, it was said.

That was one of the few rumours that became fact; and Hess came up to join us there later.

16

ALL MOD-CONS ON THE FREIGHTER
ENGLAND MARU!

The *England Maru* was a merchant ship of about 6,000 tons, British built in 1898 on the river Ouse near Selby, Yorkshire.

When we came aboard her the officers must have thought it was Christmas because they were taken off aft into a ventilated area and given room to lie down in reasonable comfort on rattan matting.

By contrast the rest of us were met by a different and particularly vicious gang of guards who immediately set about thrusting, bashing and kicking anyone who didn't move smartly across the forrard deck and down a makeshift companionway into the hold. Thank heaven I had an armband declaring that I was the senior NCO in charge, otherwise I would also have been given an 'assist' into that stinking, dark and sweltering abyss.

They wanted anyone with an armband up on deck, so, pointing out Tim Healy and other special duty men such as medical and mess orderlies and group sergeants, I used the age-old Army ploy of waving an official-looking piece of paper at one of the guards, cleared a space below the bridge and dumped our kit. My next move was not nearly so clever, though! I went back to the hatch combing to see if I could calm down the frenetic action there and all I got for my pains was a whack round the ear by a vicious sod who looked like a latter-day Genghis Khan.

I was looking down on a scene that rivalled the most lurid depictions of hell in ancient bibles, the only difference being that 'our' Satan's tormentors were weilding bayoneted rifles – not tridents – and bashing with the butts.

A three-tiered wooden decking had been constructed above the mid section of the hold from a level of about 12 feet below the hatch covers. There were two temporary companionways, one of which led to the mid-level and the other down to a lower bank of three-tier accommodation.

My first sight of all that came as the last man was being man-handled into the lower level, where he joined a layer of bodies sitting buttocks to crutch like rowing eights with the 'cox' – lucky man that he was – just able to turn and dangle his legs over the void below.

It was midday and they were at the equator, anchored in the hold of a steel-cladded vessel. They couldn't stand up and if they were ever going to be able to rest or sleep, it would only be achieved by flopping back onto the man behind.

I was told later by some Aussies that our guards were a hand-picked gang of bastards from Singapore who had delighted in hanging placards round POWs which invited all and sundry to abuse, attack – and even kill – the bearers at will. My 'Ackney cockney assessment of them was that they were a load of 'Uckfay Arstabays!' first class.

Up on deck we had little relief from the searing sun but our discomfort was as nothing compared with that of the men below. The few of them who owned shirts had stripped off and hundreds of bodies were now revealed, glistening with sweat in the light of dim electric bulbs. Their distress had been evident from the very moment that they descended into that superheated 'Black Hole'.

I had already noticed the sanitary arrangements, which consisted of a cradle-like three-person thunderbox suspended outboard on lashings from the guardrail. No-one had been given the chance to relieve themselves before going below. Many were getting the urge now but the guards had stopped everyone from coming back on deck *for any purpose*. There were several men suffering from uncontrollable diarrhoea and they had absolutely no option but to defecate where they sat. This was disgusting enough for them, let alone for those who were sitting at lower levels and being splashed with dripping ordure. All my requests for water and for regulated access to the deck were being totally ignored. Those soulless bastards were not only sadists, but also so ignorant, that they had forgotten that their emperor had asked for 500 'cattle on the hoof' for his railway, not carcasses!

About three hours of Dante's Inferno went by before I was able to attract the attention of one of the crew and, thank God, those men were of a different disposition than the guards, having sailed the world and acquired some knowledge of more civilised ways of life. I wish I could have seen the man earlier. Being at anchor, there had been no occasion for any of the crew to leave the forecastle earlier; but now – without the knowledge of the guards – he went off and fetched us some pails and rope, and it was only then that he told our bunch of moronic gaolers that I must be allowed to keep a water supply going. He didn't wait for an answer but instead took us over to a point where water was delivered at deck-level by means of a steam-pipe from the engine-room.

The same seaman must have got a message up to the bridge about our plight because the captain also arrived and he demanded that ten men at a time must be allowed on deck to visit 'traps 1, 2 and 3'. Thank God that lot got sorted out because I am sure that many of the Battalion would have otherwise been dead before the sun went down.

I think that being at anchor had been the main obsession of the guards. They must have thought that some of the men might dive overboard and swim ashore. There was now a constant flow – in every sense of the word – with the scuppers being used as urinals and those precarious squatting boxes for 'number twos'. I even managed to get the use of a sea water hose to flush down the scuppers!

When my turn came for a visit over the rails, I was able to see that the ship's side below me was caked with ordure left from previous slave trips; so no wonder the flies had been homing in on us from the land to compound our problems.

We were hungry by now and I had been trying to think out a plan with Tim Healy, Sergeant Tom Bousfield and the other NCOs for the distribution of food and any liquids that might be provided. There had been a smell of cooking coming from the port-side galley; and then the voices of Captain Apthorp and Colonel Coates were heard. They had got permission to look at our accommodation and the state of the men, after which we were to be given a meal. They had already had theirs and it was debatable whether they were glad of that after they had seen and smelt the conditions below.

Colonel Coates made his medical inspection, and when they came up I could see that they were fired up for battle. They had obviously made tracks for the bridge, because we got the further permission for men to come up in relays so long as they didn't disrupt the work of the crew.

When the meal was over more and more men started to come up on deck and those with a genuine attack of the gripes had to stay there. That brought the guards in again but ignoring all their protests, I declared that they were *takusan byoni* (very sick) with dysentery. It was another very near call for a beating for me and I was only too pleased to say *arigoto* (thank you) when they ultimately agreed. We were at last winning; and we needed to, because conditions below were still diabolical. I supposed that my 'thank-you' had elevated the bastards – in their own minds only – to the role of benefactors. (Some of my villains used to say 'Harry's garters' when they won a concession, but not me! I was already too much in the firing line to invite further trouble.)

Thank heavens we were at last moved further out into the roads and away from the flies because we had to suffer another day of almost unendurable heat. Some men who had survived it stoically so far were now being brought from below in a state of collapse. The deck became so crowded that no shade could be found for them, let alone a space in which to lie down. The best we could do was to allow them a spell of fresh air, douse them with sea water and send them below again. If only there had been a breeze! As fast as the buckets went down filled with water they came back with the demand for more.

We still did not know where we would be going but most bets were by now on Burma – and that would mean that Allied submarines would be about, and even given the opportunity to abandon ship, there were only sufficient rafts, hatch covers and other loose timber forrard to support a quarter of us.

The following day we got the good news that we were going to sail; and we had actually set off out when the bad news came that we were going right back in to Belawin Deli, and this time to tie up at the dockside again. And there we stayed for yet another day!

On the nineteenth it was (thank God) a case of 'Burma, here we come at last'! By dawn we were out into the roads again. There had been a lot of bustle among the crew during the night and an increase in lamp signalling to the shore and to ships assembling south of us. Being a signalman, it was exasperating to know that even though I could read 'our' signals by the clack of the Aldis lever alone, I would never make sense of anything sent in Japanese.

During the afternoon more signals were exchanged when two

steamships hove into sight with a naval escort – a destroyer and frigate, I believe.

They came right into the harbour and anchored near enough for us to see that the decks of the steamships were crowded with Australians wearing bush hats and loaded down with kit. We didn't know at the time, of course, but they had been sent up from Singapore to amalgamate with us and others into an eventual group of 10,000 men called 'A Force', and destined for work on the 'Burma Railway of Death'.

There were 3,000 of them, led by Brigadier Arthur Varley of the 8th Australian Army, who – we discovered later – was the only officer above the rank of colonel who wasn't withdrawn from his unit and sent to Formosa for the 'duration'.

The Japanese were past-masters at deception and everyone who came up onto the railway, other than our '500', were conned into believing that their quarters in Burma would be set in idyllic surroundings where they would enjoy (quote), 'an equable climate, fresh air billets and plenty of healthy exercise'. What a joke that was! And to sustain the vision of a beckoning Shangri-La, they encouraged everyone to bring all their possessions with them *including the kitchen sink*. Every aspect of survival as a POW was a lottery. Brigadier Varley's 3,000 had been allowed to bring all their band instruments with them, for instance, and rarely had to hump them around; whereas others on the Thailand side of the railway died as a result of being encumbered with surplus baggage: and more will be said about that later.

The Japanese were also realists. Knowing that *we* were almost devoid of kit and personal possessions, they had had no reason to make promises to us other than that most of us had a short future. There may have been some psychological advantage in having that pre-knowledge. Having nothing else going for us, we needed to have some kind of edge on the others!

Once we got moving we had the benefit of a rain squall – the precursor to the south-west monsoon. This made the guards scuttle for cover, leaving us free to occupy the otherwise 'off limits' areas of the deck with frolicking bathers; and fortunately, as soon as we were well under way, the guards relaxed into a far more casual routine.

108

By the twenty-second of May we had steamed northwards on a zig-zag course up into the Andaman sea and then to a safe anchorage off Victoria Point. This was at the southern tip of the Tenasserim Peninsula, where the long tail of Burma meets the boundaries of Thailand and Malaya. We were about 400 miles north of Medan by then but had probably steamed a further 150 miles, changing direction for fear of a submarine attack. We had been lucky because within a few months there would be a steady toll of Japanese vessels sunk while using those waters.

We only stayed off Victoria Point long enough to allow 1,000 of the Aussies to disembark before steaming north again for two days – another 160 miles. We then dropped anchor off the island township of Mergui within the archipelago of that name. It was now our turn to disembark and we went ashore in company with a further group of 1,000 Aussies led by Lieutenant Colonel Ramsay, who – being the senior officer – took command of all of us.

It was only then that the stark disparity between us and all other POWs really came home to us.

POW 'Hell Ship' – the *England Maru*

17

MERGUI CAMPS – LOWER BURMA

25 May 1942

It was pitch black, there was a chilling wind and the rain was sheeting down as I formed the Battalion up to the rear of the column.

We were cold, tired and bedraggled. Most of the men were barefooted and scantily clad in a miscellany of ragged and contrived garments. The men with dysentery and malaria were standing there griping and shivering through the agony of almost interminable recounts of our 499 officers and men. Up ahead of us stood the 1,000 Aussies with their khaki shorts, stockings and boots showing below waterproof capes which covered matching uniforms, haversacks, water-bottles, side-packs and countless other possessions. Above the capes were hoisted kitbags, and every head was topped off with a protecting bush hat.

At long last came the order to left turn and quick march. That was a bit of a joke for us with our walking sick in tow; but we did whistle and we did sing 'Bollocks and the same to you...' That went not only for the Japanese but for our colonial cousins stepping it out dry and lively ahead of us. It was sheer bravado and a touch of desperation that got us through the two miles of purgatory that ensued. There had been countless cries and curses on the way as our men stubbed their toes on the uneven and unlit dirt road that led up to the township. The locals were no doubt impressed with the well-ordered appearance of those ahead of us. However, they stared in disbelief as our ragged lot shuffled and stumbled their way into the glow of their dimly lit house lamps and then onwards to shelter within the abandoned Mergui National High School.

I am sure that Colonel Ramsay tried to see that we got a fair share of cover for the night but he was on a loser from the start.

What with the darkness and the strangeness of the surroundings, once his men had moved into their allocated rooms and found inadequate space they just forced their way into parts of the buildings intended for us. By the time we arrived and had been counted yet again, there was only one double-storeyed wing available for us. Even then the overhang to the eaves of this building was already being filled with Aussies contriving lean-to shelters out of school furniture taken from other parts of the complex. It was a situation that was ripe for trouble because by now the Aussies not only had a surplus of warm kit but some of them were also after more than their fair share of the accommodation.

There always had been hostility between certain elements of the British and Australian armies, so I was not surprised to hear that a fight had started because one of the Aussies had called one of my men a bastard. This word – which was used more often than not as an expression of endearment in Australia – was a deadly insult to any Britisher who cared to take it the wrong way, which many did, during the 1940s.

A fair proportion of the men were rookies. Most of those had been hastily recruited, inadequately trained and ill-prepared for such harsh conditions. So, a lot of the trouble that developed was due to immaturity rather than malice. The more street-wise individuals such as the Londoners and Sydneyites were able to integrate far more easily than our country lads were with the Aussies from the outback. They were often equally parochial in outlook, knowing very little about each other's country or style of living. That was my impression anyway but I realise that such generalities can mask many exceptions.

There were some great characters among those Aussies, including one of their sergeants with whom I got quite friendly. As far as I can recall, he was a regular who had progressed to his rank within their pre-war yeomanry. He was about 35 years old, big and as tough as hickory. My introduction to him came through one of the rare amusing incidents of that time. I had discovered him when in conversation with one of my lads, a pint-sized cockney, who was expounding the delights and merits of living in London where – he said – the Thames bridges were second to none. The sergeant replied that there was no bridge to compare with the one over Sydney harbour. The lad then told him about the unique and majestic buildings in the 'Big Smoke'; but, seemingly unimpressed with

111

it all, the sergeant said, 'Ah but we've got the largest ranch in the world with 50,000 sheep on it and where a man must ride on horseback for three days to cross from one boundary to the other.' This unrelated but incontestable bit of information forced the lad to surrender the contest but only after this parting remark, 'The trouble with you, Digger, is that you're just like your country! Big, wide and there's sweet FA inside you!' I found this encounter to be quite hilarious. The massive Aussie could have picked his adversary up in one hand and shaken him like a rat, but all he did was to give him one long, hard and menacing look before bursting out into roars of laughter at his impudence. He was a great man in every sense of the word and I wish I could have known him much longer than the few weeks that our units were together.

Although we had marched into the National High School last, we did have the two distinct advantages of being most remote from the guardhouse and in the only building that flanked one of the main roads through the township. The only things that separated us from the bustling town life were a low fence and a line of fruiting lime trees. This crop was no sooner recognised than it was harvested, and it must have helped to stave off the worst effects of a particularly nasty vitamin deficiency disease that was beginning to assail us.

It was fortunate also that, although the Japanese provided us with little more than rice and the occasional sack of vegetables, we soon established quite good contacts with some of the Burmese. We had been given a day to settle in. I was then ordered to provide working parties to extend the aerodrome runway and within a few days the Burmese were handing over or leaving them gifts of food along the perimeter.

Those covert operations worked contrary to the scheming of the Japanese Commandant, whose aim was to make us buy any extras in camp and take a cut for himself. As for other essentials such as medicines and hygiene materials, the first were being refused and the second granted with a small supply of lime and, often with either an hysterical harangue or a beating for good measure. There was soon the urgent need to dig latrines. We asked for shovels and picks but were only supplied with one shovel and a chunkel – the latter being a broad-bladed pick-cum-shovel. The outcome was that the fatigue party had to work round the clock and they only just got the job done as the existing facilities started to overflow. Meanwhile the whole camp had been engulfed in an all-pervading stench which fortunately affected the Japanese in their quarters and guardhouse as much as anyone else; otherwise, I am sure that they would have ignored our plight. It is probably significant that our stay at the National School marked the beginning of an outbreak of dysentery which caused the death of ten of our Battalion and twenty of the Aussies during the first three weeks of June.

This sudden outbreak prompted the Commandant to allow Colonel Coates and some medical orderlies to occupy part of the local hospital for the treatment of all the most seriously sick but it was not a humanitarian gesture. The truth of the matter was that he was scared that he might be held accountable for our losses, which would otherwise have reached epidemic level. This would have defeated the chief objective of his supremos – not least his emperor – which was to deliver as many slaves as possible up onto the railway in due course.

The Commandant was very inferior in status and intelligence to the officers of the Japanese Engineering Regiment. They had the same remit yet they were always badgering him for more men to be sent up on the aerodrome job. He was not only a Jekyll and Hyde character but a devious sod who enjoyed playing both ends against the middle. He was well in with the young Burmese militia (otherwise known as the Heigho boys) of the Nationalist Party and he had been encouraging them in their oppressive surveillance and punishment of the local populace. We were also quite sure that he was making a fast buck by pocketing a large percentage of the money allocated to him for buying in our rations. Our interpreter had told us that such corruption was tolerated to the extent that it was openly admitted to in conversation with him.

When we had soup it was always thin and usually of boiled tulip bulbs, which – because the water turned purple – was called 'Blue Danube soup'. On the rare occasions that we had any 'extras' it was mainly due to the kindness and daring of the older Burmese folk who contrived to hide gifts of paw-paws, cassava root and dahl in the shrubbery near the cookhouse. Other individual gifts were still being tossed over our fence as well.

Nevertheless, the effects of malnutrition were now apparent. They had started to manifest themselves in loss of weight, mysterious rashes, lassitude and – in some cases – hallucination. It was quite evident that we were being slowly starved. Knowing that food was plentiful in the area, Colonel Ramsay went to the Commandant and asked if we could have salt, meat and more vegetables. His response was that if we wanted salt we would have to get it from the sea and that if we wanted more vegetables we would have to eat grass. The only protein offered was a few dozen eggs daily, which we would have to pay for ourselves from his overpriced canteen.

Leaving aside humanitarian considerations, the whole concept was quite illogical. They were forever requiring more and more work out of us but denying us the sustenance we needed to carry it out.

There was therefore no alternative to making the best of what had been offered, so I had to set up sea-water carrying details. We were nearly a mile from the coast and the work was very tough for malnourished and barefooted men. The containers were halved 60-gallon oil drums furnished with wire handles. They were slung between two men on poles. It took quite a while to master the ungainly out-of-step loping gait which the natives used when carrying liquids. However, even though the men got a bashing for arriving back at camp with a diminished load, there was no lack of volunteers for the job. Their route lay through the narrow streets of the town and as the detail passed by they were plied with all kinds of gifts from the householders and shopkeepers. Many of the presents came in the form of meat, fish or cooked savouries wrapped in leaves. Other gifts (such as eggs and bananas) were either tossed directly into the filled containers or left within reach on stalls and tables.

Our men – with little to wear – had to get up to all kinds of methods of concealment. Those without shorts had sweat rags with pockets sewn in. These were then either tucked into waist belts or under the carrying poles to protect their shoulders from the grinding weight of the full containers. Failing all else the packages were hung on wire hooks within their G-strings and these would often work their way round to the front to resemble exaggerated codpieces; and when those slipped out, their stride became even more ungainly than before.

Quite remarkably, they were only rarely detected but whenever they were all hell was let loose. Any smuggling was a threat to the Commandant's canteen percentage.

However, he soon had a more lucrative racket going, which was based on our rice issue. We had to send out working parties to sweep and sack up the spillage from the town warehouse floor, which always contained dust, rat dirt and weevils. When this mess was brought back into camp and tipped into our cooking *kwalis* most of the dust and dirt stayed on the surface, fortunately, and could be skimmed off. As for the weevils, we just accepted them as a welcome additive to our intake of protein. It was a bit of a lottery as to whether we would get polished rice or another type that was greyish and had a pink fleck in it. The latter tasted far less palatable and many of the men did their best to avoid eating any of it. However, some time later a Dutch doctor was assigned to our Battalion who was well versed in both tropical medicine and food values. He told us that this greyish rice was best for us because it still retained the nutritional germ that polishing removed. Many of us had become quite protein and calorie conscious by then and, given the choice, I always went for the so-called 'dirty rice'.

It has been said that everyone eats a peck of dirt before they die. This may or may not be true but we POWs must have eaten bushels of muck in one form or another.

For instance, it was not long before we discovered that our sea water was well laced with sewage that had been flushed out from the town ditches and from the lavatories on the walkways used by the fishing community.

We had an even more menacing health hazard to contend with when the monsoon set in and the rivers were in full spate. This severe flooding brought with it not only expected debris but also the bodies of swollen and putrefying animals. There was nothing that we could do about it. We needed the salt; our water was boiled and that had to suffice.

However, one unexpected and very welcome bonus came because of the severe flooding. The force of the water had torn away seaweed from the northern shoreline and it soon came washing through with the rest of the detritus. We asked the Commandant if we could send out men to collect it, and to our surprise he gave permission. Maybe that was because seaweed was free! Financially it was another very good deal for him because he was able to cut the supply of the bulbs and put the collectors on half pay as 'in-camp' workers. Once that harvest began to come in, it went on our menu as 'shredded gas-cape soup'.

The BSM duties within a POW camp bore little resemblance to those within a normal Army Battalion. Chief cook and bottle-washer and first in line for a belt round the ear would better describe my duties. Administration and disciplines for survival were my main tasks but I also had to undertake a host of other duties that would normally have been devolved to other NCOs. I had to get involved in the minutiae of such things as rations, clothing, sick and work parades, hygiene; and also liaison with the Japanese, the interpreter and the Aussies. The Japanese had at first only seen the need for me to have an office clerk, three cooks, two medical orderlies, two batmen-cum-runners and six general duty men to keep the camp ticking over.

The NCOs and men were paid on daily rates which varied according to their rank and whether they worked in or out of camp. The officers were paid a monthly salary equivalent to 120 rupees (slightly less for second lieutenants), half of which was banked in Japan against deductions for food and accommodation. A month or two later another quarter was lodged in a contingency fund to be used chiefly for buying extras for the hospital patients. (Some further details of pay are given early in Chapter 39.) However, for most of the time – and particularly in the later camps – this Japanese money became more and more useless to us as there was less and less to buy; and devaluation made it worth little more than monopoly money.

While we were in Lower Burma I was only rarely able to get out of camp and only then in the guise of a member of one of the working parties. So, on the occasion that I was summoned by two of our guards and brought before a sergeant of the Kempi-Ti (military police), it became quite obvious that something unpleasant was in store for me.

Nobody had told me what I was wanted for. The guards fixed bayonets and escorted me out of camp. I had no idea where they were taking me and I was bustled along a pathway in silence. The sergeant was a villainous-looking bastard and he conveyed a sense of menace that was tangible. Even my escorts were ill at ease in his presence. I was beginning to believe that one of our men had committed some awful crime and that I was being brought to witness his punishment. God forbid that anyone had tried to escape because two Australians who had been recently accused of that had been made to dig their own graves before being shot.

116

In the event the outcome was far worse than I could have imagined. As we came along the last section of the path it began to rise up to the northern end of the aerodrome. We rounded a bend and there, just 20 yards ahead of me, were more members of the Kempi covering two of our men on one side of the path and a young Burmese woman on the other. Even at that distance it was quite obvious that the young lady was in the last stage of pregnancy.

I was halted about ten yards away from them and the men were brought down to explain why they were being detained. They said that the lady was one of a number who used to stand along the path with presents of food and she had given them some bananas. Once that had been explained to me, the sergeant ordered the guards to detain all three of us there. And then, without further ado he marched up the path and set about systematically kicking the poor woman to death. While she writhed on the ground she could be seen trying to give birth to her child.

I could sense that the sub-human bastard was almost willing one of us to leap forward and intervene. It would have been a suicidal act. He would have been only too happy to have had us bayoneted on the spot. The whole incident was so horrific that even his own toadies were averting their gaze as he went about his murderous attack. What was even worse was that he seemed to be enjoying it. There was nothing that I could do other than to warn our men to stand still and await their turn for punishment.

In the event it was only I who was punished. I was given a whack across my ear with a rifle butt while the bastard was telling me, 'Orrel men presento no!' This signified that I must tell everyone back in camp what would happen to anyone else who offered them gifts.

Even after 60 years I have never been able to forget the look of appeal that I saw in that girl's eyes – for that is what she was, just a young, vibrant and compassionate mother-to-be. I constantly think of how she fell to the ground to convulse so silently when I would have expected her to scream at the sheer pain and horror of her treatment; and then, to have the final realisation that none of us were going to be able to come to her aid or give her comfort while she lay there dying. I have asked myself so many times since then whether I should have dashed forward, even though I knew that it would have been an act of suicide to do so. That scene has continued – and will continue – to come back to me and nudge my conscience; and I weep with the memory of it all as I struggle to type these words. Despite having witnessed hundreds of other deaths in so many other forms, they were either as a result of conflict or through the wanton deprivation of the means to live, rather than in a manic lust for blood. God grant me some relief from the memory of it in my remaining years!

It was quite by chance that I saw that sergeant again at the end of the war but I was unable to get at him to murder him – an act which I considered to be my duty ... but more of that later!

A lot of sweeping and false statements have been made about the Burmese turning traitor against the Allies. The Karen tribesmen never did. They were much like the Gurkhas, being fiercely loyal to the British at great cost to themselves. However, their operations were mainly covert and mounted from their inland strongholds up in the hills. They were a minority and there was a mutual distrust between them and the rest of the population.

It was the young townie Burmese orchestrated by Dr Ba Maw who gave us the most trouble. He was the head of the Japanese-sponsored Burmese government and he had so indoctrinated those young men that many of them were actively spying on their elders; even their own parents. They had not only been fired by Ba Maw's rhetoric but had also succumbed to the blandishments of the Japanese. This was something far more sinister than a teenage revolt. They had no doubt turned in those two Australians for the reward of 80 rupees a head and had most likely informed on that young lady as well.

There was certainly a blitz on in the Mergui area while we were there. Perhaps it was just because *we were there*! It is therefore all the more praiseworthy that so many of the older residents took so long before they were forced to bow to the fear of dreadful retribution.

Being so close to the centre of Mergui, we were able to sense much of the atmosphere of the place. There was a constant movement of residents on the road beside our quarters. The traders also came by, pushing barrows laden with all sorts of strange merchandise. Loads of reeds, bamboo, atap and rattan mats were trundled by to the accompanying sounds of clanking pots, pans and brassware. There were also a variety of foods carried in by hand or perched on heads and shoulders. Animals were driven by, live chickens with their feet tied together dangled from poles and there was many a pig borne past us strapped to a board on the owner's head. The shoppers mingled on foot and bicycle and the occasional saffron-robed monk went by, carrying his staff and begging bowl.

It was usually while all this daytime bustle was going on that our local benefactors had got away with placing or throwing gifts through the fence for us. However, it was inevitable that one of the donors was caught in the act and beaten up. That incident was soon followed by two others, in which one man was beaten to death within our sight and another chased round a corner and shot. Even after that there were still some of the older residents who put their lives on the line by selling or donating food to us.

Strangely enough, one of the most interesting happenings that I witnessed was a funeral procession. I had been taken out of camp under escort to sort out a problem relating to the sea water pollution. We were half way to the coast when we were brought to a halt by a cortège moving slowly across the track ahead of us. Some local dignitary must have died, because the whole of the area was thronging with spectators.

The lone figure of the widow came into sight first, some ten yards ahead of the followers. She was barefooted, dressed in rags, filthy and unkempt and she swooped up and down to pick up handfuls of dust, which she tossed into the air while emitting agonising wails of woe. There then followed a procession of three flat-topped floats. The first of these carried the decked-out body of the deceased surrounded by a number of chairs. The chairs were occupied by a gathering of friends and family who were chatting and laughing away as if in enjoyment of a great social occasion. The second float carried the music makers. They were having an equally happy time banging away on drums and gongs and blowing a variety of wind instruments. Within the wind section there was a virtuoso on the paper squeaker. It was of the Christmas cracker variety that whips out to emit a high-pitched squeak before rolling back again. It seemed that anyone was welcome to hop up there and have a go, and it wouldn't have surprised me to see someone get up and whack away on a washboard or join in with comb and tissue paper. The third float was loaded with more revellers, who were seated round a trestle table piled with food and drinks, which they were swilling and gorging down with great abandon. Any unwanted bits and bones were being tossed over their shoulders in a manner reminiscent of baronial banquets.

I don't know how much further they had to go but many of them were so tipsy already that it is doubtful that they would have made it to the cremation.

That festive procession finally rolled by and the sounds of gaiety from the thronging populace behind it faded.

As we moved on down to the coast I was thinking how pleasant and sensible it had been to celebrate death in that way except – that is – for the chief mourner. However, even she might have perked up a bit later after reflecting that only 20 years previously she might have been expected to sacrifice herself on the funeral pyre.

Captain Bill Storr of our Battalion – who had served in India – told me that the practice of suttee had been widespread in Burma up to the turn of the century in order to ensure that any young wives did not poison their old and rich husbands for their money. However, I suspect that there was more to the barbaric practice than just that.

18

MOVING INTO BETTER QUARTERS

21 June 1942

Although we had only been at the National High School for a month it seemed much longer than that at the time.

No doubt that is due to my lingering memory of the appalling conditions of cramped and totally inadequate accommodation and of the almost constant rain and starvation rations.

It had been particularly bad when the working parties came back into camp needing shelter, reasonable washing facilities and somewhere to dry their clothes; or – it might better be said of our Battalion – their rags, which were fast rotting on their backs. What with the intense humidity, the heat and the rain, the working parties were instantly identified as they came down from the airfield by the clouds of steam rising from them. The cooks called it their smoke signal to get the fires lit and the cooking *kwalis* heating up.

Quite apart from being rotted and gaping with holes, nearly every article of clothing was caked with streaks of exuded salt. There were very few men in the Battalion who had boots. Most of the Aussies had two pairs. But those that were worn for working in soon mildewed and started to disintegrate. The Aussies also had polish and dubbin but that wasn't going to last for ever. It seemed sensible to keep our few boots for night movements or for a further attempt to escape.

Our COs had taken every opportunity to complain about the conditions and they had been promised that new quarters were being built for us out of town; but I don't think that there was anyone who believed that. So it came as a very welcome relief that with little warning we were paraded and moved out to a fresh location on the twenty-first of June. We were marched to the edge of the

121

town and then into a new purpose-built and spacious camp. To our surprise the amenities included a light bulb in every hut, controlled from a master switch within the Japanese HQ building.

Viewed from the camp entrance, the guardhouse was to the right of it, the HQ office was about 30 yards to the rear and most of our huts were well over to the left. There was a large parade ground front-left and the cookhouse, latrine and wash-house facilities were sited centrally at the distant end.

It was a real home from home compared with our recent makeshift quarters, and we were in fact never going to get anything quite like it again. There was ample space for parading 1,500 men, and we had a new system for *tenko* in which the parade was summoned by bugle and the numbering done in Japanese.

'Reveille' and 'Cookhouse' were usually got well out of the way before it was light. We then had a *tenko*, which was basically conducted in two parts, the first of which was held by two or three guards and myself. I formed up the Battalion, with the exception of the officers and the sick, who were counted in their own quarters. The men were assembled in three ranks and – as far as they went – within groups of 100. There had at first been a marked reluctance to occupy the front rank since everyone there had to memorise their number in Japanese and moreover, pretty smartly too in order to avoid a buffeting. The numbers were really quite easy to learn but far from easy to remember when under duress. I would travel along the line with the guard to prompt before any blows could be aimed and it was a rather comical experience for me to see the look of relief on the face of a man delivering his *ni-ju-ichi* (twenty-one) faultlessly before handing the responsibility over to number *ni ju-ni* ... and so on. The Japanese tally men also had to struggle with the fact that the *san-ju-san* call only accounted for one man and the next call of *san-ju-shee* (thirty-four) took the grand total up to one hundred, there being a blank file in our tradition of assembly.

It then became the turn for the abacus wallahs to come in for a bit of flak if the figures failed to tally first time round; and they usually did!

Once that lot was sorted out, I was allowed to call the parade to attention to salute the arrival of Captain Apthorp. This daily ritual gave him the opportunity to announce any fresh instructions relayed to him by the interpreter. It was then back to the Japanese again as I sorted out the various working parties.

The Japanese seemed to be quite happy to accept this procedure and, unlike the Aussies, they saw nothing unusual in the level of discipline that we preserved within our ill-equipped and ill-assorted bunch of humanity. Appy and I worked on the simple equation that the more we organised and controlled ourselves, the less likely we were to be hounded and abused.

It was only a matter of days before we had a new and even earlier parade imposed on us. Every morning, just before dawn, we had to assemble in front of our huts, where on the command of *kiotski*, we were called to attention while the Japanese flag was run up to await the rising sun; we were then made to bow in token homage to their emperor. Our participation was obviously intended to humiliate us. Perhaps they had expected that we would protest but if so, they were unlucky. It was a meaningless event in the day for us and as we ignored it as such, the Japanese very soon gave up the idea.

Throughout our three and a half years of POW life we were only rarely allowed to conduct a proper funeral service. So here – in Mergui – it was a great plus for us to be allowed the ministrations of a local Catholic priest. Even more unusual was that the funerals were occasionally attended by Japanese other than the one who had to be there to make sure that a body had been sewn into the rice sack and not a dummy instead.

The priest was Portuguese. I don't know if it was all part of the rites within his branch of the faith, but after tossing in a handful of earth, he would leave an offering of rice cakes. He then stepped aside in case any of the Japanese wished to add to them. This signalled the end of their involvement and the moment when the pallbearers and gravediggers could 'liberate' and share out the gifts. This did not in any way signify disrespect for the dead, but it must be said that I never had any difficulty in getting volunteers for a funeral detail. My main problem was in trying to assemble seven men in more or less matching dress; and even then, although we had plenty of spit, we had no polish.

On moving into our new camp we had been surprised to find that it was unfenced. The boundary was simply defined by a series of rickety and lopsided wooden posts connected at tops and centres by single strands of ordinary wire. This was patrolled by two guards

123

only and in such a random and desultory fashion that it was almost as if we were being invited to wander round in the area beyond.

Dozens of men were daily accepting that 'open invitation'. They would slip under the wire and worm their way through the nearby grass and scrub to meet traders who had already crawled in from the opposite direction. Quite a brisk trade was being done in all kinds of commodities. For those men who had enough nerve to go farther afield it even became possible to collect hot chapatis to order. The situation became quite exasperating for me. I couldn't join them because I never knew when the Japanese might want to see me. Moreover, I couldn't expect others to take undue risks on my behalf.

Among our numbers was a certain Sergeant Florey of the Indian Army Service Corps. He had started making lengthy and distant visits in and beyond Mergui town to meet various wealthy Indians. He had three distinct advantages over the rest of us. He was half Indian, fluent in Urdu and with full knowledge of the most appropriate forms of disguise to employ. Quite unknown to me at the time, he had (at the instigation of our Captain Bill Storr) been making enquiries into ways and means of escaping. He had later guided him out of camp to a clandestine meeting with an Indian merchant who thought that he could lay on and provision a boat. Shortly after that, Stracc and I were invited to a meeting to discuss the proposition. We were of the opinion that the plans – although well-intentioned – were a bit too amateurish as outlined and well short of our minimum requirements for any hope of success. Sergeant Florey went back out again to see if our suggested amendments could be met. There was no doubt that the merchant could be trusted because he had already loaned Bill Storr £50 in local money on the strength of a promissory note to be redeemed after the war. Nevertheless, we had no intention of just setting out on a wing and a prayer, so we sat back and waited while enjoying the unexpected gift of a curried duck while negotiations went on. *That at least got our unanimous approval!*

The Aussies were in overall charge of the cookhouse at that time and they had been experimenting with all kinds of contraband ingredients to improve the quality and taste of our meals. The improvements were very soon reflected in lessening sick and death rates.

However it didn't do to enquire too closely into what those additives were, or where they had come from. Anything was better than a diet in which the chief attraction had been the once a fortnight treat of a few scraps of dry salted fish which were usually rancid and looked like stained oak chippings. One of the Aussie specialities was what they called a 'doover' which name (I believe) was a contraction for the term 'do for now'! Some of those concoctions were cooked in fat and looked like doughnuts. The taste always had to depend on the ingenuity of the cooks and the degree of thievery required to bring the rest of the ingredients to the pot.

This spell of comparatively high living came to an abrupt halt only two or three weeks after we had moved into our new camp. I cannot believe that it had taken all that time for the Japanese to realise that we had been going through the wire every day; but eventually – and without any prior warning – we were ordered out on a snap *tenko*. Despite doing all that we could to alert the men outside at that time, three of them were caught. Although it was some consolation to find that dozens more had managed to come darting and slithering back undetected, it was of no help to the three who were caught. They were paraded before us and immediately sentenced to be executed the following morning. Two of them were Australians and the other was Sergeant 'Ned' Stead RASC, from our Battalion.

The rest of us were made to remain standing on parade for an hour after seeing the three culprits marched over to the Japanese HQ to be segregated there for the night.

Although we had acquired a new Commandant whose usual behaviour was balanced, he was no pushover. There could be no reason why he saw these innocuous trips just beyond the boundary wire as full-blooded attempts to escape. We were under the control of men who were so unpredictable that they could murder someone one day for the most trivial offence and, in a matter of a few hours after that, mete out light punishment for something far more serious. They also had the national characteristic that would never allow them to reverse a decision unless it could be done without losing face.

So, without much hope of success, I was summoned to attend a meeting of the senior officers and the Aussie CSM to see if we could come up with a reason – no matter how illogical it might be – to get the men released. It was a very urgent and serious matter and there was no way that it could be solved with Western reasoning such as pointing out that the men that had been caught, were barefooted and had no escape equipment on them. The Commandant quite obviously knew that, and the worst thing we could do was to imply that he must be an idiot. For that reason also it would have been no good telling him that the same kind of thing had been going on ever since we had moved in.

We had the interpreter standing by and time was running out when – in desperation – I suggested that our only hope might be in making us appear to be idiots instead of him. Crazy as it may seem, this was our decision! The interpreter was asked to explain that the three men – in common with many others Westerners – suffered from an overpowering sense of claustrophobia which could only be abated by being allowed to get outside the confines of the wire. Those two strands of wire – fragile and harmless as they might appear to the rest of us – were, we said, 'like iron bands in their illogical minds'.

We had no real prospect of success with such a ridiculous invention but it was now late evening and the Commandant would soon be turning in for the night. As for the interpreter, I will never know how he managed to translate our improbable story into well-reasoned and, hopefully, convincing dialogue.

The following morning it seemed that our worst fears were to be confirmed. We were paraded with the full guard in attendance. The three men were then brought out under escort to stand before us while the Commandant harangued us. He was wearing his sword. That was a thing that was only done on special occasions and it was enough to convince most of us that he was about to use it. What did seem incongruous though was that the Aussie bandsmen had also been ordered out in full regalia. So, how were *they* going to be employed at such a grim ceremony?

There was just nothing at all in this set-up that could have prepared us for what happened next. We were given the order right turn. The prisoners were led off to the front of the column, the band was moved up behind them and we were marched out of camp to the strains of good old *Sussex by the Sea*. By then the word had come down from the interpreter that we were to be marched round Mergui 'to relieve the tensions of the men suffering from claustrophobia'. What a strange and enigmatic ethos must have dwelt in the mind of the Commandant to have swallowed such codswallop – or had he?

126

So on we went to the accompaniment of other favourite tunes to which we sang the usual ribald ditties.

We had hardly time to get over our relief that the three men had been reprieved, before being launched into another bizarre situation. The local population would have heard us approaching. However, they couldn't have been prepared for what they saw as the long column of men came marching into the main street with the guards lolloping along on their short legs as they tried to keep up with us.

The pace then quickened and the locals – caught up in the euphoria of the moment – started to shout their greetings. Our Battalion was at the rear of the column and by the time we reached the town, people were stepping out to shake hands and thrust gifts of food on us. They were totally ignoring the Japanese.

The farther we progressed the less tuneful was the sound of the music being wafted back to us because by then the bandsmen were trying to stash away their loot as well. I had always enjoyed the 'oompah oompah' sound of the euphonium, so I was very disappointed when it faltered and then faded away like a deflating haggis. It was through no fault of the player, because I heard later that it had happened when someone tossed a large dollop of raw meat into the mouth of the instrument. Everyone was receiving so many gifts by then that it would have been ridiculous to try and hide them. In any case the Japanese seemed to be beyond caring any more.

There must have been good reasons why the Commandant had cancelled the intended executions. However, it is hard to understand why he hadn't taken the easy option of handing the men over to the Kempi. They would have been only too pleased to oblige.

Two days later the whole incident was ended by the release of the three men. I have no idea how Ned Stead managed it, but he soon became quite philosophical about his narrow escape. It was an event that would have shaken most men rigid!

We were settled in by now and my appointment had been confirmed. Tim Healy had his typewriter sorted out and Lieutenant Dicker had firmed up on the details of the nominal roll. We had discovered that two of our worst villains were almost certainly deserters but it would have been useless to look further for absolute proof of that. By far the most important thing for us was in the help

127

that the record gave us in administration. We had seen how various NCOs and men had shaped up at their temporary assignments while on the move. It had been an exacting test of ability and character then and it was now of great help to me in making recommendations for more permanent appointments.

Although the quotas for outside jobs were not too demanding, the work itself – which was mainly required on the aerodrome – was becoming harder to perform now. We were once again having to rely almost entirely on basic rations. The death rate had eased but now malnutrition was affecting most of us in one way or another.

The constant and perhaps most worrying thing for me was that other than Captain Apthorp and Lieutenant Dicker, the officers might just as well have been on the moon for all the men saw of them, albeit it was hardly their fault. They had been painted into that corner by circumstance. The Japanese had little employment for them without breaking an agreement within the Geneva Convention. There were very few of the men that had any unit identity with them but many who were resentful of their privileges. It was an envy born of hypocrisy, and that didn't help anyone's cause. As for the officers, most of them were introverted by now and, unknown to me at that time, there were divisions opening up between those in charge – the regulars – and the 'general service' civilians, who had no real say in any decisions.

Nevertheless, the key to contentment in our situation was in having useful employment and the purpose to carry it through without too much hindrance from our captors. We were very fortunate to have been on a slow learning curve by comparison with the POWs who were to be driven up onto the Siam side of the railway construction. Some misinformed gentleman from the dim past coined the phrase that comparisons were odious. I cannot agree with that at all! After all, 'there but for the grace of God go I' is a comparison, and there is nothing wrong with that, surely. We of the Sumatra Battalion more than most had needed our slow advance towards the Railway of Death in order to get gradually acclimatised and organised. Nobody knew it at the time but we had been on a more prolonged survival course, and that was going to do us more good than harm in the long run.

All enthusiasm for escape had died down by now. Following our triumphal march the camp had been so strictly guarded that it would have been foolish to have tried to slip out to make further contact with the Indian merchant. We consoled ourselves with the thought that our next move would inevitably be north again. The latest rumour now had it that we were destined for Moulmein.

Things then went on routinely until the day late in July when the interpreter brought us a message from the Commandant. He wanted to know if there were any signalmen in camp. If so, he would like us to find volunteers who would man their coastal stations in order to intercept Allied naval and merchant fleet messages. We were also to convey his assurance that any 'takers' would be well paid and looked after. Needless to say, neither we nor the Aussies made any enquiries of the men. The surprising thing was that when our nil returns went in the following day, they were accepted without any undue histrionics. Perhaps the enigmatic gentleman was pleased to discover that although we bore the stigma of being called the 'cowards of Singapore' we could not be charged with being traitors as well.

A week or two after that event we were told that our Battalion would be moving soon as an advance party going north.

19

NEXT STOP TAVOY!

On the ninth of August we hoisted our gear and marched down to the waterside. We went there to the accompaniment of the Australian band, the rattle of tin cans and the reassuring sight of the china pisspot. It was sad to think that we had buried 12 of our comrades in Mergui, and among that number had been boy seaman Weaver – a 17-year-old, I believe.

A small coastal vessel named the *Tatu Maru* awaited us and we boarded it at night. Nobody minded the darkness because we were fearful of attacks by our own submarines.

Our embarkation followed the usual pattern of push, shove, kick and scream. We were crammed onto the deck this time and left standing there in an overcrowded mass. Shortly after that we were heading off into rain and a choppy sea on what turned out to be a 120-mile journey up through the Mergui archipelago and into the mouth of the river Tavoy.

The journey was horrendous. We had to take turns sitting down on a wet, cold and exposed deck fouled by urine, faeces and vomit.

It was late in the afternoon of the tenth when we dropped anchor. The latest rumour had been that we were destined for Moulmein or Rangoon. We were already hungry, wet, cold and stiff, so it was with some relief I suppose that we saw two lighters arrive, giving us the hope that we were going to be put ashore. This was confirmed with an even more frenetic boarding and mishandling than we had experienced before leaving Sumatra on the *England Maru*.

Unfortunately – and just because I wore the *gunso* armband – the Japanese seemed to expect me to interpret their wishes. So, I was retained on deck to be little more than a silent witness to the barbaric scene below. The men were being pushed down through just the one small opening into each of the holds. Anyone who hesitated before entering was getting an unceremonious assist into the black hole below with a pick-axe handle.

While watching, I came in for a crashing whack with a rifle butt which fortunately – although I didn't see it that way at the time – landed across my chest first before the follow-through hit my head. It was their way of telling me that it was my turn now!

The last of the officers had been pushed into the holds and there were still about 30 of us who couldn't be accommodated. The *Tatu Maru* lowered a raft for us.

We did at least have the blessing of fresh air while on it, but nothing else. It was still raining and very cold. There were no hand-holds anywhere other than at the edge of the raft, and those of us there only had enough room to sit doubled up with knees in our chins. The convoy of three vessels was then linked up for towing by a motor launch and we were at the back. Once we got under way, every movement from the backwash made our raft dance, buck and tilt while threatening to throw us into the water. If it hadn't been for the men in the middle linking to those on the edge, several of us would have drowned.

There was only one period of relief, when the lighter ahead of our raft broke free from the tow and drifted onto a sandbank. The others sailed on while we stretched our legs and awaited the return of the towing launch to resume our journey up the estuary and eventually alongside a jetty.

The last bit of our passage had only added ten miles to the total but it had taken nearly eight hours to accomplish.

We arrived tired, cramped, soaked and dishevelled – not to mention being famished – but nevertheless thankful to still be alive. Even then, we still had to form up and be counted in almost total darkness. We were then marched the two or three miles to town and into the compound of yet another abandoned school. It was the Ann Hesseltine Home – a girls' school – in the middle of Tavoy. Once again we were in quite good accommodation, and our area had already been cleared for us by Aussies who had been there for some time.

I didn't have the strength or the will left to start allocating spaces. We just flopped down anywhere and tried to get our first sleep for two days, with the welcome promise of a meal at dawn.

The following morning after *tenko* and breakfast, I went off with Appy and a few other senior NCOs to take stock of our accommodation. We were to be housed in some stone buildings that had formed the nucleus of the school. There were several other well-built wooden buildings scattered round the perimeter of what had been the gardens and playing fields of the school. Part of the garden area was enclosed by trees and shrubs which bordered a path leading to a three-storey wooden building perched on stilts. There were some partly enclosed wooden steps at the back of it which led to the upper storeys.

Our officers were accommodated within the rear ground floor section in what appeared to have been the staff kitchen, store and wash-house area. The front was occupied by the Japanese Commandant – a repulsive man – who had been very aptly named the Frog by the Aussies.

As in Mergui, the overall charge of administration rested with the Aussies. It was based this time not so much on numbers but on the rank of their senior officer, Major Cameron, and quite rightly too in my reckoning. However, that situation didn't appear to satisfy some of our officers, who used to spend an inordinate amount of time debating the matter because it was thought – and correctly as it turned out – that we were the slightly larger group.

More important than all that nonsense was the fact that a new identity and command structure had been imposed with orders from the Japanese that we must wear new armbands and learn their meaning immediately. The most significant of these designations, though simple to learn, became difficult to apply sometimes and I had plenty of bruises to prove that. *Hon* (a hundred) meant that a honcho was in charge of 100 men in Tavoy, but in other camps he would be included within that number. There was then *kumi* and *kumicho*. The latter (in Tavoy) was identified as someone in charge of 50 men. However, quite apart from the above complication, 50 was *go-ju* in the Japanese language, and in other camps the word *kumicho* was more freely applied to mean a leader of either 50, 100 or even 150 men.

By now my hope is that you will be just as confused as we were at times; but do not despair! All that is required of you is to keep a crystal ball handy, keep your fingers crossed and keep on saying 'rabbits!' – and shinpads would come in handy too! The armbands soon rotted away but the new names remained with us for the rest of our POW existence.

This new set-up made for a bit of a shambles at first because we were soon getting orders from the Japanese that conflicted with those given by the Aussies. When in doubt I would usually follow Captain Apthorp's often dangerous course of sticking to our own routine.

Tavoy was similar in many respects to Mergui. It too had a grain store in the middle of the town but of a more modern design. It was mounted on inverted mushroom-like stones which if properly used would have kept out rats, but the idiot Japanese in charge used to leave the removable steps in place overnight. So, we had to once again suffer a diet of sweepings, rat dirt, dust and weevils. There was also an aerodrome to which details went daily. The food was up to Mergui standard and some extras were available if one had the money. We had appointed a so-called 'canteen officer' who bought in the extras in order that they could then be fairly allocated, hut by hut, for division by the sergeants in charge. I was so determined to keep my promise of fair shares for all that when items were in short supply I would see that such things as coconuts, for instance, were broken into sections before sale. We also imposed the rule that shortages would mean that men who smoked would be denied items of food.

There was, however, the difference that while the Tavoy guards kept a low profile in camp, they regularly guarded and patrolled the outside – and it was the perimeter that featured in two major events. The first of these was quite audacious but the other was horrific despite the fact that it happened to one of the guards.

I was housed quite close to the perimeter fence and shared the accommodation with other NCOs. Among them there was Sergeant Winson of the Hong Kong and Singapore Regiment and the previously mentioned Sergeant Florey. George Winson was a fitness fanatic. He had come amongst us bursting with rippling muscles developed through the teachings of Charles Atlas, who used to preach the message, 'You too can have a body like mine'. My brother-in-law had also followed his doctrine. I hadn't stayed in England long enough to see the result of his exercises, but they seemed to depend on the use of just one very strong chest expander, which I was unable to believe could produce the results that George demonstrated to us. He was still able to manipulate his bulges in a fascinating pattern that travelled from biceps to stomach and back.

Charles Atlas would have been proud of him! George must have always exercised in the sun because his skin was quite dark. He spoke fluent Malay, and Sergeant Florey – who had command of more than one local dialect – had acquired some colourful native clothing.

Most evenings they went over the fence and into town to buy up meat. Their lookouts had a cut and the rest went to the highest bidders. There was just one occasion when I was able to place an order backed by some of my remaining Malay dollars. I had been lucky to find that someone outside had valued them as a better long-term saving prospect than the Japanese rubbish. There were times when Sergeant Florey went out on his own to wine and dine with Indian families. Many of them lived outside Tavoy, so he would often stay with them well into the night and slip back into camp just before dawn. One evening I saw him go over the fence on his own, slip across the road and then hire a *gharry*. He then got the driver to take it past the camp gate for the sole and audacious purpose of executing a polite salutation to the guard as he went by. On the face of it he appeared to have everything going for him and I was surprised that he didn't just go out one day and stay out.

The other perimeter incident was an entirely different affair. We had been keeping a careful watch on the patrols in the interest of the two sergeants and had noticed that one guard was kept on duty all day without relief. After that – and still without a break – he had been kept on patrol the whole of the following night. By the next morning he had become so exhausted that he had propped himself against the fence. I saw him swaying there as he tried to fight off his tiredness in order to get going again. It was no good; he just flopped back against the fence again. Without any warning, down swooped the Frog and drawing his revolver he shot him in his head.

One of the other guards was so shocked by the incident that he decided to tell us that the poor devil had committed an earlier offence. This had been of a minor nature only but the Frog didn't like the man. So what we had witnessed was planned murder out of spite and without even a faked trial.

20

'HALLO! HALLO! – RADIO "FREE INDIA" CALLING!'

Without any doubt the most momentous event for all of us began with a routine request for me to send out ten men on a working-party in the town.

It was pure chance that Sergeant Les Bullock of the RAF happened to be next in line for leading a detail. I knew little about Les at that time and had no idea what his party was wanted for. However, he came back in that evening to ask me if he could be sent out on the same job the next day because the Japanese wanted him to repair a wireless set for them.

With memories of the recent request for Morse signallers in my mind, my immediate response was 'Not bloody likely!' However, I soon changed my mind after hearing his reasons and, moreover, learning that he was a highly skilled radio mechanic. His party had been taken out to clean up a house which had been hurriedly vacated during the recent retreat of the British Army and it was now on the point of being occupied by Japanese officials.

On arriving there he had found them fiddling about with a receiver/transmitter. It had been abandoned in haste with only a very perfunctory attempt to sabotage it. After taking a good look round, Les had assessed that there were enough parts available to provide the incomers with a modified receiver and himself with more than enough to build another set for us. So he had let the Japanese know that he might be able to repair it for them if he could come back the next day. He told me that the Japanese hadn't had a clue how to do it for themselves and that they had jumped at the offer.

This was something that would need careful planning, secrecy and, quite obviously, Appy's permission as well – and he was all for it!

It was decided that Petty Officer Jan Tucker should be sent out to help smuggle in the parts. He was not only a cool customer but one who could be trusted to keep a secret. Les and Jan were then left to select the other eight men. Appy and I spent a very apprehensive and jittery day until – with great relief – we saw all the working parties in without being searched. One of Jan's Navy lads had kept watch for them during the day so at that point there were only six of us (including Major Cameron) in on the secret.

We had decided that the only safe place for assembly and testing would be in the empty upper rooms directly above the rear of the Japanese HQ building. These were only accessible to the Japanese by going through our officers' quarters to the rear.

So, it came about that each evening Les went up the external stairway to work on the parts while Jan and the other Navy lad kept lookout. Within a couple of days we were in business. I was invited up there and putting on some earphones, I listened to faint and jangly music being relayed – so Les told me – from Radio India. The cheekiest thing of all was that everything had been done by courtesy of the Japanese electricity supply. I never went up there again. It was quite enough to know that we were on the air.

Jan used to go over there regularly to tidy away and hide all evidence each night, so it was inevitable that the other officers should get to know what was going on as well. Once the news started coming through, the whole camp would also have to know. So it was decided that no news would be released until it was ten days old and that the word wireless must never be used by anyone. There were some parade times when I was left unattended by the Japanese. I used those moments to warn that in any future reference to the wireless the word nightingale must be used. Further to that, if anyone was caught relaying the news they would have to say that they had been told it by an English-speaking local while working outside.

It was fortunate that Sergeant Florey had decided to stay with us because we needed his help to buy torch batteries for Les.

We were now sitting on a bombshell which, to the later credit of all the thousands of men in Group III (Burma), was never allowed to 'explode' despite being an open secret by then.

When we arrived in Tavoy we had adopted – as it were – some Korean guards, among whom was an ugly gold-toothed villain with an ungainly walk... Now please skip a page if you don't want to know that he had already been given the name 'F..k Face' by the Aussies. He was alleged to be an accomplished arms instructor and a group of his toadies used to gather and watch him practising bayonet drill. This was usually done before an audience of POWs who were intrigued with his antics. His advance to attack was executed by means of a series of exaggerated and comical hops.

Now we had an NCO – it was Corporal Bostock, I believe – who was both a gymnast and an unarmed combat instructor. He had kept up a self-appointed fitness regime, so I was told. I was hardly surprised therefore that one day when he was walking ahead of me on a concrete path he executed a forward somersault. He hadn't done it for show, because he didn't know I was there, so I suppose it was inevitable that FF would one day witness his skills also. However, I have no idea how they got involved in a challenge match.

The corporal seemed quite unperturbed when I went to see him about it. He had discovered that all the Koreans had been armed with captured Lee Enfields, and that appeared to be all that he needed to know. The contest had been arranged without the knowledge of the Commandant, and although there should have been only guards present, many of us had found places to hide and watch as FF fixed his bayonet and moved in on the corporal.

It was all over in moments and sweet to witness. The corporal – in a series of co-ordinated movements – swept aside the rifle, removed the bayonet and held it threateningly across FF's throat. Unfortunately for the corporal, some of FF's toadies applauded and – having lost both face and reputation in a matter of moments – he went completely berserk. He made the corporal stand to attention; and then – screaming out *buggeros* – he bashed and kicked him until he fell down to be kicked again and again.

We were soon going to discover that that kind of treatment was typical of what to expect from nearly all the Korean guards, most of whom were degenerate sadists.

Despite the agility of the corporal and of our muscle-bound sergeant, we were soon starting to come apart at the seams in one way or the other. We were all looking unhealthy and losing weight. Someone had come by a handbook written by a dietician. There were tables of foods within it which showed their various calorific values, and from that information it was estimated that we were getting little more than a third of what was needed to maintain weight and fitness. So, but for the few valuable extras purchased at our own expense, there would have been an even greater decline in health.

There had been no further outbreaks of dysentery but again, no thanks to the Japanese. They did nothing to improve our hygiene arrangements other than supplying a bit of lime for the latrines. The only means that we had for fighting disease was through the constant supply of boiled water. It was a further three or four months before we were given our one and only issue of soap. This came to me in the form of 60 blocks. Each one of those was about a foot in length and of the caustic type used for scrubbing floorboards. After setting aside 20 blocks for the hospital and sanitary staff, I measured, cut and issued one small piece per head for the rest of us. God alone knows what our camps smelt like to an outsider!

However, at this point we counted ourselves lucky by comparison with most other POWs and not least the men who remained in Singapore. Even though they had all their possessions around them, they had – from all accounts – been living a very claustrophobic life in Changi, while we were right in the middle of a bustling little town with a cosmopolitan population. It was very much like our first camp in Mergui. We could see them all moving back and forth and hear the cries of tradesman selling their wares. The Buddhist monks were there too, and as far as I could make out they spent far more time begging from, than ministering to, the needs of the local population. Some of the locals were still managing to leave parcels of food around for the men on working parties but nothing was passed by hand. We wouldn't have wished them to take that sort of risk again with the Heigh-ho militia getting more and more active by the day.

Nevertheless, if one could rise above our otherwise grim existence and forget for a while the two horrific sea journeys that we had made, it was still possible to think about other things than our shrinking stomachs.

Our wanderings could be likened to a glorified and uncompleted mystery tour in tandem with a survival course.

Appy had led us well so far. He had a caring if eccentric disposition. This endeared him to the men but gained him scant support from his peers.

The men saw him as their champion in all matters. He was always willing to challenge the Japanese on their behalf and to suffer the consequences of doing so if need be. There are no service training manuals on how to cope as captors in a POW camp. It had to be a matter of instinct only, and Appy often chose the way of confrontation.

Hindsight doesn't help anyone very much but it will be seen that his ways and the disloyalty of some of his companions led to his temporary downfall later. However, he never lost the loyalty of the men. We had set out to build a secure and shared regime and, quite remarkably, that had been all but achieved in only six months. The cohesiveness was already in place and nobody was going to surrender to chaos again. We had sound and capable men in post to support us by now. I had always had Appy's backing and, come what may, I was determined to see that he would always have my allegiance in return.

There were still a few rogues and subversives about. It would have been remarkable if it weren't so within a confined community of nearly 500 men; but we knew who they were! There is no hiding place in a POW camp. You were what you were and whether that was good, bad or indifferent it was on view to all others.

As for our survival course, that was all but over and we were about to be tested.

On the twenty-first of October, after the usual lengthy counting and a typically slapdash search, we were heading out of camp for another journey north.

That search had been particularly vital for those of us who had to get the wireless parts safely through it. Les had broken down the components into the smallest pieces possible. He was carrying a number of them himself in a false-bottomed army water bottle. Some of our most reliable Houdinis were entrusted with other bits. I had a length of aerial wire attached to the inside of my webbing belt. That still left Les with many spares on his hands; and there chance helped us. A late announcement had been received from the Japanese that several of our sick men were being allowed to come up later with the Aussies. We left Jan Tucker in charge of them. He was a more than just competent medical orderly but, taking no chances, we declared him to be sick also. Among Jan's charges were some very reliable gunners, including Lance Bombadiers Grafton, Charlie Ward and Tich Shields. We gave Jan the spares and left him to decide who should help him to smuggle them through.

In the event we went north by boat. The others came up by train, carrying not only the wireless spares but a useful collection of drugs that had been liberated from Mergui hospital earlier.

So it was goodbye Tavoy for the rest of us as we marched down to the waterfront. The Frog and his entourage had gone ahead of us in lorries loaded with their baggage and our kitchen equipment. We had buried four of our number in Tavoy and shortly after we left, Private Quarterly of the Federated Malay States Volunteer Force also died there. As for the rest of the Battalion, there was scarcely a man free from all sickness. It was just a matter of degree. I had been plagued with recurring bouts of malaria – all without remedy, of course – and by now more and more men could be seen shivering and shaking with malaria or dengue fever. Some of them were having to cope with looseness or diarrhoea at the same time, unavoidable with our bland and watery diet.

21

OFF TO MOULMEIN, AND INTO THE VALLEY OF THE SHADOW OF DEATH

We were taken out into the roads aboard those horrible lighters. There were two vessels anchored there, one of which was the *Tatu Maru* that had brought us up to Tavoy in August. I don't think any one of us discovered the name of the other vessel. All that really mattered to us was that it was much larger than the *Tatu Maru*. It was already loaded with a detachment of Aussies known as Black Force – the same men, I believe, as those put off at Victoria Point in May – but that still left us plenty of room to stretch and move about in. All of us were convinced that this was to be our last sea journey but we still didn't know where we would be disembarking.

We had come aboard to discover that the Aussies had already given a lot of thought to that and had hatched up a scheme for taking over the vessel and sailing on to India. This all seemed a bit madcap to me since nobody knew how many Japanese were aboard aft or in other places inaccessible to us; or, indeed, on the *Tatu Maru* either. There was nothing that we could do about it, though. We were in the unenviable position of being captive to the Aussies' plans.

Fortunately for all of us, the scheme fizzled out with the realisation that there was no way in which we could have captured the *Tatu Maru* anyway. The two vessels must have been in radio contact with each other (and the shore) if only for the one reason that we were going to be travelling unescorted.

That last fact alone was enough to worry about. It was an indication that while we might be expendable, Japanese destroyers and their crews were not. (Post-war archives have revealed that Japanese merchant vessels on the west of Burma run at that time had to depend solely on volunteer crews – and the Spirit of Bushido, of course!) It took us a day and two nights to trundle our way over the 200 miles up to Moulmein, where we very quickly disembarked. We had been very lucky to get through unscathed because the next POW draft that came up was bombed on the way in and suffered many casualties.

We were taken from the docks down to the perimeter of the town jail cell blocks and (as in Mergui) the locals decided to turn it into a triumphal march. They were thronging the roadside, and in total

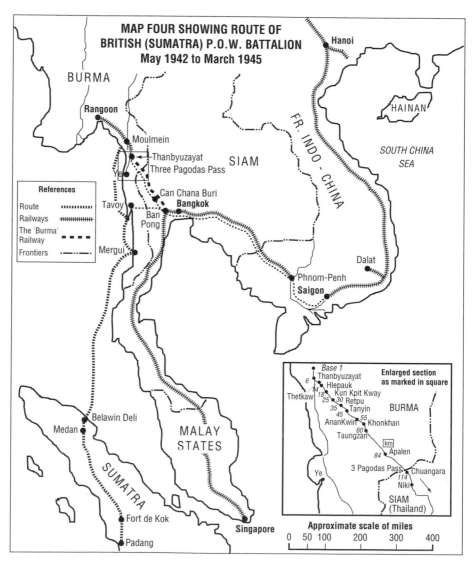

MAP FOUR SHOWING ROUTE OF
BRITISH (SUMATRA) P.O.W. BATTALION
May 1942 to March 1945

disregard of the militia youth and the guards, they came in amongst us with gifts of food. The guards were so bewildered by our reception that they had to be content with shouting a few *buggeros* and making sure that nobody tried to escape. The prison warders were also openly friendly and the Japanese did nothing much about that either. This seemed quite strange to us. They must have been infuriated with the realisation that so many of the locals – who should have been disciples of the co-prosperity doctrine – still thought more of us than of them.

There were always rumours flying about, so I was not at all surprised to hear later that during our one night stay R. A. S. Pagani was supposed to have made contact with Catholics from a local convent. This sounded like a particularly tall story to me because although we marched out next morning through another throng of locals, they were not allowed to approach us. Despite that, some of Appy's locusts left the prison precinct bearing liberated slop pails. Empty or full, durables were at a premium!

It was not very long before Moulmein railway station came into sight and there we were halted, counted and then loaded into some fiercely hot steel box cars. We were near the southern end of the Burma State Railway, destined for Thanbyuzayat and the fulfilling of Hiro Hito's promise to employ us on the noble project of railway building. How right he was going to be in his cynical forecast of deprivations and deaths and on a scale that by comparison would make all our previous sufferings look like picnic outings.

143

22

THANBYUZAYAT

Thanbyuzayat was the base HQ for 120 kilometres of new construction needed to extend the line up to the Three Pagodas Pass at the border between Burma and Siam. We were to work on that section under the planning and direction of the Japanese 5th Railway Regiment. The Siam link – from Kanchanaburi up to the pass – was controlled by the 9th Regiment and it was nearly three times as long. Much of that would have to be built over far more difficult terrain by a mixed force of British and Australian POWs. They were being sent up there on the rail network that already linked Singapore to Kanchanaburi and all but a few of them came up direct from Changi jail.

We were under the command of Colonel Nagatomo (No. 3 Group) whose chief medical appointee, Heguchi, was reputed to be a vet. The Railway Regiment had its quarters and workshops within the town. They were an intelligent group of individuals who – when outstationed upcountry – did their best to keep apart from our guards, whom they appeared to regard with as much distaste as we did.

The guards were either Japanese or Koreans and commanded by Japanese officers or NCOs. We would often wonder how those Japanese had come to be selected for such a demeaning task. My best guess was that they must have been either failed or delinquent soldiers assigned to us as much for their own humiliation as for ours; and with very few exceptions they were out and out bastards.

That was not a fair description for the Korean guards though. *They were sadistic bastards!* Whenever we came under their care it would be a near certainty that they would bash and harass – and sometimes even torture – man or beast, and often for fun. They were subject to – and despised by – the Japanese and their main functions within the Japanese army were as guards, cooks, bottle-

144

washers and the like. The evidence of this can be found in the fact that they were only allowed to form two or three fighting battalions and then, no doubt, under the total supervision of Japanese officers and NCOs. It was therefore only a short step for them to release all their frustrations on us POWs – the last in the pecking order – and quite often in far more manic and perverted fashion than that of the Japanese. As for the Japanese guards, there were just a few of them who saw more merit in using firm discipline than employing the mindless and brutal doctrinaire of their military training. The majority – who took the latter path – had a ready platform on which to develop any perversions that took their fancy.

It was only a short march from Thanbyuzayat station to the base camp. We came through the entrance into a well-established and appointed set-up that was already occupied by Aussies commanded by Brigadier Arthur L. Varley of the Australian 8th Division.

He had been selected while at Changi to lead an intended work force of 10,000 POWs on the Burma side of the railway construction, but by the time we were assembled about 300 had already been lost by attrition on the way. Our original 500 was already down to 481. The Aussies would number about 5,000, the Dutch around 4,200 and the Americans 190.

Although we had arrived ahead of the Dutch and Americans, it was already a nepotic institution in which all administrative posts had been filled by the Aussies. So for the rest of us, Thanbyuzayat was going to be the transit camp for moving us out and ever onward into the jungle camps, some of which had already been constructed for us by enforced local labour.

Thanbyuzayat flanked a section of the line that had been extended along a route surveyed and partly cleared in the thirties as a British venture that had later been abandoned. In just a few years the route had been engulfed by second-growth jungle to the extent that nearly all traces of it had been obliterated. However, by the time we arrived work had been done to clear it again.

We vagrants had walked into a dream camp which was comfortably appointed in an easily supplied town environment, to find our colonial cousins – as ever – over-endowed with kit. They also had ready access to a purpose built canteen-cum-ration store and the opportunity to acquire further supplies when employed outside. We would all have liked to take a good breather before moving out but we were to be disappointed, because other than leaving a few sick men behind with Les Bullock and the wireless set, plus Colonel Coates, we were all on our way up-country within two days. It was all rather galling but we were in no position to complain, since had we been there first in superior rank and numbers we too would have held on to any perks that were going.

During that very short stay we had been received and harangued by Colonel Nagatomo in a prepared speech that was not only ominous but also amusing in parts; the full text of which is given at the end of this chapter. After that, those of us with administrative jobs were issued with new armbands. The following day (the twenty-sixth of October) we marched out of camp and away up a rutted expanse of baked earth onto which lorries were transporting ballast, sleepers and rails.

We had started out on a journey which for most of us would be ever onward and away from base. The exceptions to that were mainly the critically sick men that we managed to send back later. Sad to relate, very few of those survived to rejoin us.

Most of the lorries that were buzzing around us were being driven by Aussies, in many cases unaccompanied by guards, and one had been released for the use of our advance party. This carried our cooks, our few heavy items of kit, the Japanese kitchen equipment and two or three guards. However, we hadn't been marching very long before another empty lorry arrived to begin relaying batches of men up to our first camp. The Aussie driver told us that it was 18 kilometres from base at a place called Hlepauk.

This bit of sensible organisation by the Japanese was a great relief to all of us. There were many men with us who would never have made it to Hlepauk without assistance, despite having been declared *sukoshi byoki* (little sick) by the Japanese vet's acolytes. There would have been even more than that but for the fact that during our six months of largely bootless life we had grown a thick layer of protective callused skin on the soles of our feet.

We were moving in a south-easterly direction more or less parallel to the coast and through partly cleared scrub. Up ahead – on both sides of our route – the more densely covered and jungle-clad hills were waiting to welcome us.

146

Something usually went wrong when the Japanese were organising things, and it did so on that day. Two more lorries were sent up to assist and the drivers mistakenly whisked 60 men off to a deserted and only half-built camp at Wegali, only eight kilometres from base. They then had to stay there overnight until the Japanese got the mess sorted out. However, most clouds quickly developed silver linings when Appy's locusts were around. When our beleaguered men rejoined us they just happened to have several items of loaned kitchen equipment with them that should have gone back to base. They had also acquired – and heaven only knows from where – two other very non-standard utensils. These were a godsend to our medical orderlies. A crude but efficient commode cabinet was constructed around one of them and the other did great service as a makeshift bedpan.

Speech delivered by Lieutenant Colonel Y. Nagatomo to Allied prisoners of war at Thanbyuzayat, Burma on 28 October 1942

It is a great pleasure to me to see you at this place as I am appointed Chief of the war prisoners camp obedient to the Imperial Command issued by His Majesty the Emperor. The great East Asiatic war has broken out due to the rising of the East Asiatic Nations whose hearts were burnt with the desire to live and preserve their nations on account of the intrusion of the British and Americans for the past many years.

There is therefore no other reason for Japan to drive out the Anti-Asiatic powers of the arrogant and insolent British and Americans from East Asia in co-operation with our neighbours of China and other East Asiatic Nations and establish the Great East Asia Co-Prosperity Sphere for the benefit of all human beings and establish lasting great peace in the world. During the past few centuries, Nippon has made great sacrifices and extreme endeavours to become the leader of the East Asiatic Nations, who were mercilessly and pitifully treated by the outside forces of the British and Americans, and the Nippon Army, without disgracing anybody, has been doing her best until now for fostering Nippon's real power.

You are only a few remaining skeletons after the invasion of East Asia for the past few centuries, and are pitiful victims. It

147

is not your fault, but until your governments do not wake up from their dreams and discontinue their resistance, all of you will not be released. However, I shall not treat you badly for the sake of humanity as you have no fighting power left at all.

His Majesty the Emperor has been deeply anxious about all prisoners of war, and has ordered us to enable the opening of War Prisoner camps at almost all the places in the SW countries.

The Imperial Thoughts are unestimable and the Imperial Favours are infinite, and as such, you should weep with gratitude at the greatness of them. I shall correct or mend the misleading and improper Anti-Japanese ideas. I shall meet with you hereafter and at the beginning I shall require of you the four following points:

(1) I heard that you complain about the insufficiency of various items. Although there may be lack of materials it is difficult to meet your requirements. Just turn your eyes to the present conditions of the world. It is entirely different from the pre-war times. In all lands and countries materials are considerably short and it is not easy to obtain even a small piece of cigarette and the present position is such that it is not possible even for needy women and children to get sufficient food. Needless to say, therefore at such inconvenient places even our respectable Imperial Army is also not able to get mosquito nets, foodstuffs, medicines and cigarettes. As conditions are such, how can you expect me to treat you better than the Imperial Army? I do not prosecute according to my own wishes and it is not due to the expense but due to the shortage of materials at such difficult places. In spite of our wishes to meet their requirements, I cannot do so with money. I shall supply you, however, if I can do so with my best efforts and I hope you will rely upon me and render your wishes before me. We will build the railroad if we have to build it over the white man's body. It gives me great pleasure to have a fast moving defeated nation in my power. You are merely rubble but I will not feel bad because it is your rulers. If you want anything you will have to come through me for same and there will be many of you who

148

will not see your homes again. Work cheerfully at my command.

(2) I shall strictly manage all of your going out, coming back, meeting with friends, communications. Possessions of money shall be limited, living manners, deportment, salutation, and attitude shall be strictly according to the rules of the Nippon Army, because it is only possible to manage you all, who are merely rabble, by the order of military regulations. By this time I shall issue separate pamphlets of house rules of War prisoners and you are required to act strictly in accordance with these rules and you shall not infringe on them by any means.

(3) My biggest requirement from you is escape. The rules of escape shall naturally be severe. This rule may be quite useless and only binding to some of the war prisoners, but it is most important for all of you in the management of the camp. You shall therefore be contented accordingly. If there is a man here who has at least 1% of a chance of escape, we shall make him face the extreme penalty. If there is one foolish man who is trying to escape, he shall see big jungles toward the East which are impossible for communication. Towards the West he shall see boundless ocean and above all, in the main points of the North, South, our Nippon Armies are guarding. You will easily understand the difficulty of complete escape. A few such cases of ill-omened matters which happened in Singapore (*Execution of over a thousand Chinese civilians*) shall prove the above and you shall not repeat such foolish things although it is a lost chance after great embarrassment.

(4) Hereafter I shall require all of you to work as nobody is permitted to do nothing and eat at the present. In addition, the Imperial Japanese have great work to promote at the places newly occupied by them, and this is an essential and important matter. At the time of such shortness of materials your lives are preserved by the military, and all of you must award them with your labor. By the hand of the Nippon Army Railway Construction

Corps to connect Thailand and Burma, the work has started to the great interest of the world. There are deep jungles where no man ever came to clear them by cutting the trees. There are also countless difficulties and suffering, but you shall have the honour to join in this great work which was never done before, and you shall also do your best effort. I shall investigate and check carefully about your coming back, attendance, so that all you except those who are unable to work shall be taken out for labor. At the same time I shall expect all of you to work earnestly and confidently. Henceforth you shall be guided by this motto.

Y. Nagatomo, Lt/Col. Nippon Exp. Force Chief of No 3 Branch Thailand POW Administration.

(*Note:* The texts or précis of other speeches are shown in Appendix V)

– ACCOMMODATION FOUND –

(Arrow shows the lashed-up remains of the author's camp bed which he 'liberated' from Fort-de-kok Barracks (see Chapter 12))

23

HLEPAUK – 18 KILOMETRE CAMP

We had arrived to find the camp occupied by Aussies under the Command of Lieutenant Colonel Charles Anderson VC, who quite unexpectedly had a British officer (Captain Bill Drower) with him as interpreter.

The Captain was a tall, well-kitted-out and amiable man. He had come up from Singapore with the Aussies, was closely identified with them and, predictably, saw no merit in moving in with a scruffy bunch of nomads. We scarcely had time to make his acquaintance before rumours started to get around about his past. The most prevalent of these was that he had worked as a civilian in German and Japanese embassies and that he had become fluent in both languages. It was said that he was so fluent in the Japanese tongue that he could speak an educated and far more refined form of the language than was used by the Japanese he was having to deal with. It was said to be 'Emperor' Japanese and likened to 'Rajah' Malay.

I don't know where all that misinformation started from but it would have been wrong to dilute the mystique that surrounded him. We needed champions and morale boosters around in our situation and the more remote he remained the greater the legend became. He only visited my office once during our stay at Hlepauk and very soon after that he was at the centre of a fateful incident witnessed by all of us.

The kind of rumours that did nobody any good – particularly the most gullible men amongst us – were those that so inflated hopes that the reality that followed had a damaging effect. A particular instance of this has always remained in my memory and the furphy (rumour) had been an Australian special. The story was that we were going to be taken into the care and administration of the Red

Cross within a neutral country. It was put over in such a plausible way that even I – an arrant sceptic – hoped (but never truly believed) that it could be true. Thank heavens I was soon back with my firm belief that it would be a long war, and for reasons that will be explained later.

Perhaps now is the best moment to say something about Lieutenant Colonel Anderson and of the thousands of 8 Div men that were commanded by Brigadier Varley. There has been a lot of contentious reporting in the press about the relative levels of blame for failure during the Malay/Singapore campaign. Soldiers do not get VCs for nothing, and such rewards usually reflect the bravery of those who fought with them. So, it always seemed quite stupid to me that the same sort of bickering attitude spilt over into our POW lives occasionally and – I might add – more often among the officers than the men. The latter took the relatively simple stance that pride of country, regiment or anything else was not worth slang-ing each other about in our situation. There was, of course, a lot of Digger/Pommie repartee bandied about but that was more healthy than harmful.

To my mind the Aussie CO was very even-handed. So, if I were to be called upon to lay blame for any friction, it would have been more with our much admired but totally intransigent CO and some of the junior Aussie officers than any others.

One thing that was incontestable was that we British were always a pain in the neck for any others who had the misfortune to share a camp with us. This was in part due to the fact that Appy was dis-missive of all but Sandhurst-trained officers of whatever nationality, but mainly because of the 'taking ways' of so many of his locusts.

However, many friendships were developed between the rest of us and a few of our near-naked men were given items of clothing by the Aussies. These were very generous acts because even though they had plenty of clothing, such possessions ranked as a 'visa' for survival in my estimation. Despite that, it was inevitable (I suppose) that some of our tramps should steal from their millionaire cousins. I would quite often hear the warning cry of 'Watch your kits' when any unvetted Pommies came too close to their huts. There was noth-ing much that I could do about it other than to issue an admonish-ment at the next parade and express the hope that the Aussies would catch and deal with any culprits themselves.

Another cause of strife between us and others was that our

152

poverty had made us more overtly anti-Japanese than the others. This was true of Appy right down to the lowest ranker, and in shared camps the others often had to suffer for our misdeeds as well. Who knows? Perhaps a little more subtlety would have served our cause better in the long run. But we were as we were!

Hlepauk was in most respects typical of the majority of camps that we occupied later. It was wholly enclosed within two strands of ordinary fencing wire except at the entrance, where the guardhouse stood to one side of a ten-foot gap. There the wire was attached to large whitened posts which (I believe) had some special significance in the eyes of the Japanese. No attempt was ever made to secure any of the railway camp boundaries in any other way. Colonel Nagatomo had been quite right when he suggested that the jungle between us and potential freedom was just as good a deterrent to escape attempts as iron bars.

Most of the camps were enclosed by jungle on three sides, with the fourth open alongside the track (or trace) of the railway. There was often a river or stream within convenient distance for water collection and there were two camps at which bathing was allowed.

The notable exceptions to this general pattern were that Hlepauk – being in a lightly forested area – stood within the boundary of an abandoned paddy field. In contrast to that there were camps where the water-carrying details had to bring in loads from anything up to 400 yards from the camp kitchen areas. That task, when carried out during the monsoon season over uneven paths made slippery with mud, was one for which I didn't find many volunteers.

The most significant and common feature of all camps was that nearly every structure within them was made of local material; 90 per cent were contrived from bamboo for the framework and folded leaves (*atap*) for the roof. These were cut, fashioned and erected by the use of forced local labour which was rarely 'local' in the true sense of that word. This was because our various camp names – although of Burmese origin – only appeared to have two villages or hamlets of those names near them. Hlepauk was once again an exception albeit only discovered by a few of us later.

There was plenty of more general labour available to be tempted, coerced or press-ganged into going up-country on what for most of them proved to be a one-way journey. Once up there, they had to live in ghastly jungle communities which for the most part were totally devoid of amenities or organisation. Most of them were taken up to the remotest points of what had been old merchant caravan trails and once there they were left to fend for themselves. There, they slaved in an environment of steadily mounting chaos, disease and death, the outcome of which will be related as the story develops.

Having digressed a bit I must now return to the time of our arrival in Hlepauk camp, which much to our surprise had a lowly Japanese corporal named Tanaka as its Commandant. He had a habit of strutting round the camp girded with belt and sword and – being a short-arse – he used to leave a trail of dust as the sword bounced along behind him. He was an altogether comical character (in aspect only) and he soon attracted the nickname of Little Napoleon. However, by nature, he was nothing more than a nasty little sod.

As soon as we arrived, all of us except the cookhouse staff and the CO were sent out on railway construction work whether bearing armbands for other duties or not. The other officers had to accompany us as *kumichos*. We were issued with picks, shovels, chunkels and baskets, and stretchers made from bamboo poles and rice sacks. The chunkel – though unfamiliar to us at first – turned out to be a very useful tool. Being broad-edged, it could be used as either a light pick, or as a scoop to lift and throw soil in the one action. Skilled locals were able to dredge ditches or chop out monsoon drains with chunkels in no time flat.

Once clear of the camp, our guard handed us over to a member of the Japanese Railway Regiment who had already been busy placing markers. These were the boundaries of stints at which groups of three men were set to dig out and carry away six cubic metres of soil per man. Each load had to be carried and dumped within the contours of a light bamboo framework that defined the size of the intended embankment.

His task completed, the engineer then went on his way without a single word to his more lowly placed countryman (our guard), who then sat down in what appeared to be total uninterest in anything much for the rest of the day.

As it was our first day, we had gone out with the intent to do as little work as possible either for ourselves or – as it were – for King and country. So, once the engineer had disappeared we lifted the markers and reset them to reduce the overall length by a quarter. This was accomplished in quick time while our uninterested guard sat smoking and contemplating his navel. There then followed a try-on by some of the men to make three of the officers work a vacant section. There were only a few – but typically over-vociferous – barrack-room lawyers in the Battalion, but they were soon making enough fuss to alert the guard. The further threat was that they might soon get the co-operation of others. They were cowards really, because when I stood firm on the principle of officer privilege and the guard bore down on us, the whole business fizzled out. I was not particularly pleased at having to intervene, but there was no way that I would flout a principle which even the Japanese appeared to accept. Our own army had set those rules and I was determined to keep to them.

I had been counted off to work with two Welshmen, who for the next two hours showed no interest whatsoever in making even a token start on our stint despite our reduced task being well within the capability of three men. I began to get more and more worried as time went by and the groups on either side of us were digging out and carrying off their loads. My two companions came in for quite a lot of banter for doing nothing at all except on the rare occasions that our guard went by. Their only reply had been 'There's plenty of time yet!' until – having been told that there was going to be a meal at noon – they at last decided that it would be a good idea to start. We were just in time because the engineer was seen coming down the track to check on our progress.

I needn't have worried, though, because after being asked to move to one side, I stood to watch those two – with the knowledge gained from a long line of miners – chop out and undercut the lower face. They then slammed into the top with a few well-aimed whacks which sent the whole of our stint thundering down round our feet before the engineer reached our section.

However, the laugh was soon on us because a colony of hundreds of black scorpions had also descended with the soil. They ranged in size from four-inch great-grandfathers to barely visible great-grandsons, and they came among us with arched stingers at the ready. We backed off while beating at them with our shovels but I was still caught by one and made to pay for our 'clever Dick' antics with a nasty swelling and throbbing pain.

During the morning our guard had come to life and announced, *'Orral haiti yasume, smoko'*, which in our commonly understood jargon translated into an invitation for all soldiers to have a rest and a smoke. This wasn't a joke because there were some of us who really did manage to smoke with the aid of a variety of props and tobacco substitutes.

I had to be content with either dragging on an empty pipe or smoking an evil-smelling concoction of dried and chopped papaya leaves mixed with Burmese cheroots which, whenever possible, was sweetened with goula or shintegar. The cigarette smokers had to rely mainly on the cheroots, which, if left uncut and untreated, were usually so dry that they spluttered and crackled in their mouths. The possible alternative for them was to roll the makings. However, paper of any sort was not only hard to come by but best kept out of sight of the Japanese, who had a mania about its illegal use for secret messages and the like. During the short time that thin paper was available, bibles were being sold off at the rate of three rupees a sheet.

There were a few well thumbed and guarded books about in most camps, and in ours I had given Tim Healy the additional task of being the librarian for a circulation of about 30 volumes which owed their survival to being unsmokeable. It was not very long before the only two smokeable books in camp were one bible and a *Pears Encyclopaedia* which I owned and kept well out of sight for use in compiling quizzes. If only I had patented the idea I might have made a fortune because they were presented on the lines of the BBC's programme *Twenty Questions*. Well, I've had my smoke, so let us get back to the story again!

We must have completed about 80 yards of embankment during an eight-hour shift broken with just one hour's rest for the midday meal. That one hour might sound like a very civilised concession, but believe me, and the Japanese knew it too, the combination of intense midday heat and high humidity was so enervating that less rest would have been counter-productive unless... Yes, there were alternatives that didn't bear thinking about too much!

Once we got back into camp, those of us who had duty armbands had to catch up on our other work. Fortunately for all of us, it took only a few days for Tanaka to realise that he couldn't run the camp properly without our full-time help. That realisation came as something of a mixed blessing for me.

There is no doubt at all that my job gave me both the protection from hard labour and the reward of being occupied on work that was mentally and physically stimulating and, moreover, solely for the benefit of the Battalion. The flip side of the coin was that I was then always exposed to punishment for any real or imagined breach of camp rules. One of Tanaka's favourite amusements was to play a well rehearsed 'yes/no game' with me.

I would be called to the guardroom to await his presence and then receive a tirade of raving and ranting which I was both expected to understand and to give the right answer to. In a typical encounter I might get the impression that (to put it mildly) he was upset about the small number of men who had been declared fit for work that day. He would end his ravings with a 'no goodtenah'. This I could think required me to give an answer of no in agreement. My reward for that would be a bash across the face with a clenched fist. His ravings would then continue. So presuming that they had been on the same subject, I would try a 'yes', which – as often as not – was followed by another whack and further ranting. Having by then used the only two responses other than *maybe* – which wouldn't have been appreciated at all – I would often be made to keep standing there while being hit by him until his hands hurt enough to make him stop. After that, I would be hopefully led off by a guard to either see the interpreter, or to visit the scene of the crime to try and work out what had upset the manic little sod. I am certain that most of those confrontations were contrived for the sole purpose of boosting his ego with the fact that he – a corporal – had bashed up a warrant officer; and he undoubtedly found even more gratification when setting about Appy.

It was fortunate for my peace of mind that I didn't have to take any part in selecting the men deemed fittest for railway work. Our Australian doctor, Kranz, had that unenviable task. There was scarcely a man amongst the lot of us who wasn't sick in one way or another, so it was just a matter of deciding to what degree by the use of the scantiest of medical aids. The unfortunate Kranz was long on sound advice but almost devoid of remedies to back it up.

Sick parades were held each evening, and if the Japanese didn't like the result they would send in one of their number who – despite being totally unqualified – bore the exalted title of 'medical corporal, Railway Regiment'. It was that body of men who were the masters, and such is life that although they imposed the quotas, it was the camp Commandant who exacted the punishments. These were rarely visited on the doctor, occasionally on Appy or myself but with regularity on any man or group of men that Tanaka selected to be driven out to make up the numbers.

During those early days there were times when Tanaka would accept the challenge of a bit of wheeling and dealing, but confrontation was out of the question unless one had a death wish. The nearest I ever got to that was much later when the railway was through and I was so ill that I did not care any more and told a Japanese to bugger off. I got lucky that day. He must have realised that I wasn't wishing him a Happy Christmas, but to my astonishment he just went on his way rejoicing.

We were only working a six-day week at that time and although the food ration was small it had just sufficient content to save us from outright starvation.

Our stay in Hlepauk lasted through to early January 1943 and during that time some small detachments were sent back to Thetkau – the 14 kilometre camp – to lay track through to where embankment work had been completed. Many significant – albeit unrelated – incidents occurred while we remained and they were heralded in with the order from base that we must all sign an undertaking not to escape. Brigadier Varley had purposely made a token refusal in order to establish the fact that when he finally signed, it would be under duress and thus make the main document invalid. There were no refusals when the rest of us were asked to sign because the Aussies had already been through the experience of the 'Selerang incident' in Singapore. On that occasion they had been made to stay out in the open with no protection from the sun and in company with all their sick men for over two days while General Percival established the same principle of duress. It would have been ridiculous to go through that again!

Quite by chance – and only a few days previously – one of our men had left camp on what was to be the only escape made which didn't result in capture *and execution*. The man was Private R. A. S. Pagani (18 Div Recce Corps), who had protested about the desecration of the chapel altar while we were moving up to North Sumatra. R.A.S. has given his own account of events in his book entitled *The Flame of Freedom*, and I commend it to you as a fascinating and compelling story of what courage linked to planning and determination can achieve.

158

Having decided to prepare secretly and leave barefooted and alone, he had for a long time been toughening up his feet, getting well sun-tanned and accumulating suitable clothing. So far as I know, Stracc was his only early confidant until (being almost ready) he had come to Appy and myself to reveal his final plan for vetting and, hopefully, our approval.

The simplest of plans are often the most successful and this one was no exception. R.A.S. would go out the day before his intended escape and hide most of his gear up the track between the camp and the work area, which was at that time within the view of the guardroom. The next morning when paraded for work he would feign sickness. Following usual practice, he would be replaced and sent off to see the doctor. Once there, Dr Kranz would create a commotion while telling Pagani that he was a malingering so-and-so. This would impress the Japanese who would send him straight out to work. The Japanese – who had already set a precedent for the procedure – would allow him to walk unguarded up to the workface about 300 yards distant. Tim Healy and the guards would then 'up the tally' by one ready for the return *tenko* that evening. There was just the one gamble: that the guards must follow their habitual indolent routine of total reliance on the tally.

I could see the track from my office. R.A.S. just walked off it to pick up his gear and that was the last we saw of him. The whole thing had been done without compromising the rest of us, and R.A.S. – as planned – would have an eight-hour start before I would pre-empt the *tenko* by declaring one man missing. My unvarying custom being to see every working-party out and back in, it was an easy matter to 'discover' his absence when called to report to the office.

The interpreter had been well primed by Appy to suggest that his absence had been an act of pique and then (with darkness imminent) to get permission to search for the poor fellow, who would no doubt be found sitting out in the jungle sulking.

The grand finale came when one of our civilian officers out with the search party was heard time and again calling out, 'Now then, Pagani, there's a good fellow! No-one will blame you! Just come back in to camp again!'

There were no repercussions. The Japanese by their laxness had shot themselves in the foot! The rest of the story belongs to Roy Anthony Stephen Pagani MM.

159

While R.A.S. had been beavering about on his own plans, five of us who had been captured from off the *Bintang Dua* went walk-about one rest day. Being a special day in the calendar for the Japanese, it had been announced the previous evening by the order *'Orral men be happy! Tomorrow resto'*. They then gave early signs of taking their own advice by drinking themselves into a stupor with hooch and saki. By the following morning they were well set to continue celebrations by means of an extended binge. The guard-house was staffed; but other than that, the discipline was so lax that men went outside to sit around the unguarded perimeter. So, we five – having decided that there was unlikely to be a daytime *tenko* – stepped over the wire and kept walking. We went off on what must now be considered as a vague and highly dangerous mission to recce the area with a view to possible escape later.

The first part of our walk took us through fairly open jungle and then, as it thickened, we continued along an ill-defined path. We wandered on, in and out of undergrowth, which thinned occasion-ally to give us distant and tantalising glimpses of the sun glinting on the sea. My compass was used for general guidance and we also took the precaution of leaving a blaze as we progressed. We were then faced with open country and the necessity to cross the railway track in order to get nearer to the coast. Thank God nobody seemed willing to risk that, because by then I had reluctantly come to con-sider myself a non-starter for any escape – overland, or by sea. Apart from recurring malaria, I was now suffering from the first nasty signs of pellagra. I could only partly open my mouth, which – as well as my tongue – was very sore, making eating both diffi-cult and painful; and my companions were in no great shape either. So, you might well ask, why were you out on such a risky trip? Our answer would have been that it is difficult to surrender all hope. However, quite apart from that, we were young enough – and daft enough – to gamble the very real chance of capture and death against the pleasure of those few hours of freedom from the con-fining influences of the camp.

We must have walked about four kilometres before the path led into a small clearing and then to a cluster of five or six huts. The largest of these was a communal longhouse built on stilts, into which we mounted by means of a log ladder. We had discovered

Hlepauk! The headman greeted us and we were invited to sit out on a bamboo-slatted verandah with him. The old boy had shown no alarm at our intrusion. That gave us the comfortable feeling that there could be no Japanese about, or for that matter any Heigho-ho boys lurking to cash in on what would have been a 400-rupee reward for our capture. A drink (though offered) had to be politely refused. It looked like something that had been dredged from the bottom of a muddy pond. We then attempted with the aid of mime and drawings to find out if he knew of a safe and direct route down to the coast and into an area of small boats; but we got nowhere with that!

During our short stay one of the villagers came dashing into the clearing to loose off an arrow at a bird in flight. We asked the old boy to call him over so that we could get a closer look at the weapon. To our utter amazement it turned out to be a beautifully patterned and inlaid arbalest which must have dated back to the Middle Ages. I still have these two unanswered questions: where and for whom was that priceless object made? And what was the history behind it finishing up in the middle of the Burmese jungle centuries later?

It was then about three o'clock so we didn't stay much longer. We had to get back in time for an early meal at five and the possibility of a *tenko* shortly after. I for one was only too glad to get going and with some haste, because the Japanese could have asked to see me at any time during the day. Appy knew that we had gone and he would have stood in for mc, but there is no certainty that that would have satisfied even a tipsy Japanese.

For me the most important incident in that eventful day happened on the way back and, moreover, quite by chance, after starting down the wrong path.

We came across a tall and sturdy tree bearing strange fruits which were similar to mangosteens, being prickly on the outside and containing a large stone within. But there the likeness ceased, because when I took a chance and bit into one it felt as though I had got a live coal in my mouth. It was obviously a citrus fruit of some kind, and despite the sting and pain it had the remarkable and almost immediate effect of freeing up the confining grip of pellagra. For almost an hour after that I was able to open my mouth fully and talk rather than mumble.

All of us had some symptoms of pellagra so it was decided to

161

indulge in something of a conker-bashing hunt by hurling up sticks to knock down and gather in a good supply of the fruit for later use. We then got back onto our path and along to the camp, to find that there were still men wandering about outside the boundary, thank God.

Shortly after our return I experimented with roasting some of the fruits on an open fire, aiming to reduce its acid sting. It was wholly successful and they remained just as effective. My stock lasted a few weeks and by then I had cured the pellagra, including its least worrying side-effect of reddening and itching joints.

I have never heard of anyone else who came across one of those trees. And I have no idea whatsoever if it is a known species. The most we five wanderers remembered about it was that it at first appeared to be some form of chestnut; and that was the only reason why we threw a stick up to bring down the fruit that I tested. How lucky can you get!

While sitting round the fire doing the first roasting, Sergeant Stead came charging in over the boundary wire from where he had been making horrible noises on a piccolo.

The Aussie band had come up from Lower Burma during November and, more recently, on to Hlepauk to rejoin us. Unfortunately one of them had had this spare instrument and sold it to Ned, and we had thereafter been plagued with his ghastly attempts to get a tune out of it. He had apparently been sitting in his hut earlier while striving to produce a melody when his hut-mates had politely requested him to 'F... off, Ned, and take that bloody thing with you.' So with feelings of offence and reluctance he had finally gone out over the wire.

He had – so he told us – been sitting out there playing and lost in the reverie of his excellence, when a snake slid out and started to rear and weave before him with its fangs flicking around ... in ecstasy no doubt. (I added that last bit because he had looked so shaken when he first came amongst us that we were convinced that his story was true.)

If that was so, it must have been the first time that he had charmed anything or anybody with his blasted piccolo. After that, Ned had a fascination – or was it hatred? – for snakes. He started to hunt them and I was fortunate enough to be given some snake steaks later at times when I would have eaten almost anything to stave off the pangs of hunger.

In our experience the strangest thing about snakes was that unless you menaced them by chance or design, they would just glide away and disappear into the undergrowth. It could be that our Battalion just got lucky, but for whatever reason it may have been, nobody to my knowledge was bitten by one even though the majority of us were barefooted at all times!

Thank heavens no large attacking snakes such as the boa-constrictor were seen. We were equally fortunate that most bamboo cutting was done by local labour; because within damaged stems there often lurked the deadliest little snake of all, the krait. There were, however, times when our working parties had to clear clumps of bamboo to make way for the track. It was then we found the bamboo itself had a 'sting'.

Its good points were that we could construct and repair huts entirely of bamboo (see sketch in Chapter 22) except for the *atap* roof cladding. It provided us with pegs for locking the crosspieces to the uprights, and lashings made from crushed, saturated and flayed out strips. The larger flattened pieces were used to construct our sleeping platforms, which were fixed at about 18 inches above the ground to protect us from the invading torrents of water that swept through during the monsoon, bearing debris, rats, snakes and other flora and fauna along with it.

However, it was in the cutting and fashioning of the bamboo that we had to be wary. If we received one cut, scratch or puncture from its razor-sharp edges and failed to treat it immediately, we were in trouble. We were particularly vulnerable because, quite apart from being unfit and in an unhealthy place, we had no medicines and scarcely anything that either looked like (or could serve as) an adequate bandage. It was essential to have the wounds cleaned, treated and then covered at all times, otherwise they would suppurate within a day. After that, if still unchecked, they would develop into an ever-deepening and spreading ulcer. The workers outside were in a catch 22 situation with their ulcers because until they became so bad that the sufferer could be declared sick, he would be made to hobble to work through either contaminating dust or mud, according to the season. The word 'hobble' is used advisably because most of the worst cuts were on legs. If they happened to be below the knee, that was considered to be a bonus by the many men who had to undergo amputations. These were performed under primitive conditions and almost invariably without suitable anaesthetic or with none at all.

Those of us who stayed in camp were fortunate in being able to properly tend our wounds and *all of us* were particularly so, when we came under the care of Dr Hekking (a Dutchman), who was assigned to us early in 1943. Up until that time all camps were having to send their most serious cases to base for conventional treatment and that often resulted in what Dr Hekking thought to be unnecessary amputations. He was an exponent of a successful, albeit painful and unconventional, treatment that was best given at the earliest stage. I am sure he was much more familiar with tropical infections and their treatment than most of the other doctors. We were very fortunate to have him with us. However, that thought came more readily after the treatment because – having announced, 'This is going to hurt!' – he would dig in with a scalpel to cut away all the dead flesh and continue down to the bone if necessary. After that he excoriated the hole until it was awash with blood. Everyone coming for treatment was asked to attend with a bandage or rag that had been boiled for 15 minutes. Following bandaging there came the habitual warning, 'Now then lad, don't let the flies get at it or you'll lose your leg!' One of our men had to sacrifice modesty for a week in order to provide a suitable bandage. Who wouldn't when it was *your* leg! Dozens of us have to thank Dr Hekking for his knowledge and dedication. I have four barely visible marks left by ulcers that had driven down to the bone on an ankle, lower leg and knee, any one of which could otherwise have resulted in amputation. Unfortunately there were still many of the Battalion who died from the ghastly and uncontrollable progress of ulcers on places that were inoperable. It will make for unpleasant reading but something further will have to be said about that later!

While it must be admitted that we were within a period of calm, there had been a few indications that a storm was on the way. The first of these was very unpleasant! A new body of guards was drafted in. They were Koreans and a finer bunch of sadists and bastards would have been difficult to imagine. They had quite obviously been purpose-trained to bash, harry and make life as difficult as possible for all of us. They were such a despicable, openly masturbating, lot of horrors that even the Japanese treated most of them with contempt. Unfortunately, that did nothing for our cause, because any aggravation that they suffered was passed on to us with interest.

This had happened shortly after we gave our undertaking not to escape. There then followed the unilateral decision to alter Japanese time, which resulted in camp reveille being well before daylight and working parties being sent out just before dawn. Japanese Blitzkrieg teams then came to weigh us and to give us compulsory skinhead haircuts.

Those barbers could have given the best of Aussie sheep-shearers a run for their money. We had to lather up with soap provided – a luxury indeed – and then it was up and over in quick time for all, as well as 'on' for those with beards. We at least got a good laugh out of it watching the production line leaving the end of the queue looking like emasculated lay figures made ready for the window-dresser. It was also comical to see the reactions of the men who had proudly sported beards and then – after a few expert swipes – were reduced from buccaneers to hairless moon men. After that we had to rely on the ministrations of the few men with scissors and of Sergeant Stracchino, who owned a cut-throat razor. The haircut was beneficial for all because with the trimmings there must have been a bucketful of lice.

The weighing was also a one-off event. The Japanese had brought in a beam balance with a bucket seat on one side and a platform for the weights on the other. The records were intended for their use only but I managed to get a good sampling, which showed that we had an average weight of around eight and a half stone. This worked out at a loss of about two stone since being captured. About four months later I rigged up a makeshift machine and by use of the balanced-off contents of a 100 kilo sack of rice, I made up a variety of weights that revealed our average to be little over seven stone. Two men – who had admittedly always been lightweights – had wasted away to five stone by then.

One of those two was Private Nutter of 18 Div Recce Corps. He had (in common with most of us) been suffering from a series of debilitating illnesses which for him had been further compounded by a long spell of acute dysentery. This had left him looking more like a stick man than a human being. He had then reached what we called the '25 visit state', which was the time when he started to pass nothing other than blood and mucous; but he was still refusing to be sent to the hospital hut. Nobody could blame him for that because we all knew that – regardless of the dedication of our three medical orderlies – it was just a quiet place in which to await death

165

for a man in his condition. He had been taking large quantities of charcoal and water – the only thing on offer – but all to no effect.

One morning his mate decided to point him out to me and said 'Do you see him Sergeant-Major? He's been sitting out there near the bog for the last twenty-four hours and the silly bugger won't die! Do you know what he wants me to do now? He wants me to strip some bark off that tree, boil it up and give him the liquid to drink. He's convinced it will do him some good!' I replied, 'Well, bloody well do it then! It can't possibly help him, but why refuse a dying man his last wish?'

You will probably be ahead of me by now when I tell you that he drank it, lived and then survived a further two and a half years as a skeletal walking miracle, to be repatriated and, hopefully, restored to reasonable health. His case has always baffled me. Did the bark have some medicinal value? Or had we perhaps witnessed psychosomatic influences at work? It must have been one or the other, presumably. I went into Bart's Hospital after the war to get the last traces of a less virulent form of dysentery cleared up. Even that took a long time to clear despite the dedicated and expert ministrations of all the staff there. Around me were other survivors who had been repatriated in only a '15 visit' state and despite all the care available some of them died.

A few days after our haircut session Corporal Tanaka started to punish the Koreans openly with full-blooded belts round the face; the spin-off being that overnight we also had to suffer a tightening of discipline verging on tyranny. It was a case of 'passed to you, Claude' with a vengeance from then on. All freedoms that we had had under the old regime of guards were now either curtailed or totally denied to us. We had been able to go unguarded across the abandoned paddy strip to bathe. This had been a particular boon for the men coming off working parties. They could linger unhindered to wash off the grime from the day's work and rinse out whatever rag, sack or G-string had covered them that day.

For many men those were the only bits of clothing possessed by them and the Koreans had noted that. The visits were soon being conducted and the Koreans began singling out any men who wore 'rice-sack' clothing. They then confiscated those pitiful and essential bits of covering and bashed up the owners for good measure. This treatment had the knock-on effect that all rice sacks that had been acquired for use as blankets also had to be hidden away to avoid confiscation and another bashing. All this was being done while the nights were getting progressively colder. The only remedy left for the dispossessed was to huddle around the fires at the hut entrances and doze there until they were thrust off out to work again in the morning. Those bastards weren't to know that we would eventually receive some clothing and blankets within two months which would quite literally be life-saving for some men. They just didn't give a toss for the rest of mankind or, in fact, for any beast either who was unfortunate enough to stray their way.

In witness of that I once watched them hack a leg off a stray dog and then gather around their rest hut to sit, watch and laugh their heads off at the howling animal stumbling around on three legs and a bleeding stump. There was another occasion when – having caught a monkey – one of them took it by the tail and whirled it around within their hut to bash its brains out on ceiling, walls and floor. I witnessed both of these events from my office, which was within sight of their hut entrance. On the second occasion I had to watch with even more revulsion as one of the guards – who obviously derived some sexual pleasure from the sight – started to masturbate.

One of the most aggravating things that they did was at the insistence of Tanaka. I had to set up a system of latrine pickets every evening after the bugle sounded lights out. This entailed working out a two-hourly detail of tally men in each hut to record how many men were away for a pee at any one time. The hut sergeants – having assigned the reliefs – then had to hope that the duty man stayed awake to see his relief in post. The Koreans made random visits throughout the night, stopping anyone else going out until they were satisfied that the incoming tally was correct – and they were more than delighted when the figures didn't agree. They would then vent their spleen on the tally man and hut sergeant and – if they felt like it – Appy and myself, later. Most of the men were ill and others exhausted and craving rest before the next day's work, so it was inevitable that the guards found and enjoyed easy pickings.

As a last resort Captain Apthorp detailed officers to take turns doing night patrols in order to check huts and hopefully get in first to give a warning if a Korean was on the prowl. That arrangement was quite effective and, moreover, a sensible use of our otherwise unoccupied manpower.

All the guards were able to pussyfoot around on patrol because their standard army footwear were boots with the texture of plimsolls and of quite unusual design. They were slit vertically at the rear and provided with hasps for latching up. The front was even more peculiar, having a separate section for the big toe. The Japanese had worn identical footwear when dashing through the Malayan peninsula to capture Singapore. They were lightweight, cheap and nasty and they only had about six weeks' wear in them when used for heavy work so they always carried spares.

Shortly after we moved into our next camp I was supplied with 137 pairs, of which more than a half were no larger than sixes and none above size seven and a half. We found just a few men who were able to squeeze their feet into the largest of them and it was they who got the first allocation if they had no other footwear. All the rest had to remain in my store-cum-office until we invented the Clomper Mark II, or what were known as 'Go-aheads' by the Aussies.

Mark I, more of a fair weather design, was made from shaped wood with a canvas strap for the toes. It looked like a crude forerunner to the style of sandal that came into fashion around the sixties. Mark II – 'the monsoon crippler' – was of a high platform variety, fitted with looped thongs for capturing between the toes. Those were painful and ungainly to wear and they more often than not got stuck in the mud as we teetered around during the monsoon period.

We were having far more success with another invention which served us well in all seasons. May I proudly present Sergeant Stracchino's invention (and named by yours truly) – the Pissaphone Mk I.* It was designed – and no pun intended – to relieve the pressure on our latrines, which would otherwise have quickly overflowed when the heavy rain set in. Every man then had to strip down to the G-string and – resisting the temptation to pee in the monsoon ditch around his hut – make a dash for the nearest 'P. Mk I'.

There waiting for him would be a battery of slanting bamboos embedded in a mounded sump, set at varying heights to accommodate all 'tackle' presented. They were both hygienic and efficient and (unlike the latrines) they never had to be shut down.

---

*The name had come to me quite readily, being a Post Office man. It reminded me of Telephone No. 1, which had a large horn-like mouthpiece which could be swivelled up and down for the comfortable use of the short or the tall! Patents have been obtained for all these contraptions. They are illustrated at the end of this chapter.

Our worst sick cases were still being sent down to base whenever we could persuade the Commandant to allow us the use of a returning lorry. However, the main sticking point on postings was the lack of guards able to cope with the mental effort of keeping the tallies properly at both ends of the journey. One of their cock-ups earned me a hell of a beating at an evening *tenko* when Tanaka was incorrectly persuaded by the guard that we were one man short. I did, however, have the pleasure of seeing the same guard being beaten for the error later.

Within a day or two of that Tanaka was promoted sergeant. He celebrated the occasion by wearing a samurai sword and, for reasons unknown to us, laying into the Koreans more than ever before; and as we moved towards Christmas there were other welcome and unexpected occurrences.

It is said that things often have to get worse before they can get better and that was so when our interpreter – Captain Drower – was called to the guardhouse one morning. The rest of us were standing on parade in response to an unexplained *tenko* and we saw him being escorted to the Koreans' recreation hut. He was scarcely inside before we heard shouting followed by the sounds of him being beaten up. Nobody had any idea what it was about and we had all got a bit edgy by the time Colonel Anderson went across to try and find out. As he approached the hut the noises got louder, the men started to murmur threateningly and then one of the Aussies shouted to his colonel, 'Do you want the mob, sir?'

I doubt that Tanaka or any of the guards understood the words but his intention was enough to have him marked down for later punishment. The next day he was singled out to accompany a guard on a fictitious hunting trip where he was shot (we were told) due to an unfortunate accident. The guard responsible was for ever after called Dillinger by the Aussies and they had him marked down for retribution.

As for the beating up, it turned out that Bill Drower had been made to take the blame for one of the men, who had allegedly sold a faulty watch to one of the Koreans. What a trivial thing for a man to have to die for!

Within a day or two of that incident the whole atmosphere of the camp changed. Christmas Day was going to be a holiday and – I was told – our Lieutenant Power would depart for base (bearing the exalted title of Canteen Officer) to buy celebratory food from Thanbyuzayat market. More surprising than that, perhaps, was that the Aussie band was to be used to provide entertainment at each camp throughout the day.

The whole affair was sprung on us with such little warning that Tim Healy and I were already well advanced in our preparations for making a Christmas cake. They had started with the 'liberation' of an empty four-gallon petrol can from the Japanese cookhouse with which to make our oven. It was already set in a nearby bank, with a cavity below for the fire and with the front hinged ready to accept our masterpiece the following day.

Our Battalion runner-cum-batman (Frank Gough) was in line for a share, having 'borrowed' a suitable tin and a metal plate from the same source. Now came the tricky bit! We had to devise a lining and grease for the tin and, of course, the ingredients. Lieutenant Power might have got us some fat and a few more eggs if we had had more notice, but we now had to make do with inspired adaptation. Tim had been busy pounding rice with a bottle and we had spent almost two months' wages on four eggs. It then seemed quite appropriate to use palm leaves for the lining at Christmas time, but we only had one source for our fat. That had been in my haversack for the seven months since we lodged for the night in Fort-de-Kok chapel, in the form of two altar candles. They were melted down, the tin was greased and the mixture – sweetened with shintegar – went into the oven for a slow baking.

Come the morning (and with the prospect of a lovely dinner in view) we had decided to have our cake for mid-morning 'starters'. It was tapped out of the tin and to our surprise it stood up in one piece to await the cutting ceremony. The knife went in, the whole lot collapsed and it had to be served up with a spoon. However, once sampled, it tasted just as expected, like a bloody awful sweetened wax candle! But we still ate the lot. Never mind the quality, just think of those eggs! And as for our digestion, well, I had remembered this story told me by my father-in-law, a merchant navy chief engineer. Whenever the convoys went on supply runs to the north Russia ports, they had (he said) taken boxes of candles for the locals, who ate them with relish and still survived to welcome the next convoy in.

The rest of that Christmas Day was marvellous. There was so

little rice in our dinner that it was submerged below a variety of vegetables and – wonder of wonders – some fried buffalo meat. After that we had a pudding made with a mixture of dozens of ducks' eggs, pap rice, milk, shintegar and fruit. There were also carefully rationed second helpings of both courses until all the *kwalis* had been scraped clean. We were then served by our resident entrepreneur with a brew of his 'hot, sweet rice-coffee' and a bread roll. To round the evening off, the band came back resplendent in matching uniforms to play a selection of carols, military tunes, including my request for *Begone Dull Care* – the regimental march of the Royal Corps of Signals; and then (without hindrance from the guards) the National Anthem.

That was the first night for many months that any of us had gone to sleep on a full stomach and I believe even the sick must have slept well for a change.

The crowning event for me had been the arrival of a guard carrying a lantern and a pack of postcards for completion and despatch the next day.

I have often wondered if the Japanese stopped to consider how over a thousand cards got filled in after the Boxing Day work parties came back, when officially there should only have been ten pencils held by the lot of us, and no pens.

It was the second card that I had sent. The first one – which never arrived – would have informed Dora (my wife) that 'We are living in fresh air billets where the climate is good! The food is good! We are getting plenty of entertainment and healthy exercise! I am in good/bad health ... etc.'

The Japanese were quite safe in the belief that none of us would have deleted the word 'good' for fear of worrying the folk at home. So, there was only the salutation section left in which to let them know that the rest was a lot of codswallop. My card conveyed 'Love to Dora' etc. and finished with 'and my best regards to Jim Blony'. Other men were less subtle with messages such as, 'And tell it to the Marines'. The best contribution that I saw was sent by Lance Bombardier Bob Grafton, in which he sent his love to 'Little Audrey', a pre-war comic strip character who, whenever told a lie, just laughed and laughed. (Appendix V includes specimen texts of POW cards and the remarkable story of how my Boxing Day card reached home nearly nine months later.) ... And now on with the story!

*　　*　　*

Many things had happened in the two months since we came up from Tavoy, some of which – occurring at Thanbyuzayat – would soon be having a direct influence on our life.

We had earlier discovered that Dr Hekking had been sent on to us after arriving down there with a large contingent of his countrymen and a group of 190 Yanks. It was now being rumoured that many of them might be sent up to us to replace the Aussies. Apart from that, wireless news had started to arrive making me determined to wangle a trip down there to see Les Bullock. Also, at Hlepauk, we had seen off the last of the 1942 rains, stabilised the disciplines of camp life and achieved the almost impossible by taming some of our guards.

These improvements had helped to alleviate the demands being made for greater output regardless of diminishing rations and our deteriorating health. Our physical condition could be likened to creeping paralysis on the verge of malignancy. During the first month we had received a scant ration of meat. More recently, though, nothing much more than a little pulse or marrow with the occasional treat of dried and salty Bombay duck had been supplied. Malnutrition was rife, owing to deprivation not only of sufficient healthy food but also of a complete lack of medicine.

The Japanese didn't provide us with a single pill for anything even though they held, for instance, practically the whole of the world's sources and stocks of quinine within the territories that they controlled. That fact alone underlined their intent to work us to death without care or compassion. Apart from the dedicated work being done by the doctor and our three medical orderlies, survival had to depend on stamina, will-power, self-discipline and, to a certain extent, luck.

Sadly, it had needed our very special Christmas meal to convince me that escape was not on any more. The surge of well-being and strength felt on that one day only had been proof that I would need a constant supply of sustaining food to stand the slightest chance of success. Stracc and Harry Adrian soon had to make the same decision. None of us had the 'go' any more and it was perhaps just as well that we realised it then, because the only two attempts made after 1942 resulted in all concerned being executed. There had been a strong rumour that the more senior NCOs were going to be sep-

172

arated from the rest of the men. Stracc and Harry had been so convinced by the rumour that Harry had swapped identities with Sergeant Pearce in order to stay together for their final attempt. However, the rumour faded and with it went all resolve to do anything other than to stay put and see what the New Year had in store for us.

But 1943 was scarcely with us before, on the third of January, we were *tenkoed*, searched, bundled into lorries and taken further up the track to the 35 kilometre camp at Tanyin.

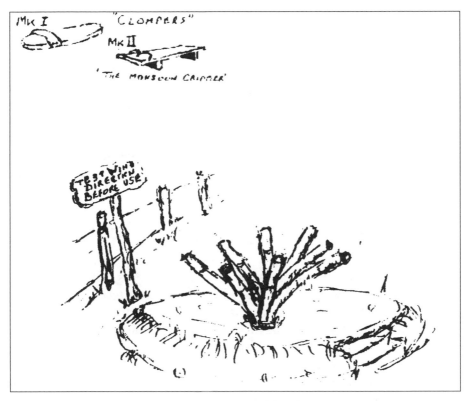

'Pissaphone Mk I'

24

TANYIN – 35 KILOMETRE CAMP

3 January – 20 March 1943

Tanyin camp turned out to be much the same kind of place as Hlepauk. We still had Korean guards, and although we were there for only two and a half months, we had two commandants. Quite unusually, they were both three-star privates, neither of whom turned out to be unduly vicious or too difficult to deal with. It was a colder place than Hlepauk had been at night. The advancing monsoon season had something to do with that but it was mainly because we were now up in the plateau that reached to the thicker jungle areas ahead.

So, it was a godsend when we were supplied with 232 locally manufactured blankets even though they were small and thin. With them, there had also come 45 12-man mosquito nets and a further small issue of those useless size six canvas boots. The latter – it was rumoured – were those that the Aussie quartermaster at base camp had found no use for. It was difficult to be charitable in our circumstances but I think that assertion to be untrue. He knew the disparity between their possessions and ours.

However, remembering how the Koreans had stripped the men of their rice sacks, cover of any kind was going to be a life-saver even though we didn't use all the items in the manner intended – and that brought more troubles for us.

The mosquito nets were blue-green in colour, about 18 by 15 feet in size, and they had a 9-inch skirt of fabric round the base. Our huts were about 15 feet wide with a 3-foot passage through the middle which had to be left clear for use by all – particularly the guards. There was also the problem of covering the sleeping platforms against invasion from below. So, they either had to be used

174

wastefully as provided, or cut and contoured to fit both sides separately. Commandant Yamamoto was sensible enough to realise our difficulty and he agreed with the suggestion that most of the nets could be better used within the hospital hut. Faced with the same dilemma, the orderlies had them cut and tailored them for the individual use of the patients. The nine inch skirts were trimmed off for use as bandages. One of the orderlies had bruises to show for that bit of innovation!

The Korean guards, for their part, didn't like this more rational approach to problems and – being low bred morons – they sought means of harassment in places where Yamamoto wouldn't see what they were up to.

There must have been about 40 kilometres of the line completed by now. Various details had been moving up and down the track clearing ahead, excavating cuttings and building embankments. The POW workforce had been considerably increased by now, the first arrivals being the Aussies released from airfield work in Mergui, Tavoy and Victoria Point. The Dutch then started to arrive in large numbers from Java. With them came survivors from the Australian cruiser HMAS *Perth* and the USS cruiser *Houston*. The US contingent of 190 men was largely comprised of members of a Field Artillery unit which had been stationed in Java.

The Dutch came up in far greater numbers. Some of them had journeyed from Sumatra and others from some of the notorious POW camps in Java, and by the time they reached us many had suffered even more hellish and prolonged sea passages than we had. The most horrific journey of all was made by a large contingent of Dutch on a freighter that took three weeks to get from Java to Rangoon. They had to run the gauntlet of Allied submarine attacks and then – when within sight of Rangoon – they were bombed by British planes. Nearly 60 POWs and about 200 Japanese were killed. Many others were wounded and hundreds of them were in such a bad state that they had to be left in Rangoon for a while. Many of them had to leave the damaged ship and come ashore in tenders, regardless of whether they had their kit with them or not.

Some of that particular group were sent on to join *us* later and we got on with them very well. The main reason for that, I suppose, was that their 'have-nots' could more readily identify with us than the bulk of their compatriots, who reached Burma safely carrying everything but the kitchen sink.

There is no doubt at all that much of the construction work on the Siam side was done over far more difficult terrain than anything that we met with. That was reflected in the numbers that had to be employed there. Apart from the extra length of construction, there were deeper cuttings and larger bridges to be engineered and much more blasting work to be done. However, we weren't to know anything about that for several months yet. Our immediate task was to complete the section that we had prepared south of Hlepauk.

It was there that Bombardier Bob Grafton was employed on what he has described as the gruelling job of rail laying and I have his widow's permission to quote what he wrote about it:

The rails and sleepers were brought up by two four-wheeled bogies onto which ten rails were bolted. In the floor of each bogie there were runners. Across each end of the rails there was a pile of heavy teak sleepers strapped with wire. The men worked in teams and about two kilometres of track were laid each day. The rails weighed about ninety-six pounds per foot length, and one gang would shoulder the sleepers and place them on the prepared track at even spaces while the laying team removed the long bolts from the rails. The bogies were then moved to the very edge of the last rail and the hand-brakes applied. Two tripods were set up in front of the bogies on each side and the signal given to take the weight of the rail, run it over the rollers and then, through other rollers hanging from the tripods. When it was clear from the body of the bogies a trip handle released it to fall on the sleepers. It was then levered into position by means of crowbars and then the gauges were set across. A team with fishplates put the bolts through to make the join and another gang drove in one or two dog spikes so that the bogies could be run on for the next rail to be laid. If the rail did not fall evenly and one end dipped, it became a live rail which had a great deal of whip. The men learned about the dangers very quickly. When a set of bogies were emptied they were tipped over onto the side of the track to be assembled at the end of the day into a small train to be pushed back to the rail-head.

Work now went on throughout the night. At first three eight hour shifts were in operation, but as the number of sick increased they were replaced by two twelve hour shifts. This was known as the Speedo period. During this period the Japanese increased the workload almost beyond human endurance. The bogies were now coming up the line loaded only with rails. On the top of the usual ten were loaded a pyramid of eight, then six, four, two and one, held together by a wire tightened by passing a bamboo stick through and twisting it. The sleepers came separately.

He also wrote the following account of a day when, after the shift had ended, he was left with several others to collect the empty bogies:

By the time we had got them all back onto the line it was sundown. There were so many that it made up quite a long train. We had over the last two days been working over a long gradient. We therefore did not have to push, as once all the brakes were unwound, the train started to gather speed and we all jumped on platforms at various intervals to control the brake wheels. The fact that the track had not been properly levelled, dog-spiked or ballasted did not make the ride an easy one. We gathered speed alarmingly and someone frantically wound on a brake in the middle of the train which caused that bogie to jump the rails and continue its journey on the sleepers shaking the riders off. By the time the railhead and our camp came into sight the train was travelling like an express and passed our screaming camp guards who loosed off into the air as if we werc all trying to escape. It was a long and weary push back to the camp.

Although I would occasionally get out of the camp in the guise of a mess orderly, I didn't see much of the rail-laying work, but I did see, and even assist with (although I cannot recall why) a pile-driving job (see sketch at end of Chapter 26). That job, as with nearly every other on the railway, had to rely on locally prepared materials and slave labour. The thudding would quite often continue throughout the night. The Japanese in charge was more often than not perched right on top of the staging, from where he counted out the rhythm for the lift and fall of the weight.

Now I was born, and had lived for many years, adjacent to a marshalling yard. I became so used to the clanking of goods trucks being shunted and hooked up that any absence of sound disturbed my rest far more than those familiar noises which, in fact, tended to lull me to sleep. This is a well-known phenomenon under normal conditions but you would have to be case-hardened to be able to sleep through the constant reminder that starved, sick and – often – soaking wet young men were being worked to destruction nearby. It may seem strange that I should be talking about young men when at that time I was only 26. However, we did have many lads who were under 20 years old when captured. A fair number of those were among the 79 RAF in the Battalion. There had been well over 1,000 ground staff stationed on the dromes and at the Air Ministry Experimental (Radar) Station who were evacuated from Singapore. They were variously dispersed among the 44 official evacuation vessels, of which 41 were sunk. The AMES men had left on the flat-bottomed river boat the *Tien Kwan* and – as on the many other vessels – they had suffered the trauma of being bombed and sunk and witnessed the resultant maiming, drowning and other forms of death. The mental legacy of such events seemed to affect the younger men far more than others in trying to cope with the near hopelessness of POW life.

On balance it was also the younger men who died first, and that, I thought, was partly owing to the fact that their bodies were still trying to grow bone and muscle on a starvation diet.

It could be that I was wrong in that particular, but not about a malaise among some – both young and old, who, as a result, had started to withdraw from their hutmates. It was Sergeant Tom Bousefield who drew my attention to this. I was doing the rounds with quizzes when I saw two men from his work shift who – although rested and fed – showed no sign of getting up to join in with the rest. I asked if they were ill and Tom said they were as fit as any of the others physically but both appeared to have 'switched off'. That condition was noticed more and more as the months went by. I called it '*atap* gazing', and I was convinced that the main cause stemmed from the fact that each of them had by then passed the time when they had expected the war to finish. We had also been getting wireless news in support of my own lengthy forecast and that wouldn't have helped their condition one jot! There must have been a great temptation for far more men to isolate themselves in that way because once it got dark – which is very early in the tropics – we had no other illumination than firelight, hardly anything to read anyway and no amusements other than what we could contrive for ourselves.

However, it was not all doom and gloom. Even when conditions were at their worst there were men whose spirit and humour were irrepressible, and that often sustained their mates. Quite obviously, humour was about the only free item on offer to us at the time. My portrayal of the incident in the food queue is typical of so many others and perhaps needs this explanation to be fully appreciated... It was usual for the so-called soup to contain nothing more than, say, 20 vegetable marrows for the whole Battalion. So, whatever was on offer had to be chopped into small pieces that either floated or dropped to the bottom of the liquid. It was alleged – although unfairly – that the mess orderlies got fat by taking more than their fair share of those bits. The hut sergeants and I were always on hand to ensure that the soup was kept well stirred and the scoop dipped well down in order to give everyone a fair crack of the whip. So on that particular day I was delighted to hear one of the Navy men – a cockney – receive his few bits with the spontaneous challenge, 'Oi, mate! Watcha fink you are? A bleedin' surface raider?'

There were, in fact, many things that we could laugh about, thank God, and not least some of the antics that our captors got up to. I cannot recall the reason why, but Yamamoto summoned the interpreter with the request that Captain Apthorp should 'ask his men not to laugh at the guards'. When Appy passed the message on at

Oi, mate! Watcha fink you are? A bleedin' surface raider?

179

our next parade we then had to be careful not to laugh again, because Yamamato was standing by to watch our reaction.

Wireless News: The Conspirators

Quite frankly, Appy and I had been content with the decision to leave Les Bullock in Thanbyuzayat with the wireless set. However, it was never ever going to be a case of 'out of sight, out of mind' for us. Having been conspirators in acquiring it, we had since had to live with the uneasy certainty of punishment if it were found. It didn't need much imagination to guess what the Japanese would do to us – and the later news that a set found on the Siam side resulted in torture (then execution) for all concerned confirmed our fears.

I only saw Les once after we were sent up the line and that was when I was made to accompany two sick men to base. By then Jan Tucker had brought the spares up to him from Tavoy and then had been retained as a pseudo-medical attendant in order to run the team of lookouts that protected Les.

Les himself had the cover of employment within a group of four doing canteen and stores work. They had been installed in the only lockable hut there because that in turn needed protection from the taking ways of the rest of the camp community. When I arrived I found that he and his companions had made themselves comfortable by installing bunk beds, benches, a table and a camp fire. To the uninformed the fire looked like a typical Boy Scout job, having two forked uprights with a bar across from which to suspend cooking and brewing pots. It was something quite different to the initiated, though! The ashes were never entirely cleared away because they concealed a metal plate, under which the battery, wireless set, earphones and aerial lead remained throughout the day. When news time came – and with a good fire burning above it – the plate was lifted and the lead connected across to an aerial, which was left in permanent disguise as the supporting frame for Les's mosquito net. And then, with earphones plugged in, he was in business.

Guards were always patrolling inside and around the camp and occasionally one of them – out of sheer boredom rather than duty – would bang on the door after dark for it to be unlocked so they could rest for a time and perhaps cadge a cup of tea. Jan Tucker and his lookouts were always nearby during scheduled periods of news broadcasts to signal the approach of a guard. When that happened, everyone inside would spring into action with a well-rehearsed drill. The earphones and lead were dumped back into the cavity by Les, the metal plate lowered and concealed with ash and fresh timber; and then (while three of them sat at the table and picked up hands of cards) the fourth unlocked the door.

The system was so well organised that Les was able to get recharged batteries on demand. They came in the guise of a spare for the stores lorry. When one was required, the Aussie driver from the Transport Depot would halt close to the hut door, where the swap could be masked by the bustle of carrying in the stores.

We usually received two monthly summaries up the line, and they reached us through trusted envoys such as Lieutenant Dicker and CPO Ambrose when returning from base with the monthly pay. There would be one copy only, the contents of which were dispensed by word of mouth via the hut sergeants.

This cloak-and-dagger stuff turned out to be vital when we later discovered a Dutchman skulking about behind our huts. I had been warned that one of their men – a linguist – was suspected of listening out for compromising bits of conversation to pass on to the Japanese for rewards of extra food. He was – as I have said – already suspected, so once apprehended he was court-martialled and given a suspended sentence of death without any recommendation for mercy. We were naturally pleased to get such a dangerous man off our backs. I doubt that he would have got a reprieve after the war!

Les and his co-conspirators had more scares and worries than any of us, though. Things became particularly hairy for him when it was announced later that he and most of the base personnel were to be moved up the line. They solved that conundrum by the simple but daring expedient of letting the Japanese take the set up there themselves.

The Japanese had announced that a lorry would be going up in advance of the main move, carrying the staff, rations and equipment for both the Japanese and the POW cookhouse. So the set went up there within a sack of rations earmarked for the POW kitchen, and the battery, as usual, as a conspicuous spare for the lorry. Which all goes to prove one of the alleged sayings of Confucius, that if you want to hide something, put it in the open!

Thank God it was not many months after that event that the set was finally declared to be too hot to handle any more. Hearsay declares it to have been buried somewhere up near the Three Pagodas Pass. With it no doubt is also hidden the unexplained reason why Les's recommendation for merititious service never received the award or acclaim that his services deserved. (see Appx IIIc.)

A Profile of Captain Dudley P. Apthorp, 6th Royal Norfolk Regiment

Everyone in the British Sumatra Battalion called him Appy! The officers did so to his face, no doubt, and the rest of us when out of his hearing.

There was scarcely a man among the rankers who did not hold our CO in the highest regard. That feeling persists to this day and it is well and truly underlined in anecdotal form in the book *The British Sumatra Battalion*, written in 1988 by his widow Ann. Appy died aged 70 in 1983, a regular since pre-war days and, at completion of his service, a major in the Norfolks.

Chapter 14 has already dealt with the formation and naming of the Battalion and of how I came to be appointed as its BSM to carry out his remit; and within seven months all his objectives had been achieved. The rebels had been given a short sharp jolt, and everyone an identity, purpose and focus to get them back into line for their own good both in self-esteem and a better prospect of survival. There was one other ingredient which in my estimation was equally important, and that was my own promise – rigidly kept – that there would be no special favours for anyone.

It was Appy's steadfastness in these matters that most endeared him to the men and which prompted me to give the following appreciation of him in Ann's book:

> Throughout the whole of my acquaintance with Dudley he led by example in the true tradition of an English officer and gentleman. He was without doubt the most obstinate man that I have ever had the pleasure of knowing. Perhaps *obdurate* would be an even better adjective to apply to his inflexible will to win through, to gain the greatest advantage for his men and to retain the best semblance of an army unit that was possible under POW conditions. Most of the thinking personnel within the Battalion could see the sense behind the continuation of the

182

essentials of discipline and of corporate purpose to achieve maximum survival. The Battalion statistics of survival alone prove that his methods were correct quite apart from the fact that we were serving personnel and therefore automatically under discipline anyway.

There then followed a passage which related to later events, before continuing:

We were extremely lucky to have a regular army officer to command us and one with such a sense of purpose. Dudley would argue work quotas with the Japanese. He would win a few and get beaten up – or otherwise punished – for his obduracy on other occasions. He would also argue for more lenient treatment of the men whether they had deservedly attracted punishment or not and that would often call down the major part of the punishment on his own head.

I can well remember the occasion when he was summoned to the guardhouse to answer for one offence. He was repeatedly knocked to the ground before the assembled parade. He kept getting to his feet and then I heard him say, 'if you want me to understand you don't keep on shouting at me in your monkey language but get an interpreter'. He then stood for hours in the sun holding a heavy boulder over his head and every time that he collapsed water was thrown over him and the punishment continued. Many of us had that kind of treatment at various times but no-one took upon himself other people's blame – imagined or otherwise – more than Dudley. As I have said before, he led by example, never asking anyone to do more than he did.

For most of the time he was shielded from physical labour by nature of his rank and duty as was I for the better part of two years. It was these duties that led to the situation in which some of the mindless ones amongst us thought that we were collaborating with the Japanese if we didn't take a course of action (or decision) which conformed to their own selfish desires. There were others who would have liked to have seen a soldiers' army i.e. a state of anarchy, in which they alone would have benefited... One thing that was preserved, thank God, was the show of discipline when the men were paraded.

183

I always called the Battalion to attention to salute the arrival of Appy on parade. To an outsider this must have appeared quite ludicrous since we were a raggle-taggle, filthy and emaciated bunch of humanity, bootless and clothed in little other than G-strings for the most part. However it was a most essential ritual for our survival that a person should be recognised as in command and with the day-to-day situation in hand.

Dudley always wore an army shirt, shorts, stockings, boots and hat and he appeared on parade clean-shaven. This duo-miracle was achieved first by the ingenious manipulation of needle and thread. He contrived to sew together scraps of cloth which he had cadged or bought from others in order to maintain the original shape of an army issue tropical uniform: and, second, with three razor blades which he kept sharpened by rotating them within the confines of a drinking glass.

We ran an orderly office and had a punishment system that awarded fines and extra duties. There were only two occasions when we had to threaten to hand culprits over to the merciless attention of the Japanese but of course, we never did so.

I am sure that all the survivors will endorse my final comment which is thank God for Dudley and for discipline. Without either we would have been lost!

The only area in which I would differ from the more general narrative in Ann's book is the description of the Battalion given in the publisher's blurb. This describes us as having been transformed into a unit with the esprit-de-corps of an *old-established regiment*.

That last bit smacks of out-and-out bullshit and, believe me, there was absolutely no place for that within a POW camp. The majority of the men were quite uncomplicated in the view of their CO. They accepted the fact that our more relaxed form of discipline should never be allowed to descend to the level of familiarity. I readily concurred with that viewpoint since there was no way in which I could be on familiar terms with a man one minute and shortly after that give him a right bollocking.

Appy had very fixed – even idiosyncratic – ideas about his fellow men and a lot of his views were freely expressed to the annoyance, exasperation and even detestation of his peers. He viewed the Aussies as his overlords but by virtue of numbers only. He dismissed their administration as nepotistic as soon as he heard that

Brigadier Varley had kept his son with him at Thanbyuzayat. He was equally dismissive of most of the other Aussie officers for the reasons that they were not Sandhurst-trained and that they allowed their men to address them by their first names. (I must say that I found no merit in such familiarity either but that was their affair.) The Aussies for their part saw him as an autocratic pain in the neck who by his cussedness fell foul of the Japanese to the disadvantage of all other groups who had the misfortune to be in a camp with us.

I had no problems with sharing his views about the Yanks. Their discipline was so slap-happy that it had to depend entirely on their senior NCO being able to beat it into them with his fists, and their senior officer was ineffective beyond imagination.

Appy had no great regard for the Dutch either. There were few of us who could understand that because they were a mild-mannered and well-disciplined body of men. Also, in spite of the aggravation that many of our actions caused them, they were for the most part both friendly and understanding of our state of deprivation.

As for the Japanese, Appy was anathema to them. Without uttering a word he could project an air of hauteur and insolence which for his captors was like a red rag to a bull. They, of course, expected total deference from all of us. Thank heavens they hadn't picked up on his reference to their 'monkey language', which by inference supported the Chinese assertion that the Japanese had originated from a liaison between a Chinese whore and a monkey. Had they done so, he would have very quickly become one of our statistics!

While the rest of us might indulge ourselves with remarks such as 'bloody Diggers, goddam Yanks and Dutch cheese-eaters', we all knew our place where the Japanese were concerned, but not so Appy. He led with the chin when most others would stand to attention, let the little sods work off their venom and stay on our feet if at all possible. That was my strategy and despite being at their beck and call more than anyone else, there were only six occasions when I was beaten up.

Appy's approach – which almost invited trouble – was described by a fellow officer who said, 'He was always correct, never departing from his profile as a British officer, always maintaining a gulf between the Japanese and himself and always treating them with very obvious and active loathing while being apparently polite, but never servile.'

And finally, a few words about how he was perceived by his fellow 17 British officers and they by him. Well, up to this point in my narrative most of our other officers were so rarely seen by the rest of us that it would have been difficult to say. They ate, slept and performed other necessary functions within their enclave, and apart from our adjutant, Lieutenant Dicker, and Captain Power, they were rarely known to stick their heads above the parapet.

Lieutenant Dicker in an earlier assessment has described them as a bunch of misfits having little common identity with one another and virtually none with the men. However, by virtue of his POW appointment, he became a very close associate of Appy and they were well able to recognise each other's faults and weaknesses. He wrote of him as follows:

> I rather liked the old so-and-so. There is no doubt that he was an awkward cuss – facially he was a cross between Lawrence of Arabia and Leslie Howard. He was very anti-Japanese (and, not noticeably pro-Australian, Dutch or American) but he was the senior captain, and under British Service Law, command of the Battalion was his responsibility. This being the case he was entitled to the absolute loyalty and support of his subordinate officers. Whether they liked him or not was quite beside the point.

And amen to all that, and on with our progress up the line.

Once all the intake had been sorted out and pushed up the line, the work went ahead more rapidly. Vast piles of ballast had been stacked by the local labour force employed near base and this was beginning to be moved up for the sleepers and rails to be put in place. The sleepers were mainly fashioned from trees felled close to the work sites and they were usually of teak. The rails were mostly taken either from other parts of the existing Burma State Railways system on our side, and the Malayan States Railways system was similarly skeletonised for the construction in Siam. Some of our track also came from Malaya and it had to be sent up to us via the Malacca Strait. There was no other route available to the Japanese at that time for heavy material, and much of what was sent was lost due to submarine and air attacks.

The Japanese – who were by nature innovative – had to resort to more recycling than they would have wished. Their most successful venture was the adaptation of all broken-down lorries as light rail trucks, which when coupled were loaded with ballast and hauled up to the advance sites by light locomotives.

We were well into January 1943 by now and under the reasonably benign care of Yamamoto, who up to this point had been used by his superiors as more of a quartermaster than a disciplinarian. He had supplied us with 104 locally made sheet metal plates and they were a godsend. There were dozens of men in the Battalion who up until then had been either sharing their eating utensils with others or eating from a variety of makeshift receptacles such as bits of cloth, leaves or sections of bamboo, none of which could be hygienically cleaned between meals.

It was the Japanese Railway Regiment who held sway locally. They had rarely intruded on our camp life previously but by now they had obviously had a kick up the backside by their superiors for falling behind in the construction programme. Nobody was talking of the big 'Speedo' yet but they were getting far more active in their demands, and when they jumped everybody else had to, or else!

However, it was a great boost to our morale now that we were beginning to get encouraging wireless news. It seemed a long time since August 1942 when the last really big events to cheer us up had been of a naval and air battle around the Solomon Islands in which the Japanese had been forced to withdraw; and – a bit later – the news of the bloody but victorious US battle at Guadalcanal. That battle had been very significant for us when we realised that the Americans – who had landed there in August had since brought up enough clout to start pushing the Japanese back towards their homeland. We didn't have to rely entirely on wireless news either during January, because our reinforcements were arriving with up-to-date local accounts of the effect that Allied attacks were having on the Japanese merchant shipping. Another bonus for us was that a considerable consignment of Dutch army clothing survived the most recent attack and we received an issue of 278 of their green straw jungle hats.

In the latter part of January the Japanese had insisted that officers must take turns as *kumichos* to accompany the working parties and by February they were wanting the officers to do a stint themselves. This was a try-on, being an infringement of the small part

187

of the Geneva Convention terms that they had agreed to. The base camp administration refused to co-operate so the Japanese very quickly gave up that idea. However, I am sure that it jolted our largely inactive officers into thinking what might lie ahead of them now that the Japanese were looking for ways in which they might be legitimately employed.

I had long since been aware of an anti-Appy faction within our officer group but up until now it had only been apparent in vague innuendoes. These had strengthened more recently into more challenging statements, such as how *they* might have handled certain situations if *they* had been given the opportunity. *They* were usually the two older captains, and before very long they became the prime movers in scheming to get Appy removed.

They started by actively backing the Aussies' assessment of him. Their next move – and one totally to their discredit – was to visit me in the camp office to try and subvert my loyalty. Even more discreditably, that was done within sight and sound of Sergeant Tim Healy. Having told them that the Battalion needed stability not disaffection, I then warned Tim not to discuss what he had heard with anyone else. That – I hoped – was going to be the end of the matter but within two months their scheming took a new turn when the American contingent led by Captain FitzSimmons was drafted in to replace the Aussies with us at that time.

It was just as well that all this officer posturing had been going on while the conditions of work were not too demanding and while we were still able to get some extras into camp to augment the basic rations. This was reflected in a drop in the death rate generally and particularly so within our Battalion. We only lost two men in January, one in February and – looking ahead – none at all during March. This was a period of stability that I was able to use well.

In early February a new three-star private, Matsuoka, had replaced Yamamoto and he brought with him a supply of 141 British Army jackets and 114 shorts. We had needed a boost in morale and there couldn't have been anything better than clothing to lift the spirits of the men, who had nothing but the scantiest of rags to wear night and day. We were further helped by the fact that most of the men then had a few weeks' employment at jobs where they were able to filch some of the rations intended for the Railway Regiment depots.

I had some very good men working for me within the camp and

there was none better than Lance Corporal Nobby Clarke of the 6th Norfolks. He was the only one with us from Appy's regiment. Appy had commended him to me as a reliable NCO and deserving of some oversight and protection within the camp staff because of his pre-capture sufferings. Nobby had sacrificed a good chance of avoiding captivity when he had stayed with Appy to help in the rescue of others shipwrecked along their escape route; and in the course of doing this work he had suffered from a severe attack of sun-stroke. This had left him slightly mentally impaired. I put him in charge of the sanitation detail. It was a very important and exacting job and he carried it out with great effect despite the scant supply of tools and cleansing materials. His team had the unsavoury but vital task of clearing up all the fouling within the camp by sick men who couldn't make it to the latrines. They also had to help the medical orderlies with cleaning and slopping-out within the so-called hospital hut.

Despite Nobby's excellent work he too had to be watched because he would often forget to clean himself before drawing his meals. So I made him report to the hospital orderlies for his food and they had to see that he used the soap that was left there for him. The sad thing about Nobby was that he survived the whole period of the railway building to within four days of our evacuation from the foulest camp of all. It was touch and go for so many of us at that time and Nobby deserved a better flip of the coin than that!

However, it would be wrong to single him out from the many others who at various times held appointments within the camp. They were the life-line for the outside workers, who always knew that they could return to camp and find everything possible done for them in the way of hygiene and care. The medical orderlies are deserving of more than a passing tribute, though.

They were LAC Bowler, AC1 Eccleston, Private Fitzpatrick, AC1 McBain and Gunner Yarwood – the latter being eventually employed in the hospital camp where he too died after the railway went through. Those men all worked tirelessly under indescribably primitive conditions and much of the time under the direction of Dr Hekking, whose medical equipment consisted of little more than a stethoscope and a few scalpels. They had to work without the benefit of medicines or bandages other than those stolen, contrived or – in the case of bandaging – by the use of constantly recycled strips of rag and, of course, without any anaesthetic. The general condition of most of their patients was so bad that it was nothing short of a miracle that any were discharged from the hospital hut after treatment. Most of them went in there reluctantly and so many with the certain knowledge that they were on a one-way ticket marked 'dedicated care only!' For those of them we got down to the base hospital it was often worse, because they lost the visits and companionship of their mates as well.

Without our medics the mortality rate would have more than doubled, I'm sure; and may God for ever damn the bastards who decreed that they should work in such conditions of deprivation!

It was a shame that while all this dedicated work was going on, our officers were still finding nothing better to do than increase their nannying and bickering. They were being orchestrated by one of the older officers, who was strong on persuasion but cunning enough to distance himself from the action. The fact that Appy was confrontational and that Brigadier Varley had the ear of Colonel Nagatomo already had him half way there in his conniving to get Appy ousted.

The first move came when we were amalgamated with the Americans. Their captain, who was junior to Appy and with a much smaller command, came in with a mandate to assume overall control. The rest of the coup was so swift and subversive that I was able to parade the men the following morning and put the full blame for it on the Japanese. Fortunately, they knew nothing of the internal plotting, and that softened the blow for Appy and, moreover, resulted in the men continuing to regard him as their real Commanding Officer.

So, we now had US Captain FitzSimmons in overall charge, Captain Apthorp down-rated and, further to that, I now found that I would have to share some of my responsibilities with a US sergeant, Martinez. We had also re-inherited Menheer Hesse in replacement for the Aussie interpreter. We had met Hesse before in north Sumatra in the Dutch civilian camp and knew him to be an excellent linguist. He had to be, because he had to think in Dutch and discourse in a mixture of English and Japanese.

Well, that was the end of the sordid affair for the time being, except that it had left the Aussies with so much control that they were apparently able to influence the decisions of Colonel Nagatomo.

190

Martinez turned out to be a quite agreeable guy and he had little effect on anything that I did other than to conduct 50 per cent of the daily *tenkos*. As for Captain FitzSimmons, he was such a laid back individual that, having taken up residence with Hesse and the Aussie officers, he worked entirely from there. His only communication with our officers was by runner via my office, which was also used for passing through any orders from the Japanese. He never addressed his command as a whole or our Battalion singly; and when he spoke to his own contingent I was appalled at their disrespect and at his apparent acceptance of it.

There were some minor problems within the ranks due to our merger. Certain factions on both sides never took kindly to being given orders by a Limey NCO one day and a Yank the next. This led to a particularly nasty incident on a day when I paraded the incoming work parties for *tenko*. The Yanks had a habit of ignoring the shouts of the guards who had led them in and making a dash for their huts to off-load their booty before reassembling for the count. They had done that a few days before when Sergeant Martinez was seeing them in. That had resulted in the guard commander racing out to lay about everyone – except the culprits! After that the whole parade had been made to stand to attention for an hour before being released for their food and rest. I was ready for them that day and shouted at them to get back out of their huts double quick. They certainly came out but one of them stooped to pick up a rock and whiz it at me in baseball style. Thank God he was out of practice. It zoomed past my head like an express train.

That incident was dealt with by their lieutenant, who was a man as wide as a barn door, and he *might well* have been a professional baseball player. He threatened the culprit with the promise, 'If you ever do anything like that again, you and I will go to the mat and there'll be a goddam awful tear-up.' There was no recurrence but I often wondered what would have happened if their sergeant, who had recently only just managed to win a disciplinary fist fight (or indeed, the lieutenant), got weakened by illness. Presumably things would have then deteriorated into a situation where Joe Doe reigned supreme and sod any discipline.

Second Lieutenant Brockman had died at the base hospital on the twenty-third of February, but with the advent of Dr Hekking and the improved conditions the general state of health remained steady. We were right on the edge of starvation, though. Men were coming back from their work looking more and more hollow-eyed each day. We had further good wireless news in early March and then – on the fourteenth – we were warned that we would soon be going back down the line to do more track-laying.

It was during our last few days at Tanyin that the Koreans decided to conduct a blitz search on our kit, and as far as I could make out, without the knowledge of Matsuoka.

I was one of the first on their random list. A guard came into the office and ordered me to tip out my kit. While emptying my small pack I managed to roll a section of bamboo containing sketches out of his sight, but after that he stood and watched every other move that I made. There was a tin box in my large pack which held several of my more personal possessions. He decided to empty that himself. He pulled out my Army pay-book, photographs, a cigarette lighter, some Malay dollars and a Dutch silver guilder and then, from the bottom, my Army oil-filled compass, which was wrapped in a cloth. He went through each item systematically until, coming to the compass, he stared at the swinging needle and then, putting it to his ear, he shook it. After that – and with a dismissive 'no goodtena' he went off out of the office, leaving me to repack. Thank heavens that guard was not only a bestial sod but an idiot to boot who didn't know the difference between a watch and a compass. Weapons, cameras, compasses and maps – and even thin bits of wire – were rated as *execution items*. About the only other thing that I had of any worth was a gold ring and that was concealed within the webbing of my pack.

There were several other banned items about that I knew of, but once the word got around, anything of that sort was quickly buried or else hidden within the bamboo structures of the huts.

This sporadic searching went on until the twentieth of March, when we were transported in lorries to the 14 kilometre camp at Thetkaw to do a short spell of track-laying.

25

THETKAW! – AND THEN, UP TO THE 25 KILOMETRE CAMP AT KUN KNIT KWAY

We arrived in batches to be greeted by our new Commandant, Sergeant Shimojo. Every one of us came in with kit and an unwelcome supercargo of body lice. Having just left a resident colony of bed bugs at Tanyin, we were welcomed into Thetkaw by another lot that was well-established within the bamboo sleeping platforms. Due to the neglect of the previous occupants, we were also assailed by a plague of flies winging in from uncleared messes around the place.

Shimojo very quickly made his mark on us – POWs and Koreans alike – with a regime of strict discipline that ensured that everyone was kept fully employed during daylight. He was a rather forbidding individual but there was a lot of method and common sense in the way he organised things.

I had only just had time to set up office when he came in with Appy and the interpreter and set down a small bamboo cup in front of me. I stood at attention while he passed on the order that the following morning everyone left in camp must cut further cups of that size which – he said – held 50 dead flies. He then produced a large container for the 400 or so offerings that I must bring to him each morning, being 50 flies per man whether he was working or not.

Although this was going to be a bloody nuisance for everybody, I had to agree that it would be a good idea if we could get rid of 20,000 potential killers a day. So, we made up a lot of swatters and got bashing. Perhaps it was just as well that we only stayed at Thetkaw for three weeks because we soon reached a state of diminishing returns in which Shimojo still demanded his pound of flesh and I was having to get Nobby to put down ground bait.

Running in conjunction with that venture I had also been given morning employment on buffalo skin curing. It was hell on the feet pounding away in a brine trough for four hours and, moreover, with no shelter from the sun.

Meanwhile Lieutenant Dicker – who on his own admission tried to keep a low profile – got mixed up in unavoidable problems. He twice fell foul of the Japanese and Captain FitzSimmons in trying to agree the parade states for the day, and our runner (who doubled as his shared batman) set off an infestation of scabies. I was one of the victims of that, and there were many others. It had started with the Japanese in their handling of the skins, which was fortunate for us since we had noticed them rubbing sulphur ointment on their hands. A large bottle of that, when left around, finished up in the *care* of Dr Hekking.

While the scabies was being treated, one of Lieutenant Dicker's fellow officers developed suspected smallpox and was – I believe – escorted by him to base when he went there for our monthly pay. He returned with the pay, a bugle that he had bought off one of the Aussies and the very welcome news that the Americans had destroyed a Japanese convoy during the battle of the Bismarck Sea.

It was at Thetkaw that I made special efforts to tour the huts in order to conduct quiz sessions. Tim Healy and I had the advantage of getting mental stimulus from our office routine. Nearly everyone else needed (and welcomed) the opportunity to keep their grey cells ticking over too, but first of all we had to have the consent of Shimojo.

The interpreter was asked to pass this through for me but it was my fault that I went in on the first session without checking if it had been given. I had just started when Shimojo walked in unannounced. We all stood up and bowed, and I with anticipation of punishment. However, he was simply interested in what we were doing. I was forced into revealing the encyclopaedia, which again had no clearance. The interpreter was called to explain that permission had been given at previous camps and then, having compared the text with my list of questions, Shimojo watched for a while and went on his way without further comment.

Shortly before we moved back up the line I was *ordered* to provide a team of volunteer footballers to go to Thanbyuzayat and play a team of Koreans. There were very few men who felt fit enough to engage in strenuous sport and even fewer who didn't take the request to be a publicity stunt. However, there were others who saw the trip as an opportunity to make purchases from the base canteen. As expected, it was an orchestrated event from all points of view. The Japanese had their filming crew ready and press-ganged cheer leaders lined up, and our team captain carried a script that ensured a dishonourable tie.

So, it was back up the line for us on the fifth of April, and for the first time we had the luxury of travel by train. We arrived at Kun Knit Kway to find ourselves with the Aussies again and unfortunately under the control of a villainous and half-crazed bastard named Colonel Naito. The Aussies told us that he was a Jekyll and Hyde character and to beware of the fact that he spoke good English.

The full story about him was that he came of a family of Japanese bankers and that he had been on business in Australia in the company of his wife until shortly before the war. He had then been recalled and, with no hint of impending hostilities, his wife had been left behind to await his return. The outcome was that when war was declared, she was interned and he was kept in Japan. However, he soon began to receive letters from his wife telling him that she was being fairly treated. That had made him so well-disposed towards the Aussies – so they said – that he encouraged them to come up with him from Changi loaded with all their possessions, which included their regimental band instruments. Since then, however, Japanese propaganda had – they said – so strongly convinced him that his wife was being maltreated that he had become quite irrational and, moreover, with a bias towards out-and-out sadism.

Those who had little direct contact with him judged him to be nothing more than an eccentric – and even amusing, after he had downed a few tots of brandy. I was one of a few who had to see him daily, though, and I very soon became aware of the brooding menace of the man.

Right from the start rations began to diminish both in quantity and quality. He hated the Koreans even more than Shimojo had and that intensified the pecking order syndrome. It soon became quite impossible to know when, for what, or from whom the next beating or other form of punishment would come. It was therefore something of a miracle that I didn't come in for at least one bashing from Naito himself.

He used to wander about the camp a lot and it was only a short time before he discovered Lieutenant Dicker's bugle and the fact that our boy soldier – Private Parker – was able to play it. Parker was immediately given the triple appointments of camp bugler, Naito's personal bath attendant and his wine servant.

Every evening the lad had to fill a tall tub for him. Once Naito had bathed and fed, Parker was required to attend with the bugle and join him in the ritual of warming up some brandy which both of them would often be seen drinking from the spout of a kettle. It was fortunate that the lad detested the taste of spirits because until I knew that, I had been worried that Naito might get him drunk and then – perhaps – get him talking about the wireless or the news.

At 8.30 exactly Parker would sound Lights Out – not that we had any lights to put out, but that was the time that Naito ordered that there must be absolute silence. It was then that he would commence to prowl around in the darkness, trying to surprise anybody he thought was up to no good. One evening he had become convinced that a man on the way to the latrine was using the darkness in an attempt to escape. So, he stepped out quietly from the shadow of the hospital hut and shot him in the back. Thankfully, he was not only a bad shot but was also armed with a low-calibre pistol, which did no more than inflict a nasty weal across the man's shoulder. If there had been any logic in the attack Naito should surely have handed over his victim to the *Kempi-Ti*. Instead of that, he was made to stand outside the guardhouse for the night.

The following morning he decided to take personal command of the daily *tenkos*, at which I normally made up the working parties and submitted the sick figures to the senior guard. I now had to give them to Naito personally and that was to be the procedure from then on. I will never know why I didn't get shot (or Dr Hekking, for that matter) because Naito was now being pressed by the Railway Regiment for fixed quotas of workers rather than only those the doctor deemed to be fit. We got away with that for about two or three days only. The next day he took me off in close attendance while he rooted around within each hut looking for trouble. I was then ordered to fetch the doctor – complete with kit and medicines – to the hut where he conducted sick parades.

The doctor didn't come willingly but he at least hoped that Naito, seeing his lack of gear, might do something about it – and he did! He fetched the doctor a whack across his face while saying, 'The Japanese Emperor gives you everything you need! Now we will go to the hospital.' I had never seen him go in there before so I was only too pleased that he should see the human wrecks within, albeit with little hope that what he saw might mellow him a little. The hut was – as in all camps and for obvious reasons – sited close to the latrine. Neither Nobby nor the orderlies ever had sufficient disinfectant supplied to cancel out the all-pervading stench within the area. As I had expected, Naito didn't stay there long and he left without comment to find more salubrious places to inspect. He had obviously hoped to find a number of fit men doing nothing. From our point of view there were none, but not in the opinion of Naito, who left the scene fuming.

That very day two suspect smallpox cases were confirmed. Naito was no fool and he quickly agreed that the men should be isolated in a small hut on the other side of the track and outside the camp boundary. Two orderlies accompanied them and I was the only person other than the doctor allowed over there. I took their meals across and, to avoid contamination of our containers, I served them into their dishes from outside the hut. After a day or two of segregation it was suspected that one man would die but the other – a Welsh farmer – was soon showing signs of recovery.

Around midday on the following day a Japanese general surprised everybody (except Naito) by visiting the camp unannounced. The guard only just found time to dash out and form a parade of honour but Naito – who had obviously hoped to catch them napping – appeared in full dress uniform.

I can only presume that the General had called in to give him a pep talk because of the further event in that unusual day. The working-party had scarcely time to get back to camp when I was ordered to assemble everyone able to stand and to have the bugler at the ready. As usual, a number of the sick men were either scarcely able to hobble out or arrived shaking with fever and needing the support of their mates. We stood there for an hour in the fast diminishing light. The Koreans were lined up too and they were on the jump to a greater degree than usual. Eventually the interpreter arrived with an order for the rear boundary posts and wire to be pulled aside. When that had been done, Naito appeared from behind the guardhouse in shirt-sleeve order and with sword slung across his chest;

and behind him there came a Korean bearing the Japanese flag on a pole. The interpreter then set the scene for us.

Naito was going to lead a charge up the hill to the rear of the camp to capture it for his emperor. We were to be driven up behind him by the Koreans while emitting bloodcurdling shrieks and *banzais* and with the bugler sounding the 'view halloo!'

Being rather stocky and not very spry – but, no doubt spurred on with a few tots of brandy – Naito set of at a smart gait until he was half way up the incline. He then stopped to wave on our screaming mob from behind and to lift his sword from its breast toggle. The sword was then swished around in a fury of mock blows at his imaginary enemy. Everybody gave him a wide berth as – still diligent with our *banzais* – we ran, shuffled and staggered our various ways up the hill and past him. It had become dark by now and those far enough away from our intrepid leader were beginning to slow down and fall about with laughter. Those who were still in his view, though, had to carry on up to the crest of the hill to witness the flag being planted in token of our gallant conquest.

By the following morning I had expected that this maniac would have worked off enough steam to allow us a reasonably quiet day for a change; but it was not to be. Things were going to get progressively worse over the next few days, starting almost at once with the morning *tenko*, when I was ordered to provide 300 men for work. The events of the past few days had prepared us for a heavier demand, so the doctor had selected the fittest 250 and 25 reserves. I had no option but to send the 25 back to their huts to collect their gear and reassemble. The 275 were then counted and marched out of camp and the rest of the parade was dismissed.

The outgoing party had scarcely cleared the camp when Naito appeared and charged over, ready for action. I was the first object of his wrath, being given a clout by his attendant and then made to fetch everybody back out of the huts again. Having selected a further 25 men, he made me line them up with their backs to a deep monsoon drain. After that I had to walk with him and witness his sickening method of interrogation, which for sheer sadism seemed all the worse for being conducted in English and – to begin with – in an unexpected gentlemanly calm.

To the first man: 'What is wrong with you?' Answer: 'Ulcers on my leg, sir!' Naito again: 'Bandage off!' And once the so-called bandage of rotting cloth had been removed, it revealed a deep and suppurating hole. Naito once again: 'You are a fit man!' And, at the same time, he delivered a vicious kick at the ulcer, which spurted with pus as the man collapsed backwards into the drain.

The next selection needed no explanation from the man but he said: 'Beri-beri, sir!', only to be informed, 'You are a fat man, work!' And with a well-aimed kick to the groin down he went into the drain.

The next man answered: 'Dysentery, sir!' And it was a bash in the stomach for him.

And so it went on through the parade of 25 men, who I now realised had been specially selected for their vulnerability to pain from a well-aimed blow. After that I was made to take them out and up to the working-party without any protection from the sun, with nothing to eat from and with nothing to cover ulcers against the hordes of flies that followed them out for a feast. I will never forget that parade and the feeling of frustration that I felt at being powerless to do anything other than watch those men being systematically taken apart.

From that day onwards we were in a catch 22 situation in which we had either to meet Naito's illogical quotas without demur, or suffer from more of his barbaric selections. Try as we did there appeared to be no solution to the dilemma. Dr Hekking protested and received a bashing. Appy for once tried reason, and all he got for his intervention was the sentence of standing before the guard-house in the sun until the working-party returned. Quite frankly, I was looking for ways in which I might murder Naito without suspicion either falling on me or repercussions on the others; and the solution came to me by chance.

I was over at the smallpox hut one morning, and looking through the door I saw one of the orderlies carefully removing pustules from the Welshman's face. So I asked the orderly to remove scrapings from the worst-affected patient, keep them for me when I revisited that evening and to say nothing about it to the others there. In the interest of my own safety I told nobody about my plan other than Captain Apthorp and the bugler, who would have to be part of it.

I collected the infected scabs as arranged and the bugler tossed them into Naito's bath water that evening. After that it was just a matter of waiting and hoping for results. As each day went by there was a deterioration in Naito's demeanour but, unfortunately, not in his health. He was now focusing his attentions on the Koreans for a change. They were so afraid of him by then that they would often visit our huts for no other purpose than to hide from him.

The end to all this came quite suddenly. We awoke one morning to discover that two off-duty Koreans had just returned after walking the 25 kilometres to base overnight in order to complain about Naito's behaviour. This must have been a decision born of real terror, and the hope that they would be believed. Events soon proved that they had been when a lorry came up the track to collect him.

All his possessions, including – at his insistence – a padded armchair, were carried out and placed on the rear section behind the driver. The last I saw of him, thank God, was his enthroned and isolated figure disappearing on its way down to Thanbyuzayat; and after that, who knows where? I will never know if what I did helped to tip the balance of his sanity or not. He had to be got rid of one way or another for the good of all of us, including the bloody Koreans!

There was no replacement for him. No doubt it was for that reason that we were quickly moved out and up to the 45 kilometre camp at Anankwin ... and before we even get there I have to say that that place also allowed us very few favours!

26

ANANKWIN – THEN, BACK TO HLEPAUK

26 April 1943

We moved in to join an Aussie group that had recently arrived from Java under the command of Lieutenant Colonel Williams. Having exchanged greetings, there followed the news that one of their men had recently had his jaw shattered by a blow from a rifle butt, and that the food was bloody awful. However, it was not all doom and gloom! Apparently approval was on the way for British bugle calls to be sounded in future.

Three days later one of the guards – who must have been reciting his message for hours – came into the office with the *order*: 'Orrer men be happy. Tomorrow Emperor's birthday.' He then handed me a rice sack full of green-skinned oranges as a *presento* from his legendary divinity and *Showa Tenno*, Hiro Hito.

It was his forty-second birthday and I offered up the prayer that by the time he was 44 we would have him swinging by his balls from the top of his favourite shrine.

The interpreter then arrived with the further order that I had to put on a celebratory show the following evening at which the Japanese would also attend.

I suspected that the Aussies had lumbered me with that job and without any consideration of how I might provide clothing or props out of our few possessions. However. it would have been useless to complain to the Japanese about that, so I first of all put the word round to the hut sergeants to see if we had any budding thespians among our ranks. Shortly after that, Sergeant Pat Fox came in to offer his help in organising and directing the show. He had run impromptu events many times within his army unit and I was very lucky to find someone so capable and seemingly unworried about the imminence of the show.

Off he went to do auditions, while I saw the Aussies and the interpreter saw the Japanese, to get the loan of items that Pat began asking for later. The interpreter returned to say that the Japanese would co-operate fully in honour of the occasion and also that I was to organise a work-party and materials for building a makeshift stage in a clearing about 200 yards north of the camp.

Pat and I went out with a guard to inspect the place by moonlight and then we called in representatives from each hut for a meeting. I had thought that the show would have to rely entirely on corny and under-rehearsed slapstick, but it was not so. Pat had already found an accomplished Aussie piccolo-player, a shadow artist and also three men willing to dress up as women to perform in a short and lewd sketch, the script of which he knew by heart.

Sergeant Stracchino was lined up to shave our three extroverts (dubbed the perverts), and Sergeant Healy and the runner to guard the various props that had started to accumulate. Come the morning we had a bizarre collection of articles in the office, among which there were three sarongs, various bits of coloured cloth and a hank of dyed and flayed-out rope for making the women's wigs. There was also going to be a second shadow act, and for this the Japanese had provided white sheets, hurricane lamps, a table and rattan screens for the stage. The doctor's bag arrived later and with it came Pat's secret weapon, the washed-out (but still smelly) intestines from an animal cooked in the Japanese kitchen the night before.

The oranges were distributed and a freshly washed flag (the Imperial Flaming Arsehole) was run up the mast. Those visible reminders of the occasion left me wondering how anyone – Japanese included – were being allowed to celebrate that day. We were now within a month of when the railway had been scheduled for completion and with less than a half of the job done.

Around seven o'clock we decamped and went out to the clearing, carrying chairs for our honoured guests. The show was opened with exuberant gusto by an accompanied sing-song in which we parodied the words of *She'll be Coming Round the Mountain* with words that had Tojo running to the mountains when the thousand-pounders dropped. This was rendered to the lively accompaniment of the Japanese handclapping to the beat and obviously unaware of the meaning of our words. We then had a remarkably clever display by a hand-shadow illusionist, which was followed by a shadow charade of an operation. The last bit had been preceded by a medical inspection at which a line of men had the stethoscope applied to most unlikely parts until one was found to need surgery. He was then tapped on the head, carted behind the illuminated bed sheets, put on the operating table and opened up. All kinds of objects including the inevitable string of sausages were seemingly extracted from his stomach. The Japanese applauded everything, and particularly so the final act, which featured a lewd portrayal of our three ladies grappling with slipped bosoms and the over-boisterous advances of their lecherous suitors.

There was a final sing-song ending with *Auld Lang Syne*, which was a favourite of the Japanese, and they accompanied us by singing it in their own language.

The most enduring memory of that evening for me has been of our men standing there in the middle of the jungle, dressed in G-strings and puffing away at Burmese cheroots. *The Man Who Broke the Bank at Monte Carlo* would have suited that scene.

After a night's rest it was back to the daily grind, to the accompaniment of early monsoon rains. Three days later we were taken back into the clearing to see a much different show and it was put on by the Japanese this time.

We had been given no warning of what they had in store for us and we arrived to find the Japanese assembled before a roaring fire. We then had to stand and listen to a typical loud, unintelligible and manic tirade from the Commandant which (even when interpreted) made little sense. We had committed a communal sin which was unexplained by the Japanese but which the interpreter thought must be our failure to keep up with the work schedules. However, there was soon no doubt at all about what our punishment was to be. We had been assembled there to witness the Commandant burn up the only consignment of Red Cross mail that had reached us so far and which for many of us was the only mail that ever did!

The sheaves of cards were slowly fed into the flames and I could see that many of the men were on the verge of tears. Quite spontaneously I gave the word to start singing and there we stood proclaiming 'Britons never, never, never shall be slaves', which was a bit of a joke if you care to think about it! By then many of us were really singing through our tears but we carried on with our act of mock bravado to show the Japanese that they would never destroy our spirits.

Whether this shamed them into a loss of face or not I will never know, but we were to hear no more about the alleged crime, or our audacious bit of singing. The tears were over and we just had to soldier on. Within a day or two we were moved out and back down the line to Hlepauk – the 18 kilometre camp – from where we had started out in January.

We had been only eight days at Anankwin!

Hlepauk

It was the ninth of May and we were back with our far from friendly host Tanaka, who was now a sergeant. Ours was to be a short-term mopping-up job, the main task being the off-loading of freight from the heavy steam locomotives onto the lighter and makeshift stock being used south of Hlepauk. Piles of ballast had to be loaded and sent forward with the local labourers who would be laying it to extend the temporary track. Once up there, very few of them were allowed to return other than the cattle drovers and

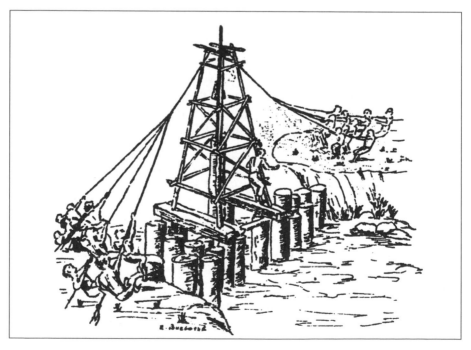

Pile-driving between Tanyin and Anankwin (see Chapter 24)

204

bullock cart drivers taking food and merchandise to off-track hamlets and storage sites. They used the ancient trade route that led over into Siam and when they returned it was with tales of countless deaths, decaying and unburied bodies, and the rumour of a cholera epidemic among the workforce there.

Although the Battalion had had the benefit of a lull in the death rate, most of us were by now suffering from a debilitating cocktail of complaints. All of those had to be survived by means of our individual reserves of strength and will-power, our communal discipline and, often, with a modicum of luck thrown in as well. I, for example, was coping with regular bouts of malaria and – in common with most others – had already seen off scabies, pellagra and leg ulcers for the time being, but never the constant looseness which resulted from our diet.

There is not much more to say about our second stay other than it only lasted ten days. However, many years later I discovered that by the time we moved out on the fourteenth of May there were already 50,000 Allied POWs at work over the advancing Burma and Siam rail routes and that nearly 35 per cent of them died up there.

27

RETPU – 30 KILOMETRE CAMP

14th May 1943

It was early morning and dark when we arrived at Retpu and we were soaking wet from a recent cloudburst. We were now to be amalgamated within what was to be known as Advance Mobile Force 2, which was mainly comprised of a mixed bunch of Dutch and American troops. We were rarely all together though at the same camp.

Our first day there gave us something to really cheer about when six high-flying Liberators flew above us on their way down to the coast and our Korean guards raced out of the camp to take cover in the surrounding scrubland.

Within a matter of a few days after that it was confirmed that after nearly three months of scheming by the Aussies and Japanese, they had persuaded two of our officers to replace our CO and adjutant and seemingly without any prior consultation with Appy. It was both a lightning coup and – so far as the other ranks were concerned – a non-event, because they stayed firmly loyal to Appy. Our new CO (I was told) was to be Captain Davies of the Federated Malay States Volunteers, and Lieutenant Villiers of the Independent Infantry, had replaced Lieutenant Dicker.

Sergeant Healy and I just got on with our daily routine as if nothing had happened, except for our mounting distaste for those of our officers who by their disloyalty to Appy had now completely surrendered the Battalion into the control of the Aussie hierarchy.

It didn't take us very long to see the proof of that when Lieutenant Dicker visited base in his reduced capacity of Pay Officer, only to find that he was – at first – not going to be allowed to see Les Bullock or *our* wireless set. Fortunately, all this officer posturing had no effect on relationships between the British/Aussie other ranks. However, the knock-on effect did harm the officers, who were now told that they would have to act as *kumichos* in charge of the external working parties. With that order there came the further directive that the work would now be continuous over a three eight-hour shift system.

It was nice to be back with the Dutch again even though their recent intake from Sumatra and Java had made us look more than ever like a scruffy bunch of vagrants. They, by comparison, had arrived in Burma looking like a fully equipped safari party. Their native troops were the bearers and they were burdened with trunks, valises, camp beds, collapsible canvas wash-stands and heaven only knows what else. Most of that was for the additional comfort of their officers and senior NCOs, of which there was an inordinate number.

Some of their excess baggage – particularly clothing – quickly changed hands without being donated. So, I thought it best to tell them from the outset that I was not going to go charging about trying to retrieve items that they left around unguarded.

I certainly profited from their arrival in two important ways. The first was by friendship with one of their under-lieutenants. He kindly offered (in what he called 'our mutual interest') to teach me Dutch in return for allowing him to practise his English on me. It was in fact a totally one-sided contract because he was already a consummate linguist, being fluent in four European languages and three native dialects. So many of the Dutch were multi-lingual, in order to trade with their more heavily populated European neighbours, I suppose. However, although it was only a short acquaintanceship we both profited from the additional and welcome mental stimulus during evenings that might otherwise have been dull. I picked up quite a useful vocabulary during the few weeks that we were together, all of which has been totally useless to me in later years. Nevertheless, it was well worth the effort at the time.

My other gain from this association was the unexpected discovery that there was a weed-like plant in the jungle that was nutritious and could be eaten either raw or cooked. One of the Dutch native troops happened to come into the hut with some of the plants when I was having a lesson and the lieutenant called him over to show them to me. He did so with great reluctance and only when I had promised not to spread the knowledge around. This was okay

207

with me because, what with the scarcity of it and the fact that I could rarely get out of camp, there wouldn't have been any around for me to pick if everybody got to know about it. This was not greediness on my part because both Tim and I had no access to – or expectation of receiving – any of the extras that the working parties might pilfer.

It so happened that my legs had started to swell up and then my face got puffy. I didn't need the doctor's confirmation that it was the onset of beriberi. It was my almost total reliance on what the Japanese provided that caused me to be one of the first to show these symptoms. Having seen what it did to some of the local labourers, I had already restricted my water intake to one army water-bottle full a week. So I now put myself onto the water-carrying detail that collected from a stream to the rear of the camp in an untrampled area where I might find some of those plants – which we later called jungle spinach. There was another plant out there that was so sensitive to movement that it would close its leaves when we touched it and open them again when we had moved on. I discovered that where they grew, there were usually a few plants of the spinach too. That discovery probably saved my life! I was cured within a month and just as well too, because I hardly ever saw any more of the plants further up-country. The sad thing about that was that others within the Battalion developed beriberi later and became so swollen that they literally drowned in the excess of their body liquid. Such is fate!

It was also fate, no doubt, that gave me another useful nudge during my period of recuperation by decreeing that the Commandant's lovely white cat went walkabout. I was sitting in my office when it strayed into the compound, slunk past the guardhouse and decided to pop in to see us. Within no time at all it had been killed, cooked, shared between four of us and its few remains consigned to the depths of the latrine pit.

As a true lover of cats, I find it hard to believe that I could have done such a thing, but hunger was urging us to any lengths short of cannibalism at that time. Apart from that cat, I ate a few snakes snared by Ned Stead, and a rat, which was both prepared and recommended to me by the native spinach collector. There was also a time when I got so famished that I broke bits of fungus off the bark of a tree and stuffed them into my mouth.

The cat was rabbit-like and tasted delicious, the snakes eel-like and rather revolting and the rat so totally revolting that I had difficulty in keeping it down despite the assurance from the provider that all the nasty bits had been cut away from it. The fungus was nothing other than something to chew on and then spit out! It was therefore hardly surprising that I – in common with thousands of other survivors – was later found to be suffering from avitaminosis due to a complete lack of stomach acids. Those acids had no doubt given up on us with the realisation that they had nothing much other than rice to work on.

With the onset of the monsoon and the general deterioration of conditions came an increase of deaths within all groups. Towards the end of May we lost two men we had (only a week or two previously) managed to evacuate to the base hospital. One of them was Able-Seaman McCaffery, who had been among our escape party on the *Bintang Dua*. In June the Battalion had a surge of seven deaths, four of which also occurred at Thanbyuzayat. Two of those were during the second of two bombing raids made by Liberators, which in total resulted in 27 Allied POWs being killed and 40 wounded. Unfortunately, none of the Japanese guards were killed. They had shelters to run to, whereas the rest of the camp community was exposed to what the pilots must have considered to be a legitimate railside target. There were no Red Cross markings!

Lieutenant Dicker just got clear of the place with our pay before the second raid swept in and within a day or two he was sent on up to the 60 kilometre camp with an advance party. I remember that day well, because having paraded and seen that draft out of camp, I had only just got back to the office when an officer of the Japanese Railway Regiment walked in. He came through the camp entrance, ignoring the guard who, in common with his colleagues, he quite overtly despised. His object in visiting me was first to air his English and then to rummage through my kit, having seen some of my webbing equipment lying around there. It wasn't a true search but I had no way of stopping him and he was soon on to my compass. He most certainly knew what it was but instead of calling the guard over as I had expected, he showed great interest in buying it.

I hadn't really got much else to divert his attention from it, but having explained to him that it was the property of the British Army and it was expected that I should return it to them with the rest of my issue kit, I eventually persuaded him to take one of my Malayan bank notes as a souvenir instead.

He accepted my offer with some amusement and then walked off out of the camp again without so much as an '*Ah so-ka*' to anyone else – and I went back into the office to change my pants!

I saw him again while we were still at Retpu and on a day when – for no reason that I can recall – we had been given a day's rest. It was certainly a special day in the Japanese calendar, though, because they were quite relaxed for a change. I took advantage of that by quite openly sitting outside the office to do some sketching of camp scenes, including one of the cookhouse. This soon attracted the attention of the guards and then – satisfied that I was not doing anything subversive – they started to turn up bearing blank post-cards.

It was hard to imagine who could have loved those sadistic and ignorant turds but they made it plain that they required me to draw similar camp scenes for sending off to their loved ones. It would have pleased them no end to boast that they had made a British NCO do the drawings for them. However, it was quite a different matter when the Japanese engineer-officer walked in again. He came to me bearing an artist's block of cartridge paper, a bottle of Indian ink, a mapping pen and a set of nibs and asked if I could do a por-trait of him.

He was a rather ugly-looking man, but regardless of that I took a chance and portrayed him warts and all. It had always been my preference to do live studies of people of character rather than chocolate box types. He posed for about 15 minutes and then, hav-ing looked at my pencilled draft, he went off again, leaving me to do the inking in and shading. When he came back again he gave me four eggs and told me I could keep the drawing materials. He and just one other – a westernised Japanese – were the only two of that despicable crew that were decent enough to see me as some-thing other than scum. As for the rest of them, the only thing that was going to keep me alive during the next few months was my implacable hatred for the whole bloody lot of them!

We had been working in blindingly hot temperatures during the past few months. Now we were in for several months of steaming humidity, almost continuous torrential rain, unremitting toil and death. When the monsoon started we had dashed out of our huts like a lot of schoolboys to whoop and frolic under the torrents of water streaming down from the eaves of our huts. It was wonder-ful to be able to wash away the sweat and grime from our bodies,

210

to feel cool for a while and to get temporary relief from the swarms of pestiferous flies while they took refuge from the downpour.

There was a stream nearby and many dried-out *chaungs* (water-courses) a bit further away. The stream soon became a river and the *chaungs* filled but, unfortunately, even that didn't bring the water supply much nearer to the camp, which would have been a blessing for our water-carrying details. It had been arduous enough having to carry in thousands of gallons of water when the paths were dry but the rain had now made the job hazardous as well. The containers were halved 60-gallon oil drums with handles of stout wire. Each load had to be carried between the shoulders of two men on a sturdy bamboo pole. Our carriers – who never had had boots – always had to rely on the man in front mapping out a route free from hazards such as tree roots. The monsoon had now turned the once hardened tracks into slippery surfaces which could only be negotiated by the fittest of men and, moreover, on extra rations. I didn't find many volunteers for the job despite the inducement of more food, because part of the contract was the willingness to accept a bashing from the guard every time water was spilled. When that happened too often, it added to the number of 300-yard journeys to be done each day and that never did please them.

The Japanese wouldn't allow me any more camp staff so we just had to get on with it by adding to the duties of anyone with free time. The more it rained the more arduous the job became. I eventually had to ask Appy to send some of the officers to assist with the problem of getting the loads up and over the perimeter embankment. This was a token enclosure only but, out of sheer buggeration, the Japanese would not allow me to cut a path through it. So once that got slippery it became impossible to get a toehold. There were hundreds of spare drums stacked at base and plenty of scrap metal from which to improvise guttering. A few drums under the eaves of each hut would have solved our water-collection problem, but for all the Japanese cared they might just as well have been in China.

Sergeant Stracchino came up with a plan for building a trestle and bamboo trough supply from the stream to our kitchen and for the erection of a canopied walkway over the latrine pit. The latrine pit was becoming so precarious to use that Nobby Clarke had had to bang in handposts at the edge to prevent users slipping into the pit. This was explained to the Japanese by the interpreter, but all to

211

no avail. So we just decided to do the jobs anyway by stealing the required material from a consignment that had arrived for the Railway Regiment. We were helped in this venture when timber supplies for the kitchen dried up and the Japanese ordered that every man working up the line must bring in a load when returning to camp. For the next few days the working parties became over-zealous in that task. Their loads of bamboo, poles and *atap* increased in direct ratio to the reduction of the Railway Regiment's stockpile and our guards – who had no time for the Regiment – just turned a blind eye to it all. In the end they were urging us to erect the structures as the best means of hiding it. The Confucius theory again, I suppose!

It was just as well that we got on with those jobs quickly because shortly after that the Koreans burnt their rest hut down and it was never replaced. A few days later one of our men came to the office and handed in a small-calibre pistol that he had found among the charred remains of the hut. My first inclination was to just toss it into the latrine and forget about it. However, I finally decided to walk over to the guardhouse with it openly displayed in the flat of my hands. I did this with the uncharitable intention of having the matter reported to the Commandant in the hope that one of the Koreans would get bashed up for his carelessness.

The sudden and frantic Speedo had resulted in the Japanese Southern Army command seeking additional labour and effort by any means. There had not only been the recent influx of 5,000 Allied POWs on our side but over in Siam countless thousands of POWs and labourers were driven up into the dense jungle areas in haste and in total disarray. One ploy used by the Japanese to recruit the labour force was the lure of free cinema shows. They took film units on to recently conquered Pacific islands, ostensibly to entertain and educate the population. Actually, though, they went in for the ease in which they could then encircle each audience and single out all the males for forced labour. Most of them were then shipped direct to Siam, relayed on by train and then force-marched straight up into the railway construction areas. Through no fault of their own they landed up there as a motley bunch, devoid of organisation, disci-pline or any sense of hygiene as we know it – and, moreover, in an environment totally alien to most of them. The outcome of this was soon seen in thousands of deaths – inevitably, mostly due to outbreaks of cholera.

The POWs had gone up there direct from Singapore. They were lured there by false promises of better living conditions, which (quite cynically) had encouraged them to bring every bit of gear with them that they could carry in support of that myth. They too were force-marched from the railhead straight up into the jungle and driven on by guards who knew that at least a third of them would be nothing less than expendable load bearers for the others. The fittest of those who survived the march were set to work immediately. All of them had to sleep rough until the sick among them – given only half rations – were able to build and organise their camp sites.

I cannot begin to know how they coped with the horrors of their situation, which were compounded by having to work over far more difficult terrain than we did. We were also helped by the fact that far more of that totally undisciplined native force was deployed on the Siam side than with us. The epidemic – which knew no artificial boundaries, of course – did spread over into Burma but, thank God, it was rarely able to penetrate our better established and more organised camps.

The native workers were mostly sent up ahead (on both sides to begin with) and it was from that high ground that many of the rivers and flash floods swept down and through to the plains. They flowed through many of our water-collecting points, carrying the excrement and vomit of the dying and the direct contamination from the unburied bodies of cholera victims rotting upstream. Our working parties began to find unburied corpses as we moved up that way and the monsoon rains soon began to expose many more that had been washed out from shallow graves.

It was fortunate that we had been forewarned of these dangers before we got permission to bathe in the stream at Retpu. We had always boiled all of our water but I now took the additional precaution of warning all bathers against getting any of the stream water in their mouths. Cholera is a disease that leads to vomiting, rapid dehydration and then death within only two or three days of picking up the infection. Quite miraculously, though, there were survivors who developed an immunity which allowed them to stay close to (and help) those who were still afflicted. The greatest danger for those still unaffected was close contact when carrying away the bodies of the dead for cremation.

Apart from the obvious pleasure of being able to bathe at Retpu, we gained a very unexpected benefit from it. The first day that we went down there, I was standing near the bank and up to my knees in water, when I felt several sharp stings on my ankles and knees. Looking down I saw a number of small tube-like fish tearing away at the infected flesh within my ulcers – and I very quickly kicked them away to begin with. However, after a few more attacks by the persistent little beggars, I realised that they had cleared all the muck out and left the surrounding flesh bright and clean. We soon came to welcome the attention of those mini-piranhas darting in for their daily pound of flesh.

We were continuing to get fortnightly news but much of it was uninspiring at that time for any but the most over-optimistic amongst us. However, quite out of the blue the Japanese started to fill in some of the gaps for us by supplying us with copies of their *Greater Asia* newspaper. This was printed in Malaya and mainly for the edification of all the English-speaking locals who were gullible enough to believe the Japanese version of the war news.

Every fortnight – but unfortunately only on five or six occasions – I was supplied with three copies. The obvious intention was to make us despondent with the accounts of their progress and prowess; and I have to admit that they had quite a lot to shout about at that time. However, where they failed was in the ludicrous presentation of their news which, when thoroughly analysed, often revealed that they were, in effect, 'advancing backwards'! Further to that, each issue had a special feature in it about the achievements of one of their fighting men. These were presented in such a child-like and comical manner that roars of laughter were heard from our huts as soon as I passed the copies on to the officers and hut-sergeants. I made sure that I was last on the circulation list once, in order to keep the copy as a souvenir, but unfortunately it was stolen, along with much of my gear, only a week or so before repatriation. So, you will have to rely on my recollection – without any exaggeration – as follows:

Our gallant pilot Lieutenant X flying over the Andaman sea (having shot down two enemy planes) was out of ammunition when confronted by a third. So, what did our gallant pilot do? He flew up alongside it, having quickly armed himself with the rice balls that had been supplied for his lunch: and then, pelting it with these, he forced the other pilot to land and surrender!

In another edition there was an account of the Japanese pilot who in similar circumstances drew his revolver and menaced the opposing pilot until he also landed and gave himself up.

Another astounding exploit told of a pilot who (having expended all his ammunition including his bomb-load) was about to return to base when he saw a British merchant vessel ... So 'What did this gallant pilot do? He flew down low over the water and as he closed on the ship he drew his sword; and then, flipping the plane on its back, he swept over the bridge and cut the captain's head off as he went by!'

It was then inevitable that we should get a story about a brave soldier. This duly arrived to tell us the deeds of Private Y, whose unit – having first destroyed half of the British Army – was finally besieged. Their wireless had been knocked out so the private had volunteered to get the news back to his general's headquarters some 100 kilometres away. However, very shortly after leaving he was ambushed and mortally wounded... So, yes, you've guessed!

> He picked himself up, dusted himself down and then ran for two days without any rest . He ploughed his way through almost impenetrable jungle, swam rivers and waded through swamps until – arriving at Headquarters – he saluted, handed in his message and then collapsed. He was examined by the army doctor and it was declared that he had already been dead for two days but the spirit of Bushido had kept him going.

The last of these papers gave the account of yet another pilot who, of course, having already shot down two enemy planes, was then forced to break off action. His undercarriage had been shot away and his fuel was running out... So, what did our valiant pilot do then? 'He circled around until he spotted a paddy field, and then, while swooping down to land, he kicked a hole through the floor of the plane, stuck his legs through, and ran along with the plane until he was able to bring it to a standstill!'

Sadly, that last masterpiece resulted in an abrupt cancellation of our newspaper delivery. It was no use complaining! We shouldn't have laughed so much. (*If any readers do not believe all this I invite*

215

them to call on the archivist at the appropriate Record Office in Singapore and get photostat copies. I would love to have one to keep as a souvenir but not for proof, because I know it to be true!)

Our own news gradually became more encouraging over the above period and that – together with the Japanese facts and fantasy – was a great morale booster for us all. The best of the news came at a time when working conditions were getting worse by the week. We really needed that bit of extra good cheer.

The men were now coming back into camp soaked, famished, shattered and, for the most part, as skinny as rakes. There had been one or two occasions during the earlier days when meat or dried fish had been supplied with our rice. Now, however, just when we were barely able to cope, there were periods when we were supplied with nothing other than rice. After that – and because of the resultant diminishing output – the Japanese resorted to a 12-hour shift system of working. These moves, more than any others in the past, clearly signalled their intent to work us to death if need be. The outcome was soon felt after we moved up to our next camp, where work became even more arduous and had to be performed in almost constant teeming rain.

Well before we moved out of Retpu most of us had been coping with two or three forms of illness at the same time. I was one of those and I am only making mention of my condition as an example of what had to be worked through without rest or medicine. Having just seen off beriberi and the worst aspects of pellagra, I was then left with constantly recurring bouts of malaria, malnutrition and the on-and-off scourge of diarrhoea. Diarrhoea plagued most of us, and apart from drinking charcoal water, nothing other could be done than just soldiering on and hoping for the best. However, I then began to feel unusually ill due to a disquieting feeling of lethargy and nausea. The doctor examined my eyes and then told me that I had got yellow jaundice. I think that I may have scored a first with that illness, as I had done with beriberi (and perhaps for the same reason). The doctor – ever the humorist – said, 'Don't eat meat, too many eggs, or dairy products such as butter, cheese or milk!' – which got the expected answer, 'Not much bloody chance of that, sir!'

Now, if there is such a thing as a typical case of Sod's Law, this must have been one, because that evening a stray bullock came wandering up the track, entered the camp and *stood on parade* out-

216

side my office. It was splay-legged with fatigue and as skinny as a scarecrow (which, incidentally, prompted me to do the cattle sketch). Fortunately, our Commandant – who doubled as an opportunist and a bastard – gave me permission to have it slaughtered but with the proviso that the select cuts were to be taken to the Japanese cookhouse.

I am not overly squeamish, but butchery took on a new meaning for me after I had witnessed that poor animal being battered time and again with a small hand axe before it succumbed, to be skinned, hung, bled and quartered. My main concern after that was whether I should chance eating some of it! So, it was back to the doctor again and he didn't disappoint me with his second session of counselling. 'Let me put it this way,' he said, 'if you eat some of it you might die and if you don't, you probably will anyway!' You'll never get better advice than that, I would suspect, even from Harley Street!

So, I had some of it despite the typical feeling of revulsion while eating it. Later that evening I found out that I had been put on the 'special rations list' when an orderly arrived with some dried blood. The doctor had sent his prescription with it, which read, 'This might really get rid of *it* . . . or *you*!'

Cattle – when they arrived – were so thin that they were only too glad to give themselves up.

That was the only special *laigi* (extra) portion of food that I ever had and whether it did me any good or not I will never know. However, my skin did eventually change from yellow back to its previous unhealthy and muddy grey colour.

One of the particularly revolting things that we all had to contend with was the continuous invasion of body lice. By preference, they delighted in extracting their ration of blood from the warmest parts of our bodies. After tanking up they would then take refuge

217

in the seams of our clothing, which during daytime was almost invariably in the waist fixing of our G-strings.

It was just as well that we were undergoing a single-sex course of education, because the resting shift-men would gather by the score completely starkers while hunting out and trying to exterminate all invaders. It had been generally agreed that clothing boiled for a few minutes would do the trick, but in practice it was not so with all of the lice. Those that were bloated with blood would shed it in the boiling but, to our astonishment, many of them – although reduced to a mere husk – would start to wriggle about again once they had cooled off. The only sure remedy was to hunt them down individually and 'zap' them between our fingernails.

It was both an absorbing and a revolting occupation but it was no worse than our nightly bug hunt. Those pests would come out of our bamboo sleeping slats in hordes to suck away at our skin. The only sure way to got rid of them was to squash them, which – if successfully done – released a disgustingly pungent odour.

One of the many other things that combined to debilitate us was the lack of sufficient natural salts in our food. We sweated away pints of perspiration, in the course of which a salty deposit was left on our clothing. One remedy employed by some of the Dutch native troops was to drink some of their urine. None of *us* fancied that method of recycling, though. Instead, some of us indulged in the far less hygienic routine of scraping the deposit from our clothes and sprinkling it into our next boiled drink with all the dust and germs that came with it. We reasoned that, once boiled, it would be just as beneficial as the weevils that came with our servings of rice.

And now – leaving aside any more fascinating culinary tips – I will present my poem on the theme of our pests and then go to Taungzan, the 60 kilometre camp beyond Khonkhan.

(*Khonkhan was 55 kilometres from base and near the site of the new Tanbaya hospital camp which eventually housed the human wreckage that managed to survive the Speedo.*)

Refrain:

> All things bright and beautiful
> All creatures great and small
> All things wise and wonderful
> The Lord God made them all.

The bugs within the bamboo
came out to nip your bum.
It did not do to squash them
'cos that would make them hum.

The 'mossies' having tanked up
sought rest when it was light.
But then the awakening 'bog-flies'
would pester you til night.
(refrain . . .)

The lice would bite and wiggle
they'd find most awkward spots
to hide around and wriggle
while caring for their 'tots'.

And with that proliferation
came unbearable torment.
So you'd crack them with your nails
until their lives were spent.
(refrain . . .)

The scorpions were a menace
they didn't play the game.
It really wasn't tennis!
But they'd sting you just the same.

The ants they were enormous
so I always found it best
to be a little cautious
when standing near their nest.
(refrain . . .)

The leaf-like praying mantis
was very infra dig.
When it wanted breakfast
It would simulate a twig.

It would grab and take its prey
into a fond embrace
and then would bite its head off
without even saying grace.
(refrain . . .)

The elephant – less harmful –
had menace in its tail.
So if you saw that lifted
you'd dash in with a pail.

There was many a dung-beetle
when waiting for a feed
got clobbered by a pailful
so, you had to take great heed.
(refrain...)

The snakes were mainly harmless
and tasty in a pie,
Some men thought them charmless
but certainly not I!

Ned Stead really liked them
he'd woo them with his flute.
They mostly liked the rhythm
but once he had to scoot!
(refrain...)

He played ad-infinitum
I'd had enough of that,
so I just went off to cook
the Commandant's white cat.

All things bright and beautiful
All creatures great and small
All things fat and edible
We really loved them all.

A parody – (with apologies to Cecil F Alexander)

28

TAUNGZAN – 60 KILOMETRE CAMP

Advance Party

Lieutenant Dicker had already arrived here with an advance party of 50 men a few weeks before the rest of us. He had marched in to find the Aussie 'Williams Force' in residence and busy burying several of their dead.

They had taken over the camp from a 'coolie group' that had been decimated by cholera. The filthy and contaminated area had then become a sea of mud due to the early onset of the monsoon rains. Despite all their efforts to de-contaminate the area in the first few weeks of their residence, the Aussies were unable to contain their own outbreak. Quite typically it was thwarted by the lack of

Elephant 'beeokee'! Six men speedo

221

medical supplies and disinfectants so they eventually had to resort to a 'clear, demolish and burn blitzkrieg', which included the removal of a layer of the surface soil from the whole of the camp.

It was fortunate for us that before our main party moved up, the epidemic had been contained and all the survivors from the still considerable Williams Force had been moved on. They were replaced by a much smaller intake of Dutchmen. If it had been otherwise we would have had to occupy the semi-derelict (and some even roofless) huts awaiting de-contamination and repair and, moreover, with the monsoon well and truly set in by then.

Early in July and while the main party was still at Retpu, the Japanese had brought a captive into the camp office. He had been sent up from base by lorry. The first thing that I noticed about him as he dismounted was that he was wearing filthy and sweat-ridden British Army tropical uniform. As he came nearer I could see that he was in no better condition than the rest of us.

Once he was handed over to me, I got Tim Healy to put him on the camp strength and sent the runner off to ask the CO to come over and interrogate him. This had to be done immediately for our own safety.

He told us that he was Sergeant J. Maney of the Royal Artillery and that his unit had been cut off during the wholesale retreat from Moulmein in January 1942. The only line of escape left to them was by swimming across the Salween River, which was otherwise secured by the Japanese at all main crossing points. Being a non-swimmer – he said – he had had to be left behind to try and cross later by means of a makeshift raft. All attempts at that failed but he was then fortunate to have been discovered and sheltered by Karen tribesman for many months until he was betrayed by the Burmese. He then told us about the tortures that he had suffered since his capture.

Early on – he said – he had been regularly interrogated and (in the course of questioning) had been beaten up with a baseball bat. He was then handed on to the Kempi-Ti (Military Police) HQ in Moulmein. They then conducted their own interrogations aboard a boat that was anchored in the harbour and well out of sight and sound. While lodged there, he said that he had been beaten up again, then tortured by being force-filled with water before having his stomach jumped on. Finally, he had been keel-hauled!

Despite hearing that horrific account it was decided that we daren't lodge him with any of the other men until we could be convinced that his story 'stood up'. We had also to consider that he might have been indoctrinated and was perhaps still under threat of death as well unless he gave the Japanese, something in return for their leniency. After all, the safety of everyone else depended on keeping the existence of our wireless set a secret. We couldn't understand why *he* had been released into our care but none of the others had who we knew to be languishing in Moulmein jail. Many of those had been captured in similar circumstances, so why had he been singled out?

We decided to put him on the sick list and lodge him in an unoccupied part of the hospital hut under the pay, rations and surveillance of the medical orderlies. After that – and until we moved up to Taungzan – his only visitors were the doctor, the CO and Sergeant Tom Bousefield. Tom's task – being himself an artilleryman – was to try and further authenticate his story.

17 July 1943

Once we had moved into Taungzan with the main party, Sergeant Maney was released into the care of the rest of the Battalion, who had been warned not to mention the wireless in his presence. By then the doctor had declared him to be just as fit for work as any of the others, albeit that was not much of a recommendation. During the next few weeks it became obvious that he was slipping back physically and – I thought – mentally also.

It must have been a great shock for him when he was thrust into the unfamiliar surroundings of a POW camp and then an even greater one when he discovered that he was never being fully accepted by his new companions. Sadly he died on the first of September without having made any close friends and perhaps through circumstances that had been partly our fault. Our suspicions of him were probably totally unfounded. Dr Hekking had found no visible signs of him having suffered from torture, but he could easily have had serious internal damage which the doctor would have needed special equipment to detect. It was very sad that a man should have to die that way.

* * *

It had been bad enough to walk into Taungzan through ankle-deep mud but even worse to find that the guardhouse was occupied by a group of bastorial Koreans. Even Lieutenant Dicker – who was given to gross understatements about our captors – had already marked them down as 'a villainous and unpleasant band of gentry', among which, one nicknamed Mickey Rooney had beaten him up with his rifle butt; and it didn't surprise me at all to find that others of our officer group (who had previously had little close contact with the guards) were now questioning their legitimacy.

I cannot recall the Japanese Lieutenant Commandant's given name. He had been passed on to us by the Aussies with the nickname Donald Duck and the false appraisement that just because he could speak a little English, that somehow made him a bit more civilised.

We were now up at the sharp end of the construction, which among other things entailed building bridges; and, we were doing two 12-hour shifts. Even without the torrential rain, the work and the longer hours would have been both backbreaking and precarious enough. The conditions were now becoming extremely dangerous and particularly so when undertaken at night in the eerie shadows thrown by inadequate arclights.

During the period when our advance party had been working with the Aussies they had been able to join with them in what was probably the most successful bit of sabotage done on the Burma side of the construction.

The bridge supports and cross-bracings were jointed together and strengthened with large staple-like cleats made by the Aussies who worked in the Thanbyuzayat Transport Depot. They were about 15 to 18 inches long and had pointed spikes at each end. Williams Force had been kept informed of consignments in which there would be a few 'specials' (either weakened or shortened) to make them inadequate for the job.

Shortly after the Aussies departed, the track was brought up, through and over three completed bridges, the last of which was the largest. They were all ready for testing when the torrents of rain – which had already destroyed some footbridges – smashed the large bridge, leaving a tangle of twisted rails and sleepers spanning the void below. The bridge was then hastily rebuilt by the Japanese engineers themselves and then – to our delight – after being tested by running a heavy locomotive across, that also collapsed. The final build stood firm but we were convinced that that was only because the Japanese had fashioned the cleats themselves.

A month or so after that we heard a rumour that a troop train had plunged over a weakened bridge beyond the Three Pagodas Pass. If that were true the Japanese must have had some remarkable recovery equipment because we never saw any wreckage when we travelled over the route later.

The most persistent rumour, though, was so bizarre that for that reason it might well have been true. It was said to have happened over on the Siam side at a swampy area just short of the ascent into the more formidable jungle workings; and the story went like this... In order to save time, money and a lengthy diversion around a swamp, an enterprising Japanese engineer/officer had designed and built a bridge out of large bamboo. The supports and struts were then pegged and lashed together using hut-building techniques. After that – and with the track laid – a locomotive was inched triumphantly onto the structure. All was going well until it got to the middle. The bridge then began to sway, then tilt, and it finally collapsed, tipping the whole lot into the swamp. The officer – having failed his Emperor – was said to have drawn his sword and committed hara-kiri on the spot.

Even though the above story may not have been true, it was one of many that was well received by believer or cynic as either a morale booster or – at the very least – something to laugh about. Such improbable stories were very welcome at that time.

It was the Aussies who came up with most of the 'fair dinkum furphies' (strong rumours) and some of them were so outrageously 'strong' that – paradoxically – they were more likely to be true than false. I believe that it was Ronald Searle who first told this next story, which reached us on the Burma side when Brigadier Varley's group came up from Singapore... Just after captivity an Australian detail was taken out to do road repairs. Their chief task was the filling of bomb craters, which then had to be consolidated by a steam-roller. The Aussies were in the care of a dim-wit Japanese guard who they had conned into believing that the steam-roller ran on petrol. Several days later (and with the job well under way) the guard discovered that it was fired and fuelled by logs and water and, that the daily supply of petrol had been sold off to Chinese black marketeers. The Aussies had expected to be caught out eventually and had gambled that the guard would be too scared to report the matter. The consequences of his stupidity would no doubt have been terminal. So, with that realisation, he took the pragmatic view that if he couldn't beat the Aussies he might just as well join them! Another furphy released to us by Williams Force just before they left Taungzan was a real gem but totally suspect, because it was said to have happened a month before in Siam at a time when none of us had made contact with the POWs there. However, I still like to think that this could have been true!

Some Aussies who worked from the transport lines in Siam did supply trips into the jungle area by lorry. Two of them were out on a regular run with their Japanese guard when – as usual – he made the driver stop near a kampong while he went off to savour the delights of one of the maidens. Whenever they had stopped there before, the Aussies had been able to buy or scrounge food from the locals. However, this time there was a difference, because the assembled traders wanted to *buy*, not *sell*; and, moreover, they were after the lorry's spare wheel. That was quickly sold. Things got quite out of control after that when it was agreed to jack up the lorry and sell first one and then the second of the rear wheels.

Eventually, the guard was seen flashing his torch as he made his way back from the kampong and that was the cue for the two Aussies to dash into the jungle. The guard went ballistic when he saw the lorry. The Aussies came back to explain that they had been *taksan byoki* with an attack of the runs and for that reason knew nothing of the crime. Much as the Japanese was inclined to beat them to death on the spot, he had to realise that he was compromised. How could he explain the loss of three wheels without confessing that he had left the lorry and those men unguarded just to satisfy the stirrings of his loins! It was the steam-roller scenario all over again but with the further complication that he still had to deliver his load of supplies, or else...! The consequences of failure didn't bear thinking about. It was fear alone that inspired his decision to walk back down the track with one of the Aussies, break into a lorry compound, steal two wheels and then bowl them back to the stranded vehicle.

Sufficient unto the day was the laughter and tonic thereof with the Speedo getting under way.

The 55 kilometre hospital camp at Khonkhan was by now being

extended to accommodate 3,000 men from our side and an expected large influx of survivors from Nikki and Songkrai. Those camps were actually within our administrative area (Japanese section 5, Group III) but due to the nature of the terrain, they were being 'worked' from the Siam side. They were in a state of indescribable shambles and pestilence following outbreaks of cholera.

The Japanese never did like to mix personnel from different sources but fortunately for the survivors from Nikki their camp was just north of Malay Command (section 9) and only 65 kilometres from Khonkhan. Some idea of the state that they were in can be gauged by the fact that the Japanese themselves had run a sick parade and those men assessed to be incurable were dumped just over the border in ramshackle huts at 80 kilometre camp and told, 'No work, no food!' It was only by the grace of God and the dedication of Lieutenant Colonel Williams of Mobile Force that they were discovered there and occasionally given food that his men stole from the Japanese supplies.

I am unable to say whether any of those men ultimately survived or not, but those who were deemed fit for the journey from Nikki to Khonkhan, were halted at Taungzan for an hour or two on one of the few occasions when I went up to the workings with the ration party. Few were able to eat much of the food that we offered them. Those of them who were capable of sitting up resembled Belsenites and many who were lying down were already dead. If those were the less sick, it would be hard to imagine what those left behind had looked like.

The Japanese were now intent on getting the job done regardless of the number of men sacrificed along the track. The Tokyo Tribunal revealed that 1,700 men from F Group alone had died within ten weeks of being force-marched up to the Siam border; and that had happened well before the Speedo was launched!

For our part – now that the Speedo was on – we were slowly building up to the state where we had 80 men down at Khonkhan who had very little chance of returning. During the next three months we were hit by the full impact of the unremitting toil and privation, losing 25 of our Battalion already down there and 41 within the work camps. Many of the latter survived only a few days after coming in from their last shift. The conditions were bad enough within the camp let alone outside, where they were horrific.

During July our railhead was about two kilometres beyond

Taungzan and the way up there was in many places knee-deep with mud. We had tried infilling with logs and branches but that often spread the flooding to adjacent areas. This made the going dangerous for our barefooted men during the day and treacherous for those going out on the night shift. More and more bodies were being washed out along the route as the rain continued to lash down. There were periods when it rained incessantly for days on end and beat on the *atap* roofs with such ferocity that it was scarcely possible to hear any conversation. The noise might then quieten, giving some hope of an interval of sunshine and calm, but on most occasions it would quicken up again into a pounding deluge that caused the monsoon drains to fill and overflow, flooding the huts. The worst downpours left a layer of liquid mud behind, which was churned up by incoming workers or those going out on their next shift. The Japanese steadfastly refused to increase the 'in-camp' staff. So I was forced to use the less sick and the partly rested men to deepen the drains and keep the latrine pits from overflowing. Despite the valiant work done by Nobby and his team, there were times when masses of maggots fought their way up out of the morass in search of drier areas in which to create our next generation of invading flies.

On the all too rare occasions that the rain did stop for a few hours, the jungle came alive. It literally pulsated with the sound of millions of gallons of water being sucked into it as if by a giant sponge. The *chaungs* filled and then overflowed to create large areas of swampland as breeding places for more mosquitoes and nurseries for the bullfrogs that later tortured us with the continuous sound of their mating calls. *It was torture too* in the sense that we were so tantalisingly within reach of an abundance of frogs' legs, but most of us were unable to reap any of the 'harvest'. The nearest swamp to our camp was close to the rear of the Japanese guardhouse and therefore out-of-bounds to all but the most daring of men, who would have been shot if discovered there.

By far and away the most revolting invasion was made by hordes of flies when food was being served up. Dealing with that could be likened to trying to hold back the tide. I had to post men at the issuing points to fan the tubs of food, and once a ration had been issued each man had to either protect it in the same way or cover it with a piece of rag until he could find a place to sit with both hands free – one for eating with and the other for waving above the food. It was inevitable that some got through the defences and when that happened a fly needed just two seconds to hover or land on its filthy legs in order to deposit a string of yellow eggs. If you had any sense at all, you then had to forget your hunger and sacrifice all of your ration that was in and around the infected area. However, *sense* is one thing but having the resolve to be sensible when starving is an entirely different matter!

(*Just in case someone should be interested, I can tell you of an almost infallible way of catching a fly without the use of a zapper, but if you ever put it to the test, first make sure that all valuable objects are well clear of the landing ground. You then have to know quite a lot about the aerodynamics of the fly. To lift off it has to rise vertically an inch or two to hover and then move forward a fraction before it can take any evasive action. The strategy then is to cup your hand in front of it, swipe forward and capture it during that split second when it is still in the 'hover mode'. One must then listen with cupped hand to ear, and if you have made a capture I recommend hurling the fly against a hard surface before splatting it. It is most unfortunate that they were not edible. If they had been I would never have gone hungry!*)

And now, a little dissertation on the subject of thievery! It cannot be denied that we of the British Sumatra Battalion were consummate thieves, or that the dire circumstances of the Speedo served to hone our skill. The Speedo also spurred some men beyond the bounds of audacity into the realms of sheer recklessness. Some would steal the 'whole' rather than an undetectable 'portion' of anything (food in particular) if it belonged to the Japanese. So, nothing could have been better for us at this time than bringing off two substantial coups that between them provided extra food for the whole Battalion for several days.

I am using Sergeant Harry Pearce's words to tell this first story about Appy's Locusts, who he considered to be 'the finest and bravest thieves in captivity':

On taking a working-party to bring in the camp rations from the railhead I noticed that it was seven or eight men short. The rations had to be taken to where those for the main store were immediately checked in between the Japanese and an Australian captain. The check was correct there and I was told that *our* rations had been sent to our kitchen … in which I was amazed at the amount of food that had been delivered there. While I had been checking with the Japanese guard the missing men had gone round the back and helped themselves. There were sacks of rice, beans and some coconut oil. We fed like lords for a couple of weeks.

The other incident was so bizarre and outrageously opportunist that even after 55 years I still marvel at how we got away with it and there is no doubt that we would not have done so without the aid of Mother Nature.

I was always on hand to see each working-party out and – 12 hours later – when they returned with their loads of firewood for the camp kitchen. On this particular day they disappeared into pelting rain and, as usual, I was rewarded with the sight of that china pisspot bouncing out on the backside of the owner.

By the time the party came back it had been raining stair-rods for hours, creating a steamy mist that made them almost invisible until they had got to within a few feet of me to halt and be counted. The Japanese in the guardhouse would have been vaguely aware of their arrival but none of them came to assist the solitary guard who had brought them in. So he made a desultory check and then scuttled off to take cover.

While I was standing and watching from the rear under the shelter of one of the hut eaves, I saw horns tossing about amongst the branches of firewood and then the backside of a bullock standing in line at the rear of the parade while the men in front stood tall to conceal it.

As soon as the guard had disappeared – and with the camp for once free from roving guards – the beast was brought right through the central aisle of the hut to the back, then slaughtered, skinned and cut up with the help of Dutchmen who were sharing the camp with us. Every container that we could muster was commandeered! The first boiling was added to our evening meal and the rest was boiled, shredded and hidden away for enriching the next day's meals with a mouth-watering soup. Meanwhile the story of the capture had been told. The bullock driver had been forced to take shelter after unhitching his two beasts and tethering them to the camp fence. The working-party had then come upon them and with inspired impulse one of them had been unhitched and – without any protest – hustled into camp among the stampede of men loaded with firewood, exhausted and hell-bent on seeking shelter themselves.

The rain still sheeted down throughout that night and continued until mid-morning when Mother Nature let up on the deluge and switched on the sun. Long before that, though the night-working parties had come in, the replacing shift had gone out and all had had a second glorious meal. Around 10 a.m. the bewildered and forlorn figure of the bullock-cart driver came in through the camp entrance to continue what had been a fruitless and exhausting search for his animal outside.

The interpreter was called and ordered to co-opt a Dutch NCO and myself to help him with the thorough but useless search that ensued. We were elated, of course, but nevertheless a bit sad that the poor chap had had to lose half of his worldly goods just to keep us happy for a couple of days.

It took all of 30 years after my repatriation to discover that Gunner Alf Perry – a regular of the Heavy Ack Ack – took a major role in getting animals mysteriously stranded within sight of POW camps. Alf had been in hospital at Thanbyuzayat when the Japanese called for volunteer drovers to take cattle up-country to the Japanese supply depots. He must have been a great persuader. There he was amongst a host of Aussies experienced in the work but he had convinced them that he had come from farming stock, despite the fact that he didn't know 'one udder from the udder'. The group of stockmen used to make their way up-country along the old trade route paths and whenever they came close to one of the POW camps they would abandon a beast. There was little fodder for the cattle while on the drive and any of them that we caught sight of were emaciated as I have depicted and often nearly dead. Presumably it was Alf who delivered the stray to us when we were in Retpu!

As we edged into August the men were just about managing to cope with the increased shift hours and the return to periods when we were getting rice, rice and nothing else but bloody rice for days on end. The credit for that had just as much to do with their remarkable resolve to survive as our non-stop fight to maintain hygiene standards within the camp. What with the constant rain and the confining nature of the bridge-building work, it had become almost impossible to make any contacts with itinerant traders while on the day shift. However, during the night some of the bolder men occasionally dodged surveillance to pillage from rail trucks and lorries halted beyond the glare of the arc-lights.

I was well aware of those activities and, despite never being able to take part in them myself, I would always rejoice with any of our locusts who got safely back into camp with their loot. So, I was more than a little surprised by the naivety of a request made by our ever-villainous gang of Scotsmen that I should put them all on permanent night-shift. Their excuse was that they had all quite suddenly decided to become allergic to strong sunlight. Being a cockney, I at first invited them to pull the other leg etc. They were then reminded of the promise that I had made to all that I would never allow anyone to advantage themselves at the expense of others. That evening I had them paraded for a medical check and Dr Hekking told them that they were all fit to take their turn at day work, and that, I hoped, would be the end of the matter.

Those four men were sick in mind but far from being sick in body! They had indulged in a collective campaign of intimidation of weaker men to thieve from them and – if necessary – to additionally bash up any of them who did not readily hand over their possessions. Unfortunately, I was never able to induce any of the victims to come forward and give evidence against them. This was not really surprising because one of them was a razor-slasher who had already done time in the glasshouse for slicing the neck of his bombardier just before the fall of Singapore. I had been told that he still had his favourite weapon to hand ready to use on anyone who thwarted him. The rest of the men knew only too well that there was nowhere to hide from vicious little sods like that in a POW camp. They themselves knew that even if they had been put on a charge, the only punishment available to us was to fine them out of their monthly pay, which – because of their activities – they never had to depend on anyway.

Apart from them, there was only one other faction that gave me cause to worry about their activities while within the camp. They were Welshmen and they somehow contrived to keep fat and fit without ever revealing how. All of the other hard cases in the Battalion quite acceptably restricted their activities to causing problems for the Japanese while at work and they, quite cunningly, took turns in owning up to accept any punishment when detected.

232

Among our sergeants was one Pinkie Tribe of the Royal Army Ordnance Corps, who right from the time of our formation in Padang had shown scant respect for anyone who wasn't 'regular army'. He was certainly not alone in this attitude, though. At least a half of the Battalion were regulars and he was one of many who were far from co-operative when it came to compiling our first draft of the nominal roll. We had to thank Lieutenant Dicker – also a regular – for the painstaking job that he did with Sergeant Healy later in firming up on that draft to compile the list that we used from early 1943 and eventually saved from confiscation by the Japanese.

Now Pinkie took his turn with all work, but well into 1943 he was still sounding off about people who hadn't got their knees brown, which inevitably included myself, a conscript. He was really nothing more than a cantankerous old sod and I told him that when he went too far and refused to go out on a working-party led by one of the civilian officers.

He and I had a confidential heart-to-heart in which I told him several home truths. I made him agree that nearly all our trouble-makers were regulars and only a few of them had seen more action than the rest of us.

Despite his attitude I rather liked Pinkie. He had a quirky sense of humour and once we had got our differences sorted out we became quite friendly. This friendship helped both of us. He was a bit of a loner, as I was, too, albeit out of duty rather than choice. We talked a lot about home and our family life and he mainly spoke of his father and brothers, who had also followed the family tradition of serving in the British Army.

I was very soon going to need a friend and Pinkie didn't fail me!

The accommodation at Taungzan was such that Tim Healy and I had had to set up shop in a makeshift office. I was lodged at one of the central entrances to a long hut and Tim within a screened area on the opposite side which doubled as the office. Ideally, both of us should have had security as well as privacy because we still had some odds and ends of issue clothing that had to be kept out of the way of sticky fingers.

It was that vulnerability that nearly caused my death. Shortly after my confrontation with the Scottish mob, Pinkie came to tell me that an informer had told him that he had heard them say that they were coming to 'get me' that night. I was well aware of the fact that that despicable quartet were – to put it mildly – displeased with the fact that I had halved their previously exclusive night-shift racket and that they were due to take their turn on day work the following morning.

This was a threat which I had to take seriously and for which I had to find a solution without compromising anyone else.

That evening I made up my bedding with a blanket filled out to look as if I was sleeping under it with my head covered. Pinkie and I then stood and waited at the end of the hut for what seemed like ages before the gang made a furtive entry and pulled the blanket aside, while the slasher stood poised to strike with his razor. I am sure that it would have been comical for anyone else but me to witness their bewilderment and then their hasty retreat into the shadowed side of the moonlit hut. However, I was now left with the riddle of how to protect myself on future nights, when they only had to wait and wear me down with lack of sleep before having another go. Pinkie remained with me for what must have been three or four hours until I was able to tell him that I had finally come up with the solution.

I saw the gang out of camp, got some sleep and then went to see our new CO, Captain Davies, who up until then had known nothing about the threat, let alone the incident. It was agreed that I would bring the men before him as soon as they came back into camp, on the pretext that he wanted to discuss their request to go back on night work. Having got them there, he then agreed that he would greet them with the words, 'You four men are going to be handed over to the Japanese for punishment ... [pause] ... if you make any more threats on the CSM's life. We have witnesses to your attempt last night and we are well aware of why it was made. So, you will now have to go away and pray that nothing undue ever happens to him – injury or death – or you will be lodged in the Japanese guardroom to await the attention of the Kempi-Ti.' Although *that* was very fortunately *that* for me, it never entirely subdued their menace or thuggery towards others until much later, when ... (but that has to be related later).

There were other men who were tough but only in the sense that they remained fit and seemed to be indestructible. One of them was Alfie Page of 18 Div Recce Corps, who was an amiable and gentle giant always ready to assist any of his sick comrades. We certainly needed men like that because the Battalion was beginning to look more and more desperately sick by now. Most of us had been strong young men averaging about $10\frac{1}{2}$ stone, full-faced and bright-eyed. Now we were fast becoming a skinny, gaunt-faced and listless bunch of human wrecks. There were very few among the lot of us who in normal circumstances wouldn't have been sent straight into hospital.

We were now under the care of a vicious group of Japanese and Koreans. Apart from always laying about any man who had slackened at work, they had more recently introduced the refinement that, night or day, they all had to be saluted. Any failure to do so had – at the very least – resulted in a bashing for the man concerned and sometimes the further punishment of everyone else in the hut. Everyone was on the jump and if just one man failed to see and salute a patrolling guard, all others would be routed out from their bed-spaces, whether awake or asleep, to stand outside for several hours. We were well into the monsoon season so men would often have to stand there naked in order to preserve at least one article of dry clothing to sleep in. When the punishment was over they would then have no option but to climb back onto their allotted bed-space soaking wet, feet covered in mud and then pray that the bastard wouldn't come back to enjoy a further round of sadism.

This dire situation was partly relieved when one of our men declared himself to be a lay preacher. He then quite unexpectedly got permission to conduct morning and evening Sunday services. Although many of us were sceptical of the man's credentials, I for one found it inspiring to look in occasionally and join in the singing, despite my new and firm conviction that salvation was only achievable through hate, fate, self-help and a bit of luck thrown in for good measure. However, there was no doubt that the 30 or so regular worshippers derived the spiritual uplift that they sought. It really mattered little whether the man was authentic or not, because he went on to give solace to the mates of the men who died and to conduct simple services at many of our burials.

I would have loved to have regained the hope – if not the conviction – that there was an all-seeing and caring God who could be relied on to punish man's inhumanity to man. Vengeance is mine, said the Lord. I wish that I could believe so! Heaven forbid that all we have to rely on are the fickle whims of such people who decided that proven murderers should escape summary justice *then* and, now that 55 years have gone by, that they should still be given the protection of age to avoid it. It had been even worse for me to discover that many such murderers were long ago given immunity for reasons of political expediency and that successive governments have preserved that stance. We certainly need a God in there somewhere because the same governments have paid little more than lip service to seeking reparation for the families of those they murdered, or for those who survived.

Quite recently they have gone even further than that by disallowing that portion of a deceased POW's war pension that should have automatically gone to his widow *just because he smoked!* The man I have in mind – who will by now be one of many – was Sapper Adrian, one of the crew of the *Bintang Dua*.

Harry never considered himself to be exceptional any more than the rest of us. The illnesses and diseases shown on my pension assessment (see Appendices – Correspondence) are also typical of those that he and the rest of the Battalion members suffered. He was also (like the rest of us) a slave for three and a half years, starved, beaten, deprived of *all* medicines, barefooted, near-naked, unwashed, sweat-ridden, fevered, etc ... but of course, *he smoked!* When? Very little at all as a POW, I can assure you, and far less than any uncaptured swattie whose supply of free or subsidised cigarettes was limitless. However, Harry smoked; and that, to the shame of the assessors, is their cop-out.

How on earth can our government balance the concept of leniency for the now aged oppressors mentioned above against such scandalous treatment for those that they oppressed? You disgust me! Your gods are political expediency and the fostering of good relations for financial gain and nothing else, it would seem. It will quite obviously cause you no embarrassment to be told that the above decision has sent a clear signal to the Japanese that you too don't give a damn for any of us either.

Today is Tuesday, the twenty-sixth of May 1998, and I have just come back from the Mall after registering my fury that Akihito – a puppet – had been awarded the Order of the Garter. It would have been far more appropriate that having awarded our Queen the Order of the Chrysanthemum, he should carry back with him the posthumous award to Hiro Hito of The Red Hot Poker!

And now, without much apology for leaving Alfie Page standing in the wings, I will bring him back on stage to go out with him for the second night running to where he was stealing food from an unattended truck.

He had been beaten up when searched the previous night but this time he got safely into camp and then down to the hospital hut, where I happened to be at the time. Alfie had decided that his mission in life was to steal from the Japanese almost entirely for the benefit of the patients. He used to bring in the food for the medical orderlies to cook while he sat around chatting to the sick about his work as a London docker. According to the orderlies, it was his visits that were far more beneficial to those men – who in most cases knew that they were dying – than a well-intentioned visit from the chaplain. Quite apart from his selflessness, I don't know how he managed to stay so many hours close to men shrouded within the sickly sweet smell of death and decay.

It was those visits that sparked off the idea of organising talks about the pre-war experiences of just anyone who would tell us their story. Almost anything was better than nothing at all to keep our minds off the stark realities of the Speedo. Alfie was our first and a willing volunteer. He told us how some of the dockers used to spirit out food that was on ration at that time. There were some who had to push their bicycles out of the gates because the tyres were stuffed with contraband, and another character had his loot hidden within the tubular frame. There was yet another – who will remain unnamed – whose mother lined the inside of his clothing with pockets. His main target was the crates of orange pekoe tea and he had become adept at tipping one to fall on a corner to burst it open. When he got home his mother would have already covered the floor with bedsheets in order that – so he said – he could stand on his head to tip out the tea for bagging up and sale on the black market. Alfie wasn't much of an orator but he could certainly tell a good tale.

Our resident hot sweet coffee merchant – another cockney – had always boasted that he had never had the need to work more than

15 days a year to make his living. He achieved that by employing cheap night labour to make up mountains of exorbitantly priced sandwiches and rolls for sale at the five 'Classic' horse-race meetings. He had plenty more spiv stories with which to top up his sessions.

It was a great pity that we had had to wait until the Japanese forced our junior officers out from their reclusive lifestyle, because once they were made to work as *kumichos* they became far more accepted by our hard-liners. It was then that we were able to hear interesting things about their pre-war employment in Malaya. One of our civvy officers overcame his problem with deafness to give us a lively account of his employment as a hangman. Perhaps lively is not an appropriate word for describing Lieutenant Tallent's job, though! No wonder he in particular was only too pleased to be able to sew a pip on his shoulder in order to gain the protection of the Army when retreating to Singapore.

Unfortunately the talks petered out as the Japanese became more and more obsessive about demanding salutes.

Our despicable Commandant Donald Duck had been given that name because he was short, fat and had an exaggerated waddle which left us all speculating if he had got an 'undischarged load' left in his baggy pants. However, there was nothing else that was comical about him as he directed his willing band of Koreans – Gold Tooth, Liver Lips, Cat's Eyes, Mickey Rooney, Silver Bullet and Dillinger (the assassin) – into more and more acts of violence.

The only good fortune that came our way during his oppressive reign was the build-up of good news as the Americans made a succession of landings and conquests in the Solomon, New Guinea and Gilbert Islands. We needed all the encouragement that we could get now as malnutrition, coupled with the Speedo, took us into our worst spell of pellagra and a marked increase in the number of men suffering from oedema and the onset of beriberi. Some of this hit me in the form of mild pellagra, oedemic swellings round newly erupted ulcers and, finally, dry pleurisy. The only effective remedy that I found for the pleurisy was in wrapping a warm puttee round my chest in order to free up the phlegm. We all had to soldier on and, if possible, find our own cures, but for many – like the worst of our beriberi cases – it was already too late. They filled up with water to such an extent that some of them had to walk splay-legged to accommodate massively swollen testicles that all but obscured

Gibraltar 1923 - The battleship HMS *Barham*. A vintage shot of her 15" guns being sponged out after breaking off action

IWM A 2277

HMS *Barham* at anchor in the Mediterranean 1942   IWM DS 595/15

Priggi Rajah at the mouth of the Andragiri River   Photo courtesy of Stanley Saddington

Rengat. The first 'Organisation' staging post 100 miles up river

Photo courtesy of Stanley Saddington

Sawahalunto. The final lap from the plateau to Padang, and capture

Photo courtesy of Stanley Saddington

Captain Dudley Apthorp OBE, CO

Lieut H.G. Dicker, Adjutant

The Author, BSM

The Author, October 1945, in
Rangoon awaiting repatriation

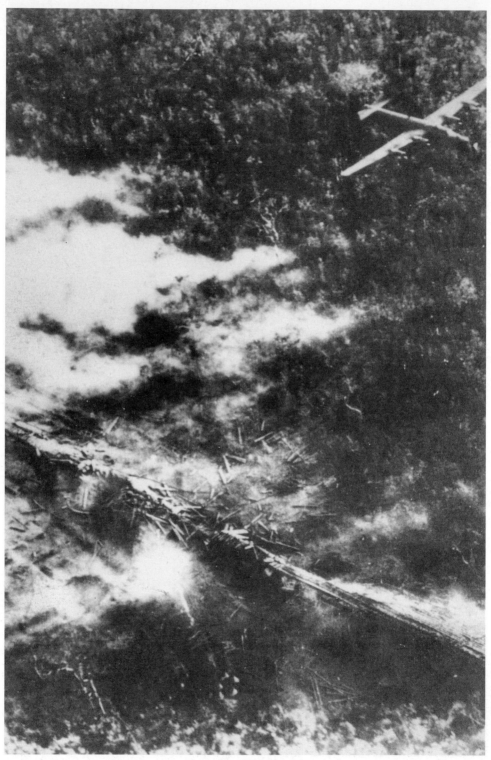

An allied aircraft bombing one of the wooden trestle viaducts   IWM HU 67811

At WAMPO - the longest viaduct bridge on the line   IWM HU 67810

Wooden 'Bridge on the River Kwai'   IWM HU 28599

The 1982 reunion at Blackpool
Left to right:
Ashley Sedgbeer, stoker - Prince of Wales, 'Bob' Grafton, Bdr 30 HAA - FEPOW rep.,
The Author, Dudley Apthorp, Major retd - 'Appy' our revered CO,
Levi Thomas, L/Bdr 30 HAA

their penises. It was a mercy for such men when they died by drowning in their own body fluid, and an equal tragedy that, given moderate medical facilities, they could easily have been saved.

Despite the squalor, aggravation, saluting, searching and beatings, there were still moments when we were able to get a laugh out of our situation, thank God. Even more reassuring than that was the unbelievable morale of so many of the men in their refusal to be cowed either by the Japanese or by the conditions in which we had been forced to live.

I remember the day when one of the Koreans who, having swooped into a hut for a random search of a man's pack, departed far more quickly after grasping a snake. It was oven-ready but he didn't know that! Another man was discovered with a stolen fish stuffed down his G-string. However, it was not all laughter because one of the Koreans had by now imposed on us the much-favoured Japanese punishment of lining everyone up to slap each other whether a crime had been committed or not. This was sheer bastardisation and fortunately only lasted for the few days until he was confronted by Corporal 'Curly' Neame of the Argyll and Sutherland Highlanders. Curly refused to either stand up or salute. It was then that the guard realised that he had challenged the same man who had defied him a month or two previously. On that occasion he had lunged at Curly with his bayonet, hit him in the stomach and drawn blood. That had scared him *then* and – as before – he decided that discretion was the better part of bastardisation and withdrew. Curly was a very brave man. He always confronted his troubles head on, but he was very lucky. Had there been another guard around to witness either of those incidents, *face* would have been lost and *discretion*!

Shortly after that event 'our' Koreans were thinned out a bit in order to strengthen those slave-driving outside where a few men had found opportunities for revenge and minor sabotage. Lance Bombadier Bob Grafton wrote this account of one such incident:

At a later stage in POW life when the line was completed and the Japanese were transporting their troops into Burma in box-cars, it was found that they were also carrying spare rails on bogies in the same pyramid fashion as used before; and, because they put a box-car between each load of rails, the POWs thought out a method of sabotage. They loosened the wire at the end nearest the engine and then, because of the speed of the train, the rails would drop and dig into the ground causing the back end to smash its way through the box-car with horrifying effect on the troops inside. In fact, so ghastly were the injuries caused that some of the men refused to participate.

Bob was there when this happened, having been kept back for maintenance work after the rest of us had moved on into Thailand, and when the rest of us arrived there in January 1944 we heard about another gang that had dropped a length of rail on the feet of a guard who had been constantly terrorising them. My reaction to the story – which differs little to this day – was to give three hearty cheers for the fact that some of our sufferings had been repaid.

I was still going out with some ration parties on occasions, and we always made sure that the sickest of the men went back to camp with the empties in our place. It was always a revelation for me to see what was going on out there, and one day when the three bridges were still under repair I was summoned by an officer of the Railway Regiment and told to replace a sick elephant with six men. (That incident is depicted in one of my cartoons, which shows a typical scene of a short-arsed Japanese trailing his sword in the dust, to which I added a wheel to help it along.)

The elephants were a joy to watch as their mahouts worked them back and forth to collect and drag massive teak logs down to the bridge areas. The logs were secured by a chain wrapped round at the front. This left a triangle between the log and the chain which, but for the dexterity of the elephants, would have snagged on the standing stumps left in the ground. The wise old beasts knew that and it was they – not the mahout – who manoeuvred to avoid them. Also, no matter how much he might urge them to go onto swampy ground, they would steadfastly refuse to do so until they had tested ahead with a cautiously placed leg. On one occasion they had to come right through our camp in order to get to the rear. This entailed negotiating a route between two long and low-eaved huts and only allowed them a few inches' clearance between their swaying bellies and the all too likely catastrophe of demolishing the sleeping area of about 200 men. I stood, watched and marvelled as they lumbered and wheezed their way through so deftly that it was accomplished without disturbing one blade of *atap*. As each of them passed me they sized me up with a knowing look in their eyes. You didn't need to know elephant language to interpret the message: 'We're clever old sods, aren't we?'

Apart from bullocks, the only other large animals up-country were wild and most of us never caught sight of any of them. Quite sensibly the 'wore-wore' monkeys stayed well clear of us, otherwise they would have finished up in the pot. Their predators – the Burmese tigers – were alleged to have been seen carrying off the remains of cholera victims on both sides of the border. All that can be said about that is that it was more than likely true because that was their main habitat.

From the 60 kilometre camp onwards we were not only advancing into primary (primitive) jungle but heading into a more deadly malaria belt. Our ultimate responsibility was to be the building of a further 54 kilometres of track up to the Three Pagodas Pass which – along its 35-kilometre length – cut centrally through a range of hills that rose from the coastline to a height of about a kilometre and a quarter to north and west of it. Very few birds were heard or seen on the way up there other than the presumed migratory ones that flapped around in the canopy above us for a day or two. However, once the monsoon broke, the whole area began to rejuvenate itself beneath with extravagant growth and life. A greater variety of insects and flora emerged, the latter being mainly large and flamboyantly coloured. Most of them were of species unknown to us other than the orchids, but all of them were so profuse and vigorous that they were even able to take hold in well-trampled camp areas.

It was something of a mixed blessing for us when increasing heat and humidity 'fathered' insects in profusion, most of them were of unidentifiable varieties. Those familiar to us were always larger than we had ever seen before but, fortunately, mainly harmless. Enormous bumbling May-bugs and fruit-bugs made aimless sorties into our huts and we invented names for some of them, such as the Clockwork Beetle. Nature had also 'manufactured' enormous ants in approximately three equal three-quarter-inch sections (head, thorax and abdomen), and half of them had come off the 'conveyor belt' programmed to forage or to scout ahead for followers

241

carrying eggs. When they decide to move, they do so with the determination and direct approach of an incontinent making for the nearest public lavatory.

One day I was walking out with the ration party along a footpath that had diverted from the usual route because of flooding. The rains had then eased off for a day or two, leaving the path trampled and rutted with streamlets. It was a day of haze, fierce heat and humidity, in fact the kind of weather that can easily induce hallucination. The sunlight was filtering through the canopy and flashing on what I thought to be a stream. However, on getting closer I stood in amazement – and a certain amount of fear – to watch the reality of hordes of ants on the move and with the sun glinting on their backs. When they met water, they continued in an undeviating line over a sacrificial bridge of the kamikaze scouts that had preceded them.

I have enjoyed this interlude in which to talk about nature for a change. Neither I, nor you, the reader, I suspect, would have wished to have an unrelieved account of blood, guts and death. However, it is now time to move ahead with the rations past a familiar corner where a cluster of exposed skulls grinned at us from the side of the track and then on to deliver our offering of rice and wishy-washy soup.

We replaced four men that day, one of whom died two days later. The Dutch were working up the line from us, breaking up rocks for ballast. They had been made to make their numbers up with sick men that had to be carried out on stretchers. When they came back into camp that night they were carrying the body of one of them who had keeled over and died of exhaustion.

Our men were at the sidings loading two hundredweight sacks of rice across from a store to a string of box-cars. After the midday meal I stepped into line with a crocodile of our slaves humping them over. Each sack was swung up onto our shoulders by two 'lifters'. When my turn came, the impact sent me sprawling onto my knees. Fortunately, another one was quickly hoisted up before the guard could get over to give me a bashing. I had been advised to lock my spindly legs at the knees throughout the 'carry', which ended with a steep walk up a ramp to the doorway of the wagon. Mercifully, when half way up, two other pairs of hands reached down to swing the loads in. It was sheer bloody hell for men who

– having already done five hours of loading – still had another five to go before being relieved.

Early in September a large contingent of 'Williams Force' Aussies were marched in to stay with us for a few weeks. They had been shunted about from camp to camp as a mobile unit and many of them came in carrying tools. They arrived at the time when our cookhouse staff were hacking away trying to split a long thick tree trunk that had been dragged in by an elephant. We had never been supplied with tools other than a saw and two hand-axes for the kitchen and two shovels and a chunkel for the sanitary staff. The axes were locally made and untempered and I had seen our men banging away with them and getting nowhere for some time.

Shortly after the Aussies' *tenko*, one of them arrived on the scene with what he called his 'swayed-handled plumb axe', I believe. He turned out to be Brum, a Birmingham-cum-Tasmanian world championship axeman. He took over the task and it was a joy to watch an expert at work. He walked the length of the trunk and then – having eyed it up – he took our hand-axes and whacked them into the end grain at obviously selected positions. Then, in line with those, he slammed down a few times with his plumb axe. It was finally left buried in the wood and he turned away theatrically as if in disgust. There was then a series of pops and cracks as the tree slowly split open down its whole length. What a show that was!

Once Brum had settled in, I looked him up in order to hear about the championships. He said that to win an event he had to cut notches to the exact size needed for platform wedges to be inserted and to mount before lopping the top off a tall standing trunk. All that had to be done within a scarcely believable few minutes, as far as I can remember.

One of his 'cobbers' chipped in with the comment that Brum was so expert that he could split a matchstick down its length. I was then treated to an incredible display of his accuracy as the cobber spread two fingers apart on the top of a tree stump and Brum whacked his axe down between them.

It was quite by chance that I met both of them 12 months later in Singapore – the cobber with all fingers intact. They were both very friendly and genuine men and my hope has always been that they got home safely. However, my fears are that they were among the thousands of Allied POWs whose ships were torpedoed when they were en-route for work in the Japanese copper mines.

We were half way into September before the rain eased off, and that was the only good thing going for us at the time. We had no illusions about the impending rise in deaths with so many of us looking like scarecrows but still being driven on in manic and uncaring fury.

Captain Apthorp had earlier predicted that the time would come when a list must be made of the few valuables and sentimental items left by the dead. It had been our practice to hand them over to mates on trust that they would eventually get them back to the families of the deceased. By now, though, some of those mates had also died, so the record was set up – albeit in semi-official form and controlled by one of the officers – and, not a day too soon.

There were already 80 of our men down at the hospital camp by now who – unlike the less sick, who stayed with us – were under the direct control of the Japanese and only receiving half rations. Our only representatives there were one trained orderly – LAC Bowler, I believe, and Jan Tucker, who was still the 'minder' for the radio. It seemed inconceivable to us that anyone could recover the strength to return to us when existing on half of what we were getting. I, for instance, seriously thought about boiling up and trying to eat the leather tongues of my army boots. Even those of us who were deemed to be the most fit looked ghastly, and the less fit were so emaciated that within another month or two many of us resembled animated skeletons. God alone knows what our average weight was by then!

Sometime during September the Aussies took full responsibility for the radio and that enabled Jan Tucker to be sent up to join us. We never had any need to get Jan motivated! He brought in the latest news, dumped his kit and straightaway went off to see how he might help our medical orderlies.

I was only too pleased to pass on some of my responsibilities for the sick and dead to him. The deaths were few when he arrived but within a month he was voluntarily engaged in making crudely fashioned crosses for graves and helping at burial services. The crosses were made from whittled-down firewood lashed together with whatever he could devise and inscribed in poker-work. Nails, wire and finished-prepared wood did not 'grow on trees'! So, it was all down to ingenuity. Jan had plenty of that – and dedication. (There is an appendix of citations in this book, which in the case of Jan also highlights his additional work with the radio and his care for our naval ratings. He was awarded the Military Medal.)

With the Battalion fragmented and with no representation at base any more, it now became impossible for Tim Healy to know with any certainty who was still alive down there. Tim had been an operations clerk attached to General Percival's staff and nobody could have done our recording work better than he did. He had come to Appy's notice quite early in 'the piece' when he and Corporal North had been rescued from rowing boats onto Appy's junk – the *Hiap Hin* – shortly after leaving Singapore. It was good to have adventurous men like them around when the going was hard but even Tim with all his expertise never got to the end of the 'railway' period with a hundred per cent record of our Battalion state. After that, he was only able to account for the men who remained with him when we were permanently fragmented in May of 1944. By then our recorded deaths were 151 (30%). They were all young men who had been trashed out of their lives by the 'non-caring' bastards of Japanese, who I was now hating with a greater intensity than ever before.

'The summer never came for them again!
Just September, last September, in the rain!'

29

APALON – 84 KILOMETRE CAMP

Mid-September 1943

Sergeant Bullock had made another move up-country by the time we arrived at Apalon. By then the wireless was wholly and thankfully (but not, in my opinion rightfully) under the control of the Aussies.

September to October was going to be the last phase of the Speedo, it was said. There were more and more indications that that might be true by the increase in Japanese troop movements, of freight and of the sick, between the Burma and Siam railheads. We were greatly involved in all of this and in the building of the last of the bridges on our side.

It was worrying to know that our efforts were frustrating the Allied cause but our focus was by now almost totally on self-interest. Completion of the job spelt survival and – in the state that we were now in – any undue delay would have finished us all off. The building of the last bridge had been more than enough to prove that to all of the workers engaged there at night during the last of the monsoon rains. The work had been hazardous there at all times but it became even more so after completion, when the track had been extended beyond it and the rolling stock started moving over it.

If there had ever been anyone who thought otherwise before, they now realised that they were totally expendable. The Japanese had their teeth bared and their eyes on nothing else but completion for their emperor, regardless of the consequences to life and limb. There was no co-ordination, or care taken, when shifts were exchanged at night. It had always been difficult to distinguish sleepers from the gaps on bridges at night but things were far worse now. Many men

246

had near misses from being swept into oblivion by locomotives driven by unsighted and reckless crews. They were caught up in the dilemma of whether to do the stupid thing and make a run for it to the other side, or to drop down between the rails and hang there until the train had gone by above. Lieutenant Dicker and others with him were very nearly victims one night. So, although Apalon was a bit of a dump, we were all glad to move up there beyond the last big bridge and, moreover, with the bonus of being in a camp that had been free from cholera.

One thing that we focused on more than any other now was our stomachs. Some men were still stealing successfully despite the tighter and more manic supervision. The reward for success was obvious but the punishment for failure was getting so severe that thievery had become an undertaking for the desperate and the brave only. Gunner Charlie Ward was one of the Battalion who combined bravery with artifice. He was also one of those indestructible characters who was predestined to survive. He did that but, unfortunately, only at the price of steadily deteriorating health up to his death in 1987. We corresponded several times and in his letters he wrote to me about some of his POW experiences.

He was very ill when he wrote this one, and although that shows a bit, I think it is far better that I should use his own words:

I used to go for a walk in the jungle there; came out of the jungle once onto the line and saw a Tamil crouching on the end of the sleepers; spoke to him, no answer; gave him a push, he fell over, he was dead, so I left him at the side of the track; had a look later, he had gone; presume his mates picked him up [the letter continued in what I thought to be non-sequential form, but sadly although I have written *When?* on it at several points, he had died before I could get any answers. However, I now find his off-the-cuff remarks most helpful as reminders about things that I should have written about earlier. So, on we go Charlie!] We were at the 40 kilo camp; forty of us went back down to the 18th kilo camp to unload trains and build sidings; we had been working all day; the Japanese then picked us out for a night job – 8.30 start. We unloaded the lines and sleepers; – about 1.30, but the guard didn't want to go back then – (he would have had to go out in the morning) – so he said 'tenko 3.30!'. I had a scrounge round, picked up some

247

sweet potatoes and rice and fell asleep; a train woke me up; heard the guard shouting; don't know how long they had been standing there; gave my light bag to a mate and told the guard I had been asleep; I saw the rifle coming and I dodged most of it but got a broken nose and a gash across the top of my eye, – got a kick on my shins. I thought I would get done over at the guardroom but he dismissed us; when I woke up a couple of hours later, I was covered in blood. Went to Jock Fitzpatrick he cleaned me up but couldn't do much; after a couple of days my shin started to ulcer and the gash on my eye was going that way; a mate of mine came into the camp, Alf Perry; he was driving cattle from camp to camp. He was going back to Thanbyuzayat; he said he would see me on the return journey; he did! He had got hold of some yellow powder, Iodoform; put some small amounts on my shin and eye, within three days they were better; the guard was Gold Tooth; he also had one tooth next to it missing; I kept my eye on that guard all the time I was a POW, he would not have gone back to Korea when the war finished!...

I was in a camp called Tumy; we had finished a runway in the jungle; must have been 60 miles south-east of Saigon; we dug a trench round the camp 9ft by 9ft, the Japanese said we were going in there if the Yanks bombed Tokyo. Got back to Saigon, the Japanese guards had vanished, so Ron Matthews and I joined the MPs; the Japanese regular guards were still guarding us... [and then he wrote about his repatriation].

Charlie's potted history of events typifies a few days in the life of a POW: being beaten up; the chance encounter which enabled Alf to treat his wounds with about the only medicine capable of curing him; the desire for retribution and the ever-present threat – which would have been our destiny but for the atom bombs – that we were to be written off if the Japanese had been threatened with defeat solely by conventional means of warfare.

My mother was entirely to blame for the fact that by now my most persistent dreams were about Marmite. I was given my first taste of it when an infant and I was well and truly hooked on it before I could even read. She would point at the label and say how good

248

yeast and vitamin C were for building bonny babies. You all know how mothers will go on and how receptive their 'little treasures' can be during their formative years! So now, just when I needed bulk as well as content, all I could recapture in my dreams was a batch of six or eight large jars of Marmite and the words on their labels. It used to be only four small jars before I got so hungry!

Even though I might drift my way into sleep by counting sheep and hoping to eat them in my dreams, it was always those bloody jars of Marmite that got stuck in front of me once I had nodded off. It was not fair at all that nearly everyone else in camp was able to dream of juicy steaks and such like and then wake up still salivating with the sense of meat, two veg and lashings of greasy gravy on their lips. Surely somewhere in the whole of Burma there must have still been a few jars about which had been left by our retreating colonials in 1942! The Japanese would not have known the value of it any more than they had of the tins of butter that they had used for greasing the lorry axles in Fort-de-Kok.

I still have dreams about those days, and some of the better ones are only about the hunger that we suffered then. In one recent dream I was fantasising about a group of Buddhist monks being founding fathers of a present-day fetish of rubbing Marmite on the head to induce the growth of hair. I then jerked awake with the pictures of Graham Gooch in my mind and of some other character – who shall remain unnamed – who tried rubbing the liquid from boiled watercress on *his* bald patches.

However, there had been some sense in all that hallucinating in the past. A year before the Speedo, when discussing an escape plan with Captain Storr and others, I had said that I would pay a hundred pounds a jar for Marmite. But now – at the height of the Speedo – I would have given thousands for such a food, which in small amounts could flavour my rice for months, provide vitamins and – just as importantly – be free from invasion by foraging insects and germs.

Well! That ends the commercial, so you can switch on again!

Our most constant diet now was little else than pap – boiled slushy rice – for the morning meal and ordinary rice in the evening, of which very little now contained the valuable germ that I wrote about earlier. It was, however, still of the mainly filthy, dusty, rat-dirtied and weevil-ridden variety, which we were now having to glean from the floors of railway box-cars. Cooking it was scarcely a challenge for Bud Flannaghan, our newly appointed cook-sergeant. His most constant concern was in keeping a supply of water boiled up for drinking and sterilising. Thank heavens the disciplines started in Lower Burma had since been so well learned as to be automatic, now that cholera was rampant among the native workers. Nobby Clarke and his team were still keeping hygiene up to standard against all odds and with the exemplary co-operation of everyone else in camp. The reduction in both quality and quantity of supplied food had by now made the issuing of it even more of an exact science than before. It would have been quite unacceptable to have had either long *laigi* queues, or to run short before everyone had had their ration. Food was on everyone's mind all day and every day and not only did the mess orderlies do a good job but, to the credit of all, nobody ever tried to double-up no matter how hungry they might be.

Another big obsession for most of us was how to cope with the smell of extra food being cooked by our fraternity of master thieves. It was theirs by right of their legerdemain and daring, but knowing that did nothing to still the rumblings coming from the empty stomachs of the rest of us. Some men used to hang around in the hope that there might be a few crumbs offered from the rich men's tables. Most others – and I was one – would get away from the sight and smell of it as quickly as we could. My problem – as ever – was that I had no opportunities for stealing, while even our officer *kumi-chos* could from time to time pick up bits of food spillage from in and around the marshalling points outside. My only break came in opportunism – not stealing – and then only due to the adversity of Stoker Reg Keast when he went missing from a morning *tenko*.

Although it was I who had first discovered and reported his absence, it was as usual treated by the Japanese as an attempt to escape despite Reg having no kit beyond what he wore other than a blanket which was still on his bed space.

The Japanese Commandant-Sergeant made the men stay on parade while he took me off under escort to search for him beyond the rear boundary. I expected to find him just outside the wire and either seriously ill, or dead, but he was not there. The search then widened, and on moving into a small area of open land I saw a patch of jungle spinach. Within moments it was stashed in the pockets of my shorts and down the front into less salubrious regions. Shortly after that I was again searching with the guard in close attendance and the *gunso* looking elsewhere, when I heard a faint noise and then saw Reg curled up under a bush. He was whimpering softly like a baby.

The guard had just beaten me to the discovery. He had his rifle aimed, the safety catch released and, to my mind, was about to shoot.

I shouted, '*Gunso, sono haiti taksan beokee*,' and then, tapping my head, added 'damme-damme, malaria' as I swept the rifle aside. Fortunately the sergeant got my meaning, which in our disjointed lingua franca was 'Sergeant, this soldier very sick – out of his mind with malaria'!

I was then made to pick Reg up in a fireman's lift and stagger up the hill to the boundary wire. Once there, the inhuman bastards made me lower and drag him under without assistance before lifting him again for carrying through to the parade ground. I had run out of strength by then, so – still without any help allowed – I could do no more than sink to my knees and dump him. The sun was fierce by now and we were made to stand out in it for another two hours. The Japanese would not allow Reg a drink or medical attention and the only way that I was able to help him was to stand where I could protect him from the sun with my shadow.

The sick had been made to stand out with us and many of them flopped out during the next two hours. I am sure that I would have done so also in my exhausted and dehydrated state but for the protection of my old Dutch army 'straw'. Finally – and typically – without any explanation, I was allowed to get Reg off down the track to Khonkhan on a lorry. My diagnosis had quite obviously been accepted at last and thankfully also my hasty action in knocking the guard's rifle aside. I would have loved to have been able to swap my limited command of their language for the full understanding of their mind. That I am sure would have saved us from a lot of grief on many occasions!

Well, I boiled the spinach up and shared it with Tim, sparing him the knowledge of where most of it had been nestling while we were standing on parade. Many years later I discovered where Reg lived. On visiting him, I reminded him of the incident, but he didn't remember a damn thing about it! As for the spinach, that was the very last *laigi* that I tasted until after the railway was through and we had been evacuated to a place where my dream came true and I at last tasted yeast.

The rest of September and through into October remain as a nightmare period in the minds of all who suffered the final thrust of hell, starvation and inhumanity that led to the completion of the Railway of Death.

Thankfully, I neither need nor indeed intend to spell out the ghastly details of all that had happened and continued to happen up there until the survivors were evacuated. Those events were well documented many years ago and never more starkly than by Lord Russell of Liverpool in his book entitled *The Knights of Bushido* (1958), which with its subsequent editions, gives details of all the Japanese atrocities – some illustrated – and of the resultant war crimes tribunals.

Someone had to do that, and I am grateful to him – and others like him – for freeing me to continue with my story in my own way. Fortunately, that does not require me to put names to events that could still shock the families of those who died. No-one to my knowledge came home 55 years ago to tell them of the realities of the manner in which 'their man' died.

I (as did many others of the Battalion) went to see two or three families in order to hand over the possessions left in our trust. The inevitable questions came up. 'How did he die?' was the first question, and my stock answer would be that he suffered many illnesses like the rest of us but *died peacefully in the end*. That was an outrageous lie in so many cases. 'Where was he buried?' would be the next question, and then perhaps, 'In what manner?' The first part was easy to answer from the Battalion records, and it was always kindest to add – true or false – 'He was buried with due ceremony but, unfortunately, our crude crosses would not have survived.' I can and will spell out some of the facts as this story develops, but I will never mention the names of those who died in agony, or of the many that we were forced to bury without respect.

It may seem impossible to believe that there was one occasion when we actually showed compassion for the Japanese. Perhaps I had gone a bit soft in the head by then because it was I who sparked it off, despite my more abiding hatred of them.

252

The men were loading up wagons when around mid-morning a train drew up alongside, full of sick and wounded Japanese soldiers. It was still there when I came out with the ration party, to be told by our sergeant *kumicho* that they appeared to be unattended and distressed. We all knew what it was like to be halted in the sun and roasted within those wagons, but our Korean guards didn't appear to care a toss.

Perhaps it was that that led me to consult the others, and they readily agreed we must offer them some of our food and drink. It was such a spontaneous thing, and by doing it we scored more than just a moral victory. We had shamed the Koreans and shown the Japanese that though they might be barbarians, we were not. Further to that, when I went back into camp a far more liberal and nutritious replacement was cooked up for us in their own kitchen.

Their soldiers were on average younger than ours and – astounded by our action – many of them had responded with an '*arigato gozaimashita*'. Until that day *arigato* (thank you) from a Japanese had rarely been heard by any of us, and *gozaimashita* (very much) never. Although I had acted on impulse I was certainly not naive. They would never have done the same for us! Knowing that, I was soon cured of any further compassion for them and back to my basic belief that they were nothing more than a lot of barbaric bastards!

There were many of the Dutch and Aussie groups ahead of us at this time, and all of them were also being driven mercilessly to near destruction on starvation rations.

Until quite recently the Sumatra Battalion had remained for the most part united within one camp except for those at the base hospital; but now the Japanese had divided us so much that the administrative cohesion – at first only threatened – was finally fragmented. We never fully recovered from that position, and but for the fact that the railway was completed in October few of us would have survived.

Our deposed CO and our adjutant – Captain Apthorp and Lieutenant Dicker – had been left at Taungzan with the doctor and the *light sick* – a misnomer if ever there was one! Sixteen of the Battalion were literally worked to death there. They had been made to carry heavy loads of supplies over long distances and when any of them faltered they had been beaten into line.

253

None of us stayed very long at Apalon. The survivors from Taungzan were eventually brought up by rail to join us, and within a few days they were evacuated together with our heavy sick to the infamous 114 kilometre camp at Chaungara-La.

Heavy and light sick had never meant much other than a division between those totally incapacitated or expected to die on the one hand and, on the other, the dreadfully sick and emaciated men who somehow managed to keep going. Once the Taungzan contingent had moved off I was left with the so-called fit, who were mostly a skeletonic bunch of men capable only of working to see each day through with enough resolve and stamina to take on the next. Their chief concerns were the avoidance of any further injury or illness that would put them in our hospital. That place – and they knew it – was nothing more than a quieter hut in which to await death. In their perception, evacuation down to Khonkhan would have been even worse. They would have been on half rations there and remote from their friends. Unfortunately, it was for the latter reason that some who should have reported sick and left for 114 camp with Dr Hekking concealed their injuries instead. We were now left with only one medical orderly, who – apart from sympathy – had little else to offer than hot water, crushed charcoal and a few recycled rags.

We were all being constantly bitten by bugs, lice and mosquitoes. The great temptation had always been to scratch at the bites which irritated our skins to the point of distraction. That had to be resisted at all costs. Some of the men had obviously scratched and, whether done in their sleep or consciously, the result was always the same. The scratches became small ulcers and then, inevitably, developed and deepened right down to the bone. Any injuries that they had often went the same way because we had no means of checking them with proper treatment at any stage. The 'Hekking' treatment had cured ulcers and wounds on all parts of the body, but for some men left with me now it would be far too late to save them by the time we caught up with him again.

It would be wrong to entirely avoid talking about such things in detail but – as I said before – it is best done without mentioning names and places; so, where better than here at Apalon, where none of the following events took place.

There was more than one camp where I was unable to have privacy all the time and it was in one of those that I remember being involved in two cases that were typical of so many others. We were closely confined there for several days (and in unspeakable conditions) before I could get things sorted out. During that time we had been allowed little space in which to set up a large enough sick bay, so the overspill of patients had to be housed with the rest of us. When it wasn't raining many of us slept outside the huts to avoid the stench of the unattended and the cramped space. We had no lighting and I knew little of my companions until one awakened me in the half-light of an early morning. He was one of two Geordie mates whose spaces were about ten feet from mine. 'Sergeant-major,' he said, 'my mate isn't very well. Could you come over and have a look at him please?' I worked my way there, crawling over other men still asleep, and with every foot gained, the horrible stench increased. His mate turned out to be both conscious and rational, which, on examining him, astounded me. 'Sergeant-major,' he said, 'my arse doesn't half hurt!' We turned him over, pulled through the flap of his G-string away and then a piece of rag that was soaking wet. I was confronted by an ulcer of tea-plate size squirming with maggots within a mass of stinking pus. It was an horrific sight! He should have been in agony – if not already dead – with an ulcer like that. 'Well, Bombardier,' I said, 'you've got a nasty wound there but nothing that the orderly can't sort out. However, you will have to leave your mate for a couple of days to stay in the sick bay for treatment.' He was dead within 48 hours at most and – so I was told – he died peacefully and still lucid almost to the end.

We were in the same camp when I discovered that two of our men had (against orders) been supplying water to another who was 'blown up' with beriberi. They had also been getting his rice which was mainly in the form of pap. I was asked to see him too, and as before, when it was too late to save him. He had holed up in an otherwise uninhabitable shack in which he sat throughout the day dressed in nothing other than a Dutch army jacket. When I went in and sat beside him I was immediately aware of an unpleasant rancid smell. He had been eating very little of the pappy rice, but in his delirium, what he had left over had been stuffed into his pockets. He also died within a few days grossly swollen in literally all parts of his body. There were *some* remarkable recoveries, though, where men came back from the brink in much the same way as Private Nutter had earlier, and without the benefit of boiled bark liquid.

255

Dr Hekking never performed an amputation but he was fortunately able to loan his scalpels and assist an Australian doctor with a last-chance case. I witnessed that through circumstance only. I don't think that anyone would have been there given the choice, including perhaps the two medical orderlies and most certainly neither the patient nor I. I had been volunteered in with an Aussie to stand by in case the patient needed restraining, but, remarkably, the orderlies managed on their own by the use of some strapping on the good limb and an occasional whiff of ether. The doctors did have some surgical thread and that was a godsend. Apart from that, the whole operation was so primitive that the man shouldn't have survived, but somehow did so without any post-operative infection.

I was told that the same Aussie doctor had removed a man's appendix. Having no scalpel, he had improvised with the razor-sharp edge of an old-fashioned army mess tin. Also – as with the amputation – he had no gloves and had only been allowed to operate after dark by the light of a guttering palm-oil lamp and, inevitably, with his perspiration dripping down and around the incision area.

I had remained in Apalon with one of the junior officers and a small work-force of about 60 men. All surplus materials had to be cleared away and stacked, as far as possible, out of sight of aircraft surveillance. This was being done at night for this reason. It was soon completed, and then we also were on standby for a move.

Our advance party had been taken forward by train but I had been told to prepare for a night march of unknown distance in the company of just one stooge guard. The prospect would have been daunting even for men both fit and with footwear, let alone us. Just a few of us had boots and the lieutenant was the only one of us with socks that still looked like the original article. Our physical state was even worse. We so-called fit would hardly have passed muster within a geriatric unit. We were an emaciated and spent force.

However, we did at least have two days free from labour in which to prepare. In anticipation of casualties, we had stolen a number of rice sacks with which to make up stretchers, some of which were earmarked for carrying our equipment. We were also fortunate in having such a docile guard. Previous ones would have denied us the rice sacks and also gone ballistic when we finally loaded up with the rice buckets and cooking *kwalis* without asking permission.

Having divided the men into parties of eight for each stretcher, I took up the rear and the officer led off with the guard, who we just had to hope knew his way. It was pitch dark for most of the way and we stumbled along unfamiliar jungle paths snared with tree roots. It was around three o'clock in the morning that we at last reached a more open and moonlit path which led up to a ramshackle bunch of huts. It was then that I discovered that Bud Flannaghan (our cook-sergeant) was missing.

Apparently he had been with us right up to the point when we had left the main path. Quite unknown to anyone else other than two of his cookhouse orderlies, he had been lurching along on auto-pilot, delirious with malaria and assailed with diarrhoea. He had then presumably kept straight on when we branched off. I told the guard and then took two men with me to search for him.

We soon reached the main path, and then a bit further on it widened into an open roadway darkened with the shadow of the jungle on one side and eerily moonlit on the other. Having gone about one kilometre, calling all the time, we were startled to find ourselves right opposite a camouflaged Japanese stores depot with an armed sentry posted outside. He had obviously heard us approaching long before we came near him, but even so, it was quite strange that he continued to stand there without challenging us. I went over nearer to him and tried him out with the same '*ichi haiti taksan beokee*' jargon that I had used when searching for Reg Keast, but, instead of answering or shooting us, he just totally ignored me. It was all rather weird.

A bit further on we discovered Bud still lurching along and, for-tunately, still on the road, or we would never have found him. It was even more weird that he also hadn't been challenged as he went by. I can only surmise that the guard must have thought that we were locals and that Bud was tipsy.

Bud, poor chap, had defecated while on the move. Thankfully his fever had broken and we didn't have to carry him because, apart from the smell of ordure, he was soaked and sweat-ridden. I got his mates to clean him up and appointed two others (who wouldn't be handling him) to look for water and get some of it boiled up.

We wrecked out a hut for firewood and lit it from the nurtured embers of a fire that we had brought along with us in one of the

257

kwalis. Everyone else had by then flopped out to rest until daylight, including the guard, who I discovered sleeping propped at the end of an empty hut. His rifle had slipped from his hands and dropped to the ground. I too had been looking for somewhere to rest, and as I entered he jerked awake to the realisation that I had caught him napping. I went to another corner and drifted off within moments, all the more happily in the knowledge that he would now be forcing himself to keep awake.

Our temporary cookhouse staff – exhausted like the rest of us – still managed to have a meal of rice and dahl ready by daylight. After that (wonder of wonders) we were served with a 'presento' cup of tea by courtesy of the guard. He had already committed two heinous crimes, for either of which he could have been shot. Apart from falling asleep on duty he had not *tenkoed* us on arrival the previous night. Who knows! If I had told him about the sentry he might have thrown in a few biscuits as an additional sweetener to keep us quiet.

My conviction has always been that he was made to guide us on his own as some form of punishment. It certainly was not because he knew the way. We had had to backtrack twice. As guards went, he was a one-off docile character and quite obviously knew nothing about POW management.

Among our casualties we had other men suffering from malaria and a variety of stomach disorders. We also – and not unsurprisingly – had two men who had broken toes on tree roots. It seemed that we had been left so much to our own devices that we wouldn't have eaten but for our own foresight and might yet starve, because we had very little left.

Sometime during that morning a truck came up from the direction of the depot driven by an Aussie and with two Japanese guards – one a corporal – aboard. I spoke to the Aussie while the corporal was having a heated set-to with our guard. It turned out that the guard and I had been sleeping in a hut that had quite recently been cleared of the bodies of local cholera victims and fortunately (as the Aussie put it) I had been on the side from which survivors had been rescued. We were then told to put Sergeant Flannaghan and one or two other sick men on the truck, which (he said) would be passing the 55 kilometre hospital later on its way down to Thanbyuzayat.

If we had ever hoped that we might be sent *forward* on other empty trucks it was not to be. We had to remain there for the rest of the day and then, after an early breakfast the following morning, we were once again on safari, stumbling and cursing our way along in a pre-dawn mist. Apparently we had walked about 20 kilometres the previous night, and if that were so, the depot – as I found out much later – had been only part of a much larger complex somewhere between Kyondan and Anganan.

We had no idea where we were going to or how far that might be. Our physical state was pitiful by now. Three men had to be loaded on stretchers by the time it was light. That slowed us right down because I now had men who should have been on stretchers themselves having to take turns as best they could in helping to carry others. We were struggling along on an ill-defined path that led uphill all the way to the border plateau. That slowed us to a crawl and made our docile guard come to life and lash out in an attempt to urge us on. That had no effect on us at all because by then we just basically didn't care any more whatever he might decide to do.

It was around 11 a.m. that we topped the last rise, where the path opened into a large clearing around which was stacked pile after pile of logs, *atap*, bamboo and ballast. Right in the middle of that lot there was a tall stack of sleepers, from the top of which a Japanese instructor was leading a batch of soldiers in PT.

At last we were told by our guard to take a very welcome *sukoshi yasume* (little rest) and we thankfully flopped to the ground. It was indeed *sukoshi* because we were hardly settled there before a group of Japanese soldiers came over and made all of us except the stretcher cases assemble again to await our turn for PT.

I don't think that there was ever a time that I felt more angry and full of hate for the Japanese than then. We were indeed 'The Tattered Remnants' by now, albeit of their making and in fulfilment of their emperor's promise to work us to death. We had already been reduced from young and fit men to weaklings but yet that bastard on top of the sleepers obviously wanted his bit of fun as well.

He led us off with Swedish drill and we were soon tottering about like disjointed marionettes, to the derision of his cronies but not – in fairness to them – very many of the Japanese troops. The strongest of us tried to keep up with him but that was only done to prevent the Japanese from laying about the others for not trying.

I had never been more than average at PT except at press-ups, when I could take on the best; and that was our next exercise. We

259

all lacked strength but it was knack that allowed me to keep going. Each time I raised myself I got a view of that sadistic bastard above, lording like a rooster crowing on top of a dungheap. I can also quite clearly remember my thoughts at that time. I was praying that a flight of Liberators might wing in and blast him to hell off his perch, but there were no avenging angels up in the Three Pagodas Pass. He kept us at it relentlessly until we had all collapsed into a panting and gasping heap. Even then the gyrating bastard kept going awhile in a final display of contempt.

After that, we were allowed to pick up the stretchered men and move off. We crawled our way along for about four kilometres and finally crossed the railtrack to halt and be *tenkoed* at a guardhouse perched above a steep path. About a hundred feet below us within the jungle lay the squalor, pestilence and death of 114 kilometre camp, nicknamed Shangri-La.

30

CHAUNGARA-LA – 114 KILOMETRE CAMP

November 1943

Our main party reached 'Shangri-La' on the fourteenth of November to join large contingents of Aussies and Dutch. We arrived about ten days after them. We didn't know it then but for most of us, it was going to be our last railway camp: – and thank God for that!

Once the roll call was over we went through the posts marking the camp boundary and then straight down a steep jungle slope into a large area of tumbledown and scattered huts. Our Battalion – having been the last in – had been put in huts shored at the rear to level them against the hillside. I reported to the camp office, which in my absence had been set up by Tim Healy in the only place available to him, a triangular sloping space beneath one of the huts. The officers had been accommodated in the same manner and we late arrivals had to cram in above.

Chaungara-La was dank, depressing and gloomy. The sun only reached it fully by mid-afternoon. For the rest of the day the only light we got was random flickering through the jungle canopy. Living down there could be compared to being at the bottom of fish barrel; and I make that comparison advisedly because the place stank with pestilence, gangrene and death. That wasn't because they had lapsed in hygiene – although they had been stretched to the limit to maintain it – it was due to the rampant cholera epidemic within the ranks of those who had preceded us, POWs and locals alike. There were places where POW survivors had been forced out before they could properly close down camps by cremating all of their dead. Makeshift burials had been attempted here and there by infected men who had been left by the Japanese to tend their comrades until they too had died.

261

The thousands of Burmese who had been driven up there without any organisation or discipline – 200,000 it has been estimated – had left thousands of unburied dead. The poor devils had had no communal hygiene in place anywhere as far as we could discover. The matter and manner of disposal of their dead could be seen everywhere within the three categories: 1. a very few, competently; 2. thousands, random and shallow; 3. thousands just left where they had died with no thought of the consequences to those still living.

The surviving Burmese were now living all around us and were becoming a greater threat to us than ever before. Our area had no boundary other than the guarded plateau and track above. We were otherwise able to wander about below on the hillside. Sometimes we would meet them, though never by choice. They threatened us with contamination at every encounter.

Bob Grafton, whose hut was merely divided from some of them by an eight-foot *atap* screen, wrote:

The death toll among them was far greater than ours. They had no officers to speak up for them or any system of discipline to fall back on. They also lacked the indefinable stamina of the British.

They had very little sense of hygiene and were therefore prey to all kinds of diseases in spite of their advantage of natural immunity. The Japanese had paid them in the usual 'Mickey Mouse' money, with which they could buy nothing and therefore gambled and quarrelled among themselves to all hours of the night. The dead and the sick were pushed under the sleeping platforms, attracting millions of disease-carrying bluebottle flies. No kind of medical aid was provided for them although I did hear that there was a small British RAMC unit working among them somewhere along the line against impossible odds. It was a common occurrence for us to find one of their number either dead or dying in the bush anywhere along the whole length of the line. Their habits were a constant threat to our own efforts to keep down contagious disease. When we shouted at them for leaving one of their number under the bed slats dying and covered in flies, they showed complete indifference.

Another man wrote to tell me of similar scenes in more remote parts of the section and of one in particular where two men were drinking and laughing amid the stench of decaying bodies. It is difficult enough to understand how they could have been so uncaring for their dead let alone for their own safety.

There was certainly an air of malaise about the place which had been felt as soon as we walked down to the gloom below. The Japanese were openly afraid of descending amongst us and only did so in order to check that our reported dead *were dead*. If they wanted any work done I in particular was within sight and call for making up work parties or requesting them from the Aussies and the Dutch. Fortunately, only a few men were required on most occasions because even those were difficult to provide.

All but a few were at the end of their tether when I arrived and things got steadily worse over the next few weeks. The food was as bad – and sometimes even worse – than anything we had ever had before. The quantities were also less than before because so few were working. We could have well done with *more* than previously, if only for the fact that we were now in the hills and the nights were colder.

Death was peering over the shoulders of everyone and our toll mounted steadily each week. It was the same in the other units and remarkably so, considering our deprived beginnings in comparison to those of the Dutch and the Aussies, who were still overburdened with surplus kit. Quite unexpectedly and equally sadly, one of our earliest losses was Alfie Page. I had seen him looking more fit than most one day and, on the next (the eighth of December) he was dead. Our losses then took off, increasing to a further 38 before we left for Siam and nearly as many again after we arrived. All losses were directly due to the toll taken on their young bodies over the previous year.

As for the rest of us, most were so sick that by mid-December I could scarcely muster 20 men on any one day for outside work, and finally it was only 12, of whom one or two had to double as grave-diggers. Charlie Ward was one of them and it was a mystery to me how he managed to keep going.

Pinkie Tribe died on the second of January, mainly due to beriberi but compounded by a cocktail of all the other things that he suffered before. Shortly after that, we lost Nobby Clarke. They, like the rest who died, had unwittingly slaved to better our chance of survival.

I was as sick as any of the survivors at times and there was one

263

occasion when I had expected to die and another later when I most certainly would have, but for our timely withdrawal to Siam. Shortly after coming to this dreadful place I had had a touch of the runs. This was a common complaint that thousands of us had regularly suffered and taken in our stride. But then, things got rapidly worse as I progressed to the dangerous 15 to 20 visit state, beyond which so many of our Battalion had previously gone and rarely survived. But then I *moved back* – a very apt expression in the circumstances – on the Richter scale to the point where I was able to walk about with a little less caution. I can remember as if it was yesterday, sitting on the bed slats and making the momentous decision to risk a fart. After easing my backside up slowly (and with a fixed stare on my face) I released a plaintive but glorious WHEEP! What a wonderful reprieve! I was going to live! I didn't find the situation particularly amusing at the time despite liking lavatorial jokes.

My mother had to take the blame for my dreams about Marmite but it was my father and a young uncle who gave me my preference for 'farty' humour. My father started it all by insisting that my brother Dick and I should accompany him to see widow Barley (a herbalist and friend of the family) who was by then too old to continue in business. We would have far preferred to play football than walk from Clapton to Mare Street, Hackney. When we got there Dad knocked on the door while we (at first) stood uninterestedly out of sight listening to the welcomes and the enquiries about health. It was not very long, though, before we realised that the dear lady – afflicted with flatulence – was punctuating her remarks with a series of spontaneous and staccato BROOMPHS. Whenever we were asked to go there again we went willingly. Aren't little boys nasty young devils?

An incident in which my young uncle was involved came about when my two brothers Alf and Dick and I accompanied him to the Congregational Church at Watford. Uncle Ernie was both a cellist and the organist at his own church. He was also quite uninhibited and a bit of a wag! We were standing in a half-pew right at the back of the church. The service had commenced and the first hymn was about to be announced, when Ernie whispered to me, 'Eric, drop your hymn book – I'm about to fart.' Ernie was a fine musician but he obviously lacked synchronisation in the wind depart-

264

ment. My book whacked on the floor and then – at least half a beat later – Ernie came in with a sustained and unaccompanied blaster on the 'arsolio'.

Dick and I slid out of the pew and into the foyer nearly bursting with suppressed laughter. Ernie and my eldest brother Alf (who was trapped at the end of the pew) remained to glare and stare in mutual accusation at the folk who had turned round from the pew in front of them. Happy days! Memories of events like that were more than just a blessing for everyone stuck in this godforsaken place.

There was one other event I recall that though macabre, was nevertheless a matter of laughter for most of us, as we were by now almost inured to death. I was in a dreadful state of debility but still one of the few who could face a day's work in and around the camp. Fewer and fewer of the men were fit enough to mount the steep slope either to work outside or to act as pall-bearers or dig graves, so I had been doing some of that. It was therefore with relief that I was told that Appy particularly wanted to attend one of the funerals himself and would take my place. The cortège ascended, walked to the graveside and lowered the body. It was then that Appy became quite perturbed that it was lying humped up in the middle and he questioned why. One of the diggers told him that the ground was hard and there was a large boulder down there which they couldn't shift. In typical Appy style he said, 'You'll have to get him up again and dig the boulder out, we can't leave him like that! He doesn't look at all comfortable down there!' Good old Appy, say I; but I won't tell you what the gravediggers said!

The following gems come from Bob Grafton:

Throughout the night there was a constant traffic of sleepy men heading for the Pissaphone to urinate as the cold night contracted the bladder... It says something for the discipline of those sleep-drugged men that they staggered through the camp to urinate in the proper place in the name of hygiene ... I was visiting the latrines half asleep when I became aware of a bulky figure standing nearby at the next Pissaphone in the line. As my eyes became accustomed to the light the hair stood up on my head as I realised that this was an orang utang standing within a few feet of me. I had one further occasion to remember Pissaphones when I looked down and saw a giant praying mantis about to sink his fangs into my John Thomas. A well

265

aimed stream spoiled his lunch and he disappeared down the
pipe!

Bob must have been among the 12 so-called fit that I led out of
camp to work down the line at a camp near Nikki. I was in a worse
state of health that day than ever before and would not have gone
out except that the Japanese came down and grabbed me. I had a
badly swollen ankle which throbbed with the pressure of unreleased
pus from two ulcers which stubbornly refused to discharge. I was
also suffering from an overwhelming malaise and with breathless-
ness, due to all the other illnesses both of the past and those recurring. I needed two gasping stops on the 100 yard slope up to the
guardhouse, where we were given some tools and a large container
of water before moving off. We had been given no hint of our destination, or of the job to be done. I would normally have welcomed
the brightness and heat of the sun after the gloom of the valley
below. However, that day my leg throbbed more and more as the
sun got hotter – and the glare was making me dizzy.

We had only gone about one kilometre along the track when we
saw a Burman coming towards us. He stopped some way short of
us to reach into a bush and pick a bunch of leaves; and then – when
we were nearly level with him – I saw him start packing them round
a leg ulcer. That was enough for me! It was a case of 'when in
Rome' etc. So, ignoring the urgings of the Japanese, I too picked a
supply and secured a pack of them round my ankle with a sweat
rag.

Very shortly after that we got onto a path and, rounding a corner, we were confronted by two tattooed Thais engaged in a strange
form of boxing-cum-judo. They were leaping and lunging at one
another with leg strikes that stopped just short of contact. Whenever
a strike went close it was accompanied with a tap on the body of
the striker as if to say, 'I would have copped you a nasty one there
if it had hit'! We watched for a bit and moved off again to complete what was going to be a momentous and terrible day for us all.

We went on a little further before being halted opposite an abandoned camp. I was led over to the entrance, where a shallow trough
filled with disinfectant had been installed, and then along the boundary wire to view the grisly and grossly misshapen remains of
cholera victims scattered within. There were so many bits of bodies in there that it resembled a ransacked charnel house.

I didn't need any instructions to know what had to be done. The Japanese stayed over on the far side of the path with masks over their faces while we went through the trough.

We had walked in past unburied corpses and others washed out from scrapes where an attempt had been made to cover them. Beyond that we could see an area littered with the blackened bones of a cremation site. The whole place was reeking with infection. I have already mentioned being inured to death, but it was self-preservation – not callousness, or being brutalised – that caused me to say, 'If you see *anything* sticking out of the ground that can't easily be dug out just cover *it* over. Don't touch anything, don't lay your tools on the ground. All the loose bodies will have to be dragged over to burn above, and then be dropped into, the latrine pits.' The only way that I could cope with the situation was by seeing them only as *things* that threatened our lives. I gave instructions for some sleeping platforms to be removed and used as sledges for dragging the human debris over to the pyre while I went off to get matches from the guards.

It was a day-long task, during which we had nothing to eat, although in fact we wouldn't have wished to do for more than one reason. We went outside the camp to draw water from the large container which was boiled outside and drank from our own vessels cupped within leaves. The leaves were then burnt to ensure that we would take no contamination back into camp. There had been no possessions, clothing or identity discs found with any of the remains and the Japanese either couldn't, or wouldn't, tell us the nationality of those who had died.

It was nearly dusk when we came out through the entrance to disinfect ourselves and the tools. We took a last look at the glowing column of smoke and then we set off back towards Chaungara-La.

We had only gone a short distance before I realised that my leg had ceased to throb and despite all the activity of the day, I could walk instead of limping along. Having handed in the tools and purloined the container, we went below and warned that we might be contaminated. The only soap available was held by the orderlies in the hospital hut so we went there to wash ourselves in near-scalding water. In the process of washing myself, I had had to take the pack of leaves off from round my ankle. There was no longer any redness there or swelling and nearly all the muck had been drawn from the ulcers. The ulcers never erupted again and today the scars are scarcely visible. Whether there was any medicinal value in the leaves or not, I will never know because nobody could identify the bush.

All the time we were stuck below on the slopes we could hear the movement of trains above, for security reasons mostly after dark. The working parties had seen thousands of troops de-trained, rested, fed and then re-assembled for the journey through to the battlefronts. The opening ceremony had long since been conducted with some well-dressed POWs in attendance to hear the usual claptrap and the fulsome praise (see Appendices – Speeches) for the countless thousands of men sacrificed to the cause. It had been a great engineering feat but it never did live up to the expectations of the Emperor in any other respect than the number of dead per sleeper laid. The Japanese had expected to move up to 700 tons daily but they rarely achieved more than 300 because of the terrain and the threat to daytime movements.

The nightmarish conditions at 'Shangri-La' were getting worse and worse throughout December 1943. We had lost our second officer in early November and that set off a train of deaths that went on for three months more among the other ranks.

I hope to God that all our surviving officers fully realised what they owed to those men. I certainly did. Captain Apthorp had been 'up front' with me daily and we had 'fielded' our share of the 'flak' but there had been little input at any time from any other of the officers than Lieutenant Dicker. All the rest was achieved for us by the unremitting toil of the NCOs and the men. Every man who died on the railway made their sacrifice for the rest of us. They would not have seen it that way but that does not alter the truth of it. Each day that a man survived he was making a contribution to the relief of the others who would otherwise have been made to work harder and longer. There were times when some other units had been kept on 48-hour shifts.

Our recorded losses up to April 1944 show 2 of 19 officers (10.5%) and 149 of 481 men (30.1%). That first two-year period covers all losses directly attributable to the Railway of Death and it is estimated that a further 30 men died after that. I was inclined to just let those statistics speak for themselves in order to highlight the marked officer/men comparisons. However, there have been some ill-advised statements made by one officer that must be chal-

268

lenged, otherwise – intentional or not – they diminish the suffering and sacrifice made by the men. It is alleged that the Japanese had the same rations as we did, *the only difference being that they knew how to cook rice properly.* That is utter nonsense! The quantity, quality of additives, and their ability to supplement them by personal purchases, gave the Japanese a massive advantage over us. Where, may I ask him, were the emaciated guards suffering from vitamin deficiency diseases or, for that matter, our own officers, who, suffering from *any* diseases, had them compounded and the value of their food further diminished by gut-wrenching slavery?

Other statements made by the same officer were that the Japanese sick and wounded were reduced to half rations and that they were given the same sort of punishments as those given to POWs. Again nonsense! Half-truths fail by their omissions and those also fail on the grounds of quality and degree. Yes! the Japanese sick and wounded that we saw were hungry and had probably gone without food for many hours, but they would be getting rest, medicine and good-quality food at the end of their journey. What did we get? Also yes! it was the habit of the Japanese to slap one another in descending order of rank – from general down to private if need be – on a 'passed to you, Claude' basis, in admission of their shared guilt. No doubt a lot of that was done when the completion of the railway was delayed; but, where is the likeness between that trivial admonishment and the constant and sadistic battering of POWs either to get the last ounce of work out of them, or just for the fun of it?

Such statements do no good. Apart from being ludicrous they imply a false parity with the sufferings of those who, unlike the officers, died without the benefit of a protected lifestyle.

The last two or three weeks of our stay in Burma brought a mixed bag of events. The food did improve slightly but far too late to stem the increasing toll of the dying. There were also further reports of discoveries of POW graves, one of which was a mound surmounted by a cross recording the burial of a large number of Highlanders – Argyll and Sutherland, I believe. There were three other, but diminutive, mounds up there – the cairn-like pagodas that marked the pass and the boundary with Siam.

The only wireless news that I recall getting at 114 camp was of the Teheran Conference meeting between Churchill, Roosevelt and Stalin. However, the lack of news was more than offset for us by the sound of our planes heading for Siam on bombing raids.

We received our first (and for most of us our only) Red Cross parcel which when divided, amounted to seven items of food between fourteen men. I issued these to the hut sergeants, who then had to dispose of them by lottery. Tim and I shared a tin of Spam. Our next surprise was the arrival of Red Cross mail – *just one letter only*, for Gunner Yarwood, and he, poor fellow, died a few days later.

Christmas was celebrated with a sudden reduction of rations, which if anything, were even less for the following few days. There was no explanation from the Japanese, of course, but we suspected that they thought we had been sufficiently nourished by our half tins of Spam and the like.

I must confess that I was almost beyond caring by then, being not ill in the strict sense of the word, but so dreadfully weak that during the first days of January I was scarcely able to get up the slope to attend the burials. It must have been about the fourth of January 1944 when I went to the CO and told him that he should think about appointing a new BSM because I doubted that I could last another week.

We had not been able to weigh ourselves for a while but I guess that I was little above six and a half stone and, even then, heavier than many others much taller than me. I was dizzy with malnutrition and starvation and during my last walk up the slope, I was swaying and pausing to let the horizon swing round to catch up with me again. There were scores of men in the same state as I was – and many a lot worse – wondering when their turn would come to be carried up above. It would have been wrong to talk about 'atap-gazers' at Chaungara-La because those men who spent hours lying down there had not given up on life, far from it! Life had given up on them, young as they all were.

The Americans had joined us by now and they had come in with a last small detail of our men who had been clearing up a cholera camp down the line. Their story was that we were being reunited ready for evacuation. There had been several rumours of a move down into Siam but that had been the first real indication that it might be imminent.

It had been nearly two years since I had rowed out of Singapore

270

and in writing about it I mentioned that my brothers had alleged I was so lucky that if I fell into a sewer I would come up with a gold chain round my neck. Well, Chaungara-La was a sewer! I had been into it, but now fate was offering me a 'last chance link' that would enable me to escape death by the skin of my teeth.

The move was confirmed on the eighth of January. From that moment it was just a matter of summoning up my last reserves of strength to organise the evacuation. Stretchers were made for getting the sick up to the line, we had our last meal in Burma that evening; and then, we were on standby for the move at dawn.

It was the Japanese, of course, who had the last say about how we were going to depart. Before first light on the ninth a guard came down the slope and told the interpreter that our train would be leaving at 7 a.m. and that we were to start moving up at 6 a.m. Now whether this was sheer buggeration on the part of the Japanese or just officialdom between their 5th and 9th Railway Regiments we will never know. The train had already been halted 300 metres south of us and we were going to be made to claw our way up a slope there to get to it.

The interpreter did his best for us but he couldn't budge them. The border was there and that was perhaps the significant and literal point. Everyone (officers, men, the sick) who was not stretchered had to help with the 'carry' along the bottom and then with the 'lift' up the rugged face of a slope that was almost devoid of hand or footholds. We had to cling to bushes to hand the stretchers on and up.

It was sheer desperation that got us to the top with only 15 minutes in hand in which to be *tenkoed* and then entrained – 30 men to each wagon.

31

DOWN TO KANCHANABURI, THAILAND*

9 January 1944

The Japanese had told us that we were being sent down out of the jungle into a pleasant camp where the food would be good and the work light. We had heard that kind of thing before but for once it was going to be true.

However, first we had to get there. Our journey got off to a bad and very sad start. The train had just started to move when the guard had to flag it to stop. Signalman Bennett (Royal Corps of Signals) and Lance Corporal Nobby Clarke (6th Norfolks) had both died within minutes of being put on the train and they had to be carried back down the track to be buried alongside the other 37 men that we had lost in Chaungara-La. I was in no fit state to attend. One of our officers, the indefatigable Charlie Ward, and some of his mates were sent to conduct the ceremony and to back-fill graves that by now were being dug in advance. Signalman Bennett had earlier survived smallpox and Nobby Clarke had been our valuable hygiene NCO but fate had not offered *them* any last chances to escape the Railway of Death!

We at last got moving along the 430 kilometres of track that we had helped to build between Thanbyuzayat and Kanchanaburi.

A Japanese pre-war planning junta had estimated that it would take five years to join through at Kon Kuta, which was a few kilometres down the track from where we were starting now. Instead it had been done in ten months only and over some of the worst and

---

* With the railway completed and having crossed the border, this seems to be the appropriate moment to start calling Siam by its new name – Thailand.

most pestilential terrain that could be imagined, and throughout an entire period of torrential monsoon rain which in $3\frac{1}{2}$ months averages 40 inches a month. The impossible had been achieved with the losses of over 100,000 (50%) of a press-ganged local labour force and around 19,000 (30%) of the Allied POWs.

Before us now lay the 300 kilometres of track that we had heard about but which none of us had seen before. It was an awesome revelation! Despite our own preoccupation with sickness, heat and dehydration on the journey, there would have been few of us who didn't also marvel at the work done on the Thailand side. No-one but a maniac would have attempted to proceed faster than a slow crawl over the track leading to the plains below. Our route followed the meanderings of the river Me-Kwai-Noi, which in many places was flanked by an ancient and ill-defined trading path. At various points where these met, the Japanese had set up field kitchens, staging posts and transport depots. Everyone including ourselves was fed from the kitchens, and although the fare was always basic – substantially rice – the ration was both generous and livened up with vegetables, dried fish, soy sauce or other tasty additives.

There was no doubt at all that we were receiving Japanese army 'in transit' rations, so bang go those ridiculous assertions made by our laid-back officer. There is also no doubt at all that most of our 500 officers and men would have survived to make this remarkable journey, and done so earlier, if we had been given the same level of rations regularly. That thought would not have been a happy one for the Allies, though – particularly for those of our Forgotten Army, who were now about to suffer the direct consequences of its completion.

There was a rear locomotive attached to the train which was being used to brake our descent when necessary, and that was quite often. We lolloped and crawled our way over bridges that creaked with the weight of the train, causing many of us to think about the sabotage that must have been done by the POWs. There were large structures that were buttressed into the sides of slopes that had been blasted out to carry most of the weight on one side but depended entirely on a complicated structure of large timbers on the other. We crossed and re-crossed the river and its tributaries until we came to Hintok and Kanyu (named Hellfire Pass by the POWs). Hintok was the most awe-inspiring place of all and it needed no imagination to appreciate what it must have cost in life and endeavour to get the

273

Hintok 'Pack of Cards' bridge built. The men who worked there would have had no chance to scrounge off and hide (or thieve) in the vicinity, as ours had when doing similar but far smaller-scale work.

Medical reports and other archives (such as the details of the War Crimes Trials) have revealed that around 70 men were beaten to death while building this bridge. It was in five tiers, reaching to a height of 80 feet and shored into the cliff face at all intermediate stages by giant timbers. It took a further toll of deaths due to falls, crushing and other ghastly accidents.

By contrast our A Force – all of which was employed on the Burma side – had had a far better opportunity than most of those in Thailand to establish organised camps, and that was mainly because we were deployed in September 1942 before the 'heat' was on.

It was F Force on the Thailand side that suffered the greatest attrition. There were already about 50,000 POWs on railway construction when the Japanese – on the sixteenth of April 1943 – lured them up there on the usual pretext of a trip to well-appointed sites with good climatic conditions. They were mostly British troops that had been retained in Changi by reason of being older, the most sick or suffering from war wounds. There were 7,000 of them. They were brought up to Thailand and from there force-marched to the remotest parts of the jungle. They were driven along relentlessly to (and beyond) the existing construction areas, loaded with kit and other comforts for use in their promised land. At each nightfall the fitter men flopped out to await stragglers before eating their ration of cold rice together, tending the sick and wounded and then sleeping rough. Most of the men discarded kit in order to reserve their strength for the next day's purgatory. Those who fell out on the way had to be sought and assisted in by their mates. The poor devils who were finally unable to carry on had their skulls bashed in by the Japanese rearguard. Of the 7,000 men 4,000 were dead within six months. Many of them were caught up in the cholera epidemic, the survivors from which we had seen being evacuated through our side to Khonkhan.

That is the truth about those evil sods who controlled us. Even the above march pales into insignificance against that of B and E Forces. Those men – Australians, and finally totalling 3,000 – had been phased down to Borneo from Changi between July 1942 and

274

March 1943. Once their task was completed they were then marched and marched on to *complete annihilation except for six men* who escaped and hid up with hill tribes until the end of the war. That was not an isolated case of men being marched to death either. There were several similar marches carried out all over the Pacific in varying numbers and with the same intent. The only difference between them – apart from numbers – was that Japanese in their 'mercy' shot all the stragglers in Borneo instead of battering them to death. We were indeed lucky to have been taken prisoner in Sumatra and assigned to Burma, albeit we didn't think so at the time!

It was just as well that we already had experience of slave travel over long distances because this journey was going to be as bad as any other before in many respects. Apart from the more spectacular sections, there were intermediate stretches of the route where we just drifted slowly along through a swathe of vegetation that was close enough for us to pluck leaves as we went by. It was inevitable that many of us would be caught short and then have to suffer the disgusting and hair-raising indignity of being supported at the door entrance while relieving ourselves. For those who were stretchered it was even more disgusting. A space had to be set aside and padded with leaves on which they had to defecate, and then the mess had to be cleared away. Several of those men would unfortunately see little more of Thailand than those jungle trees, and after that, a few days of fruitless care in Kanchanaburi camp before they died.

We continued down through the jungle over a large viaduct, across the *real* bridge over the river Kwai Yai and finally through to the plateau below scattered with rich and fertile fields of rice and other crops.

(Just for the record it should be known that Kwai Yai translates as a large tributary, and in this case, of the Mae Klong river. The original bridge was long ramshackle and made of wood. It was ultimately replaced by steel span-sections brought up from Java and assembled about 60 yards upstream; and from the day it was installed it suffered from a series of bombings which lasted through to VJ Day.)

It was nearing dusk on the second day of our journey, when we had cleared the last of the thick shrubland, that we suffered our first death in Thailand.

Our second locomotive had been released for its return journey as soon as we were (thank God) clear of the pest-ridden jungle, and where we might at last get soap with which to clean up our stinking bodies and clothes and free us from the ever-present attentions of body-lice.

It was around 9.30 p.m. and quite dark when we saw the lights of Kanchanaburi. Shortly after that we were coasting along towards a darkened camp and the sounds of temple gongs being beaten to the accompaniment of chanting priests. The train halted a short distance from the camp, where we were *tenkoed* and then marched up, handed over to the resident guard and bundled into four huts.

It had been an eye-opening but disgusting and tiring journey. No-one greeted us on arrival. So, having located the latrines for the benefit of all and the sick bay for the orderlies, I went to join Tim Healy, flop out, and be lulled into sleep by those distant and persistent temple gongs.

The world goes none the lamer,
For aught that I can see,
Because this cursed trouble
Has struck my days and me.

The stars of heaven are steady,
The founded hills remain,
Though I to earth and darkness
Return in blood and pain.

Farewell to all belongings
I won or bought or stole;
Farewell, my lusty carcase,
Farewell, my aery soul.

Oh worse remains for others
And worse to fear had I
Than here at four-and-twenty
To lay me down and die.

A. E. Houseman

In Memoriam

PART THREE

32

KANCHANABURI – ALIAS KANBURI – ALIAS THE 'AERODROME CAMP'

14 January 1944

We awoke around dawn to receive the happy news that breakfast was being prepared for us by a Dutch force that had been in residence for some time. They had things well organised and as each contingent arrived from Burma its nominees were integrated with camp workers doing medical, cooking and hygiene jobs.

It has been estimated that there were eventually about 40,000 Allied troops scattered in and around Kanburi. Within our half of what was a strictly divided complex, we were soon meeting batches from all the units who had been with us in Burma. The survivors from the original American force of 190 had got in shortly before us with men from Dutch units that we had never met before.

We had marched in the previous night along the outer perimeter of a tall palisaded fence that enclosed three sides of an adjoining camp which held some of the British POW survivors from the Thailand camps. Although the inner fence was lower and of far more open construction, the Japanese had ordered that there must be no fraternising between the two sides.

One of the reasons given for that was that the men on the other side had already been *vetted* for onward transit to Japan by Heguchi (*their horse doctor*) and his staff. Presumably they were guarding against cross-contamination from us, in the interests of all within the Land of the Rising Sun. That was sensible, of course, but they had no hope (if that also was their intention) of keeping us from exchanging news or renewing friendships.

I can recall every detail of the events of that first day in Kanburi and I will give you the bad news first.

It was Gunner Harris of 30 Battery RA who had died during the last leg of our journey. Captain Apthorp had by then re-assumed command in the eyes of all but the Japanese and he decided that we must keep quiet about it in order to ensure that he would get a proper burial; and then Fusilier Cree of the Northumberlands died shortly after we arrived and an urgent double burial service was necessary. Before the end of January another 16 men of the Battalion had died. There was similar attrition in all the other units.

The previous night when I was arranging accommodation for our sick, a Dutch orderly had told me that one of his men had committed suicide on the railtrack that ran into the back of our camp. The unfortunate man had just received news of the death of his wife and a child who he had been forced to leave behind in an internment camp. I have many times since then thought with some amazement that none of our Battalion committed suicide, went mad, or, for that matter, indulged in cannibalism, as some of the Japanese fighting men did later. Russell Braddon, who wrote *The Naked Island*, tells of the time when survivors from the native work camps came to Kanburi and how they were abandoned to die there with little food and no medical facilities. Dozens of them had dashed out in groups to throw themselves on the track, leaving the rails so slippery with their remains that the trains had to struggle to regain traction.

However, in so many respects Kanburi really was a Shangri-La. Breakfast arrived in the form of rice well laced with shintegar and the ration was generous. I was seeing the food queue through when a Dutch NCO told me that we newcomers from the railway were to be given an *extra* ration of yeast that day and – wonder of wonders! – any surpluses would *as usual* be on sale at 10 cents a tot. I discovered that the kitchen contained three large vats of yeast and that everything that could ferment was being added to them. This reminded me of the time when we had stayed in Cape Town for a few days, where it was alleged that the illicit stills were topped up with all kinds of gruesome additives that were best not enquired about too closely. I am sure that everything was well regulated in Kanburi, though, and boiling would in any case take care of the less savoury elements of the brew. Yeast conjured up visions of my obsession with Marmite and because it was not popular with many of the men, I was able to indulge in four or five extra tots on most days. I was at last able to spend my Japanese Monopoly money to good effect and within a few days my health started to pick up.

That first day was spent in a rush of both purposeful and happy activity. Having been *tenkoed* and informed that no-one would be required for work parties that day, Tim and I set about organising the integration of our 'in camp' staff with that of the other units. The amenities were still quite basic but with this air of new hope we thought that anything like occasional miracles might yet happen to save a few of our sick men, and they did! Our medical orderlies had discovered that a small supply of drugs and some medicines such as quinine and sulphanilamide were already being smuggled into camp. Purchases were being made on promissory notes for payment when the war was over. It soon became well-known, and an equally well-kept secret from the Japanese, that all such items were being brought in by a very brave Chinese trader* who had been allowed to set up shop in the adjacent camp.

The Japanese had to allow us controlled access into that side for water, and our carriers were soon coming back with almost unbelievable tales about a canteen stocked with such things as eggs, sugar, pomelos (a kind of grapefruit), dried fish, Thai sweetmeats, soap and tobacco. Much later (when the men destined for Japan had moved out) we got far more direct access to that side. However, it was during the first day or two that our needs were most urgent for getting some of our worst sick off the danger list. I was only just pulling away from a life-threatening state and, with no access to the other side myself, I had contacted a sergeant there and offered him a percentage to buy things for me. I am far from being naive but that seemingly genuine character just took my money and never returned to the fence again. Such men were pariah and they rated no better than one of mine who was discovered stealing the blanket off another dying in the hospital. Fortunately for us, the Dutch had established an orderly room and a camp jail. I had already taken the drastic action of naming and shaming the man before the assembled Battalion, despite the fact that he was wheeled in to the orderly room later. It took two NCOs to restrain him and, while he was being charged, he attempted to pick up the bamboo table and hurl it at the CO. The outcome of that was a surprise to all and not least the offender. The Dutch must have had equally violent men to deal with before we arrived so they had cross-braced the table legs and sunk them deep into the dirt floor.

* After the war he was awarded a well-deserved decoration for his work.

All orders from the Japanese came via the Dutch, whose senior officer was in overall command, which was just as well for the Sumatra Battalion because our own officers had resumed their fannying about. We NCOs kept aloof from their posturing and saw no good reason why we should give other than token allegiance to the faction that we regarded as usurpers.

Two or three days after our arrival Captain Apthorp decided to take our parade and we found that we were one man short. Although we knew that he had gone over to see mates in the other part of the camp, it was decided to report him as *takusan byoki* and in the *benjo* (very unwell and in the lavatory), hoping that he might yet get back over the fence in time for the parade.

It was a fifty-fifty gamble but, as it happened, we had walked right into trouble because the Japanese already had him in their custody. He was paraded in triumph before us by some of our most despicable Korean guards from Burma. The outcome was predictable!

All the officers and I were brought before them for special punishment. First of all we got a beating with bamboo canes from the 'parade guards' and then from those in the guardhouse. After that we were put into two facing ranks and made to slap one another about the face. My clearest recollections of that demeaning procedure were of Captain Davies carefully removing his spectacles, and myself asking my opponent (a reluctant second lieutenant) not to hold back. The Japanese would have been only too pleased to extend the ceremony if anyone had slacked. We were then paraded with the rest again and made to watch the culprit being beaten up.

I am sure that the man would not have thought so at the time, but he was lucky (so the Dutch told us) in comparison to previous offenders. There were men in our side of the camp who had been made to stand night and day within a four-foot-deep pit filled with water and without food or drink for as long as their sentence lasted. Inevitably there were some who succumbed to sunstroke, fever or exhaustion, and when they drowned they were left there for a day as a visible warning to others.

They had a total disregard for our dead. Twenty-six of our number died in Kanburi, and once I was up and running again I led out four burial parties. The first part of our journey was by lorry, across the flat and rather featureless plain west of Kanburi – the so-called aerodrome strip. The rest was done on foot along the raised ground of what appeared to have been sections of reclaimed paddy fields. We had a two kilometre carry to the rear of the cemetery to a line of graves dug ready for the day's intake. We brought the bodies to the graveside on the usual bamboo and rice-sack stretchers and then we were made to release one side and tumble them in. There were no boards or ropes with which to perform the job with dignity and respect. We were not allowed a preacher or time to pay our respects properly to them. The best I could manage was as much of the Twenty-third Psalm as I could remember while the guard shouted his *kuneros* and *buggeros* for us to get off the site. No markings were allowed and very few of the men had identity tags. Long may those Japanese rot in hell for their unfeeling behaviour!

It was tragic to see so many men of all the nationalities being taken from the camp on their last journey while the rest of us were rejoicing in our new-found plenty. What with the canteen, the vastly improved climate and no great demand for heavy or sustained work, most of us were soon improving in both health and disposition. Recreation was organised and welcomed and it could be said that we invented the forerunner of what later became the BBC's *Just a Minute* programme.

The British, Australian and Dutch were challenged to provide contestants. Each man in turn had to draw a subject and then immediately talk about it for three minutes without any hesitation. There was already a large raised stage in our part of the camp. A prize of six eggs had been put up for the winner from the three specially selected contestants who were to appear for the finale.

I can only remember one of those three. He was an Australian doctor of philosophy and the eventual winner. Quite notably he had managed to learn Japanese to such a fluent and high standard (and without the benefit of textbooks or dictionary) that the Aussies had been using him as their unofficial interpreter in preference to the well-schooled and officially appointed Dutchman. Unfortunately, he was very sick in hospital and expected to die. However, his mind was still in top gear. When his turn came he was carried up onto the stage, placed on a chair and supported by two of his mates. There will be very few of the hundreds of men who witnessed his act who have forgotten it and perhaps even fewer who knew the meaning of his subject when asked, 'Say all you know about conchology.' I still retain a mental picture of him launching into his discourse on the subject of shells for three minutes without hesitation or repetition. It was a remarkable performance by any standard, and particularly so when we heard that soon after being carried back into the hospital he had died without getting a taste of even one of his eggs.

We were now so closely integrated with the other groups that the extent of their possessions was on open display more than ever before. What a bonus it would have been for our men while in Burma to have owned not only the many changes of clothing that we already knew about, but also some of their books, playing cards and board games. The Dutch in particular were now bringing out their chess sets and challenging some of us in organised competition. We had very few competent players and nobody at all in the same league as one of their officers. He took on eight of our best players at the same time and beat the lot with ease, making his immediate responses to their moves as he walked past. He also took on the best of his opponents individually and unsighted, playing on a board that was lettered across and numbered vertically in order that moves could be communicated while his back was to it. He won those games easily as well.

The Dutch had another outstanding character, who practised hypnosis and reputedly was able to control and immunise his subjects from pain.

As far as I know I was the only member of our Battalion who had taken the trouble to learn Dutch, and only then in order to stimulate the grey cells. Otherwise it was a rather useless occupation since most of the Dutch were quite competent in the English language. However, it was no doubt due to my very basic knowledge of their language that some of them preferred to see me if they wanted interpretation of things that they had heard said in English but misunderstood. The most memorable request came from a Dutch cook, who asked me to explain something said by one of ours.

'Sergeant-major,' he asked, 'what did your man mean when he said *the fookin fookers fooked*?' My Dutch teacher would have been convulsed with laughter both at my attempt to elicit the circumstances of the event and at my endeavour to explain the words. I knew our man, of course, and moreover, that he was a Geordie whose conversation revolved around a dialect laced with almost unintelligible oaths. Having finally discovered that he had been stirring rice with a large 'paddle' that had broken, I then had to convey the meaning in Dutch. It went something like this: 'The fookin fooker *het rijs-schep was*; fooked, *is het zelft als gebroken*', which

I hope he understood to mean that the 'fookin fooker' was the rice paddle and 'fooked' meant broken. I believe he got the message but he left me with the hope that if he came back with further questions they would be about something far less complicated, such as explaining the rules of cricket.

I had been sending out small working parties quite regularly and became envious of them when they returned with tales about the life outside and the many opportunities for buying extras.

The time finally came when I felt fit enough to go out. I had assembled a working-party of about 20 men outside the camp to await transport by lorry. The day started well. We were waiting beneath a large tree burdened with ripe figs, which we very soon harvested.

The lorry took us to a Japanese HQ two miles away on the other side of Kanburi. We were under the care of a tame and miserable little scroat of a Japanese guard who tried to act big but was in fact all wind and wee-wee. We had to move various shrubs about within the grounds to the rear, and the men were soon making the most of our docile guard. Childish as it may seem now, they were working off their venom for the whole Japanese military by inviting him – among other well-chosen phrases – to 'F—— off, you little yellow bastard!' We were not doing war work, so the Japanese would have had every right to make me join in with the others. However, my own protest was in making it clear that I would only work if I thought it was good for my health. We had been working for about an hour and during that time I had noticed someone leave the main buildings, move our way and then disappear behind some shrubbery. From that position – and quite unsuspected by any of us – he had moved up under cover to within about ten yards of me to watch and listen to us.

I was therefore quite startled when he stepped into the open, and calling in immaculate English asked, 'Who is the senior NCO in charge of this party?' Guessing that he must be a man of rank and importance, I did at least have the presence of mind to reply, 'I am, sir.' He then stepped back more closely into the bushes and beckoned me over to stand there with him. My first thoughts were that I was going to get a nice and private beating-up and then, unless it was my lucky day, be handed over to the Kempi for further treatment.

It was indeed my lucky day, because all he wanted to do was question me about my views on the outcome of the war, and the manner in which he led up to the subject was astounding.

He started by saying, 'I heard everything your men said when they were swearing at and abusing that soldier.' Before I could make any reply to that he said, *'Just think yourself lucky that you don't (as I do) have to eat and sleep with such men!'* There then followed an explicit assessment of the average Japanese soldiers that he had to associate with daily, who, he said, were mainly brutal, disgusting in their general habits and many of them perverts of the lowest order. There was no answer to that, and, in any case, he had much more to say to me before I was expected to reply. 'I just happened to be in Japan on business when war was declared,' he said, 'having recently arrived from England, where I had lived with my British wife in Manchester for twenty years. I was first detained and then, – because of my knowledge of English – recruited for service within various Japanese HQs. While working in those places I have been appalled by the callous, bestial and sub-human behaviour of my associates, most of whom I am ashamed to acknowledge as fellow countrymen.'

He carried on in this vein and I was only too happy to continue listening, while trying to decide if this was just a clever line of talk aimed at getting compromising disclosures from me later. He did eventually ask questions and then I had no choice but to reply.

The first were about our work on the railroad and how we were treated, to which I only gave factual replies about starvation and deaths due to deprivation. I also told him that he was asking me to take a great risk in speaking the truth to him because my opinion had never been invited before, and had it been volunteered, I would have been beaten up. 'Who do you think is going to win the war?' was his next question. There was something in the furtive way in which he had been hiding himself from view from his HQ building that finally made me realise that he also was putting himself at risk and therefore must surely be genuine. I decided to give him my blunt opinion but at the same time to lead into it as diplomatically as possible.

'There is no doubt,' I said, 'that Japanese forces are seasoned, dedicated and brave and that they will be hard to beat. However, as soon as the United States had been forced into the war by the Pearl Harbor attack, there had never been any doubt about the outcome.

For every plane lost they can produce another ten if need be, whereas your output can only diminish.' And then, with an 'ah so' and a bow, he turned and went back through the bushes to rejoin his detested countrymen.

That meeting for me was the second (and the most remarkable) exception that proved my conviction that our captors – as a whole – were a lot of bastards.

33

RUMOURS, INCIDENTAL EVENTS AND PARTINGS – KANCHANABURI

February/March 1944

Almost from the day of our arrival there had been rumours that we would be off to Japan in a few days. There was also the other oft-repeated rumour that the officers were going to be moved out into another camp and then compelled to work. Much of that was eventually true.

During late February a large contingent was moved from the other side to a camp about five kilometres away. A week or so after that the interpreter told us that we were to be injected against cholera, given a blood test and tested to see if any of us had dysentery, and that set off a more sinister rumour that – with the railway job done – the Japanese were about to exterminate us by means of a lethal injection. There were some gullible men who swallowed that yarn hook, line and sinker, but reason alone convinced most of us that it couldn't be true, because those who had left us earlier had had the same treatment and we saw some of them from time to time.

The day before the vet Heguchi was due to examine our 'herd', I told the men that we were all going to be given a jab, prick and a shufti – the latter word being Arabic for a look-see (thus, the further British Army word 'shuftiscope' for the instrument used for rectal examination and the even more explicit Aussie army phrase, the 'dung punch'). I told the doubters that they should view these treatments as a 'passport to freedom', and that the bad news for any would-be objectors was that every man would be issued with a numbered identity tag which must be handed back to the Japanese tallyman.

The following day we gave our smear of blood, endured having a wide-bore horse-needle being jabbed – in some cases thrown like a dart – into our buttocks; then came the pièce-de-résistance! The last vet assistant rammed a thick piece of bent fencing wire up each backside with obvious personal delight and total disregard for any internal damage that might be done.

At the end of all that, most men viewed the treatment as *anything but* a passport to their freedom. Among those can be numbered the inevitable few who flaked out at injection time and the many who leapt into the air as the wire got to the parts that no other wire had reached before!

I did not volunteer myself out on any other work-party. On reflection that may have been a wise decision because many of those who did go suffered illness through eating badly cooked or contaminated food, particularly river shellfish.

The food in camp was good anyway, and what with that, the yeast ration and our vastly improved mode of living, I was soon putting on weight again and must have reached eight stone by early March. The most abiding memories for me are of the continual chanting and gong-bashing from the temples and the rumour (which unfortunately turned out to be true later) that some men had been tortured and then killed for running a wireless set. There but for the grace of God etc. ... and one of the most incongruous things was witnessing the slap-happy interaction between the American Captain FitzSimmons and his command.

Our Captain Davies didn't rate great respect in the eyes of most men of our Battalion but they responded when called to attention as he joined us on parade. In contrast to that, FitzSimmons was treated with total disrespect and never did anything about it. I recall seeing and hearing him one day as he relayed the day's instructions to an outgoing work-party assembled in line about ten feet in front of him.

'The goddam Japanese,' he said, 'have ordered that you must salute their officers both in and out of camp! What do youse boys think?' His 'boys' were hunched before him in slovenly disarray and as each of them gave their opinion it was accompanied with a gobbet of spit that plonked into the dust near his toecaps.

* * *

289

Shortly after that incident came the final fragmentation of the Battalion as the Dutch Commandant received orders to assemble 500 men identified by Captain Heguchi as suitable for sending to Japan.

Captain Davies (who still clung tenaciously to his joint and nominal last few days in control of the British/American contingents) ensured that Captain Apthorp left with our first draft of 80 men, taking Tim Healy (and the Battalion records) with him to the main assembly camp at Tamarkan. We had left about 50 men back in Burma and they were sent down direct from there to join that party. Also, Sergeant Pat Fox (who had been sent back up to 114 camp with 30 men to do maintenance and clearing-up work) came down to Tamarkan later and stayed there during a time of severe Allied bombing. There were still about 70 of our men left in Burma doing similar work under the command of lieutenants Pocock and Power. That group stayed on there well into 1945 and just how many of them survived has never been exactly determined.

I had taken a calculated decision in holding back from the first Japan selection, since included within it were the two gangs of rogues who I would be only too pleased to be parted from. Eventually just a few of our very sick men were left in Kanburi. I was sent off as the *kumicho* in charge of 150 men, of which only about 10 were of the original Sumatra Battalion. It turned out that we were also part of a Japan party being sent via Singapore, where we would first be staying for an undetermined period to work on the docks. An officer with limited medical knowledge accompanied us, Dr Hekking having already been drafted out to Tamarkan.

So that was that. 'The Tattered Remnants', 'Appy's Locusts' – call them what you will – were now scattered to the winds and I was the poorer for having lost the chargeship of a remarkable, loyal and stoical band of men.

I estimate that about 60 per cent of us got back home, half of whom I caught up with again a few weeks before repatriation.

PART FOUR

34

THE FINAL BREAK-UP AND THEN, OFF TO SINGAPORE

26 March 1944

The medical that we had was a lot of nonsense really. Although the injection was welcome the yardstick for selection rested on whether you were a sufficiently fat member of the herd to endure the sea journey to Japan and arrive there still tough enough to do slavery in their mines.

Of the 2,000 men selected, nearly all eventually started out but for various reasons only a very small number of them actually arrived. However, more about that later!

I could have only been excluded from the earlier drafts due to my light weight, because, although I had dysentery at that time, it couldn't have been detected during that crude inspection or I would not have keen kept on their list for this later draft.

On the twenty-sixth of March we too were readied for moving out. We were assembled alongside the embankment-cum-platform at the rear of the camp to be searched. That – as for the groups that had already left – was to be a special search conducted by the much feared Kempi-Ti, who were well known to be ruthless and, supposedly, astute. When it came to astuteness they were never in the same league as Appy's Locusts. After all, we had for the past two years – and to a very considerable extent – been surviving by thievery and deception.

Knowing that the Japanese had rarely moved us without at least one false start, and also how lax they became on completion of a search, our evasions were just as simple as on previous occasions. The Kempi searched quite thoroughly and then, quite predictably, having found nothing, they just formed up again and marched out of camp, leaving us in the care of our guards.

After that we were left to wait and wait until the bamboo gateway over the track was opened to let in our train. Long before that happened our guard had – as ever – become more and more slack until those of our men staying behind just mingled with us to fraternise and hand back the 'hot' items that we had left in their care. Among those were my few personal records of Battalion events, sketches and compass. The only check made after that was a further *tenko* to ensure that 151 bodies got on the train. Then, amid a chorus of farewells, our engine shuddered and hissed its way out onto the branch line that led to the main Thai–Malay route via Bampong and Non-Pladuk.

The wagons that we left in were only used on that branch line and we enjoyed a comfortable and uncrowded journey on them. When we transferred to the main line we were bundled into those familiar and dreaded steel boxes to endure the further 1,200 miles down to Singapore. *That* journey was a four-day nightmare of overcrowding, almost unendurable heat during daytime, and then cold at night, once the wagons had cooled.

As usual, no water had been provided for us and we were having to alternate squatting and standing to allow lying space for the sick. Two of them died, perhaps for no other reason than, though fevered and dehydrated, neither they nor their companions had any water left. (We had travelled longer than expected without halting on the first day and had no means of forcing the train to make an unscheduled stop.)

During scheduled stops we fed at wayside townships from Japanese field kitchens as we had done in Sumatra when going north to Medan two years previously. There was always some sort of liquid provided with our rice ration and the more watery it was on our present journey the better. Other than that, the Japanese only doled out about a half a pint of water per man, and that was sweated out of us again within minutes.

One of the first things that we did – even before queuing for our food – was to stop by the engine to catch the watery droplets from its oily steam-vents and then walk beneath the bowser to cool ourselves and catch the spillage from it as it was swung over to top up the boiler. We were all so desperately thirsty that we drank any water caught without caring that it might be contaminated. It was Hobson's choice! We had no means of boiling anything, except during two life-saving stops when we were shunted off the main line to let more urgent traffic through.

The most memorable event on that terrible journey was when (on pulling in for food) we ran slowly past a halted Japanese 'comfort train'. Each windowed compartment of it framed a full-faced and rouged-up young girl on display to a waiting column of Japanese troops lined up ready to gang-rape them. I shall never forget that scene. The girls' faces reminded me of a set of brightly painted wooden dolls owned by my sister Nancy. They too were somebody's sister or daughter, and I remember my hope that at least some of those men would be satisfied with only talking with them and wait for other comfort when offered without compulsion.

Our journey followed the old east coast route flanking the Gulf of Siam and then crossed to the west of Malaya and onwards down to Johore. The earlier gatherings of civilians seen in Thailand and the northernmost part of Malaya had seemed contented and in reasonable shape. However, the further south we went the more we were confronted by disillusioned and half-starved people, in particular from among the Chinese communities. When trading they were supposed to accept our devalued Monopoly money only. So one far-sighted trader became quite ecstatic when I bought up the whole of his stock – for a share-out in our wagon – using one of my 20-dollar Malay notes. He voiced the disillusionment of all the other traders with the inequalities of the so-called Co-Prosperity Sphere. He told our Malay-speaking officer that the Japanese always demanded the best and expected to pay little or nothing in return. We were, of course, selfishly pleased to hear that, hoping that that short-sighted policy would hasten their downfall.

Even the Malays were losing their *tidak apa* (another day will come) carefree attitude to life with every mile that we travelled towards Singapore.

The final evening was spent covering the last 200 miles approach to the causeway, and if ever there had been a right time for me to reflect on the past and look into the future, it was then.

Rattling over the 30-foot-wide link from the mainland to the island seemed symbolic to me of the final cut with a past over which I had had considerable influence and input. In contrast (on reaching the island) I had to pick up the challenge of a new venture, in the company of a largely unknown band of men and moreover, within the environment of austerity and starvation that had been signalled to us on the way down.

However, despite those thoughts, once we had disentangled our stiff limbs, detrained and *tenkoed*, my mood changed. The familiar humidity of an early Singapore morning greeted us. Thankfully, though, it was accompanied by a light breeze and with it came the pleasant smell of the sea. We had already been told that we would not be going to Changi jail. That at least pleased us, for we knew it to be both crowded and claustrophobic.

In the event, that and the sea air were about the only pleasing things on that first day – particularly for me.

We had only just started marching away from the terminus when the shattering thought came to me that we had arrived within a few hundred yards of the point that I had escaped from. So, after two years and journeys totalling several thousand miles, I had gained nothing but the doubtful benefit of experience.

That realisation alone would have been bad enough for one day but there was even worse to come.

Our route followed the sleazy roads and lanes that led towards Chinatown and the invading stench of a low tide within the River Valley estuary. There were no balmy breezes to greet us from that direction. We marched right into the heart of the area before being halted before the guardroom and tall gates of a palisaded complex called River Valley Camp. Two years previously I had motor-cycled down that way from Bukit Timah through a bustling, frightened and frantic community facing surrender. Now it was deserted by all but a few residents who were moving about furtively and with down-cast eyes to avoid any suspicion that they might have any feelings of compassion for our plight. It was a desolate scene outside the camp but there was far worse to come inside it.

35

RIVER VALLEY CAMP

1 April 1944

It was the first of April and two years to the day since I had been captured, when the gates of River Valley Camp were opened to let us in.

It was stinking, filthy, unhealthily sited and quite obviously badly organised. The accommodation – which had at some time served as coolie lines – had by neglect become an absolute shambles. As it was just a transit camp, no previous newcomers had seen any good reason to do other than basic repairs, and badly at that. The last occupants had departed leaving gaping holes in the slatted sleeping platforms and rickety hut supports needing urgent attention; one of them collapsed shortly after we moved in.

Some British prisoners were already there. They had been left behind after being rejected as too sick for onward transit to Japan. With them was a sergeant-in-charge, also sick. They were all scattered randomly over the levels of the two two-tiered huts that were to be our home for the next eight months.

Once they had *tenkoed* us the guards just pushed, kicked or otherwise persuaded our men into them to fill up the vacant spaces before departing through a lych gate to their guardhouse outside. All of that unnecessary chaos had to be urgently unscrambled in order to get the sick men together in one group and the various mates who shared possessions into others. Having dumped our kit, the officer and I got the sergeant to show us the rest of the camp, which, apart from a small parade area, amounted to little else.

The only water point consisted of a continuously leaking tap mounted on a standpipe and the immediate area around it was awash with mud. At the southern end of the compound to the left of the entrance there was a run of low and open-fronted hutting which served as a toilet. Within that we found a cesspool of ordure and urine flowing unchecked from the tops of metal containers housed below low platforms that were also caked with excrement. Millions of maggots were crawling up and out of this filthy mess and flopping down into the vast pool of spillage. The resultant foetid morass had to be crossed in order to get to the platforms and the only means of doing that had been by performing a balancing act over semi-submerged bits of timber and rattan frames. The water spillage was separated from this filth by little more than ten feet of dry earth and would soon be merging with it. No wonder some of the sick were suffering from dysentery. The situation was ripe for an uncontrollable epidemic. It was then made even worse by the withdrawal of our medical officer, leaving me with just the one orderly who had come down with us from Thailand.

Somehow – and without any tools – one of our REs managed to tighten the tap enough to reduce the flow to a trickle. That, for the time being, was the best that we could manage at short notice.

And now for the good news! The basic food ration (though practically devoid of vitamin value) was better than the worst that we had had while in Burma although much worse than we had had in Kanchanaburi. More importantly, though, it was cooked for us hygienically within a well-ordered section of the complex occupied by a company of Gurkhas, who were divided from us by a tall internal gate. They, like the rest of the Allied personnel that had remained in Singapore, were called Resident Troops and they were not allowed to fraternise with us.

Despite that ruling we soon managed to pass notes and verbal messages to their *subhardar* via the orderlies who brought and served our food. Those loyal little men were neatly dressed, well-organised and still equipped with many necessities that we vagrants craved. They also had the knack – given notice – of liberating anything else required, so we soon had the use of some plumbing tools and spades to clean up the parade area and trench round the latrine. Even then it was several days before the containers were emptied by a chain-ganged group of convicts sent in from the local gaol. It was a pitiful sight watching men who were even lower on the pecking order than us carrying a ball and chain around while they went about that filthy task.

It became quite evident that the Gurkhas were not only respected

298

but also (despite being captive) still feared by the Japanese and, moreover, with good cause. For those reasons they were rarely allowed outside the camp on work details, and then only when under the strictest supervision. That restraint had little effect on their activities or their reputation for fearsome stealth. Hardly an evening went by without one or two of them getting over the fence, across the adjacent creek and then into the Chinese quarter. The story was – and I can well believe it – that they picked up buried kukris on the way out to guard against surprise by roving Japanese sentries, who, if met, would then – as it were – go 'absent on leave'.

I once saw two of them leaving the camp dressed as women in order to avoid patrols. Heaven help any amorous Japanese who accosted them! I can well imagine that they would have been separated in very 'short-arm' order from their vital accoutrements.

Their *subahdar* did his best to augment our rations with spices and other additives concealed beneath our cooked rice. Also, to their credit, he and his men still regarded us as comrades-in-arms despite the fact that most of our *kumi* were bootless and looked like tramps. They took many risks on our behalf, and I, for one, received the very welcome gift of some pipe tobacco – the real McCoy- when two of them were sent in by the Japanese to give us an up-and-over haircut.

Meanwhile our officer (who had been over in Changi) had rejoined us in time to take responsibility for the selection of the men going on work-parties. That was a godsend, because it not only released me from an unenviable task but also made it possible for me to go out of camp daily.

Before he came back I had been out just once with a small party that was taken by lorry for work in a quarry to the north of the island. Thankfully the job only lasted two days because it was both hard and dangerous work. Our task was to drill out holes for explosive charges by means of spike, hammer, water and handpower only. We had a particularly nasty gang of bastards in charge of us who amused themselves by giving us little warning of the detonations that showered and lacerated us with dirt and stone chippings. Each evening we had to cut and bring in firewood for the camp kitchen. We were working with a cross-cut saw, trying to fell a rubber tree, when the blade started to jam in the running latex. There was a small Aussie party working at another task nearby with which we had started to exchange news. Our guards – who neither liked

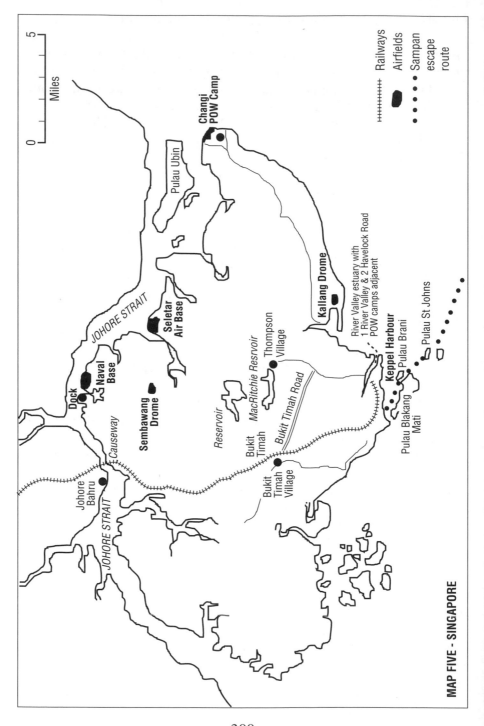

MAP FIVE - SINGAPORE

Railways
Airfields
Sampan escape route

Miles
0   5

Changi POW Camp

Pulau Ubin

JOHORE STRAIT

Seletar Air Base

Kallang Drome

Naval Base

Dock

Causeway

Johore Bahru

JOHORE STRAIT

Sembawang Drome

Reservoir

MacRitchie Resrvoir

Thompson Village

Bukit Timah

Bukit Timah Road

Bukit Timah Village

River Valley estuary with 1 River Valley & 2 Havelock Road POW camps adjacent

Keppel Harbour

Pulau Brani

Pulau St Johns

Pulau Blakang Mati

damage to tools or fraternising – were beginning to get edgy when I heard a familiar Aussie voice. It came from that remarkable axeman Brum advising, 'Go in and out fast with a first cut and then quickly right through just below that with a second one.' We did that and he was right, of course! Brum told us that he was in the Havelock Road camp near ours and that was not good news.*

A few days after the quarry job the Gurkhas told us that we were shortly to be employed solely on work at the docks. Heaven only knows where they picked up that bit of information because it only became official two days later when I was ordered to parade and lead out a party of 100 men.

*Sad to say, with the dreadful losses from his group of Japan-bound *kumis* later, he was probably among the hundreds aboard the ill-fated *Rakuo Maru*, which in September 1944 was torpedoed with an 85 per cent loss of life. A brief account is given later (see also Appendix IV – Vessels).

36

WORK ON SINGAPORE DOCKS

There was no frantic Speedo here as there had been on the railway. The daily requirement of only 100 men allowed rest and recuperation for all who needed it. There were always sufficient and willing volunteers among our half-starved fraternity to make up the numbers, which made our officer's job a picnic compared with the grim task of selection that our doctors had had in Burma.

With the 80 or so sick that we had inherited, we numbered about 230 men, so there was also plenty of scope for attrition through severe illness. Those who became seriously ill were escorted to Changi by the officer, and once there, none of them ever rejoined us. We know that a few of them subsequently died there, and it was a blessing that we didn't have to witness their decline. We had seen quite enough of that while on the Railway of Death.

It was also fortunate that after two years of POW life we had learnt the lesson of survival through self-imposed rules of communal behaviour. We numbered a few hard cases but none of them were out-and-out villains.

Counting myself, we always totalled 100 as we formed up to be marched out of camp. Quite often that number would have the guard working frantically with his abacus because of the blank file which contained only one man. We must have caused great amusement among the local populace when they first saw our bunch of scarecrows emerging from the camp. As I came level with the guardhouse I had to give the command *kashira-hidari* (eyes left) while saluting the 'flaming arsehole'. (There were, however, a few occasions, like on Sunday or when the wind was in the right direction, when it might be referred to as the 'fried egg'.) It never did worry me unduly that I was paying homage to Hiro Hito because all orders from the Japanese were performed under duress. Not so however, our spontaneous and derisory rendering of *Colonel Bogey* which began as we cleared the gates to head off south down River Valley Road.

On we would go towards the docks with our motley collection of eating utensils clanking and bouncing from a variety of belts and nether garments held in position by string. At the rear of the column were our mess-orderlies carrying four empty four-gallon petrol tins slung on poles, a handful of big-leafed china tea and an assortment of scruffy and *very visible* old rags. The rags were part of an illusion designed to convince the Japanese that they were necessary for our midday tea-making ceremony and thus to expect them to be there again when we assembled to return to camp later. The more filthy and sweat-laden they were, the better for making our guard reluctant to handle them when searching us before leaving the docks. The tins draped with the rags would then be ostentatiously set down in front of the guard and myself as I lined the detail up in open order of three ranks. From then on our tactics could well be compared with a game of Russian roulette.

We only rarely filled all tins with loot, and then only when we had been coaling or handling tin, rubber, scrap iron or machinery and nothing else. On these occasions the guard would take us out of the docks and back past the camp guardhouse with just a *tenko* at both ends. It was then that things that had been stolen and hidden up within the docks on the good days for pilfering could be taken out in bulk to be divided out later. (These were the more durable items of food such as rice and dahl swept up from around the dockside.)

Other most favoured receptacles were of the well-tried hidden pocket variety, water bottles with false bottoms and, of course, stowage within our G-strings, into which only the most ardent Japanese searcher was willing to thrust his hands. Overall there was very little to thieve in the food line because large bulk cargoes of it were fast diminishing due to the loss of merchant vessels. What little did arrive became more and more difficult to break into because, once discharged, it was rarely out of sight of the vigilant dockyard police force of collaborating captured Sikhs.

I had been quite surprised to find the Sikhs there, imposing in their traditional dress, when I first marched my tattered band of vagrants through the dock entrance. There was a rumour in common currency about them at that time that they had never had any great regard for the British and had been only too willing to embrace the concept of the Co-Prosperity Sphere after the fall of Singapore. I neither wish – nor intend – to elaborate on that theme and it is only fair to add that much better things had been said in their favour.

The Aussies who came up to work with us on the Burma side of the railway arrived with a story about the great bravery when the Sikhs – with all others – had been called on to sign the undertaking not to attempt escape. By standing firm against that, a number of them had to endure the agony of having their hair and beards set alight. Quite apart from the pain, this was the ultimate affront to their religious belief that their hair had to be left long in order that they could be raised to heaven by it when they died. Death *was* the next stage of their barbaric treatment as the Japanese – after a one in ten selection – used those victims for live bayonet practice.

No doubt history will have recorded the full truth of these things by now. However, what is totally undeniable is that most of them who were appointed as dock police went well beyond just passive compliance with the orders of the Japanese Command by actively enjoying their new role of dominance over us. That was quite another thing and in my capacity of *kumicho* I made no attempt to hide my contempt for them.

They were inscrutable in their demeanour and looking into their dark eyes could be compared with gazing into the unfathomable depths of a muddy pool. The fact that I escaped personal punishment from them rests more on luck than any lingering respect that they might have retained for a British senior NCO. However, it was quite a different matter for many of the other ranks, who were abused, reviled and reported upon on many occasions. The Gurkhas told me that some men who had been in our camp before us had been pulled aside and raped by them.

About two months after we came to work there one of our corporals got into an argument with one of them, who then threatened to strike him. The corporal retaliated with his own threat – a verbal one – saying, 'Before long the Americans will be over here to bomb you bastards off the dockside, so just you remember that you are living on borrowed time!' – or words to that effect.

There then occurred what must have been the most unfortunate

304

and once-in-a-lifetime coincidence for the corporal because, only two days later, a flight of three Flying Fortresses came winging in majestically over the city. It must have been a rest day because I remember that all of us were in camp at the time and gave a great cheer when we saw the glint of the sun shining on those vast wings. There was no sound from the engines as the planes thrust through the air at high altitude, and because of that, the contrails were giving the illusion that they and not the propellers were pushing them forwards. They stayed above the island for about 20 minutes, making a leisurely and taunting cruise around, well aware of their safety from enemy attack, and then departed without dropping a single bomb.

Very few of us had witnessed or heard about that altercation at the docks but retribution was soon upon us. Around midday I was made to assemble everybody, including the sick, for an identity parade. The Sikh was brought in, but after failing to pick anyone out, we were just left standing there in the sun throughout the hottest hours of the day waiting for someone to own up. Nobody was allowed water, food or shade and we were still standing there when it had got dark, having seen many men flake out throughout the day.

The Japanese had us over a barrel, knowing that nobody would inform on the culprit, who they well knew would eventually have to declare himself.

We had been standing there for nearly seven hours when the corporal finally stepped forward. Even then, we still had to stand for a further hour or more until the Kempi came to take him away. Thankfully he survived and was released to rejoin us about five months later, and this is an account of the way he was treated.

First of all they took him off to their HQ in Orchard Road, where he was interrogated and given a merciless beating-up. They then dumped him, more dead than alive, into the hands of their warders guarding the Outram Road gaol. He told us – and this was no surprise – that the Kempi were well-practised in all kinds of refined tortures. They regulated them either to the point where they stopped just short of breaking bones, or, at the whim of their superiors, brought their victims to the state of screaming agony in order to force a confession. In the true tradition of all such barbarians, it then mattered little whether the confession was true or false. The only explanation that he could give us for receiving the lesser punishment was that it must have been decided from the outset that he

305

was to be released for going on to Japan with us later. Lucky man! But he wouldn't have thought so earlier. It was inexplicable to most of us who had so many times witnessed men being battered sense-less for only minor infringements of camp rules, and moreover, not at the hands of the Kempi.

However, his punishment didn't stop at physical abuse. He had to suffer almost unendurable psychological affronts that were designed with the aim of reducing him to the lowest levels of degra-dation and bestiality. After his first beating-up he was lodged in a communal cell with about ten other inmates, mainly Chinese crimi-nals and already brutalised, except for just one old man who was trying to preserve some sense of order within the group. Communication was difficult but fortunately the corporal and the old man shared a few words of English and Malay. No words were necessary, though, for anyone to learn the routine within that hor-rific place. They slept on a stone floor that had a gully at one side into which they had to urinate and excrete. Their food was pushed through to them on two communal platters and quite often with the gleeful assertion of the guard that he had urinated or spat on it. To begin with, the corporal had to literally fight for his share. Sometimes they were left chained together all day despite the fact that the door was locked. Only occasionally was there sufficient water supplied with which to flush their excrement into an outside drain. There was also the certain knowledge that at least one of them could be taken off for further interrogation at any time of the night or day. When that happened, some would be returned unharmed, others beaten up, and some never came back again.

To the credit of the corporal and his Chinese ally, they eventu-ally managed to organise some decency and comradeship among the others.

Apparently the Kempi had had a fixation that he had somehow been in contact with British spies rumoured to have been put ashore on the east mainland by submarine. They always refused to accept his version of the story, and the rumour persisted right through to the day when we embarked for Japan. So was there some truth in it after all? Subsequent events gave us good cause to think so!

It was about three-quarters of a mile from the camp to the point on the dockside where we halted to receive our daily orders from the

Japanese *sergeant-dockmaster* (that being my exalted title for him since I never saw anyone there of superior rank and authority to him). He spoke English with a pronounced Yankee accent, having visited and hostelled in San Francisco as a peacetime merchant navy man. His command of our language was quite good and he liked to brush up on it a bit when talking to me. He was a tough character but nevertheless far from cruel, as indeed were nearly all merchant vessel crewmen that we met. They were a quite different breed, in fact, from the army scruffs who brought us to the docks. It was a blessing that our guards were all Japanese because we had rated the Koreans in the railway camps as the lowest form of animal life.

I had to leave two men at the sergeant's office, to boil up water for the various shifts at work within the holds. The men sometimes worked two ships on the same day, with half employed in the hold and the others resting. Those merchant navy men didn't push us beyond these limits, knowing full well that anything more than a two-hour stretch in the hold of a ship anchored at the equator would have caused deaths. Because of the ferocious heat in the hold. the crewman usually only stayed down there to get work started before coming back up again to control progress from a shady spot on deck. Our camp guards were given no role at all in these daily proceedings, only taking responsibility for us again for *tenko* and our return to camp.

When we worked two ships I was the only person allowed to move between them. I went unaccompanied but wore a distinguishing armband. No doubt the dock police kept an eye on me as I walked along the dockside, but no more than that, because they were barred from boarding any of the vessels. That strange and rigid form of apartheid helped us considerably! It was very useful to know that each group of the opposition had well-defined limits of operation and authority and we milked that knowledge to the full.

Metaphorically speaking, there *was* one thing that really was milked, and constantly.

A small bulk-liquid container of palm oil had been shunted onto a siding adjacent to where we ate our midday meal. It was a pinkish viscous fluid (reputedly only meant for use in lamps) and had a rather nauseous taste, somewhat akin to that of liquid paraffin. Despite that, reckoning that any fat or grease ought to aid our digestion, we tapped it for about six months. Whether it did us good or not nobody will know, but most of us survived to tell the tale. My

307

own ration was tapped off into a false-bottomed water-bottle that had been contrived while I was in Burma to dispense water separately from the top half.

There was another additive that I kept constantly by me and that was guaranteed to skin the lining of an elephant's throat if eaten rashly. When working at the quarry I had stripped out the yield from a bush of small and wild green chillies. I had then made the mistake of biting into one to test its strength. Sampling live coals couldn't have been worse than that experience! I must have gleaned about 50 of those fiery little devils, each of which when pared down was adequate to serve for six meals. There was a theory that they were *good for* malaria but, as Professor Joad of the BBC *Any Questions* days would have said, 'It always depends on what you mean by *good.*'

One of the earliest jobs that we were given on the docks was a split one, in which half of the party was put to trimming coal on one vessel and the other half on an adjacent one filling hoists with baled tobacco for unloading onto the dockside. Each of the bales was comprised of a cubic metre of compressed leaf. As each shift came up on deck for a breather, it was quite noticeable to me that the majority of the men had arrived there with enormous bulges in their G-strings.

Shortly before we were due to descend to the dockside for our meal, the crane-driver had decided that he too had done enough for one morning. He – careless man – went off to get his own dinner, leaving an overloaded slingful of bales swinging close above the deck guard-rail. As an invitation for thievery it was willingly accepted. We turned the sling until a bale was repositioned to where it would topple overboard as soon as the crane-driver got going again.

After that, everything went even better than planned. The tobacco detail had just returned to its task and I was bringing down the coalers for their meal, when the crane was restarted and a bale hurtled into the water between the vessel and the dockside.

Men who had been coaling were allowed to bathe in the harbour and on that day, one of them shunted the bale along and wedged it by the steps before joining us at our meal.

By the time he arrived I had already had my food and had decided to tell the Japanese sergeant about the crane-driver's *accident* and how we had managed to rescue the bale. I pointed out that the leaf would already have been ruined by immersion in the sea water, so – if he agreed – we would all like to have a few leaves to take back into camp with us. To my surprise he readily agreed, so I told the men to help themselves before they assembled that evening for return to camp.

It was quite a normal day in every other respect as I stood to watch the midday antics of the men who already had loot to hide. One by one they would disappear with the excuse that they were going for a *benjo* before heading off – hopefully unobserved – to their individual hiding places for non-perishable goods. There were so many places for concealment of loot among the go-downs, rail trucks and dockside debris. My favourite ploy was to wrap what I had stolen in a filthy bit of rag and jam it under an unused and rusted section of rail track near the palm-oil wagon. Fortunately for us, much of what we had stolen while on the tobacco ship that morning had already been hidden for bringing into camp the following day.

When the afternoon shift was finished, I joined the others for a wash and the chance to openly grab off a further supply of leaves to take back with us that day. However, when we assembled for *tenko* it became clear that something unusual was afoot. For the first time our second guard had been brought back from camp to help with a search, whereas we had expected to be waved through without one. Despite all our legerdemain and switching of positions in the ranks, the two guards proved to be one too many. They did not entirely outwit us, though, because the men already had an agreement that on discovery various groups would off-load onto individuals who would take the rap for their mates.

I could have hidden my own loot easily by slipping it to the end man in the front file as I rounded it with the guards for their search to the rear. Instead of that, I openly displayed it and then took one of the guards to show him the damaged bale and did my best to explain that we had been given permission to take some of it. It was all to no avail. Those of us who had been caught with tobacco were marched separately back to the sergeant's office by one guard and the others were then brought up and halted nearby.

There were eight of us in that first group and there was no doubt at all that we were about to be punished and, moreover, by the sergeant. My first reaction was to brand him as a two-faced bastard. He had already had all the other dockyard workers, Malay and

309

Chinese – who had never previously been allowed near us – brought up by the Sikhs to gather round. He then called me over and announced, 'You will be punished with your men first and then, on your own!' He then lowered his voice and said to me, 'And make it look good!'

It was no good reminding him that he had given us permission to have the tobacco, because he knew that, of course. I can only guess that we had been seen by someone of higher rank to him and he would then have been compromised if he had shown overt leniency.

For the communal punishment we were made to crouch down and then caper about meowing and barking while we circled around. This delighted our audience but we ignored their laughter and cat-calls. Naturally our feelings were hurt, but nothing else; but that wasn't the end of it for me.

I was made to kneel down on some paving and then – after inserting a long iron bar behind my knees – the sergeant and one of his men started to jump on each end. I had seen what was coming! Gripping the bar with both of my hands, I tensed to take the bulk of the pounding that would otherwise have smashed my kneecaps. Surprisingly, my scrawny arms were able to cope with a lot of the shock. Even then, the main thing that saved me was that they were rarely able to synchronise their jumps to land on the bar at the same time.

When the punishment was over, I had to be lifted back up onto my feet and then I somehow managed to hobble back up the road into camp. My legs were aching and covered with multi-coloured bruises and my right knee has never fully recovered to this day.

During two days in camp recuperating I had plenty of time to think about the sergeant's remark, 'Make it look good.' On returning to the docks, we resumed our relationship without any further reference to the incident. However, later – and even while I was still a POW – I could never really believe that the sergeant had maliciously deceived me in order to have a bit of fun at my expense. Now, with the benefit of over 50 years' hindsight, I have a much greater understanding of the rigid codes of conduct that governed that earlier generation of Japanese.

My belief now is that the Japanese navy, its associated airmen and their merchant navy compatriots had far more 'clout' than any others with the Japanese hierarchy, so the sergeant felt compelled

310

to tell the ship's captain about his concession. It would then have been the captain who would have had the overriding authority for what ensued. If that indeed was the case, I must feel grateful that the matter wasn't referred to the Kempi to sort out. I have read only recently of an incident that occurred in Saigon; a Japanese merchant navy captain refused to obey an army order to embark several hundred POWs for work in the Japanese copper mines, and it was the Japanese army who backed down when the fur started flying.

We were rarely dealt with viciously either on the docks or at the River Valley camp. Personally speaking there was only one other time that I was bashed about during our stay in Singapore and I can blame nobody but myself for that.

I was marching our working-party back up the road to the guard-house. As usual, I had my pipe clamped firmly in my mouth; although rarely lit, it was habitually left there in anticipation of things to come. My mistake was in still leaving it there when I came level with the guardhouse and saluted the flaming arsehole.

It was an aberration that I paid for very dearly because the whole of the guard came out to systematically beat me up. Whenever I fell to the ground they put the boot in. Despite the pain of it all, I somehow managed to get back on my feet again to avoid their manic ritual of going berserk had I stayed down. I finally stayed up to endure fists, boots and rifle butts thumping in. They had earlier whacked the pipe out of my mouth, smashing the stem, which then parted company from the bowl. How I treasured that pipe! I can clearly remember calling on the men to salvage the pieces before the Japanese got the idea of trampling on them.

It was no good trying to explain that I had not been stupid enough to have deliberately insulted their flag, or that starvation often resulted in temporary lapses of concentration.

There is no doubt at all that we all deserved a lot more punishment than we received while working on the docks and that was mainly due to our long apprenticeship at evasions while working on the railway. However, even if we had been punished more, there would have still been no lack of volunteers to continue working there. The place offered us two bonuses, the obvious being the chance to get more food but, equally important, was the daily escape from the claustrophobic camp environment.

311

About the only sound that we heard from outside during the evenings was the distant music coming from the Happy Valley amusement area some two kilometres away and across the river towards Chinatown. We led a far more exciting, entertaining and, indeed, even amusing life down on the docks. Much of that can be attributed to the demarcation lines already mentioned and typified by the following events.

The first of these occurred when we had nearly cleared the holds of a ship bringing in machinery, when we uncovered the back of the ship's lazarette. The noise of our unloading activities allowed us cover to break into a treasure trove of lovely white socks, pants, singlets and other new clothing and prize items such as cigarettes, cigarette papers and tinned food. Aided by slack supervision and the knowledge that the ship would be changing its berth that night, we had carried off far more loot than we could have reasonably expected to conceal. To start with, the men only got off the ship safely by the grace of God and my vigilance in acting as 'sweeper' to pick up the oddments that they dropped.

We had been assigned a young, inexperienced and docile guard for the day but even he could not have missed the exaggerated contours of some body parts paraded for search. We lined up, to be watched by a contingent of Japanese soldiers squatting around on adjacent piles of railway sleepers. However, quite typically – although highly amused at our antics – they never said a thing to the guard about those of us who got away with hiding loot from him.

Although I had been quite modest in my 'take', a pristine white sock hidden beneath the sole of one of my feet had worked its way out of one of those flimsy Japanese army canvas boots that I had brought down from Burma. The soldiers saw it trailing there and, fortunately, one of my men warned me, so I kept behind the guard all the time that the search was on and then managed to tuck it back out of sight. None of us had soap or owned new clothes, so what we had liberated was easily discovered – unless well concealed. So, what with that and the revealing bulges that I mentioned earlier, the guard had a field day on that search. He came back to the front of the parade to display an armful of stolen items. That, however, was not the end of the side-show for our audience by any means. The guard then used me as a lay figure on which to demonstrate the various hiding places used, by slapping at my body.

I was wearing torn and sweat-stained shorts and shirt, the pockets of which were filled with the items that I had scooped up from the deck. Every time his hand came down in the vicinity of the pockets I had to squirm like an eel to avoid discovery of *my* haul. By then the soldiers were rolling in the aisles.

The guard did not report the matter either there or at the camp, as far as I know, but he told me to address the men about their misdemeanours. So I told them, 'I have a solemn announcement to make so none of you must laugh! The guard has asked me to tell you that you have been very naughty, and that you must follow my example and never steal!'

The recovered loot was then distributed among the soldiers and that was the end of that! Presumably the hoard hidden within the hold had already been stolen by the ship's crew, who would then have quite obviously decided to keep quiet about our villainy.

There was one other occasion when we broke into an illicit store of treasure trove hidden away in the hold of a ship. That time I was so deeply implicated that I shudder to think about what would have happened to me as leader of the work-party if I had been discovered.

We were working two ships that day. I had just walked between the two and up the gangway when one of the men asked me if I would smuggle down three 200-packs of American Chesterfield cigarettes onto the dockside when I returned to the other ship. He wanted to get them off before the break-in could be discovered and I was the only person able to do that. My reward was to be one of the packets, without any further responsibility for getting them back into camp. Believe me, I didn't hasten into the arrangement. It was, however, quite obvious that this was another illicit cache of items stolen from abandoned American stores during one of the earlier battles on the Pacific islands. It was that conclusion, and the fact that I was carrying my side-pack with a groundsheet in it due to recent heavy monsoon rain, that decided me to take the chance.

I hid the groundsheet behind a life-raft, crammed the three packets into my pack and, telling the crewman that I was going back to the other vessel, set off towards the head of the gangway.

Just as I was about to descend, a Japanese army sergeant came bustling up from the dockside towards me. I had never seen this character before and he was quite obviously unaware of the fact that I was allowed to walk about unaccompanied. His immediate reaction was to shout, '*Naka*', which we POWs variously interpreted as either 'What are you up to?' or 'What have you got there?' My response was also immediate! Believe me, it nearly always is when the adrenaline is flowing and you've had the fear of God put into you. I had realised in an instant that the only hope that I might have of bluffing my way past him was to annoy him. So, drawing upon one of my limited but often used store of Japanese phrases, I said, '*Gunso, nani ji deska*' (sergeant, what is the time please?) – and then, saying, '*Ju ichi ji*', I showed him my arm band and then pointed to indicate that I had to be back over at the other vessel by eleven o'clock.

He then got so mad with me – a lesser being – having dared to ask him those things that, forgetting the reason for his original challenge, he just shouted, 'Bugger off out of it!'

I have mentioned before that the Japanese are said to have no swear words in their language, but if that is so, '*Buggero, kunero*' was enough for me to take my leave thankfully. Then down I went to the dockside (steeling my nerves not to give myself away by descending with undue haste) and then scuttled off to hide the packets in the gutter on the far side of a low derelict go-down.

There were, of course, many days that went by when we were unable to steal more than a few grains of rice or loose pulse of various kinds that had spilled from split bags. However, some of our coups were both audacious and memorable and, even hilarious in their execution. The two most notable that have forever stuck in my mind need to be told.

The first of these happened when we assembled to leave a ship for our midday break. The ship's cook had already been seen preparing the meal for the crew. He then came past us towards the deckhouse cabin carrying the captain's dinner. As we lined up there for *tenko*, I had seen that dinner steaming away on the captain's table within easy reach through an adjacent porthole. In went a hand and out came the meal, to be devoured within seconds. The plate was then skimmed like a Frisbee out into the harbour before we beat a hasty retreat down onto the dockside for our meagre ration of rice and our tot of china tea.

Once again, there were no repercussions. Perhaps the cook discovered the loss in time to replace it with his own meal! If that were so, he most certainly would not have told either the captain or his mates about it. During the afternoon I caught his eye as he was preparing more food for their next meal. I thought it best not

314

to linger too long when he ostentatiously picked up a large meat cleaver and tested the blade with his finger-tips.

The pièce-de-résistance, though, was the following episode, which was also linked to a cook and his galley.

He emerged carrying half of a large savoury roly-poly pudding on a tray and making for the crew's quarters forrard. I was standing on the port side with some of a shift of men that I had brought up on deck for a breather. Other men were enjoying their break near the starboard entrance to the galley.

The cook came along the port side and had just reached us when he must have sensed movement behind him. Turning quickly, he saw one of our group entering the galley, in which he had left the other half of the pudding. He then made a fatal move! In order to give chase he put down the half that he had been carrying and hared off back there. Before entering he checked back our way, only to see bare decking where he had just left the crew's portion. Once in the galley and finding that the officers' half had also disappeared, he dashed right through to the starboard side in a vain attempt to try and rescue it. He was far too late! It had already been rushed forrard and lobbed down to the shift working in the hold. Within seconds the whole of that pudding had been stolen, gobbled down and the trays consigned to Davy Jones' locker.

It may seem unbelievable but we never heard any more about that incident either.

I have often wondered if the cook lived long enough to see the funny side of it all, because we had been loading that vessel! By late afternoon it slipped anchor and lined up in convoy ready to head east after dark. Within a few days it came back under tow and anchored near enough for us to see that much of the superstructure had been shot away. The galley had been reduced to matchwood!

The above incidents – if nothing else – serve to show the difference in temperament between the men of the much-travelled Japanese merchant navy and the gang of vicious bastards who had terrorised us while in Burma.

By September 1944 it became clear that shipping traffic was diminishing and that we were being wound down ready for our move to Japan. Small indications when put together had been painting the full picture for us.

All of our sick were being taken off to Changi now and one day I went over with them on a return visit to have a tooth extracted. It was the one that had been wrenched when the pipe was smashed from my mouth. While over there, I was interested to hear that my other teeth were typical of the majority seen by the dentist, being in what he called 'an arrested state of decay'. That, he said, was the useful and only benefit we gained from our bland and sugarless diet.

Our officer and our only medical orderly were with me and we were all able to pick up bits of news and, of course, rumours. Only one guard accompanied us and, once there, he then had the impossible task of ensuring that none of us fraternised with the inmates. On arrival we had passed through the guardroom entrance and were then escorted along the side of a ward containing rows of stick-men who had 18 months earlier been sent up young and fit to work on the railway. There were others there, the ERTs – English Resident Troops – who had never left the island and who were supposed to be the lucky ones. My opinion, though, was that they had fared just as badly mentally as any of the Sumatra Battalion nomads had – and solely because of their institutionalised environment. Possessions and a sheltered life didn't appear to have done most of them much good physically either, except that their sick enjoyed regular – though still basic – attention without any harassment.

Despite these comparisons, our medical orderly was now only too pleased to see his charges put in their care. He, more than any others of us, needed relief from the task of trying to provide care and comfort with scarcely any resources at all. Without his dedication and the general assault on the pestilential squalor that had greeted us on arrival at River Valley, few of us would have survived. Within just a few months we had turned the situation round. Despite being weak, starved and skinny, very few of us were dying now.

We came back to the camp that night bearing welcome news in confirmation that the Pacific battle areas were closing in on us. Our officer had also received a message from his still loyal plantation foreman that the Japanese had abandoned proper management in the interests of quick gains. That too was welcome news, even for the officer. It was a good indication that the Japanese were getting desperate for supplies as well as being careless about the resources or feelings of their so-called Co-Prosperity allies. That sort of dismissive attitude had already been seen to help our own Allied cause by increasing the discontent among the locals.

316

My own gain from the visit to the dentist was to hear that a batch of prisoners had left for Japan about ten days earlier. It was alleged that they had marched to the docks dressed in a motley assortment of civilian clothes, looking more like holiday-makers than POWs.

Unlikely as that had seemed at the time, it was in fact quite true.

Many of them were men who had been housed within the nearby Havelock Road complex for a time. British from the Thailand side of the railway and – I believe – Aussies from both sides had been put there on hold for embarkation to Japan. From there hundreds of Aussies had at first been sent out daily to work at the construction of a new graving dock. The conditions there (on what was called Jeep Island) were so horrific that the Aussies at least would have been only too delighted to leave. Unfortunately, my old mate Brum was likely to have been among them.

Unfortunate is in fact an understatement of the horrible toll taken of POW lives while at sea at that time.

In order to get a full appreciation of the losses during 1944 I must draw on the rumours – now known facts – of that time, the revelations published in 1947 within our Battalion and, much later, the full published details. Even then, the following events take no account of those that I have already written about.

The first sinking on the twenty-fifth of June 1944 occurred when a convoy of six vessels was attacked by the British submarine HMS *Truculent*. One of those six was the *Harikiki Maru* (3,800 tons) with 724 British and Dutch POWs aboard. They had left Belawin Deli, Northern Sumatra (which incidentally, was the port from which we had sailed two years previously on the *England Maru*).

She and two other vessels were hit and sunk and, despite the efforts of the others to save those in the water, 178 POWs were drowned. The survivors were taken to Singapore and stranded on the docks virtually naked. They then stayed there for two months before being taken back to Sumatra for construction work extending their railway network. During that two months they were given no more than starvation rations and as a result many more of them had already perished on the docks.

It then took me more than 40 years to realise that we had seen those unfortunate men from a distance without being aware of their plight; and it happened like this. In 1990 I was still trying to find out more about what had happened to the men we left behind in Padang. Then, about two years later, I was put in touch with Taff Long, who with two of his mates Pat O'Brian and Wilf Farley – all survivors from HMS *Dragonfly* – had been selected to stay there when we set off for Burma. He wrote me a nine-page letter which in essence linked to both the above incident and the fate of all who stayed to work on *their* Railway of Death.

I feel that his account (although an aside to this story) will be of interest to living survivors as well as the families of those deceased who had any connection with Padang during World War Two. For that reason I have placed an almost verbatim copy of Taff's letter in the appendices of this book.

The second submarine sinking brings this account right back to my late September visit to the Changi dentist. Once again full confirmation of all the details had to be awaited. First of all Captain Apthorp had continued logging events in the British Sumatra Battalion diary for a further year after I left to go to Singapore. That gave the dates, disposition and final selection from about 2,800 men of the ultimate 2,218 who left Havelock Road and elsewhere for embarkation at Singapore Docks. All of those men had been relayed down from French Indochina and Thailand earlier in the year and by good fortune one *kumi* (mainly comprised of our Battalion members in Saigon) was stood down just before those moves started.

More important for me was that my *kumi* – also ultimately designated for a move to Japan – were employed as replacements for some of the above who had been working on the docks. They then went over to Havelock Road from the River Valley camp to work elsewhere while awaiting embarkation. So for the umpteenth time, there, but for the grace of God went I!

By the sixth of September the convoy had been finally assembled. It was a large one, among which were two passenger-cargo vessels carrying POWs. There were 900 British on the *Kachidoki Maru* (10,500 tons) and 600 British plus 718 Aussies in the *Rakuyo Maru* (9,500 tons). All the POWs were as usual housed either within or adjacent to the cargo holds, where conditions were cramped, airless, stinking hot and for long periods without water. There were Japanese civilians in the cabined mid-sections and one hold of the *Rakuyo Maru* contained wounded Japanese soldiers.

The convoy steamed on for six days before being cut to pieces by an American submarine pack. Both ships were torpedoed and sunk, and of the original 2,218 men the total rescued – many after several days in the water – was 785. In addition to that about 1,000 Japanese civilians and soldiers were picked up.

There are only two people that I knew who were definitely on those ships. Brigadier Arthur Varley, our overall commander from Thanbyuzayat days, was one – and he was drowned. The other was Ray Disspain who became a colleague of mine in civvy street about 20 years later. He was among the 656 rescued by the Japanese and later transferred to the whaling ship *Kibibi Maru*, which then sailed on via Formosa to Kobi arriving on the twenty-fourth. Certainly many other Aussies who were with us in Burma would have drowned too.

(Appendix IV – Vessels – lists many more details relating to that convoy. Those who wish to know more about it are recommended to read the full and compelling account in the book *Return from the River Kwai* researched and written by Joan and Clay Blair, Jr, published as a Penguin volume in 1979 and, later, the subject of an epic film.)

On the eighteenth of September 1944 there occurred the third and greatest shipping disaster involving POWs during the whole of the Pacific war.

At 16.15 hours the British submarine *Tradewind* attacked and sank the Japanese vessel *Junyo Maru* – a 5,015-ton freighter carrying 7,850 men en-route for slave labour in Sumatra. The complement was comprised of 1,750 POWs (Dutch and British), 600 Ambonese and 5,500 coolies, who the Japanese referred to dismissively as *romushas* (lesser people). The latter were in fact largely made up of students and other young people from Java and Sumatra who had been rounded up for slave work. The vessel was hit by two torpedoes when close to the coastline of Sumatra south of Emmerhaven. While the destroyer escort was releasing depth charges, no attempt at rescue could be made. Eventually just 888 were saved – 276 Dutch/British, 312 Ambonese and 300 of the young Javanese and Sumatrans). Priority was naturally given to Japanese crewmen and guards.

These figures reveal an appalling loss of 5,200 of the 5,500 youngsters. They would have been crammed into the lowest parts of the hold. Their contemporaries who reached Sumatra on other

319

vessels were always treated worse than cattle, being given no shelter, very little food and, if sick, abandoned to die without food or medicine.

It is just as well that most of the above could only be guessed at at the time. During October and November 1944 the docks started to fill up with not only badly damaged vessels but many others that came in to anchor and stay there. By that time the Chinese dockworkers from other areas were making it their job to let us know that fewer convoys were leaving.

There was a German submarine moored within 200 yards of our work area. During the last eight weeks of our stay that too never moved. We were well aware of the reverses that they had suffered, right from the time when Rommel was ousted from Africa in early 1943 to the December, when their battleship *Scharnhorst* was sunk. However, they were still very much in the war in 1944 despite the June D-Day landings.

We were of the opinion that the submarine commander had either lost heart or that the Japanese had by now forced him to remain non-operational. Whenever any of the crew came along our strip of the docks, we gave them the benefit of our opinions about their collaboration with the Japanese. Our hostility mounted to the extent that the commander set up a machine-gun post between us and his craft.

Apparently we did the man a disservice and – in doing so – ourselves also. Because, years after the end of the war, I read that when he had been tied up elsewhere (before October 1944) he and his crew had gifted food and clothing to men from the Havelock Road camp. We also heard that one of his crew had been bashed by a Japanese who mistook him for a POW. He must have been stripped off and raggedly dressed for the mistake to have been made. The story goes that the Japanese was then promptly picked up bodily and thrown into the harbour. I wish that we could have witnessed that and, of course, shown more forbearance in our attitude towards the Germans.

Our life in the River Valley camp was mundane compared with that of the unfortunate men caught up in the shipping disasters. However, there were none of us who were not both skinny and suffering the result of untreated diseases. We had no doctor in the camp and there were still men who worked one day and then, for no apparent reason, became too ill to work the next and died within days of being sent to Changi.

I was still suffering from recurring bouts of malaria; I would have a day or two in camp to get over the shakes and then carry on.

It was during one of these enforced rest days that another of our sick men gave me a pipe which – as he put it – his mate would not be needing any more! Quite apart from having been broken by the Japanese, my old pipe was so burnt down at the bowl that it looked like the rim of a spent volcano. I had carved – and to this day still own – a bowl made from the root of a tree while we were in Burma but, with the lack of tools, I had never been able to make a stem for it. The previous and unfortunate owner of this new one must have either smoked a far better grade of 'compost' than I did, or very little at all, because I was still smoking it on VJ Day.

During December we had even fewer vessels to load and were put to work tidying up the dockside with a reduced work-force. By then it was quite noticeable that most of the incoming Japanese troops were much younger than earlier intakes.

Strangely enough, by December 1944 it was the Japanese and the Gurkhas who were supplying us with the most authentic news of the progress of the war. Some of our guards became quite boastful of the fact – as they saw it – that they were now taking on the rest of the world almost single-handed. For their part, the Gurkhas had somehow got news of the fact that our *bête noir* – the Apalon bridge in Burma – had been bombed in November. It had then suffered more intensified bombing that made the railway unusable for long periods.

By January 1945 we were beginning to fit the pieces together and to sense that the battle areas were closing in on us. We then had further evidence of that when three more Flying Fortresses drifted in over Singapore for another look-see. As before, they made a leisurely aerial survey of the island and, despite all the shipping tied up in the harbours, they made no attack.

When we got back into camp that evening we were told that the next day would be our last for work on the docks.

Two days later we were heading off out of the camp for the last time en-route for embarkation and (it was rumoured) a spell of work in the Japanese copper mines.

PART FIVE

37

THE LAND OF THE RISING SUN BECKONS US

It was about the seventeenth of January at around 4 p.m. when the Japanese concluded their habitual round of counting, recounting and false starts. The whole procedure of searching was once again so casual that I was able to hide (then retrieve) my compass for taking on the next stage of our wanderings. We then moved out through the open camp gates, but only to be halted before we cleared them. A debate ensued during which our lead guard said the sergeant had at first intended taking 'orl men back campoo!' Fortunately, we had had a substantial midday meal prepared for us by the Gurkhas, because with all this farting about it seemed highly unlikely that we would get any more to eat that day. And so it turned out!

Once on the move again, we went straight to the dockside to be hustled up the gangplank of a clapped-out merchantman without getting the chance to read its name. The whole move was made in such haste and disorder that men were still being pushed down into the hold after the anchor was weighed. Then we were thrashing our way out of the harbour to join a convoy that was already on the move. Meanwhile, I had been ordered to issue each man with a block of rubber to use as a life-belt. These measured about 15 inches square and 9 inches thick and had a moulded strap on the side. They would not have supported anyone in the water and the issue was nothing more than an ill-disguised ploy to get more cargo aboard.

More men were able to stay on deck than had been allowed on our previous sea journeys, but only because our forrard hold was already well filled with cargo. For those who had been pushed down there, the conditions were little better than we had suffered while on the *England Maru* in 1942. The head-room was just as restricted and the atmosphere just as hot and foetid. The only definite advantages were that the men had a little more room in which to stretch out. Few of us were suffering from diarrhoea and none from active dysentery at that time. If any sufferers had been discovered before leaving, they wouldn't have been allowed to embark, but we had all passed another ludicrous Japanese medical in which we were declared fit if our foreheads were not hot.

As usual I had no choice of accommodation, being fortunately made to stay visible and on call just forrard of the deckhouse. My vantage point offered me the mixed blessings of fresh air at all times but blistering heat throughout most of the day. I was well placed to watch what was going on above deck and soon realised that we had some Japanese civilian families aboard.

Just before dusk the younger children were being dressed up in all-weather gear for bedding down under awnings flanking the deck rails. A few of the older and bolder of them crept forward to peer round the deckhouse at the scrawny, hungry and half-naked beings that were to be their companions on the voyage. They didn't stay there long, though. There was soon quite a hubbub as distraught mothers appeared to haul them back into the safety of their own quarters.

At about 10 p.m. we ran into a light rain squall which caused our guards to retreat into the same area. While they sheltered there I was able to get out my compass to check the general direction of our passage. We were altering course in such a regular pattern that the Navy lads had already remarked that any submarine would be able to just stay abeam of us to wait for a target to come into its sights.

We scarcely had time to digest that bit of unwelcome information when there was an ominous thump and one of the two merchant vessels in station with us slowed. Shortly after that, what had just been a dark silhouette on our port side lit up briefly and then began to break up. In a matter of minutes we had slanted off across the bow section of the crippled vessel, gathering speed as we went by and able to see it quite inexplicably still riding high. There had then been a wave of panic and confusion among the civilians and crew when dashing about to assemble aft at their lifeboat stations. Meanwhile, our escort came hounding in to scatter depth charges.

The men below had felt the thump of the torpedo strike and the shock wave bounce off our ship's plating, but thought that that too had resulted from an exploding charge. The last thing that we wanted was a more general panic, so I turned for advice from a Navy lad who had done a short spell on submarines. He assured me that the sub would now either be lying quiet and submerged or it would have got to hell and away out of the area.

Some of us who had had earlier experience of travel on Japanese hell ships had already discovered that we had no lifeboats forrard. There were, however, six life rafts within reach of us and those, with the hatch timbers, the thunderboxes and, perhaps, even the blocks of rubber as well, might keep us afloat until rescued. So, saying nothing about the sinking to the men below, I sent a sergeant to find out if we could quickly force another exit from the hold if need be. He came back with reassuring news. The cargo could be stacked higher in one corner up to a section of half-boarding but the external tarpaulin lashings above would have to be released as well.

We soon found a man possessing a cut-throat razor and positioned him at the forrard starboard corner of the hatch combing with orders to slash the area immediately if we were hit. I then went below to let everyone know that a companion vessel had been sunk and what our plans were. I also had the thought – but not the conviction – that there had been some liaison between the Fortresses and the sub-mariners that had ensured our safety from attack. However, it did little harm to let that thought circulate as a near certainty.

POW life offers few opportunities for the captives to plan for their own future. So having done that with satisfaction, we then let the Japanese do any further worrying while we slept.

Once the panic was over, the convoy – at first – re-formed to resume its zigzag course. It then adopted and held a steady course to port for what seemed to us a dangerously long time until we must have been close to the Malayan coastline.

Very few of us would have slept for long on deck because we were being soaked with intermittent bursts of squally rain. Long before dawn we were also griping with hunger but happily aware of the activities around the galley area.

It was around 6.30 a.m. and barely light when we saw a row of tubs being filled with steaming rice and with a rich soup. Our mess orderlies were assembled and – well before they were called to collect the food – they had estimated which of our scoops should be used to ensure a ration for all of us; and I had the *laigi* list ready. When the soup arrived we tested it and – praise God – it plopped with the sound of plenty of solids. Basically it was Blue Danube (brinjal and lily root) soup but there were also bean shoots, soya and some savoury lumps of what appeared to be a tinned fish paste. We cadged a few of the empty tins from a Malay cook-assistant. The only recognisable marking on them was in Japanese lettering surrounding a rather crude fish shape. So for all we really knew it might have been pet food but it was quite tasty.

It was only after we had got that lot inside us that any further thought was given to the events of the previous night. The more we mulled them over, the more we were inclined to believe the old rumour about Allied agents having been put ashore about 150 miles south of where we were sailing now. Post-war knowledge now makes it all the more feasible that survivors from the *Rakuyo Maru* had tipped them off about camp locations and the intended movement of more POWs to Japan. Whatever the truth of that may be, it was a cosy thought to speculate about at the time.

The indisputable truths on that day were that we were going to both witness and sometimes also suffer more from the attentions of our own forces. *C'est la guerre!*

There had always been two large factors that came into the equation for personal survival: to have a fair degree of luck coupled with the right mental attitude. Some of us now enjoying this Japanese pleasure cruise were up in Burma when that empty train pulled in above us at the 114 camp, and that was certainly *my* biggest slice of luck. As for mental attitude, I also had the great advantage of being given the responsibility for others and thus had little time left for too much introspection.

None of us, of course, could be sure that we were over the worst but, significantly, we also had none of those unfortunate *atap*-gazers among our party. Everyone was 'switched-on' despite the fact that I still maintained my original forecast of another nine months of slavery. Nine months would be a long time for men in our condition and I was still depending on my innate hatred for the Japanese to sustain *me* over the last lap.

* * *

If only we had known that two months previously the Americans had bombed Tokyo I might have reduced that forecast. But no such luck!

Dawn came with the discovery that we were hugging the coast of Malaya in company with another old rust-bucket and a frigate, while the rest of our convoy was fast disappearing over the horizon to the north-east. So, the intriguing topics of conversation now were, 'Where now for us? What of the returning civilians aboard? And of the valuable cargo of rubber?'

I suppose we were willing to believe anything told us at that time and in particular if it seemed to be to our advantage. However, when the cook-assistant found another opportunity to sidle up to us no-one questioned his news. Pointing to the departing main convoy, he said, 'Japan!' and, to us, 'Saigon!'

There was nobody among us who had more than the vaguest idea of where Saigon was. We did have men with us who had fought in North Malaya, though, and they, as it turned out, were rightly convinced that we were on course for the Gulf of Siam.

All things considered, this was really good news because none of us had fancied running the gauntlet of submarines through and beyond the full length of the South China Sea.

Things really began to look up for us then. Bodies that for months had been screaming out for some decent nourishment were rewarded with another good meal. We were also beginning to benefit from the cooler and fresher sea air. How tenuous are the margins between survival and death! Anyone from outside who had been thrust into our still disgusting but now less evil levels of deprivation could not have survived for long. It was quite remarkable what we had been able to get used to by the process of a long apprenticeship. As proof, I only needed to think back to when Sergeant Maney was captured and thrust in amongst us and how short his life had been after that.

Over the remaining days of the voyage we traversed the eastern coastline of Malaya, past the island of Kau Samui and then slightly east of north to anchor within sight of a Thai township which must have been Rayaung. We had arrived shortly before dawn and then saw the light from another vessel appear round a headland and close on us from the west from the direction of Bangkok.

We fully expected to be taken ashore either at Rayaung or into Bangkok and then onwards to one of the Thai POW camps, but the

Malay had been correct. It was the civilians who left us, at about 10 a.m., to swelter and dehydrate throughout the rest of the daylight hours. Nature really switched on the heat for us at this anchorage. We were close to being fried on deck and the men in the hold were being drained of all moisture and energy. The level of humidity there was diabolical and the stink of sweaty bodies and foul bilge-water nauseating. So it was Hobson's choice for any men who decided to swap around for relief.

I had no choice but to stay put as usual and be thankful for the blessed relief of temporary shade when the vessel swung round on its anchor to place me in the shadow of the deckhouse. Although some of us had enough clothing to cover up exposed skin, there were many who still had nothing much more than their G-string and a bit of rice sack to rely on. Thankfully many of them had long since been tanned as dark as the natives of the area. I would never have survived such exposure.

We eventually sailed at dusk and worked our way steadily south-east, keeping close to the land. By the twenty-fifth of January we had rounded Cape Ca Mau to head north-east and up into Saigon harbour.*

---

* Singapore docks were bombed on the twenty-fourth of February, either destroying or damaging most of the foodstocks stored within the go-downs.

38

SAIGON

January 1945

It would be an understatement to say that we were astounded by the scene that greeted us on arrival. The harbour itself and the whole of the dockside installations were in a state of devastation.

We had to creep in while being nudged by a tug to find a mooring by sliding past, or being backed off, to dodge a graveyard of sunken ships. Masts, funnels and other bits of superstructure were all about us.

Getting ashore was an equally chaotic experience but the great reward for us was to be hailed by some of the Sumatra Battalion already lodged in the area under the command of Captain Apthorp. Although we were not allowed any direct contact with him at the time, the details of the bombing raids were recorded by him in the Battalion diary as follows:

... about Christmas 1944 another large batch of POWs arrived in Saigon docks. They moved into the old Hospital Camp and were just in time for the first big raid on January 12th. It came early in the morning while Saigon was still obscured by ground mist. 140 dive-bombers flew in from the sea and commenced to attack by shooting down the only three Japanese fighters to leave the ground. Meanwhile the sirens had sounded and the POWs – who knew the drill for taking cover – moved out into the marshes at the back of the camp. It was generally assumed that this was just another of many false alarms but once outside the camp we were clearly able to see the planes circling like vultures... They attacked the aerodrome first and then three broke away and headed for the docks. They were soon followed by many others. An uncomfortable few minutes were spent in wondering if our camp location plan and nominal roll smuggled out some months before – had reached allied hands. This question was soon answered. The dive-bombers – which were greeted with a tremendous volume of ack ack fire from ships and ground defences – bombed and machine-gunned all round us but left the camp area alone. A tanker that was about four hundred yards away, caught fire and was soon a mass of flames. There was a terrific explosion as an ammunition warehouse blew up and then clouds of black smoke gradually drifted over the whole area.

Now more bombers were arriving. The sun glinted on their wings as they turned to dive. Two destroyers in the docks put up a tremendous volume of pom-pom fire and one bomber caught in it turned away and then disintegrated. However, the majority of the ack ack fire soon became inaccurate when shortly after 12 noon the destroyers were sunk. By that time a large part of the dock area was burning. It was difficult to assess the damage because smoke continued to obscure almost everything. The attackers were apparently satisfied though, for after gaining height, they flew off in an easterly direction.

The POWs had just got back to camp for the midday meal when the sirens sounded again to signal an even heavier raid. This time there was not so much to see but the sound of heavy explosions told their own story. A few ack ack guns opened up but they were hardly noticeable above the noise of exploding ammunition and the roar of burning oil. This second attack lasted all afternoon. Then, as the light faded, we saw the bombers leave one by one until only two remained to circle over the aerodrome before turning to dive low over the docks and disappear behind the clouds of black smoke.

The Japanese came out to inspect the damage which was an enormous tally of over thirty ships sunk in the docks and river, one hundred and twenty shattered and burnt out planes on the aerodrome, warehouses destroyed and the more distant oil-storage tanks at Narbay left burning furiously. In the words of one of the Japanese, Saigon all finishou!

How we would have liked to witness that great feat of selective bombing and strafing ourselves! However, we had arrived just in time to see the next raid and this time by SuperFortresses which made a 3,200 mile round trip from India to deliver their cargo of bombs around the dock area. It could have been very nasty for us if the raid had been a day earlier but by then we had been marched out to a dilapidated and abandoned camp about a mile inland from the docks.

We were on the outskirts of a city which was host to a cosmopolitan mix of eastern races similar to Singapore except that there was an entirely different feel about the place. Saigon projected an atmosphere of purpose and well-being which was due no doubt to an unchecked abundance of produce in the area. The locals enjoyed far more freedom of movement than had been allowed in Singapore. The relatively small French population, however, had been forced to capitulate to the Japanese. By declaring an allegiance to the Vichy French from the outset, they had at least been able to avoid the worst forms of repression. Nevertheless, they were constrained within a curfew – the conditions of which could have been far more strict, except that the Japanese had honoured an earlier treaty with them.

Some British POWs had been lucky enough to arrive and then stay in French Indochina from 1943 onwards. They were well kitted out and had been housed in hygienic accommodation lit by electricity and they had been favoured with supplies of good food. These were the ERTs (English Resident Troops).

It has been conjectured – and I would say correctly – that all POWs who came later to Saigon *and stayed there*, benefited from the French presence. It was a most useful place for the Japanese in which to demonstrate their alleged care for all prisoners at the expense of the French Red Cross, which was occasionally allowed to provide food parcels, books and even musical instruments. It was there that the few International Red Cross visitors were brought to see them at Sunday church services and concerts and resting on every tenth day.

All this had been going on for nearly two years before we arrived. Just when we might also have benefited, Sod's Law decreed that we should be denied all those concessions except for the days off, and then only because there was a surfeit of men for the work required.

Over the next week or so, we had a few opportunities in which to exchange news with men from other camps. They told us of the pickings to be found in some of the smashed buildings but I do not recall much of it coming our way during the brief time that we worked there. We had little contact with the locals and none with the French colonials, who, in any case, were confined within their houses at dusk. However, I did have good contact with the Japanese – but only in the form of a severe beating-up.

There is no doubt at all that the Japanese were not best pleased with the progress of the war and they set about us whenever it took their fancy, and that was quite often! My encounter came when I was personally required to take out 100 men. In Singapore that request had always meant that there would be 100 in the party including myself. So that was the number that went out! When we assembled for our return to camp I was expected to produced a 'Saigon hundred' of 101 men. The little bastard who had checked us out in the morning then threw the blame on me for the alleged deficiency and, bringing other guards to the scene, they all took turns in bashing me about. It was no doubt his way of saving face but it didn't do any good to mine.

We saw the Indochinese as a gentle and contented race and with no good reason to be otherwise. The whole area was bursting with rich produce gleaned from around the mighty Mekong river and the hundreds of miles of tributaries that flowed into its delta. It was an entirely new experience for us ex-jungleites to see plenty. In Burma our scanty provisions had had to be brought in over long supply routes, and had suffered from pilfering, whereas in Saigon there was an abundance of fruit, vegetables, fish, meat and dairy products to hand. There could have been no reason other than bloody-mindedness that we went short of the good – and cheap – food that was available. Carts laden with produce streamed past our compound on their way to the city markets.

It was perhaps just as well that we didn't stay very long in that camp to witness these tantalising scenes of plenty. Rumour had it that we were destined for a trip into the more mountainous areas north where 'orl' was said to be 'very goodka'.

39

THE NOMADS LEAVE FOR DALAT

Our rumoured destinations were by now becoming regularly true.

We started our migration with a move out of the city and into some run-down coolie lines adjacent to a railway halt. This ramshackle and ill-equipped lodging was called a holding camp and we were soon hoping that we were not going to be held there for long.

My recollection is that our numbers had by then been reduced by 55 to a total of 225, which I then had to split into parties A, B and C. Within a few days of our lodgement I was ordered to make an evening move by train with A party. We then had what turned out to be an almost interminable stand-to, waiting unfed by the track for a train that never turned up. The next morning I had to assemble group B, which after waiting for hours was about to be recalled when a train did arrive for them. It was made up of wooden freight wagons and flat cars. Two of the wagons had been left empty to receive our human cattle, while others contained livestock and produce. Interspersed between them were flat cars carrying machinery, an ack ack gun and crew, and others carrying light military equipment, around which soldiers were resting amid their personal equipment. It was around mid-afternoon when B scrambled aboard and then they were away.

In the dark and early hours of the following morning we heard a train approaching the halt from the north. Sadly it turned out to be carrying B party back as a mixture of unscathed and wounded men. They had been shot up by Allied planes when only a short way down the track and the dead – I believe there were seven of them – had been buried near the scene of the strike while a railway maintenance unit cleared the wreckage and repaired what remained.

I had by now lost count of the number of times that fate had intervened to my advantage; and now, we were about to play another game of Russian roulette, based on the order of moving. The wounded were sent back down the line. C party was made to stand-to but were quickly stood down again to be replaced by A. And then – God alone knows why – the whole procedure went into reverse, with C re-alerted and sent on their way on a journey that was completed without incident.

It now became crunch time for A party again. During all this swapping about we had been counted many times and now we had been searched for the second time. We had no chance to hide and then repossess forbidden items on the second search because it was done out on the track. Despite that, there were very few confiscations. The search was cursory, mainly (I suppose) because most men still had very few possessions and had had very little opportunity to steal anything since coming ashore. In contrast to most others', my kit was still quite substantial and I made a great play of laying it all out while making no attempt to conceal any of my sketches that showed scenes of camp life. However, I was still determined to take my compass along with me and, moreover, not to compromise anyone else. So, not for the first time, this rather heavy item had to nestle uncomfortably where the bespoke tailor is wont to thrust his tape measure.

To the surprise of everyone – the guards included – our train arrived on time and it moved off promptly, hauling a typical assemblage of wagons. The uninjured men from B party joined us and two more box wagons were added to give us five strung out behind a flat car containing the ack ack detail.

The five would have been adequate for us if our guards had travelled with us but they had taken one of the wagons for themselves. That – as ever on such journeys – meant that we could stand or squat but none but the sick were able to lie down.

We set off east and then north-east, keeping parallel to the coast, travelling through a flat, well-cultivated and rather treeless area. Much of it was covered with a patchwork of small hedged and ditched fields reminiscent of the English countryside during the thirties. There were some larger areas of light green cultivation linked by irrigation ditches, which were more than likely paddy fields. We travelled slowly and had ample opportunity to take in the occasional sights of rambling farm buildings and of labourers working in fields close to the railtrack. It all seemed rather idyllic and a bit feudal. Apart from the occasional bullock cart trundling along, we saw little

336

else that was wheeled and nothing much mechanised to assist them in their work.

After about four hours we slowed at the approach to Phan Thiet. Just beyond the town we picked up a meal, took on more fuel and, from a weird assortment of containers, warm water was doled out to us, which we just had to hope had been boiled. Some of the locals must have been expecting us. They approached us from the 'blindside', so, unknown to our guards, we were at last able to trade some of our new Monopoly money – cents and piastres – for eggs, fruit and *goula malacca*.

When we travelled on I was one of the 'squatters'. There were the usual groups standing at each doorway taking in fresh air and watching the scenery when the wheels started grinding and squealing.

At first – according to the watchers – all was well because the engine had come into view negotiating a long curve in the track. We then felt violent jolting and heard the louder sound of complaining metal as the brakes were applied, followed by a startled shout that the driver and the fireman were out on the footplate, and then that they had leapt out onto the track.

We were still sliding along with the wheels locked when the ack ack gun swivelled in the direction of the coast and started to fire; and then we saw planes sweeping towards us from the east.

I would never have believed that all of us were agile enough to leave our trucks in a matter of seconds and, moreover, before they came to a standstill. We just tumbled out of the door onto the track and did a 'Linford Christie' across a small field towards a low hedge and ditch. By god we were lucky! The planes were US Lockheed Lightnings and as they came streaking in towards the far side of the train they were loosing off their cannon shells. The ack ack gun kept on firing until there was a thump as the planes thundered through and away to turn for another run. We had no casualties but I am sure that many would have found it necessary to wash out their G-strings as we crouched within the security of the ditch. The hedge was little more than 100 yards from the trackside, but even then many of us had still been diving into the ditch as the shells scythed their way over and amongst us.

The planes had by now turned for a lengthways attack, and some unfortunate men were now within their line of fire. Stray bits of metal went zipping over their backs but, once again, we had no casualties. Not so the Japanese!

We found little pleasure after the firing had ceased to see the bodies of six men scattered about the flat car that had housed their gun. They were fighting men who had bravely stood their ground against an attack of terrifying intensity with little hope of engaging such a low-level run.

Most of us had had a go at low-flying planes with our rifles and sten-guns while fighting in Singapore but I have yet to hear of anyone who brought one down. However, we would have had more chance of hitting them than those dead Japanese had. One of my daftest actions was when I stood up to fire an anti-tank rifle at a lone Japanese recce plane. The only – and quite predictable – result was that I was knocked arse-over-head backwards by its recoil. However, if that formidable round had hit, the pilot would certainly have been blown rapidly upwards to meet his ancestors.

With the action over, one of our guards emerged with the message 'takusan haiti finishou' (many soldiers dead) – and shortly after that those who survived began to get organised. After dealing with their dead, we were called to help with clearing the wreckage and righting derailed wagons with the aid of emergency gear brought in by a repair unit. There were many dead and trapped animals amongst it all. Meanwhile, the driver and fireman had returned to check over their charge. It was still on the track but gasping with the sound of steam escaping from unfamiliar places.

We finally got going again amid three hearty cheers for the US Air Force and a few private prayers that they would not return again until we were well clear of the area.

It was a short run before we holed up in a wooded area to await a second engine to assist our wheezing wreck. At about 2 a.m. clanging and jolting announced the arrival of the relief and, once coupled, we ran on at a steady pace to a town – presumably Phan Rang, considering the large number of locals present there at such an early hour.

If there had been a Japanese field kitchen functioning in the vicinity, it wasn't working for us; but fortunately the Japanese had enough to worry about without chasing off the itinerant traders who greeted us. There were some people among them who had heard that we were coming when the relief train was called out, and they had a meal ready for us.

All that we had to offer them was some of the Japanese Emperor's trash money, which they accepted when the guards were about but promptly returned to us when unobserved. That was a wonderful gesture from the kind community, who wouldn't have known that we had had only odd scraps to eat during the previous four days of emergencies and false starts.

None of them could speak English or French but they got the meaning of our sign language and pointing down the track, they said, 'Dalat', but that didn't mean anything to us at the time. If we *were* at Phan Rang it would mean that there was only another 50 miles to go but we didn't know that either, or that Dalat would be the terminus to a branch line.

It was still dark but my compass – and my nose – told me that we were still near to the sea, and more than likely not far from aircraft carriers servicing the Lockheeds ready for another attack.

Well, we left before dawn but our journey of only 50 miles seemed interminable. There were constant stops after first light at points where we were obviously hiding up due to air raid warnings, but I couldn't work out how they had been signalled to us while on the move. Once we left the coastal region we began heading north-west and up into the foothills of a range of plateaux and mountains that extended for hundreds of miles beyond. It took us seven hours to get from Phan Rang to Dalat terminus, which backed onto the first rise into the hills.

There was the inevitable *tenko* before we were given some unboiled water, which in our parched state just had to be drunk regardless of the risk. Then came the message, '*Orl men meshi campo*' which we interpreted as, 'No food until you get to the camp'.

The camp (it was said) was somewhere up in the hills that towered above the town, and we would have to get there with the aid of just one shuttle lorry. The first lift went off at around 2 p.m. and we had to be thankful that the worst of our sick cases went with it. It was stinking hot when the rest of us were led out of the station to a mountain road with a gradient that must have averaged one in six. It rose in a series of hairpin bends that flanked a torrent of water streaming down from the heights above us. It would have been a lovely place for a picnic in ordinary times, but on that day we were engaged on an endurance test. Our progress changed from a march to a slow march and then to the point where we were almost marking time as we panted our way up. The fittest of troops could not have kept going up that gradient let alone our bunch of scarecrows, who were all knackered within 300 or 400 yards. After that – and despite the urgings of the guards – we just gasped, wheezed and scrabbled our individual ways upwards.

We hadn't gone much further when – rounding a bend – we found the lorry halted, with radiator boiling and incapable of negotiating the next bend. That was a godsend for all of us, in fact, because we had to rest while the engine cooled and the radiator was topped up. Meanwhile, the stragglers caught up with us. Then while they rested, everyone else had to take turns pushing to inch the lorry up and round a one-in-four bend to a level point where it could be given an assisted start.

We had walked about a third of what eventually turned out to be a five-mile journey before the lorry was found waiting at a turning point for the next relay to climb aboard. And so we progressed, staggering ever upwards, until I was left with the last of the stragglers. Having spent three hours of torture in fierce heat and without water, we found the road at last levelled a bit.

Sod's Law had decreed that the last of us would be getting relief when least needed. We could hear the lorry making its way down to us from a long way off. In a totally 'no care' mood we – not the Japanese – decided to take an unofficial *yasume* while awaiting its arrival.

Flanking the road was a fast-moving river tumbling over rocks as it hastened to join the torrents and falls that we had passed below.

We were soon picked up and then driven over the last mile of a rapidly levelling road, to turn right, past a guardhouse, over a moat and into a dream camp.

A reception party of Japanese quickly *tenkoed* us and then we were handed over to the care of a group of well-dressed British NCOs. They were headed by a 'regular' CSM who had quite obviously been hard put to it to welcome the earlier arrivals from our tattered band. If ever there had been a classic case of *them and us* this must have been it! We had walked into the camp of a contingent of ERTs who had known little of hardship and nothing of the horrors of the Burma/Siam railway camps until we arrived. Perhaps the biggest culture shock for him was when I – the acting sergeant-major of the *us* group – came in to present our nominal roll. He, immaculately dressed in clean tropical kit and well-polished boots, had suddenly been confronted by a scarecrow. The little clothing that I wore was a rag-bag collection of mismatched garments, torn, dirty and streaked with salty sweat stains. The only things 'British Army' about me were split and filthy boots laced with string, my webbing belt, side pack and water bottle, and a contrived CSM wrist-band.

He must have been sorely tempted to put me on a charge for being improperly dressed but instead took me off to inspect our quarters and clean myself up.

The 'thems' had quite sensibly retained separate accommodation and (to begin with) separate washing facilities, because few of us were entirely free from lice.

We were at last called to a meal, which to our amazement contained carrots, new potatoes and – wonder of wonders – chunks of meat which had been stewed in a tasty salted liquor. After that I remember having the greatest difficulty keeping awake to make the acquaintance of some ERTs who gathered around to hear our stories of death and deprivation. Once they had left us I claimed a bed space and was asleep within minutes.

The following morning we awoke to begin a new and far better era of POW life than ever before. The day began with *tenko* and then – luxury of luxuries – another wash with soap and the invitation to attend second breakfast because we were to have the day off.

40

DALAT – THE CAMP AND THE AERODROME

March 1945

Our hut was on the northern side of the camp and remote from the
guardhouse. It was two-tiered, open-fronted and ramshackle. Facing
it there was an equally dilapidated fence which did nothing other
than mark the inner boundary to a 'no-go' area. Immediately beyond
that was the moat – the main deterrent to escape. It was seven feet
deep, twelve feet wide and constantly patrolled. It was perfectly
clear that anyone found over there would be shot. North of that was
a well-wooded area frequented by barking deer, 'whippoorwill'
monkeys and other creatures which, although small, were remarkably vociferous. The loudest and most persistent of the insects was
our old acquaintance the 'clockwork beetle'. There were a few large
trees shading a cluster of admin huts, one of which was our CSM's
office.

Over to the north-west it was just possible to hear the ERTs working-party that left earlier to work on the nearby aerodrome, which
had been levelled and was now being provided with camouflaged
perimeter bays. There was no frantic Speedo on and presumably that
was because the Saigon raid had left the Japanese with very few
planes to be relocated.

I had already called in at the office. The CSM had the camp
organisation well under control. He had established a rapport of
quite unusual mutual respect with the Japanese Commandant which
spilled over into the demeanour of the guards, who were efficient
and alert but never vicious. It was obvious that I would have no
place in the hierarchy other than to act as *kumicho* for outside working-parties. The CSM was a bluff and far from erudite individual.
He informed me that he didn't want any 'argy-bargy' with any of

us. That was one of his favourite expressions and there was a time when I heard him ask his orderly sergeant – without any hint of humour – to pass him the 'incredible pencil'. Lucky chap, I didn't even possess an indelible one, while he seemed to be equipped with everything bar the kitchen sink!

I had left the office when the camp lorry came in from Dalat with a small detail of POWs aboard. They had brought up food for the Japanese cookhouse and some local purchases, made by the guards, which they later sold on to our canteen at a high level of profit. What little did come in that way was very welcome, since no vendors were allowed to approach us when we worked outside and there was nothing out there worth stealing.

I was at the south side of the camp by now, near the guardhouse and in sight of the road that we had toiled up the night before, and I heard water cascading over rocks spanning the river beyond. We were going to be allowed to bathe in there each evening. It was idyllic compared with all that we had suffered before!

Well, we had had our day of relaxation and the following morning I – with a hundred men – were put on breakfast number one before marching off for work on the 'drome, which became the more regular routine. There were other smaller jobs to be done and on one of those I experienced a day of most unusual events.

I went out on a lorry with a Japanese driver, a guard and about 20 men to collect wood for the camp kitchens. We drove off straight past the turn to the aerodrome, across a plain and into a thinly wooded copse. It was a fiercely hot day but it was quite pleasant in there. We were at the boundary, cutting and stacking timber to be taken by lorry back to the camp. When a few loads had been sent in, it was arranged that we would wait out on the plain for the lorry to return and take us over to a new site.

What happened next was both painful and comical. We were all barefooted and had been assembled for a *tenko* along a dry sandy path which was baked hot by the sun. As soon as we stepped onto it we started cavorting about like cats on a hot tin roof. None of us could stand long enough in one place to be counted and we were circling around, taking turns in occupying each other's shadow. The guard finally had to give us best and hold his *tenko* back in the copse.

343

Our new site was far more shady within a stand of tall trees close to an area of mossy bogland. We were cutting there and had got two fires going for boiling water, when the lorry returned with our midday meal. Everyone was busy and we were taken wholly unawares by an invasion of leeches. They had obviously got the smell of blood and came 'looping' along towards us from all directions to lock onto our legs. Thank God for the fires! We pulled brands from them and went into a counter-attack, burning them until they dropped off. That was the only time that we had encountered leeches and strangely so, considering the dank and boggy nature of the Burmese jungle during the monsoon season.

We still had one more surprise to come. While eating, we saw a small group of pygmies moving towards us through the trees. They came boldly up to stand and stare at us – as we did them, I suppose! Apart from having a few possessions tied to girdles, their own 'dangly bits' – men and women alike – were given a full airing. They were no more than four feet tall, their bodies dry with unhealthy grey skin and all of them pot-bellied. I imagine that they had already seen the 'Haves' from our camp and were both surprised and curious when they saw our near-naked group in their 'Jap-Happies'.* They were looking for handouts or barter but few of us had either.

I noticed that one of them had a small section of bamboo and a skin bag tied to his waist and pointed at it, for it to be shown to me. Words would have been useless and, in his case, impossible. He had been trying to talk to me while masticating a mouthful of wood lice wriggling around between his teeth. The bamboo held thistledown and a bag of flints, which he 'sparked' onto the thistledown and then blew until it glowed. I swapped a Dutch guilder for that bit of cave-man ingenuity.

It was a far from usual day!

The aerodrome was at camp level and situated about half way up a series of undulating heights reaching to over 5,000 feet. I went out there most days with a working-party of 100 men. Most of our tasks were not unduly physical, and after the engineer had set them for the day and then left us, I would quite often join in. It would have been boring to sit around in total uninterest as our guards usually did. The men worked industriously enough when the guards

* So named because the Japanese also wore them as underpants to contain all that made their lives happy.

approached but eased right off when no-one was about. We were usually hidden away in the taxiing bays anyway, with a limited view of the runway.

However, there was one special day when we were taken out to the edge of the runway to tidy up ready for the official opening ceremony. Japanese bigwigs were to be flown in for the occasion and some aircraft were already parked on the runway.

We knew the big moment had come when officers from the local command assembled with a guard of honour. It was late morning when we heard the drone of a plane approaching from the direction of the hills and saw the reception party being readied for the salute. It came slowly into view and descended towards the runway as it cleared the last of the overshadowing peaks. We were idling away as no more than interested spectators until one of our group shouted, 'Bloody hell, it's got four engines and the Japanese haven't got any of them that I know of!' Then, we were waving and cheering as it levelled to shoot up both the parade and the aircraft and then went onwards to the south of the runway, where it attacked the Ack Ack defences.

The plane – now recognised to be a Liberator – turned full circle to make another run at a level of no more than 200 feet and loose off its guns. We barely had time to get into the entrance of a run-off bay before a hail of bullets scythed into the area.

I and two others had dived behind a small steamroller, and as we lay there we felt warm liquid running over our backs. Once again fate had decided that we would all survive. We three were being sprayed by warm water from the riddled tank above us.

However, it was a far different story out on the runway, where planes were wrecked and burning among the many Japanese wounded and dead. There hadn't been any air raid warning where we were, but presumably the Japanese bigwigs had been warned and had landed elsewhere.

From that day onwards we had frequent visits by a lone Liberator. It always made saucy, arrogant attacks at low level to 'duff up' the defences at the southern end of the runway; and we always dashed out to the perimeter to wave it through. The day came when the Japanese must have accepted the fact that their cover was blown. There never was any serious attempt made to bring combat aircraft onto the 'drome during the few weeks that we worked there.

My most abiding memory is of the last run made by the Liberator.

It made no attack but, as usual, swept casually down the runway. It was quite obviously a farewell visit because as it came level with us we saw that one of the crew was standing on view within the protection of a rear nacelle in order to wave to us. It drifted so slowly past us and so close to the ground that I found myself shouting for him to lower a rope and hoist me up and away to freedom.

During our short stay my group was never wholly integrated with the ERTs, or I, within their hierarchy. I suppose it was inevitable that we 'Railwayites' should remain – as it were – on the other side of the track. We were no longer scabrous or lice-ridden but the have/have-not syndrome could never be fully overcome.

For instance, none of my men were ever given the opportunity to go down to Dalat market with the ration lorry. It would have been both a novel experience and a great opportunity for them to make personal purchases from the traders there. We were living under a remarkably benign Japanese regime, which (compared with that of *our* past) had always been commonplace for the ERTs. That situation had made them tenacious of their rights to the extent of selfishness. (I wonder what my attitude would have been if the position had been reversed? Not much different, I suspect!)

However, the disparity was really brought home to me when I came back into camp one day to discover that the CSM was out in the forest with the Japanese Commandant hunting for deer. Good luck to him, but I hope that he has never published his memoirs, or voiced the belief that we should forgive and forget, purely on the evidence of his experiences.

We others have to be thankful that the Commandant was one of a very few enlightened Japanese we came across. The credit must go to him alone for seeing that we got good and sufficient food and that nobody was unduly punished for infringement of camp rules. He was also a realist who, in my opinion, foresaw early defeat. If so, that alone might explain why none of us were punished for dashing out to welcome the raiding Liberator. Towards the end of our stay, a batch of lightweight American army boots was sent to us via the French Red Cross. He could so easily have confiscated them but instead – and quite by coincidence – issued them to us at a time when the only American in camp had decided to escape and live rough outside.

The Commandant was not a pushover. The escapee very soon realised that he had miscalculated the duration of the war, the worsening weather and his ability to survive unaided. There was no way that we could have hidden him if he had got back into camp again but we were able to send out food to him with the working-parties. We heard that he had got down to Dalat twice but each time he had been frightened off by the attitude of some of the locals. One of them must have been an informant, because the daily search patrols were stepped up. There is no doubt at all that the Commandant would have executed him if he had been caught.

It was around that time that rain squalls began to sweep into the Central Highlands from the direction of the South China Sea. These were the precursor to violent and unpredictable typhoons that I now know to be a regular feature between June and September.

We were returning to camp during one early June day when a mother and father of an electric storm started brewing up to the east of us. Having reached the turn-off into the camp and with the weather still sunny, we stripped off for our usual bathe. Recent rains had turned our stream into a river and the gentle flow into a torrent that cascaded over the rocks. By the time we got into it, the storm had reached us. The cracks of thunder intensified and then became almost continuous as they struck the mountainside and echoed their way down its walls to the valley below. That alone would have been bad enough because it was comparable to close and sustained artillery fire, but the sizzling and streaking lightning that accompanied it was awesome.

By then we had all decided that discretion was the better part of valour and it would be sensible to get out of the water PDQ and across into the safety of the camp. However, none of us made it in time. We were scrambling up the bank to gather up our clothes when a four-foot sphere of light like a massive soap bubble came rolling down the road towards us. It passed us, going on slowly beyond the entrance to the camp and – thank God – just clear of the water that some of us were still standing in. It was a luminous ball and one could easily imagine that several thousand volts of electricity had missed us by a whisker. Whether that was so or not is immaterial; it was a sight both beautiful and frightening.

There was a recent TV programme about a group of American scientists who seek out and enter storm centres in order to measure their electrical energy. They stated that fire-balls never exceed one

347

foot in height. Well, gentlemen, you are so wrong, it is just that you have never been lucky enough to see one! However, don't despair, because since the Central Highlands were defoliated by bombing with napalm, the storms in that area have been more violent than ever before.

It was only a few days after the storm that I was ordered to parade our group ready for a return journey to Saigon.

41

THE LONG TREK SOUTH

June 1945

Having been searched, we were soon on our way down to Dalat without the support of either rations or cooking equipment.

From there we were hastened onto a train to journey onwards for about 70 miles, until damaged track forced us to continue on foot. We had then only walked a short distance before being confronted by a jumble of wrecked wagons and more twisted railtrack.

There were three guards with us. They halted us beside the wreckage to consider what should be done next. There was a lot of discussion, and while that was going on we were busy examining the inside of an uptilted wagon. Most of it had been cleared out but all along the lower side there was a scattering of rice and dahl amid emptied sacks.

It looked to us as though there had been a very recent attack on the train, otherwise it would already have been gleaned by the locals. It had been heading towards Phan Thiet and Saigon, so the likelihood was that the railway staff at Phan Rang – our last stop – had been unaware of the attack or we would have been held there to await repairs.

It was quite obvious that the guards had also known nothing but, instead of taking us back to Phan Rang, they now decided to leave us to trek onwards in the care of a solitary guard. He turned out to be such a diminutive and timid specimen that it was easy to see how he had been talked into doing the job. I could sense his apprehension at being left alone with us. The first thing he said to me was, 'Germany all finish!' We already knew that! I didn't tell him so and accepted the remark with a show of astonishment and little joy. It had been silly for him to tell us without first thinking of the possible implications for himself. I had realised long before he did that he was likely to be alone with us for the rest of our journey, no matter how long that might be. He was presumably pinning his hopes on the arrival of a relief train from Saigon, whereas it seemed obvious to us that the Yanks were in full control of train movements by now.

We had our own worries, the most important of which was to get together the essentials for a long trek. In order to convince him of that, I showed him the food that we had gathered in from the first wagon and then pointed out to him that we needed more if possible and also containers for carrying and cooking.

It was fortunate for us that he had no emergency rations either, so it was an easy thing to convince him that we were now together on a potential survival course. We filled his mess tin with our gleanings and then – having first made sure that the other two guards had disappeared – he readily gave permission for the rest of the train to be searched.

None of the other wagons had contained sacks of grain but we found some more spillage on the floors and a little more on the ground. Our most useful discoveries, though, were two buckets hanging in the fuel tender and some useful lengths of wood for making up stretchers. The cab contained a shovel and an axe as well as the gruesome evidence that the crew would have no further use for them.

Having made six NCOs responsible for twenty-four men each, I apportioned the loads and then we were on our way stepping from sleeper to sleeper. Our American boots were quickly found to be something of a mixed blessing. Several of the men had been forced to accept ill-fitting pairs rather than none at all. None of them had been supplied with laces and I must have been one of a very few who had the recognisable remnants of a pair of socks stolen while we were working in the Singapore dockyard. So, it wasn't long before the choice had to be made between either blistered heels or the hazards of walking barefooted.

During the afternoon we had to divert to a lane in order to hide from planes looking for more targets along the track. They swept by and continued south-west towards Saigon, their progress being accompanied by thumps and machine-gun fire. So, finding our way onto a larger track that paralleled the railway, we stayed on it until ordered to halt within sight of a village. The guard, having decided that we would bivouac for the night in a nearby field, just left us to our own devices until the following morning.

We expected him to go on up to the village for the night but, instead of that, he started off back in the direction from which we had arrived. My belief is that he needed to sleep somewhere near us but was too frightened to do so in our company.

With the light fading fast, I got wood- and water-collecting parties organised. We cooked rice in our two buckets, and the group NCOs had to make their own arrangements for cooking beans.

I suppose that it could be said that I had brought my luck to our table and to the benefit of all. We were doing our cooking along the rear embankment of a one-acre field that was filled with a planting of sweetcorn nearly ready for harvesting. It was only necessary for us to reach out to pick some of it for afters and then later, to strip out the rest to add to our reserves.

We were all tired and many men felt ill as a result of that day's exertions. It had really found us out! However, one thing was for sure and that was that no one was going to give in now. We didn't know or really care where that Japanese had holed up for the night. It was enough for us to have the unexpected freedom to do as we liked. We had eaten well, it wasn't raining, 'the Yanks were coming' and all was well with the world for a few hours at least.

There was a lot of chat going on that evening and most of it centred on our families, about whom nearly all of us had heard nothing for over three years. Other than that, there was the usual speculation about how and when the war might cnd. It had always been my conviction that there would be a day when I would have to make a dash for freedom. My abiding premonition was that we would be made to slave until the Japanese had no further use for us and then that we would be killed off. The recent withdrawal of our officers had only confirmed me in that belief.

Our few weeks in Dalat under an unusually benign regime never clouded the issue for me. Everything that we had witnessed or heard about the Japanese while in captivity had only served to underline what I already knew about them in pre-war days. In the mid-thirties their prime minister Tojo had spelt out the sinister philosophy that sooner or later the Japanese would have to indulge in major warfare.

Talking about their over-population and the need to expand their territory he said, 'Whether we win or lose is largely immaterial. If we win, we will get the extra territory that we need! If we lose, we will have in any case reduced our surplus population.' That was the essence of his statement, and a frightening one when you consider their fanatical willingness to sacrifice themselves, en masse if need be. So, why should they concern themselves about anyone else?

I was thinking of all these things, and in weighing up my chances of survival, I came to the conclusion that it would be stupid for me to keep my compass any longer. I had never had any real cause to use it and had twice been discovered with it, as recounted earlier. So it was that before I settled down for the night, I had made the decision to get rid of it the next day.

Just after dawn the guard came back to seek me out and order us to move off without preparing a meal. I didn't feel inclined to argue with him since it would not be long before the poor farmer turned up to find his crop harvested and the stalks pulled and trampled into piles of improvised bedding. As soon as we had been *tenkoed* we left, carrying our rations and heavier items of kit on stretchers. Every available container had been filled with boiled water and every man had been issued with some boiled sweetcorn. Nearly every one of us was barefooted by preference now, but I was giving my old British Army boots a try-out. Although they gaped open at the welts like the mouth of a hungry shark, I had stuffed them out with dried grass and strapped them into shape with bits of webbing.

A few miles down the road we came to a small township that had a communal well by the roadside. The local women were busy there, winding up buckets of water. We all had a drink from our boiled supplies and then replenished the containers for carrying onwards. While leaning over to watch the action, I dropped my compass to the bottom of the well. It is probably still lying there in the sediment and still serviceable within its oil-filled waterproofed casing. I don't remember the name of the place but I am sure that I could find it again.

The most important things that we gained there were the discovery of an empty building with a disused hearth in it and getting our goon's permission to use it for preparing a meal. The locals were very helpful in supplying us with wood, although very reluctant to take our devaluing paper money in exchange for the few extras that we were able to buy.

We reckoned that we had walked about 20 miles by now and also that it was around 150 more down to Saigon; and no Japanese organisation in place to get us there. It had been estimated that we had basic rations for a further three days only and that illness and disability would inevitably slow us if our stretchers had to be used.

Thankfully, due to our lone and persuadable guard, we were at least able to dictate much of the pace and method of our progress. We had a reasonably uneventful though arduous time on that second day of relentless footslogging. Even though we spent most of the time walking along bullock tracks, we were never far from the railway. That was the mode of our progress for the next three days, which were punctuated by the sound of distant bombings. We had the rather dubious joy of seeing more wreckage along the track but nothing among it that could be improvised to re-rail for use as a trolley. By then all our carefully rationed stocks of food had been used up. We had had drenching rain during one day but thankfully on our fourth night we had all managed to get shelter under a hedge and in a small empty barn.

Each night our guard had disappeared to hide up and bivouac on his own. This gave us the freedom to scavenge at will in adjacent fields. Very little extra food had been found so far and practically nothing at all could be purchased. We were facing the prospect of a foodless day ahead and having to carry a few stretcher cases, when once again our luck started to turn. One of our number had found a pile of damaged and sun-scorched sweet potatoes along the side of a nearby field. There were men among us who knew that 'greened-up' root crops could be dangerous to eat, but with nothing else on offer, we decided to take a chance and, what's more, got away with it!

By the fifth day we had degenerated into a slow, starving and straggling group of individuals plodding along the railtrack for most of the time. We were carrying two stretcher cases, and by mid-afternoon were having to help along others who were in the last stages of exhaustion.

I will never know whether it was fate, luck or God on our side that day, but as we were approaching a cutting, we saw the wagons of a short train backing out to come slowly and lumpily over some repaired track to pick us up. The train then went back to hide up until dusk, before taking us through to the transit camp that we had left two months previously. We got there just in time to join in the evening meal, which we ate to the accompaniment of a heavy downpour lashing the roof above us. How lucky can you get!

It appears that we had been somewhere near Bien Hoa, which was about 20 miles north-east of Saigon. So, but for the arrival of the train, we could easily have had to trek on for another 40 miles, and some of the men wouldn't have made it. Most of us were moved on to yet another holding camp closer to Saigon but about 30 of our sick had to be left behind.

42

O SONS OF MANY FATHERS – YOUR 'COME-UPPANCE' IS NEAR!

July 1945

Our new camp was on the eastern outskirts of Saigon and it had none of the amenities that the ERTs were still enjoying within the town. To make matters worse, we were back in the care of a villainous gang of Japanese and Korean bastards, including some who had been with us in Burma.

There was to be no more holiday camping or conducted tours with a tame guard for us! I had arrived with about 120 men, to adopt about 30 more already in residence, the latter being so sick that few were capable of doing work. My party had to be thankful that they had had six weeks of comparatively good living to prepare them for the hardships of our trek. We had certainly needed that bit of luck. There hadn't been any deaths but many of us had come back from Dalat in little better shape than when we had gone there. Fortunately for us, there were usually enough men available from other camps to do the heavy work outside. However, that left us with few opportunities to get reliable news about the progress of the war or to improve on our rations, which were once again little better than pigswill.

None of the camps had doctors because all officers had been withdrawn, and while the ERT camps had some medicines as well as RAMC orderlies, we had none. Our so-called hospital hut was a shambles devoid of all facilities and the only help that I could offer the sick men was the care from two untrained orderlies and a hygiene detail to clear up and dispose of any messes with tools improvised from discarded petrol cans.

Our only real lifeline was the news which had to be gleaned

at great risk, mainly by French civilians from their illicit radio sets.

Early in July we had heard of the liberation of the Philippines and, after that, that warships had attacked the Japanese mainland. Apart from that, our POW grapevine had spread the news of further bombings of the Burma–Siam railway and the more recent withdrawal of front-line Japanese to various defensive positions along its route. Two of my men got badly beaten up while getting that last bit of news to us. They had been caught talking to members of other working-parties, which was more than enough provocation for our gang of sadists to wade in.

Despite all signs to the contrary, many of the Japanese remained convinced of their invincibility and accepted their reverses with oriental stoicism. This was particularly true of their High Command based in Saigon and headed by Count Terauchi, C-in-C Southern Army. There could hardly have been a more dedicated band of fanatics than that group of men. They were still hounding POWs into situations where they had little chance of survival.

Some had been sent back to Burma to assist with the withdrawal of the Japanese into various defensive positions along the railway route, which was by now being constantly bombed. Those unfortunate men were once again working under Speedo conditions, starved, abused, and (against all agreed Conventions) made to participate in active war work. They were denied personal shelter during air raids. Hundreds are known to have been killed, and among them would have been some of the Sumatra Battalion that we had left up there in early 1944. There were other ventures set up by the above Command in which thousands of men were deployed on road building to parallel and replace the railway, which was virtually rendered useless by early 1945. One road was designed to go 85 miles through the dense jungle of the Tenasserim peninsula and on to Mergui, and another – nearly twice as long – through to Tavoy. The losses on the road jobs were, if anything, worse than those suffered on the defence work. Of the few men who survived these tasks, many were in such a bad condition when liberated that they never made it back home.

And now, it was my turn to resume a nomadic life. An interpreter had been sent down to our camp from Terauchi's headquarters with the message that an advance party of 20 men was to be sent off to Phnom Penh in Cambodia and that I was to be in charge of them.

That alone was surprising enough, but the scheme that we had been chosen for – if his message could be believed – was the most crack-brained that they had thought up so far! We were being sent off to build a canal across the Tenasserim Peninsula.

43

A CANAL TO LINK THE GULF OF THAILAND
TO THE ANDAMAN SEA!

Mid-July 1945

I suppose this story had to be taken seriously, daunting as it was. They would have had no reason for indulging in kiddology, as they had in 1943 when enticing the men from Changi up to their 'so-called' rest camps in Siam and Burma.

In May 1942 we had steamed up to an anchorage off Victoria Point, where 1,000 Aussies were disembarked for working on a nearby airfield. They came up to join us later on the Burma–Siam railway, so some of us already knew of the waterway down there and of the nature of the hinterland. There is a similar inlet on the eastern side of the Tenasserim peninsula in the Gulf of Siam which contains the township of Chumphaun. Chumphaun and Victoria Point are about 60 miles apart. Both places have navigable waters inland from them but the hinterland between them is hilly if not mountainous.

So, if this was to be linked through by a canal, the Japanese must have been desperate for alternative lines of communication and convinced that, despite their setbacks, they still had a chance to win the war. Or were they just crazy? No doubt we will have the answer to that before long because hitherto secret archives are beginning to be made public.

It must have been about the twenty-first of July when we were searched and taken southwards by lorry through Saigon and then across the ferry near My Tho to the south bank of the Mekong river. From there we were transferred onto a waiting river trading boat of about 40 feet length and 9 feet beam, carrying a local crew.

We had been brought there by five guards. They all boarded with us, which seemed to bear out the story that we were the nucleus of a much larger party which would follow.

The vessel had a large but mostly empty hold left open in readiness for our stores; and thankfully, once stowed, the hold was closed and we were left on deck to fit in where we could near the stern.

The ferry had been pulled across the river, and once we started to head up towards Phnom Penh, we realised why. It was just possible to beat our way up against the slower current near the bank but only with the assistance of the crew. Our vessel – and many others – were equipped fore and aft with small outboard platforms. These often had to be mounted by pole-men to fend us away from small rocks and the shallow water close to the bank. It seemed quite remarkable to me that we made any steady headway at all, despite the undoubted strength and skill of those men. Out in midstream, all the craft were racing past us in the other direction (towards the estuary) with no assistance other than by their steersmen to keep them on course.

Our food was cooked within an open-fronted galley by a gap-toothed member of the crew who looked so piratical that we would not have been surprised to see him wearing a cutlass. However, he was a genial man and a fine cook.

It was obvious that the food was going to be the best feature of our mystery tour, so we made the most of it. We were mainly served with well-cooked rice, vegetables and fresh fish. This was made all the more enjoyable for us when our chef told us that the Japanese had been given the same but far less of it. They had no need to speak because their body language spoke volumes about their disenchantment with the Co-Prosperity concept; albeit they had never been greatly enchanted with the French colonial regime that it had replaced, either.

What an unexpected luxury it was for us to be able to doze and gaze our way along for those few lazy days. There was plenty to look at along the banks of that vast river, which was still over a quarter of a mile wide at the end of the 150 miles that we travelled. Drifting along so close to the bank often brought us within close hailing distance of farm folk in the fields or silhouetted against the skyline as they trundled above us on their bullock carts. With all that abundance it would have been difficult to believe that within

359

12 months there would be two million dead from starvation back in the central and northern highlands beyond Dalat.

We continued up-river – mooring at night – until on the afternoon of the fourth day the novelty and pleasure of our journey ceased abruptly with disembarkation and the introduction to our new quarters. Those can best be described as open-fronted concrete pigsties!

The last occupants had long since departed, leaving rotting and stinking rat-infested litter spread over the cobbled floors and the low concrete platforms and walls inside. Outside, the yard was covered in stinking riverside detritus.

The Japanese invited us to spread our kit and make ourselves at home within. With visions of bubonic plague, I surprised even myself by refusing to settle down there without clearing the place out. Instead of getting a bash round the ear, I was provided with shovels from the cargo hold, which was another surprise!

We had seen some rats scampering about the yard when we first arrived but, once we started the clean-up, they began to race from within in hordes. The few that escaped from us made for the river-bank. It was dark inside the building and we kept on finding remote niches swarming with more nests of the vermin. There was about another hour of daylight left when we started to clear the yard and it was dark when we were taken back to the boat to collect our meal.

The evening was spent in burning the piled up rubbish and collecting water, which had to be carried across from the far side of a wide boulevard that separated the city wall from the river. I never went over there myself to see whether it was piped or came from a well; but, however it was supplied, no contact was allowed with the citizens – French or native – who were rarely seen outside the walls anyway.

There we stayed for over two weeks, with the boat tied up and no sign of anyone coming up-river to join us.

It must have been the tenth of August, when I had a small working-party up on our side of the boulevard sweeping up and burning rubbish, that one of the men called down to ask if I could speak French – which I could with reasonable competency. A Frenchman

360

had been shouting across to us from the far side of the boulevard, but nobody had been able to understand what he was saying. So I went up the bankside to join them, and in case he should reappear I decided to stand with my back to the city and reply while pretending – for the benefit of the Japanese guards – that I was haranguing the men for not doing their job properly.

The Frenchman did reappear and my bit of subterfuge worked for a while. I shouted my greetings and immediately got the reply that the war was over. That on its own was wonderful news but I wish he hadn't gone on to say that it was all as a result of dropping two large bombs. Unfortunately Hiroshima and Nagasaki came over loud and clear and, of course, equally intelligible to the Japanese. They must have been already well aware of their emperor's offer to surrender and would realise that the story was now out.

I got a prompt, painful and thorough beating by the corporal, and while that was going on the unfortunate Frenchman was being dragged back within the city walls.

So there we were, left for another day in our riverside dump with that tantalising but hardly believable bit of news, while most other POWs would also have known the full sequence of events that led up to it.

The eleventh was still just another day for us except that we were taken back onto the boat and by midday we were charging down the midstream current towards Saigon at a fast rate of knots. By the following evening we had been taken back to the camp that we had started from. I found the interpreter there. He had already arranged a complete turn-around of procedures whereby Captain Suzuki, the Japanese Commandant, had been made to provide us with as much extra food as he could and to continue guarding the camp, but to see that his men saluted any of us who had dealings with them.

It had occurred to me that the Japanese corporal had beaten me up *after* the offer to surrender, so I asked the interpreter to insist that he was punished; and also to demand that we were moved into better quarters as quickly as possible. By then the Commandant must have known that we were pressing for unconditional surrender and, in common with other Commandants, he was falling over backwards in order to co-operate. He asked if I would like to punish the corporal and I told him to do it himself.

By the following morning it had already been arranged that we would be moving to a much better camp on the other side of the city, which – by chance – was occupied by many survivors from the Sumatra Battalion. I had paraded our company and we were about to move out, when one of the men drew my attention to a guard who, he said, had been patrolling on duty all night. It was the corporal lurching around with one arm broken and one of his eyes hanging out on his cheek. Fortunately for my peace of mind, there was a sequel to that event which brought more punishment on the officer than he had meted out and which, by a strange coincidence, also saved the life of the corporal – but more about that later.

When I had boarded the boat to come back from Phnom Penh I had found that one of the crew must have stolen my large pack. That had meant a lot to me at the time but now, only three days later, the only loss that worried me was of some of my Burma sketches and a personal loose-leaf diary of happenings there.

Once we had moved into our new accommodation we were caught up in a kaleidoscope of far more important events. We were in a well-built hutted camp lit with electricity and reasonably equipped to deal with the cooking of food that was being supplied in over-abundance by then. It was the fifteenth of August and the most memorable day for all. The news came in that the Japanese had been forced to accept unconditional surrender, and with that came the still mystifying confirmation that it had been brought about by the dropping of just two enormous bombs. We were in a state of euphoria and most of us dazed by the suddenness of it all. I was so overcome with emotion that I sought refuge in the darkness outside our hut and wept uncontrollably with the sense of relief that it was all over at last; and I have to confess that typing these words brings all the memories back and causes me to weep again with the recollection of all it meant to me at that time. No doubt there are many others of us who have such feelings. It doesn't do for anyone else to be present either when I see TV presentations of the release of prisoners from the German extermination camps, Changi gaol and the like. One has to have experienced such things to understand how the memories of them are an unfailing counter to the 'stiff upper-lip syndrome'.

I remember coming back from my private moment behind the hut, to discover that a lorry had arrived and delivered thousands of eggs and rashers of bacon. We had already decided that we had quite

362

enough food available for the cook-sergeant to deal with, so this lot was stacked outside to be cooked on a help-yourself basis. So, I gathered up six eggs and some of the rashers, fried and ate them, and was promptly very sick. It was not long after that, though, that I did the same again and kept them down. Despite all the warnings that it was unwise to eat too much too soon after being starved, it never seemed to do me any harm, which was quite strange considering my family's history of stomach complaints.

The rapid end to the Japanese war had caused instability in many areas. With the realisation that Allied troops could not be brought in quickly to deal with it, the Japanese had to be left armed in order to defend us from roving bands of local mercenaries taking advantage of the situation. We were, in fact, no sooner out of one war than into the beginnings of the Vietnam/Vietcong conflict.

There had been French Legionnaires interned in Saigon barracks but their 'other ranks' had already broken out and marched north just before the Japanese surrender. This came about when the Japanese tricked the officers into coming to a dinner at their HQ, at which they had been promptly arrested. So now, just a day or two into the wait for their own troops, there was a total vacuum in authority which the various local factions were exploiting by looting and by murdering French civilians on the streets of the city.

The Japanese were doing very little to control the situation and some had even gone north themselves to join with rebels. So, in an attempt to fill the vacuum, we had mobilised a 'presence' of unarmed patrols for the reassurance of the law-abiding citizens. We had three senior NCOs in our part of the camp, the rest being occupied where the desperately sick and dying were under the care of a few RAMC orderlies. We made three daily patrols, and it just happened that I drew the short straw when there was most trouble.

Each of us had a patrol of ten men, and all were equipped with boots, shorts, webbing belt and attached water bottles. We also carried home-made Indian-style lathi truncheons secured round our wrists. On my second – and the last – day of patrolling, I was out with the late afternoon detail and we had just dismounted from the camp lorry as sporadic firing started up to the north-east. We had scarcely formed up and started to march up the main street, to the accompaniment of French civilians clapping us from their doorways, when we heard the unmistakable rattle of a machine-gun. Bullets were soon whistling down our way, and, mentally saying, 'Bugger this for a game of soldiers', we beat a hasty retreat. Grabbing up a lone and very distinctively dressed Frenchman, we then had no option but to get back onto the lorry. He was in white tropical clothing and had possibly been the intended target of the machine-gunner, but we – being unarmed – didn't stay there to ask any questions.

We had just rounded a bend in the lane leading back to camp when we were confronted by a large band of locals bearing long bamboo poles sharpened like lances and slanted towards us.

Apart from our driver, the rest of us were standing within a clutter of containers to the rear of the cab. He was forced to slow down and I shouted to him to stop, while pushing our passenger to the floor where his clean clothes would not be seen.

The gang moved forward to bring their weapons right up to our chests but, fortunately (with little room to get past us), none of them came further to look over the sides or tailboard of the lorry.

Someone among them spoke French and I told him that we were starving British prisoners-of-war who had been seeking to buy food when the firing had started, and now that we had been forced to return empty-handed could he tell me of any safer place to go. He wasn't at all helpful but, thankfully, after exchanging a few remarks about '*les sanglants Français*', he waved us through.

Once we got back into camp, I had to apologise to our passenger – Monsieur Marcel Graviou – for the necessity to appear to be on the side of the wicked, in order to get him through the road-block safely.

Poor Marcel, he then had to spend a vigil with us that lasted throughout the evening and well into the early morning before it was safe enough for him to return home. Quite early on he had at least managed to bribe a local into getting a message back to his wife Yvette. That was very little consolation, though, for then having to suffer the company of a host of germ-laden scruffs and, the smells coming from the nearby hospital hut. He, like many of his compatriots, had had their businesses and estates destroyed by the mismanagement and neglect of the Co-Prosperity. Now, with the advent of insurrection as well, he was already making plans for returning to his family home in Normandy for good.

* * *

I was now back among the familiar and welcoming company of our Battalion members – except, that is, for my ever-villainous hard cases. The razor-slashing gang had long since been subdued by our Navy lads who, once able to confront them on equal terms of fitness, had given them a thrashing. However, our disreputable blanket stealer was still bearing a grudge. I was sitting with Marcel when he came in roaring drunk from an over-indulgence of (of all things) wood alcohol. He took a swing at me, which I managed to dodge before he landed another one that went straight through a nearby solid partition door. He then collapsed in a stupor, which resulted in him going temporarily blind for a few days. There were others, it was said, who stayed blind as a result of drinking that hooch. Just how moronic can a man be that, having survived three and a half years of POW existence and with the prospect of going home, immediately seek to destroy himself by other means!

We had to all intents and purposes liberated ourselves and were now waiting our turn for the RAPWI (Repatriation of Allied POWs and Internees) teams to be flown in. There were dozens of places, though, where far more deprived and abused communities than ours were needing urgent relief. So, quite understandably, we just had to soldier on for a few weeks. It soon became known that Lady Edwina Mountbatten had flown into some locations in advance of the ultimate surrender date to demand immediate succour for many who would otherwise have died. I am sure she will have known how much we admired her for her courage and, indeed, despised the so-called 'soldiers of the IRA' who later killed her husband.

Things then quietened down in the city for a while, so I went there to meet some of the French residents. I visited Marcel and Yvette and also met up with a Jewish antique dealer named Leopold Althousen. This happened to be just at the time when some of the most ghastly revelations about the German extermination camps were made public.

As soon as he had heard from Marcel about our state of deprivation he had sought me out, so naturally we had a lot to say to each other about man's inhumanity to man. He had come to deliver an invitation for me and five others to a dinner with the family of one of his Chinese business friends. Having thanked him and asked him if we could have 24 hours in which to tidy ourselves up for the occasion, I was somewhat embarrassed to find that he had already thought of that! He loaned me a shirt and gave me one of only three sets of underwear that he possessed, and a pair of socks.

The French were very appreciative of our bearing and behaviour. So, pardon our blushes when I quote part of an extract from the *Temps de Saigon* of the twenty-fourth of December 1945.

> Our town has changed a lot since the official end of the war. Armed Forces have relieved the disarmed soldiery; occupation troops have replaced the ex-POWs. The Dutch left last in full daylight amid the cheers of the town – but others had left before, unnoticed, from the airfield (then inaccessible to us), our friends the British POWs.
>
> Those British left something unforgettable behind them... Who among us can ever forget what they did that 2nd of September when the town seemed given up to hordes of Ammanite fanatics? They, only just out of their evil imprisonment, hesitantly tasting the little comforts we were able to offer them (which even then seemed to overwhelm them), still worn out and unarmed, everywhere, without exception, placed themselves in front of their new friends only made the day before. Truly they can hold their heads high. The smoke-screen of this War has sometimes veiled the true face of England from us. Here it has appeared in those of her sons, POWs in the Far East. We have recognised the type portrayed by their immortal jungle poet, Kipling; we understand the true greatness of the British Empire, of every empire, our own also – we understand this mystery, sometimes intangible, which grows from the bravery of the men who build empires, bravery of which we have been able to admire the exceptional quality.

A bit over the top that last bit, perhaps! But nevertheless I am proud of the fact that we had no lack of volunteers from Appy's Locusts.

The date for the dinner was set and we duly arrived primed to observe the rules of Chinese etiquette. The meal was sumptuous! Among many other things there was a whole deboned pullet for each of us, which, with other delicately seasoned foods, were served up on request. There was a large bowl of steaming rice set down in the middle of the table and we had been warned to ignore it since any request for a serving would have been an insult to our host. It had been cooked solely for distribution to the poor later and to have asked for any of that would – in his philosophy – have been like telling him, 'You haven't offered us sufficient of the special foods, so we must top up with a helping of the basic.' One of the most memorable things for me about that lovely meal was the requirement to eat it to the accompaniment of appreciative belches, which were acknowledged by beams of delight from our host.

Meanwhile, the Japanese had been trying to make capital out of their period of extended authority.

When the Japanese Commandant had beaten up his corporal in such an horrific manner, he was attempting to signal a message for when RAPWI came in, reading, 'Look what is done to our soldiers who maltreat their captors!' It was futile, of course, and by the same token so was their hope that plying us belatedly with an over-abundance of food would impress RAPWI, who had told them to see that we were well fed anyway.

Their latest (and perhaps far more understandable) ploy had been to start substituting the most vicious of our guards with older and more docile stooges.

Some of the Koreans who had been with us in Burma had remained with those of the Battalion that I had recently rejoined. Four of their most sadistic offenders were still with us. Our Japanese Commandant – being well aware of that – was anxious to get rid of them. However, he was unaware of the fact that we already knew the manner in which others had been spirited away from nearby camps – presumably on Count Terauchi's orders. They had been given civvies and a handful of the now quite useless Japanese money, and told to clear off back to Korea under their own steam – some 3,000 miles overland.

A day or two before RAPWI arrived, my tamed gang of four rogues came to tell me that they had saved 'our lot' the trouble of making that journey.

If their story was to be believed, the Koreans had been caught that evening while attempting to leave from the back of the camp, and they were now reposing at the bottom of a well. However, callous it may seem to the reader, my immediate – *and only* –

concern was in getting the assurance that our water supply had not been contaminated. That is the only reason why – knowing the unreliability of my informants – I took two men out with me the following morning to search the area.

We found no sign of the overgrown disused well that they were said to be in, but there was a lot of waste ground beyond the camp boundary. We didn't check there.

I have never had any guilty conscience about the affair but wouldn't have written this except that *our* four villains have long since departed. My abiding hope has always been that they *did* do that distasteful but equally necessary task for all of us. The four Koreans had long overstayed their welcome in this world, having willingly connived at the destruction of 151 of our young men.

There was one Japanese who I would gladly have sent to keep them company, and that was the Kempi-Ti sergeant who three years previously had forced me to witness him murdering that young, innocent and compassionate Burmese girl. I am almost sure it was he who drove past me in Saigon with a Japanese security patrol. Given the certainty and the means to react, I would not only have killed *him* but first made sure that he knew why!

44

RAPWI ARRIVE AND SOON AFTER, WE DEPART

September 1945

It was about the eighth of September when RAPWI arrived to sort us all out, and I will never forget the arrival of the contingent that came to our camp.

The man in command was a young naval lieutenant. Leaving his staff to get on with the paperwork, he asked to be shown round the hospital hut. It wasn't very long before he was out again, fuming at the enormity of what he had found in there and demanding that the Japanese Commandant was brought out to see him. When he appeared in shirtsleeve order, he was sent back to get properly dressed in full uniform and then made to listen to an interpreted indictment of his neglect. We POWs had become so inured to such things that we were taken totally by surprise with what happened next.

The lieutenant reached down and, drawing the Commandant's sword from its scabbard, he beat him left and right across his face with the flat of the blade.

You have to remember that Saigon had been the Japanese show area for the *fair* treatment of POWs to imagine what the lieutenant must have witnessed elsewhere. All of us were underweight human wrecks and many of those in the hospital, though free at last, would never see their homes again; and to try to imagine the depths of the Japanese inhumanity and depravity in the jungle camps could well be beyond most people.

Those of us who were fit enough to leave were paper processed and then allocated spaces on a fleet of clapped-out Dakotas that took us off to Bangkok for delousing by a team of Gurkhas. We were made to bathe and given instructions to surrender *all* of our

369

possessions for burning, but there were very few men who totally complied with that order. I kept the rest of my sketches, my original tattered and sweat-stained Army paybook containing a photo of my wife, the unfinished pipe that I fashioned in Burma and (perhaps strangely) also the pair of boots that I marched down in from Dalat; and I still possess all of them now.

Having been given a haircut, I was then invited into the massage parlour. My skeletal backbone was thumped from top to bottom for starters, and after most other parts had been given similar treatment my neck was attacked with wrenches that made it crack alarmingly. I came away from that lot feeling as if I had been run over by a steamroller. I was then given a cup of hot sweet tea – which I am sure must have been doped. A stretcher had been prepared for me on which to rest, after which I was told the aches would wear off to leave me refreshed. I fell asleep and astonishingly awoke several hours later to find that to be true.

We only stayed one night in Bangkok before being drafted back onto Dakotas again for another short flight, this time to Rangoon for a 'medical' to see if we were fit enough to journey on.

Our first pilot had told us that the Dakota was a reliable old warhorse though of basic design – the latter being well demonstrated! We occupied the stripped-out shell, clutching whatever inner struts came to hand and juggling to open K rations as we bucketed through the sky. What we didn't know was that many of the planes had had scant servicing when called into use for the formidable task of getting us quickly out of more than 250 camps. To achieve that, the pilots – all volunteers – had to make do with far too little rest.

The sadness of all that was that, having ourselves flown safely over the dense jungle area in which we had slaved, our flight arrived to find that one of the planes was missing. Even worse than that came the later news that it had contained several men who had survived amputations under the most primitive conditions in the same jungle as they had now been returned dead. The canopy would have opened to receive them and then closed to engulf them – and, probably, forever! Where in all that is there a God who, supposedly knowing what is best for us, denied them the chance of reunion with their families?

That question had to be asked then, and I, like many others of us since, have never had a convincing answer to it.

PART SIX

45

RANGOON

17 September 1945

On the thirteenth, just before leaving Saigon, each of us had been allowed to send one air-letter home. Four days later I was in tented accommodation within a British 'Reinforcement' camp in Rangoon and eagerly awaiting a reply, when a batch of 11 '20-word' POW cards were delivered to me. The earliest of them had reached the Japanese censors on the twenty-fourth of August *1944*, who had then held on to them for no other reason than sheer bastardisation. That delay meant that I had gone through my entire POW life without receiving any news from home!

I was lodged with a group of lucky 'A to Ks' who earlier that morning had been cleared by a 'medical' in the Rangoon General Hospital as sufficiently fit to be sent home.

On the way back to camp we had been overtaken by a staff car bearing Lord Louis Mountbatten. The car stopped ahead of us and his aides jumped out and set up a platform of wooden boxes, which he mounted to address us. He was fresh up from Singapore after taking the surrender of the Japanese South Asia Command and additionally 'armed' with the overall terms of surrender of the second of September taken in Tokyo by Douglas MacArthur, Supreme Commander Allied Powers.

It was immediately after the 'Tokyo' surrender that Lady Edwina Mountbatten had flown in to some of the remotest POW camp sites to enforce compliance with the following clause:

We hereby command the Japanese Imperial Government and the Japanese Imperial General Headquarters at once to liberate all Allied prisoners of war and civilian internees now under

Japanese control and provide for their protection, care, maintenance and immediate transportation to places as directed...

Lord Louis' main message for us was that we should not feel any
personal guilt for our part in the abortive defence of Malaya. We
had, he said, 'made a valuable contribution to the war effort by
diverting a large force of Japanese for those first few vital months
that had been necessary to get our troops into position along the
defence lines in India and Burma'.

I must confess that I was little more convinced of that then than
I had been when escaping from Singapore or when writing later
about the 'shame of our defeat'. Hindsight can be a very salutary
weapon and I have since read that in November 1941 General
Wavell had already told Winston Churchill that he considered the
city to be untenable!

We had only just got back into camp when we found that some
Japanese – now prisoners – were working in the NAAFI and receiving the same privileges as ourselves. No doubt the CO saw it as his
duty to treat them all humanely no matter how barbaric they might
have been. However, for us ex-POWs – so recently released from
their 'care' – it was such an affront that I went to see the CO with
our genuine and unanimous offer to put off our repatriation for three
months if he would allow *us to care for them.*

Despite there being thousands of men of 'The Forgotten Army'
long overdue for repatriation or leave who were being made
to delay their releases in the interest of us, I am convinced that
our offer further hastened our departure. Within three days of
our protest we had been kitted out, loaded with handouts from our
fighting men, given a casual payment from an 'imprest' account
and, on the twentieth of September, embarked on the troopship SS
Orduna.

It had been very hot ashore and, being still very sick, we hadn't got
much 'steam' left in us for sightseeing. Once again – viewed in
hindsight – it had been a sensible decision to move us out quickly,
because it would have done none of us any good to indulge in
fortuitous revenge on Japanese prisoners about whom we knew

nothing. It is unfortunate, though, that few of us had been given the chance to sightsee other than one quick visit to the area of the city which was dominated by the massive Shwe-Dagon pagoda.

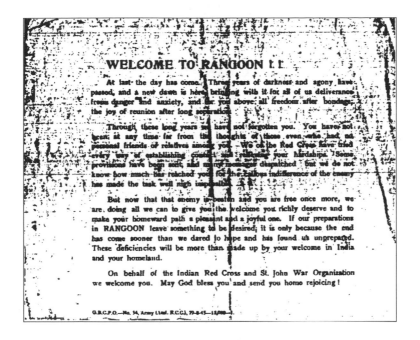

WELCOME TO RANGOON ! !

At last the day has come. Three years of darkness and agony have passed, and a new dawn is here bringing with it for all of us deliverance from danger and anxiety, and for you above all freedom after bondage, the joy of reunion after long separation.

Through these long years we have not forgotten you. You have not been, at any time far from the thoughts of those even who had no personal friends or relatives among you. We of the Red Cross have tried every way of establishing contact and relieving your hardships. Some provisions have been sent, and many messages dispatched but we do not know how much has reached you for the callous indifference of the enemy has made the task well nigh impossible.

But now that that enemy is beaten and you are free once more, we are doing all we can to give you the welcome you richly deserve and to make your homeward path a pleasant and a joyful one. If our preparations in RANGOON leave something to be desired, it is only because the end has come sooner than we dared to hope and has found us unprepared. These deficiencies will be more than made up by your welcome in India and your homeland.

On behalf of the Indian Red Cross and St. John War Organization we welcome you. May God bless you and send you home rejoicing !

G.B.C.P.O.—No. 54, Army Ltd. R.C.C.I, 79-8-45—12/500-I.

46

CEYLON, SUEZ, GIBRALTAR AND HOME!

So cheer up my lads bless 'em all
The long and the short and the tall
Bless all the sergeants and WO 1's
Bless all the corporals and their very sons
'Cos we're saying goodbye to 'em all
The long and the short and the tall
You'll get no promotion
This side of the ocean
So cheer up my lads bless 'em all.

21 September 1945

We were off to Colombo and just before weighing anchor I received an air-letter reply from Dora.

She wrote to say that it had taken two years from autumn 1941 – when I was in Ahmadnagar, India – before she had any substantial hope that I might still be alive. Up until then I had been reported as 'missing believed POW', but *where* had to be anyone's guess. No doubt my escape had further obscured that riddle! Then, in the autumn of 1943 and out of the blue, she received the charred corner of a POW card that I had written to her from Hlepauk railway camp on Boxing Day 1942.

This is illustrated at the top of page 377, and the history of how it reached her is described in the appendices by the Post Office historian who did the research.

After that she only received two of four other cards that I sent and had herself sent off many other than the 11 mentioned previously. Those also failed to reach me and none of that really surprised me when recalling the 'Anankwin incident' of April 1943 when the Japanese paraded us to watch the burning of our incoming mail.

Sadly Dora's father James – the chief engineer – had recently died but all of our other folk had survived, including, remarkably, her brother Dave, despite four years' service as a pilot-officer. Her sister Vera was a Wren and by great coincidence I would soon be making arrangements to meet her in Colombo before she moved out to join Lord Mountbatten's HQ in Singapore.

What with all this home news, the world news and trying to adjust to freedom again, things were crowding in on us far more quickly than we would have wished. It would be impossible to fully describe our feelings at that time to anyone other than the few who had actually witnessed our release from the horrors that had been imposed on us by the Japanese. However, ultimately, those experiences did strengthen the character of most of us. They taught us to cherish the true values in life. Not one of us – even if we had wished it – would ever become the same person that we had been before being taken prisoner.

It was the first time that our skipper had had such an unusual lot of passengers, so he can be forgiven for putting rice on the menu for our first meal. Fortunately for him, we all had such a respect for food by then that few of us even now can bear to see it being wasted. That feeling was just one of the 'traits' and 'isms' that we brought back with us into our strange 'new' world of wonderful nurses, bright lights, freedom, clothes, books, news and the unstinted love and care that was lavished upon us. Predictably, we all hated the Japanese so much that – having vowed never to knowingly buy any of their exports – we still have very few defectors in our ranks.

A few hours before anchoring at Colombo on the twenty-fifth, I got off a ship-to-shore message to Vera. When traced, she then had to come haring 40 miles across the island from her base in Katakarunda.

I had already been ashore for two hours waiting in a reception centre, when a vision, submerged beneath an enormous sun-hat trimmed with chiffon, swept in right past me and went over to the enquiry desk. She was then promptly referred back to an unhealthy, spindly-legged individual that she had passed on the way in; and that is how we met!

After that, the Royal Navy took us over and they did us proud. We were escorted to a Naval officers' club and served with a lovely meal while they made special arrangements for me to return to the *Orduna* on the last picket boat, which was normally reserved for mail only.

It was an overwhelming experience for both of us and perhaps, for me in particular, being able to get first-hand news of home. I didn't have much to say about my own experiences so I had no idea how the sight of so many physical wrecks had got to Vera until after her own repatriation from Singapore.

She had been descending a staircase in the Raffles Hotel when a Japanese prisoner, who had just started to ascend, tried to push his way past her. He was very promptly returned to the bottom again! She was put on a charge for that but, after explaining the reasons for her action, her CO – who had already seen the horrific state of the men who were released from Changi – was sensible enough merely to say, 'Don't let me *see* you do that again!'

The rest of our journey became a leisurely cruise during which I lazed, ate far more than I had been advised to and revelled in thoughts of home and 'civvy street'. We were also enjoying many other things that freedom had returned to us; high on my list of luxuries were cold, unboiled and safe drinking water and toilet paper. What a relief those two items were, albeit to different ends of our anatomy. (A war on prickly pear leaves headed my homecoming agenda!)

We were typical of thousands of other ex-POWs heading home on other ships at that time. Predictably, there were some men who lapsed in health and had to be nursed on the way, but, the fact that the rest of us got by on pills and potions alone made me marvel at the extent to which the human body is able to heal itself. As for mental stress, I have already written of my wonder that none of the Sumatra Battalion went mad or committed suicide. However, all of us had been scarred in one way or another and only a very few of us would ever become free of the marks.

Undoubtedly the slowness of our journey, and the sea air, also aided our recovery and acclimatisation.

By the second of October we were in the Gulf of Aden, heading for the Red Sea and our next stop at Port Tufik, which would only be a brief one for shopping and stretching our legs, while stores and mail came aboard. After that, it was off to Gibraltar, where we only stopped long enough in the 'roads' for Services counsellors and solicitors to embark, bringing the news that we would be docking at Liverpool on the nineteenth.

These were their only good tidings! There must have been about two dozen unfortunate men amongst us who either had to be told about members of their families killed in the Blitz or, worse perhaps, that their wives had either remarried thinking that they were dead or had just cleared off regardless. Poor devils! We had all set out from Rangoon in joyful anticipation of happy reunions, but the rest of the voyage must have been purgatory for them.

We arrived at Liverpool loaded with equipment, winter clothing and gifts, and we did so bang in the middle of a dockers' strike.

The Paymaster General had only advanced payment of £5 per head. Nevertheless, with the addition of generous handouts I – and most others – had our kitbags crammed with cigarettes, tobacco and chocolates as well as nylons and suchlike which we had bought in Colombo and Port Tufik. Fortunately, an advance warning of our arrival had brought hundreds of volunteers to the dockside to assist us with our baggage. My luck still held! By chance my volunteer 'porter' was a brigadier and he, unknowingly, sailed through Customs carrying my kitbag stuffed with loot.

From there, we went off to a dispersal unit where we were fed, issued with 'civvies', documented and billeted for the night. Our papers and rail passes were issued the following morning and then it was off to Euston, Watford and home for me.

It had been agreed that only Dora would meet me at the station. Any other arrangement would have been unbearable! Except for marriage and a week's leave four and a half years previously, we – and countless others like us – had been thousands of miles apart from one another.

The Bet

My CQMS, Tim Healy, thought we would be free by Easter 1944. Being a realist not a pessimist, I made him insert 'Being of sound mind'! The witness – Second Lieutenant Tallant – was an officer/civilian whose occupation was public hangman, Federated Malay States. He and five others had been given army officer status to hide their real identities from the Japanese.

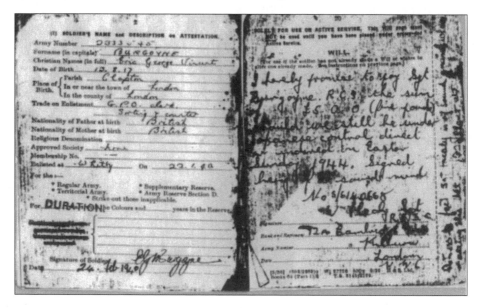

I witnessed many bets made by the Aussies. One of them related to a cockroach race. Another was a bet on how many times a 'clockwork beetle' would chirp before it needed rewinding. One of the bets was backed by 500 sheep. This was to be honoured by the family of the loser if he never made it back. There was no 'being of sound mind' endorsement on that one!

47

REUNIONS – REFLECTIONS AND CONCLUSIONS

1945 – 1999

Throughout the evening of my homecoming I was caught up in a whirl of visits to and by members of both sides of my family, which culminated in a late visit to see my mother and sisters in Bushey before walking back to my mother-in-law's flat in Watford, where we would be living for the next two or three years.

It was only after that and a further round of reunions that I was eventually able to concentrate on *my* programme for rehabilitation and recovery, which rarely involved me in further reunions.

Over the past 54 years I have neither joined the Far East Prisoners of War Association (FEPOW) nor could I be persuaded to attend any of their reunions – even as a guest – until the early 1980s. That was my 'therapy', and I was far from being unique. I had decided on that course while coming home and my stay in Bart's Hospital a few years later in the company of many other ex-prisoners just strengthened my resolve.

There were far too many 'do you remembers' in such encounters for me. My problem was – and still remains – trying to forget. It was all a matter of 'horses for courses', I suppose!

During the whole of our POW life, and particularly so while we were engaged on the 'Railway of Death', I had rarely been able to relax from total involvement. In consequence of that it would have been quite remarkable if I had been able to come home and put all of my memories on the back-burner. Every day there are events in my life that spark off reminders of the physical wrecks that I paraded daily for slavery and of the countless horrors that resulted in so many of them being trashed out of existence by barbarians. Their faces, and the manner of their going, continue to haunt me, and never more so since 1988, when I felt an obligation on me to write this book. That has not only placed a burden on me that I could well have done without but also exasperated my family with my present obsession to get the whole story down before it is too late; and thanks be to the God that I have sought to denounce and renounce that job is nearly done!

However, I was never wholly out of touch with Battalion members. I received and sent letters, and the first of many visits – sometimes reciprocal – was made by Tim Healy, during which he honoured the £5 bet which he made with me in Burma. The remarkable and chance feature of that bet was that although I hadn't possessed a crystal ball as well as a compass, my forecast of the duration of our POW existence turned out to be correct almost to the day! Soon after Tim's visit, Tom Bousfield came to see me. I also discovered that Reg Keast (ex-Navy stoker and survivor of the sinkings of the cruiser HMS *Repulse* and the Customs launch *Hung Jao*) lived in Devon. When I went to see him he couldn't remember a damn thing about the day when I hauled him out of the jungle, delirious and under threat of execution. I wish that *I* could have a few such '*do you not remembers*'.

Bob Grafton must take all the credit for tracking down and keeping in touch with a large number of our ex-Battalion survivors. It was not until 1982 that he was at last able to persuade me to attend a FEPOW National Reunion at Blackpool as a guest. Once I heard that Appy – by then major, retired – would be there and that a side room had been booked for our survivors only, there was no holding me back. There must have been about 40 of us there.

Although it was a day burdened with reminiscences, I will never regret having gone there, because I only saw Appy once more, a few months later at his home near Saxmundham shortly before he died.

It was a sad meeting in many respects. I could see that although he was not well he was still trying to gather in material to write his own story of the British Sumatra Battalion, but he never did. Among his papers he had assembled copies of his recommendations for meritorious service and apologised for not having made a strong enough case out for me. I told him that after 37 years I was too far down the civilian road to worry unduly about that, but spared him the knowledge that my Army number 2333545, had not been shown correctly anyway. I sincerely hope that there was no similar error in the case of Les Bullock, considering the unimaginable risks that he took while running our wireless set!

The truth of the matter probably resides in the facts that our recommendations were considered jointly with Captain Davies and – apart from all but one other – 18 months after we had been separated from the rest of the Battalion.

I only attended one other reunion after that. It was held in Bournemouth in 1988 when Ann Apthorp's book was being launched. My brother-in-law Dave lived nearby and, having driven me to the assembly building, he was greeted by seven of our Navy 'lads', who said, 'If it hadn't been for him we wouldn't have been here now!'

Although the circumstances were embarrassing at the time, I had no problem with accepting that accolade because in reality it was directed at all the men of the *Bintang Dua* who had stood by Appy 46 years previously when the Battalion was formed. *We* were the catalyst around which others were then able to rally and *they* – by and large – were excellent men who willingly responded to our lead. So I have to be proud of the fact that I was not only one of that nucleus but that I also kept my promise to deal honestly and fairly for the benefit of the whole. There were few men who subsequently failed us and none who were ever allowed to become like the renowned 'King Rat' of Changi, thank God.

While we individuals had been busy sorting out the early years of our rehabilitation, the governments of the Allied Powers had been trying to sort out the 'Peace'; and what a mess they had made of that!

Unconditional surrender can be a potent weapon if properly used, but the reality is that it is usually blunted by a succession of missed opportunities; and never more so than when 'emperor' MacArthur marched into Japan.

He arrived encumbered with his government's obsessions that the Japanese were on the verge of 'going communist' and that the British must never have an empire again. So, what ensued?

Too little focus was put on ensuring that the Japanese should make *full reparation* for the enormities of their crimes and, moreover, as a priority condition of aid towards their recovery.

History has shown quite conclusively that the dropping of the atom bombs alone – though an unfortunate necessity – did little to make them confront their barbaric past. I join with the almost unanimous majority of people who have sympathy for the innocent victims of the bombs but no more than that! To borrow a phrase, 'their nation sowed the wind' but they have never been made to reap the whirlwind of their iniquities. In fact, viewed dispassionately, it becomes obvious that those two atom bombs did more for salvation than destruction in the long run. The resultant deaths were 150,000, whereas if the war had gone to a conclusion by conventional means, the aggregate of additional deaths could well have exceeded a million.

The outcome of the soft approach was that the Japanese were not only let off the hook but enabled to rebuild their industries and economy by courtesy of millions of dollars of American support, while we were left to struggle along with clapped-out machinery and a requirement to sell territory in order to help pay off some of our debts.

Over and above that the War Crimes Tribunal – another potent weapon – was misapplied in a programme of leniency and a naive neglect of justice for the countless thousands of individuals who also sought reparation and apology for their losses and sufferings. After all, the Allied Powers must have surely known the nature of the 'beast' that faced them. If not, there were 250,000 unarmed and unavenged men, women and children massacred in the 1937 'Rape of Nanking' on record to remind them.

Lord Russell, in the preface to his account of their atrocities committed during World War Two, made this apology:

> I regret that it has been necessary to include so much that is *unpleasant* but it would have been impossible to have done otherwise without, at the same time, failing to achieve the whole aim of the book, namely to give a concise but comprehensive account of Japanese war crimes. Nevertheless, for every revolting incident that has been described, a hundred have been omitted!

I have already recorded my thanks to him that his one per cent still said enough to save *me* from having to go into too many 'specifics'. However, no thanks are due to the Tribunal members for omitting to make the punishments fit the crimes (as he also said) by their pleas of 'superior orders' and 'military necessity'. What atrocious cop-outs they are, and I could add to those 'political expediency', all of which have allowed so many monsters to escape retribution. Lord Russell was no doubt right when he added that such pleas have no foundation within military law anyway. The following little scenario is typical of what so many of them were allowed to get away with either entirely, or for which their sentences were greatly reduced later.

'What did you do in World War Two, granddad?' 'Well, dear, it was 1942 and I was driving a herd of prisoners-of-war up to work near the Burmese border. Each day there were several of them who collapsed due to disease, malnutrition and exhaustion. So, being a dutiful barbarian, I bashed their skulls in and beat up their officers because they refused to do it for me!' 'No wonder Showa Tenno (the Japanese emperor) decorated you for your bravery and grandma and mummy are so proud of you!'

Records from the British War Crime Courts alone reveal that although they convicted 800 such beasts only 200 of them were hanged and the other 600 all had their life sentences commuted to less than 11 years.

Those latter-mentioned were mainly the small fry among a monstrous whole that quite independently organised the death marches, the prison hulks, mutilation and vivisection. There were also instances in which they feasted on the remains of their victims.

In November 1998 the BBC *Science at War* programme gave details of live experimentation done by a Major Shiro Ishii on prisoners; he first contaminated them with bacteria and then studied their living reaction while various organs were being removed – and he is just one of several on his team who were given immunity from prosecution in exchange for their research papers!

No wonder the representatives of the various Far East Prisoner-of-War and Civilian Internee groups have been steadily losing their battle to get compensation and apology over the past 50 years. Our successive governments have done little to dispel the belief held by most Japanese that when Hiro Hito paid us £76 a head in 1951 it absolved them from all further payment. John Major ducked the issue with a 'softly softly' approach to Aki Hito in 1993 because the 'economic climate' would not have favoured the Japanese. So what! – and as if that wasn't enough, the POW associations were more recently left to go it alone in a contest with the Japanese judiciary – and lost – after which, Aki Hito visited and in full panoply and ceremony was awarded the Order of the Garter.

I wish that I could say that that was the last of the futile interventions by our government, but not so!

Having been to Tokyo with his wife Cherie in January 1998, Tony Blair not only failed to make any headway on the subject but then came back to deliver his opinion that: 'Now is the time that *we* should forgive and forget.' Who the bloody hell are *we*, Tony? Just you and Harriet Harman, who associated herself with the statement, I hope! What further arrogance are your spin doctors going to come up with? That statement has now sent a clear message to the Japanese that the British government doesn't care a toss for our cause any more. They will love you for that!

So, having put up and made a balls-up, we survivors recommend that you should shut up, pack up and join your pal 'Big Willie' in America *and don't ever come back!*

We also have got your message, Tony, which in essence was

No cheer for you lads, 'F—— you all!'
The long and the short and the tall
Bless all the widows without any funds
Bless all their children and their very sons
For them I'll be doing 'F—— all!'
The long and the short and the tall
There'll be no compensation
Try fraternisation!
And once again lads 'F—— you all!'

PS: We – the widows and survivors – are at last going to receive reparation but I make no apology for the above! Funds which had been earmarked for paying us at the cessation of hostilities were withheld and since then conveniently forgotten, whereas the Australian and United States survivors were given £600 and £1,200 respectively at that time, when it was needed most.

You – the generality of the British taxpayers – now have to foot the bill, so I hope that my portion (which is dedicated to the publication of this book) will be some recompense to all who read about *The Tattered Remnants*.

APPENDIX I (A)

BRITISH SUMATRA BATTALION – NOMINAL ROLL

Rank	Name	Unit	Deaths/*Other Information*
MSM	Ackland A.R.	RASC	Died 18 Sep 43 – 30 km Camp
Gnr	Acock A.	9th Coast RA	Died 22 Sep 42 – Tavoy
Gnr	Adams C.T.	30 HAA	Died 27 Jan 44 – 114 km Camp
*L/Bdr	Adamson J.T.	3rd HAA Regt	
Spr	Adrian H.D.G.	41 Fortress RE	Harry
L/Cpl	Agan V.	R C Sigals	Died 5 Jan 43 – Thanbyuzayat
*O/S	Allison D.H.	Royal Navy	Denny
CPO	Ambrose F.G.	Royal Navy	
Sgt	Anderson R.S.	80 A/Tk Regt	
*Capt	Apthorp D.P.	Royal Norfolk	*Commanding Officer* 'Appy' *May 1942 – May 1943, March 1944 – March 1945 (Saigon, 51 Kumi)*
L/Cpl	Armstrong H.K.	41 Fortress RE	Died 30 Jan 44 – Kanchanburi Ken
Pte	Arnold H.	4 R/Norfolk	Died 25 Nov 43 – 55 km Camp
Spr	Arnold S.	41 Fortress RE	
AB	Attersoll J.W.	Royal Navy	Died 30 Oct 43 – 60 km Camp
*AB	Austin J.E.	Royal Navy	
Gnr	Bachl W.C.	30 HAA, RA	Died 15 Nov 43 – 55 km Camp
Pte	Bailey N.C.	4 R/Norfolk	Died 4 Oct 43 – 55 km Camp
AB	Baldwin E.A.W.	Royal Navy	
Gnr	Ball F.	30 HAA	
LAC	Barker J.	Royal Air Force	
LAC	Barker W.	Royal Air Force	
LAC	Barley A.	Royal Air Force	
OS	Barnes H.	Royal Navy	*Grasshopper*
R/M	Barnes V.P.	Royal Marines	*Prince of Wales & Trang* Tom
AB	Barugh R.	Royal Navy	
Cpl	Bateman E.H.	Royal Air Force	
*L/S	Beattie A.	Merchant Seaman	
Cpl	Beatty R.J.	Royal Air Force	
*Gnr	Beckman J.F	7 RA	
L/Bdr	Bedworth G.R.	30 HAA	Died 26 Jul 44 – Kanchanburi
*LAC	Bennet A.J.	Royal Air Force	
Sgm	Bennet D.	R C Signals	Died 9 Jan 44 – 114 km Camp
AC1	Benson J.	Royal Air Force	
Gnr	Benton W.T.	9th Coast RA	Died 17 Jan 44 – Kanchanburi
Gnr	Bicknell S.	30 HAA	Died 3 Oct 43 – 55 km Camp
AB	Blake W.I.	Royal Navy	

Rank	Name	Unit	Deaths/*Other Information*
AC1	Blaklock E.J.	Royal Air Force	
Pte	Bland J.	2 Cambs R Died 13 Nov 43 – 55 km Camp	
Pte	Blockwell T.	6 R/Norfolk Died 22 Jun 42 – Mergui	
*AC1	Blont J.A.	Royal Air Force	
Pte	Bolam J.W.	RASC	Died 15 Dec 43 – 114 km Camp
L/S	Bone J.H.	Royal Navy	
Pte	Bonham J.	1 Leics R	
Cpl	Bostock D. 1	Manch Regt.	Died 13 Nov 43 – 55 km Camp
L/S	Bourne A.A.	Royal Navy Alex	
Sgt	Bousfield T.W.	11 Coast Regt RA	
*AC1	Boute T.L.	Royal Air Force	
*LAC	Bowler L.S.	Royal Air Force	
Gnr	Boycott W.H.	30 HAA	
*L/Cpl	Boyett L.	RASC	
*L/Bdr	Boyle B.J.	30 HAA	
*AC1	Bracewell S.	Royal Air Force	
Gnr	Bradley J.P.	7th Coast RA	
Gnr	Bradley R.W.	30 HAA, RA	Died 16 Sep 43 – 55 km Camp
Gnr	Brain R.C.	30 HAA, RA	
Pte	Brandon J.W.	1/5 Sherwood	Died 16 Feb ?? – Kanchanburi (John)
*Gnr	Breslin J.	9th Coast RA	
2/Lt	Brockman G.	Gen Service	Died 23 Feb 43 – Thanbyuzayat
Gnr	Brookes H.G.	30 HAA, RA	Died 16 Nov 43 – 114 km Camp
AB	Brown C.T.	Royal Navy	
LAC	Brown H.V.	Royal Air Force	
2/Lt	Browne F.G.	Gen Service	
Cpl	Bruce S.B.	Royal Air Force	
*Sgt	Bullock L.W.	Royal Air Force	Les
Stok	Burbridge R.W.	Royal Navy, *Royal Sultan*	Died 11 Mar 44 – Kanchanburi
*Sgt	Burge S.W.J.	RASC	
Sgt	Burgoyne E.G.V.	R C Signals	*A/Battalion Sergeant Major May 42 – Aug 44*
AB	Burroughs B.E.	Royal Navy	
Gnr	Burton J.	30 HAA	
LAC	Bush R.J.	Royal Air Force	
AC1	Bussey R.T.	Royal Air Force	Died 21 Jan 44 – Kanchanburi (Reg)
Cook	Byrne P.	Royal Navy	
*Pte	Campbell W.	RAOC	
L/Bdr	Cart A.	30 HAA	
AB	Carter J.E.	Royal Navy	
*Gnr	Cartmell G.	137 Field Regt RA	
Cpl	Chadwick H.A.	R C Signals	Died 29 Dec 43 – 114 km Camp
Bdr	Chambers G.	7th Coast RA	Died 6 Jul 44 – Kanchanburi (George)
LAC	Charlotte R.A.	Royal Air Force	Died 6 Jun 43 – 30 km Camp

Rank	Name	Unit	Deaths/*Other Information*
AB	Chatfield A.C.	Royal Navy	Died 16 Mar 44 – Kanchanburi
Spr	Cheadle J.	RE	
Sgt	Chippendale K.J.	Royal Air Force	Died 2 Jul 42 – Megui
Pte	Clarke G.	Gordons	
L/Cpl	Clarke J.E.	6 R/Norfolk	Died 9 Jan 44 – 114 km Camp 'Nobby'
*Gnr	Clarkson W.	9th Coast RA	
OS	Cleaver F.	Royal Navy	
Bdr	Clements W.	7th Coast RA	Died 15 Aug 43 – 60 km Camp
Stok	Clifton E.	Royal Navy	
Lt/Col	Coates A.	AIFSMO	*Australian Surgeon (Later Sir Arthur Coates – see note)*
AC1	Coffey C.	Royal Air Force	Died 13 Nov 43 – 84 km Camp
AC1	Coglan W.H.	Royal Air Force	
*Spr	Coles S.	RE	'Butch'
Pte	Collins F.	RAOC	Died 27 Sep 43 – 60 km Camp
Pte	Cook S.	6 R/Norfolk	
AB	Cooper W.E.	Royal Navy	
L/S	Copping N.	Royal Navy	Died 25 Oct 43 – 60 km Camp
Sgm	Copson A.J.	R C Signals	
*LAC	Courts H.	Royal Air Force	Harry
Spr	Coutts G.	RE	
Fus	Cree N.A.	Northbld Fus	Died 12 Jan 44 – 114 km Camp
*LAC	Cremin D.	Royal Air Force	
*Sgn	Cripps R.W.	R C Signals	
*L/Bdr	Crofts J.E.	30 IIAA	
Sgt	Cummings E.	85 A/Tk Regt T A	
2/Lt	Cummings J.	Gen Service	
Bdr	Cummings M.	85 A/Tk Regt	
LAC	Cusack D.J.	Royal Air Force	
Gnr	Daines C.	30 HAA, RA	Died 2 Oct 42 – Tavoy
Gnr	D'Arcey F.J.	137 Field Regt RA	Died 21 Jun 42 – Mergui
*AB	Darrighan S.	Royal Navy	
AB	Darrighan W.	Royal Navy	
Cpl	Daunt H.	RE	
Cpl	Davey J.E.	Royal Air Force	Died 27 Dec 43 – 55 km Camp
Gnr	Davies B.	30 HAA, RA	
Capt	Davies D.J.	FMSVP	*Temp. Commanding Officer May 43 – Jul 44*
*AC1	Davies K.E.	Royal Air Force	
Cpl	Davies L.V.	Royal Air Force	
Gnr	Davies S.	7th Coast RA	
Bdr	Davies T.	30 HAA, RA	Died 29 Jan 44 – Kanchanburi
Gnr	Davis R.G.	9th Coast RA	Died 1 Jun 42 – Mergui

389

Rank	Name	Unit	Deaths/*Other Information*	
Cpl	Dawson J.	Royal Air Force		
Pte	Devine W.W.	RAOC		
Lieut	Dicker H.G.	30 HAA, RA		Harold
Cpl	Dirs C.R.	R C Signals		'Lofty'
Pte	Dixon H.	1 Leics R		
LAC	Dobson F.H.	Royal Air Force	Died 9 Nov 42 – Thanbyuzayat	
Pte	Ducket W.	18 Div Recce Corp		
OS	Dunmore M.N.	Royal Navy		
AB	Duthie C.J.	Royal Navy, *Royal Sultan*	Died 19 Mar 44 – Kanchanburi	Charles
AC1	Eccleston C.	Royal Air Force		
*Pte	Edmunds T.A.	R C Signals		
L/S	Edwards D.W.	Royal Navy		'Bungy'
Pte	Edwards J.	2 Cambs R.		
Cpl	Ellery D.	Royal Air Force		
Sgt	Ellis A.C.R.	R C Signals	Died 25 Feb 44 – Tamarkan	Alexander
*D/S	Elsmore C.B.	Royal Navy		
Pte	Emmott D.	18 Div Recce Corp	Died May 44 – Nakom Pathom nr. Bangkok	
R.M.	Esbester R.T.	Royal Marines		
AB	Escott J.W.	Royal Navy		
AB	Evans A.M.	Royal Navy		
*Sig	Evans E.M.	R C Signals		
*Gnr	Evans F.	9th Coast RA		Yento
Bdr	Fairchild D.	30 HAA		
AC1	Fantarrow E.	Royal Air Force		
Bdr	Faulkner L.S.	1 H K S	Died 20 Dec 43 – 114 km Camp	
*Gnr	Fagan P.J.	9th Coast RA		
Spr	Fenn A.	RA		
Gnr	Final E.A.	30 HAA, RA		
L/Bdr	Fisher M.	30 HAA, RA		
Pte	Fitzpatrick S.J.	2 A & S Highlanders		
Cpl	Flannaghan C.	18 Div Recce Corp		'Bud'
Sgt	Florey E.	I A S C		
Gnr	Foden R.C.G.	30 HAA, RA	Died 27 Nov 43 – 114 km Camp	
*Gnr	Foster J.F.	30 HAA, RA		
Gnr	Foster R.N.	30 HAA, RA	Died 4 Jul 42 – Mergui	
OS	Foster S.A.	Royal Navy	Died 22 Dec 43 – 55 km Camp	
Sgt	Fox P.	1 Leics R		
*Gnr	Francis G.	30 HAA, RA		
LAC	Frazer R.	Royal Air Force		
*Pte	Freeman J.	2 E Surrey Regt		
Gnr	Fulham J.	30 HAA		'Paddy'
Sgmn	Garnett P.	R C Signals	Died 1 Jan 44 – 114 km Camp	

390

Rank	Name	Unit	Deaths/*Other Information*
AC1	Gerrish A.E.	Royal Air Force	
*Stok	Gerry F.	Royal Navy	
AB	Gibson E.	Royal Navy	
*Gnr	Gilhooley R.	7th Coast RA	
Gnr	Gill H.	30 HAA	Died 26 Oct 43 – 60 km Camp
Pte	Gillett T.	18 Div Recce Corp	Died 7 Jun 42 – Mergui
*L/Bdr	Gillies K.	7th Coast RA	
*L/Bdr	Gomer K.	30 HAA, RA	
AB	Goode J.H.	Royal Navy	
Gnr	Gough F.W.	30 HAA, RA	Died 14 Nov 43 – 55 km Camp
L/Bdr	Grafton A.W.F.	30 HAA	'Bob'
Capt	Graham A.	FMSVF	
Gnr	Graham L.	9th Coast RA	Died 12 Jun 45 – Thanbyuzayat
Gnr	Gray R.B.	30 HAA, RA	Died 29 Aug 43 – 60 km Camp
*Gnr	Green E.P.J.	30 HAA, RA	
L/Bdr	Green F.	9th Coast RA	
AC1	Green G.C.	Royal Air Force	Died 26 May 43 – 30 km Camp
*L/S	Gunn L.	Royal Navy	
*Dvr	Gunter L.	5 Field Regt RA	
L/Bdr	Guppy F.J.	30 HAA	
OS	Gutteridge J.	Royal Navy	
Bdr	Haigh W.	30 HAA	
*AC1	Hall J.	Royal Air Force	
Cpl	Hall R.A.	Royal Air Force	
Pte	Halsey C.C.	2 Cambs R	
Pte	Hamilton T.	RASC	'Jock'
Gnr	Hardy T.F.	14 S/L Regt RA	Died 21 Oct 43 – 60 km Camp
Cpl	Hargest A.J.	Royal Air Force	
Gnr	Harris F.	30 HAA	Died 16 Dec 43 – 114 km Camp
Gnr	Harris T.H.	30 HAA	Died 11 Jan 44 – Thomas Kanchanburi
*Gnr	Harrison S.	30 HAA	
2/Lt	Harrison J.H.	H K S	
Gnr	Hart G.F.	30 HAA	
Cpl	Hart N.E.	Royal Air Force	Died 27 Jul 43 – 30 km Camp
AB	Haslett N.F.	Royal Navy	
*Pte	Hatton E.	1/5 Sherwood	
Gnr	Hatton W.C.	9th Coast RA	Died 18 Oct 43 – 60 km Camp
*Spr	Hawkins H.	RE	
Sgt	Hayday W.	Royal Air Force	
LAC	Haynes E.	Royal Air Force	Died 2 Jul 42 – Mergui
Sgt	Healy W.W.H.	RASC	'Tim'
*Gnr	Heppell T.	9th Coast RA	
Pte	Hewardine F.	2 Cambs R	

391

Rank	Name	Unit	Deaths/*Other Information*
Pte	Hewitt S.	18 Div Recce Corp	Died 3 Jan 44 – 114 km Camp
AC2	Hill D.R.	Royal Air Force	
Gnr	Hill L.C.	30 HAA	Died 25 Jan 44 – Leonard Kanchanburi
Cpl	Hill W.R.	Royal Air Force	Died 22 Jun 42 – Mergui
Pte	Hindley A.	18 Div Recce Corp	
Pte	Hinks J.	5 Beds & Herts	Died 3 Dec 43 – 114 km Camp
Pte	Hinton A.	18 Div Recce Corp	
Cpl	Hodgkinson D.G.	Royal Air Force Kanchanburi	Died 14 Jan 44 – Donald
AB	Hodgson J.	Royal Navy, *Dragonfly*	
LAC	Hogarth J.S.	Royal Air Force	
Bdr	Holden W.	9th Coast RA	
LAC	Holme A.	Royal Air Force	
L/S	Hopkins R.H.	Royal Navy	Died 22 Nov 43 – 55 km Camp
Stok	Horsley B.	Royal Navy	
Bdr	Hughes B.K.	1 HAA	Died 14 Nov 42 – Tavoy
*Gnr	Hughes G.	30 HAA	
Gnr	Hughes H.	30 HAA	Died 20 Jan 44 – Kanchanburi
AB	Hughes J.H.	Royal Navy	
Sig	Hughes W.J.	R C Signals	Died 10 Dec 43 – 114 km Camp
AB	Hull R.	Royal Navy, *Prince of Wales*	Died 22 Jan 44 – Richard Kanchanburi
Gnr	Humphrey H.J.	30 HAA	Died 1 Nov 43 – 60 km Camp
*Gnr	Humphries R.	85 A/Tk	
*Gnr	Hunt M.	30 HAA	
Gnr	Hutchinson N.	7th Coast RA	Died 15 Nov 43 – 55 km Camp
Pte	Hynds J.	2 A & S Highlanders	
*Pte	Ingham W.	RASC	
Cpl	Jackson H.	Loyals	
*Sgt	James D.F.	9th Coast RA	
*AC1	Jarvies W.	Royal Air Force	
Pte	Jarvis C. 4	R/Norfolk	Died 31 Dec 43 – 114 km Camp
Pte	Jenkins T.E.	RASC	
*Pte	Jewell P.	2 E Surrey Regt	
Gnr	Johnson C.B.	30 HAA	
CSM	Johnson T.H.	2 Cambs R.	
*Gnr	Johnstone E.	30 HAA	
Stok	Jones A.H.	Royal Navy	
LAC	Jones E.L.	Royal Air Force	
*L/Bdr	Jones G.	7th Coast RA	

392

Rank	Name	Unit	Deaths/*Other Information*	
AB	Jones K.	Royal Navy		'Davy'
AC1	Jones R.	Royal Air Force		
L/Bdr	Jones R.T.	30 HAA	Died 15 Feb 44 – Kanchanburi	Richard
LAC	Jones W.	Royal Air Force	Died 22 Jan 44 – Kanchanburi	
*Stok	Keast R.	Royal Navy	*Repulse* & *Hung Jao*	Reg
Gnr	Kehoe T.	9th Coast RA		
LAC	Kelly N.	Royal Air Force	Died 23 Oct 43 – 60 km Camp	
Gnr	Kelly S.	30 HAA	Died 30 Dec 43 – 114 km Camp	
Gnr	Kendell H.N.R.	9th Coast RA		
*Gnr	Kennedy J.	88 Field Regt RA		
*AC2	Kenney L.M.	Royal Air Force		
Sgm	Kenny E.A.	R C Signals		
L/Cpl	Kernick E.	1 Leics R		
Gnr	Kerr J.	9th Coast RA	*Left at Medan, NE Sumatra 15 May 42*	
*Gnr	Kershaw H.	2 H K S		
Gnr	Kidd W.H.	7th Coast RA		
Pte	Kings W.F.	18 Div Recce Corp		
L/Bdr	Laird G.	30 HAA	Died 22 Dec 43 – 55 km Camp	
LAC	Landeer E.	Royal Air Force		
Gnr	Larvin G.	7th Coast RA	Died 1 Nov 43 – 60 km Camp	
Pte	Leatherland A.	2 E Surrey Regt		
Pte	Leenbrugger	FMSVF		
Gnr	Lewis H.	30 HAA		
*Pte	Little W.H.	R C Signals		Bill
L/S	Livermore C.	Royal Navy	Died 3 Jan 44 – 114 km Camp	
AC1	Loggie W.	Royal Air Force		
L/Cpl	Lonsdale J.P.	2 A & S Highlanders		
Gnr	Loundes J.	85 A/Tk Regt		
Stkr	Luckhurst E.A	Royal Navy		
*Pte	Lydiat T.	RASC		
*Pte	Lynch J.	30 HAA		
Gnr	Maddison C.W.	30 HAA	Died 31 Dec 43 – 114 km Camp	
Gnr	Maiden C.	9th Coast RA		
Sgt	Maney J.A.		*Captured & joined British Sumatra Battalion July 43. Died 1 Sep 43 (see Chap. 28)*	
Gnr	Mann W.	30 HAA		Alvin
Gnr	Marsden D.	30 HAA	Died 20 Oct 43 – 60 km Camp	
Gnr	Mason J.G.	9th Coast RA	Died 5 Dec 43 – 114 km Camp	
*Gnr	Mathews A.R.	30 HAA		
*L/S	May F.	30 HAA		
Stkr	McAffee J.G.	Royal Navy, *Royal Sultan*	Died 24 Jan 44 – Kanchanburi	James

Rank	Name	Unit	Deaths/*Other Information*
AC1	McBain F.C.A.	Royal Air Force	
AB	McCaffery R.C.	Royal Navy	Died 21 May 43 – Thanbyuzayat
Cpl	McCall J.	2 A & S Highlanders	Died 26 Jan 44 – James Kanchanburi
*Tel	McCall J.A.	Royal Navy	
LAC	McDougall A.G.	Royal Air Force	
2/Lt	McGlashen F.	Gen Service	
*Cpl	McGowan A.	2 A & S Highlanders	
Sgt	McKenzie S.	RASC	
AB	McLachan E.J.R.	Royal Navy	Died 10 Nov 43 – 55 km Camp
MSM	McLaren J.	RASC	*Sir Hugh Frazer*
*OS	McLauchan I.	Royal Navy	
*Gnr	McLean A.	80 A/Tk Regt	
*Bdr	McQuade J.	30 HAA	
Stok	Meldrum W.W.	Royal Navy	
Pte	Mesha D.	E Surrey Regt	
AB	Michael S.	Royal Navy	
Bdr	Milburn W.	30 HAA	Died 20 Dec 43 – 114 km Camp
CPO	Mill W.G.	Royal Navy	
AC1	Miller H.	Royal Air Force	Died 25 Oct 43 – 60 km Camp
Gnr	Mobsy C.F.	18 Div Recce Corp	
Gnr	Moore A.	30 HAA	Died 24 Jan 44 – Arthur Kanchanburi
Sgn	Morley W.	R C Signals	Died 8 Jun 43 – Thanbyuzayat
LAC	Morris A.J.	Royal Air Force	
Pte	Morris W.C.T.	18 Div Recce Corp	Died 1 Jan 44 – 114 km Camp
(CSM	Munroe A.R.	FMSVF	Co-opted into the Battalion in 1944)
*L/Cpl	Murray J.L.	Loyals	
Gnr	Murray W.M.	7th Coast RA	
*Cpl	Musk E.	2 E Surrey Regt	
L/Bdr	Musset E.F.	30 HAA	
L/Cpl	Neame P.A.W.	2 A & S Highlanders	'Curly'
Cpl	Nettleton H.	Royal Air Force	
Spr	Noble E.A.	RE	Died 3 Jan 44 – Tamarkan Eric
Cpl	North R.	RASC	Bob
*Pte	Nutter J.G.	18 Div Recce Corp	
*Gnr	O'Brien E.	30 HAA	
Ptc	Ockelford E.J.	R C Signals	Died 30 Dec 43 – Tamarkan
*L/Cpl	Oldfield G.	R C Signals	Died 13 Jun 43 – 30 km Camp
*Gnr	Oldroyd	9th Coast RA	
Lt	Oliver E.D.	1 HAA	
Dvr	Oliver J.	88 Field Regt RA	
Cpl	O'Neale L.	Royal Air Force	

Rank	Name	Unit	Deaths/*Other Information*	
Pte	Pagani R.A.S.	18 Div Recce Corp	*Escaped Dec 42*	'Ras'
Pte	Page A.J.	18 Div Recce Corp	Died 8 Dec 43 – 114 km Camp	
*AB	Parker A.H.	Royal Navy		
Pte	Parker L.W.	18 Div Recce Corp		
Gnr	Parker R.F.	30 HAA	Died 7 Dec 42 – Thanbyuzayat	
Gnr	Parrott F.W.	30 HAA		
Gnr	Parsons W.T.	30 HAA		
Gnr	Parton W.	30 HAA		
L/S	Patterson R.	Royal Navy		
Gnr	Payton C.	30 HAA	Died 13 Dec 43 – 114 km Camp	
Sgt	Pearce H.P.	30 HAA	Launch *Joan*	
*Gnr	Perry A.E.	30 HAA		
LAC	Phillips A.P.	Royal Air Force		
Gnr	Philpott A.J.	9th Coast RA	Died 20 Dec 43 – Tamarkan	
Gnr	Philpott J.C.	9th Coast RA		
Gnr	Pickford R.J.	9th Coast RA	Died 26 Dec 43 – 114 km Camp	
Cpl	Pleavin B.	Royal Air Force	Died 8 Feb 44 – Kanchanburi (Basil)	
Pte	Plumb D.	2 Cambs		
Lt	Pocock E.I.	9th Coast RA		
Lt	Power R.C.	122 Field Regt RA		
Gnr	Pratt J.G.	30 HAA	Died 18 Feb 44 – Kanchanburi	John
Gnr	Prendergast J.A.	9th Coast RA	Died 18 Dec 43 – Tamarkan	John
Dvr	Prescott A.W.	R C Signals		
Gnr	Pullen J.T.	30 HAA		
Pte	Quale F.	5 S/L Regt RA	Died 8 Jul 43 – 30 km Camp	
Pte	Quarterly E.	FMSVF	Died 24 Oct 42 – Tavoy	
Gnr	Radcliff F.L.	30 HAA		
W/Mn	Rasmussen A.C.	Royal Navy	Died 22 Jun 43 – 18 km Camp	
*Spr	Ratty L.	RE		
*Gnr	Ravenscroft E.	30 HAA		
*Gnr	Raymond E.A.	85 A/Tk Regt RA		
Gnr	Reast R.E.	30 HAA	Died 4 Jan 44 – 114 km Camp	
Sgt	Reed G.	RASC	Died 22 Dec 43 – 114 km Camp	
*L/Bdr	Rees E.	9th Coast RA		Ernie
Gnr	Reeves G.E.	85 A/Tk Regt RA		
AC1	Richards B.	Royal Air Force		
L/Bdr	Richardson H.G.	1 HAA	Died 4 Nov 42 – Thanbyuzayat	
*LAC	Ridett R.E.	Royal Air Force		
*Gnr	Rivers R.I.	30 HAA		
Gnr	Roberts C.	85 A/T Regt RA	Died 20 Dec 43 – Tamarkan	Caradoc
Bdr	Roberts F.C.	1 H K S	Died 28 Nov 42 – Thanbyuzayat	

Rank	Name	Unit	Deaths/*Other Information*
Gnr	Robinson H.	30 HAA	
Pte	Robinson J.H.	4 R/Norfolk	Died 12 Jan 44 – Tamarkan James
Sgt	Robinson J.K.	30 HAA	Died 27 Jan 44 – 'Chinky' Kanchanburi
L/S	Rodgers S.	Royal Navy	Died 18 Dec 43 – 114 km Camp
L/Bdr	Rodgers W.	30 HAA	
Gnr	Rogers A.	30 HAA	Killed 25 Jun 45 – Thanbyuzayat
*Gnr	Rosbotham J.	2 H K S	
Gnr	Ross G.	7th Coast RA	
*Cpl	Rounding J.	Royal Air Force	
Gnr	Rowsell T.J.	30 HAA	
Pte	Rundle L.G.	RASC	Died 3 Dec 43 – 114 km Camp
Gnr	Rush P.	85 A/Tk Regt RA	
Gnr	Russell F.	30 HAA	Died 14 Nov 43 – 55 km Camp
*AB	Ryan T.H.	Royal Navy	Died 26 Aug 44 – Saigon
LAC	Saddington S.W.	Royal Air Force	
Gnr	Salt J.	30 HAA	
*Gnr	Sankey W.G.	30 HAA	
AB	Sarney J.H.	Royal Navy	
*Gnr	Saunders W.J.	9th Coast RA	
AC1	Scott B.	Royal Air Force	Died 20 Jun 42 – Mergui
Stok	Scott F.G.	Royal Navy	Died 9 Feb 44 – 114 km Camp
Gnr	Scriven I.	30 HAA	Died 24 Dec 43 – 114 km Camp
*Cpl	Seager	4 R/Norfolk	
Stok	Sedgbeer A.	Royal Navy	*Prince of Wales* & Ashley *Hung Jao*
Bdr	Sennet H.	1 HAA	
Gnr	Shaw J.E.	30 HAA	Killed 15 Jun 43 – Thanbyuzayat
Gnr	Shaw M.	30 HAA	
Gnr	Shelton G.O.	30 HAA	Died 26 Jan 44 – Gerald Kanchanburi
Bdr	Shepherd J.W.	30 HAA	
Gnr	Shields G.E.	30 HAA	
Cpl	Shrimpton R.	Royal Air Force	
Gnr	Siemers C.W.	30 HAA	
Gnr	Sigsworth H.R.	30 HAA	Died 30 Dec 43 – 114 km Camp
Gnr	Sills H.	7th Coast RA	Died 5 Jan 44 – 114 km Camp
Ck	Simcock H.C.	Royal Navy	Died 1 Oct 43 – 55 km Camp
*Gnr	Sims S.	30 HAA	
Stok	Smale W.T.G.	Royal Navy	
*Bdr	Smart D.	9th Coast RA	
Gnr	Smith E.J.	30 HAA	Died 29 Dec 43 – 114 km Camp
Gnr	Smith E.W.E.	9th Coast RA	
AB	Smith G.H.	Royal Navy	
Cpl	Smith G.W.R.	2 E Surrey Regt	

Rank	Name	Unit	Deaths/*Other Information*
Gnr	Smith H.W.	5 Field Regt RA	Died 23 Dec 43 – 114 km Camp
Gnr	Smith J.L.	30 HAA	
*Pte	Smith S.	2 K & S H	
Gnr	Smith T.H.	9th Coast RA	Died 6 Dec 43 – 114 km Camp
Gnr	Smith W.	30 HAA	Died 17 Nov 43 – 55 km Camp
Stok	Smith W.T.O.	Royal Navy	
*L/S	Smyth W.	Royal Navy	
Cpl	Spears S.	Royal Air Force	
Lt	Spriggs E.	5 Beds & Herts	
*Gnr	Springett J.F.	30 HAA	
Pte	Squires H.	2 E Surrey Regt	
Cpl	Starling E.A.	Royal Air Force	
Sgt	Stead W.P.A.	RASC	Ned
Gnr	Steenson T.R.C.	7th Coast RA	
Bdr	Stephen P.W.	1 H K S	
Gnr	Stephens D.G.	7th Coast RA	
L/Cpl	Stephens E.H.	R C Signals	
Lt	Stephens M.T.T.	Sher Foresters	
*Spr	Stevenson A.C.	RE	
Gnr	Stimson F.	30 HAA	Died 28 Dec 42 – Thanbyuzayat
Capt	Storr W.G.	RASC	
Sgt	Stracchino G.	41 Fortress RE	'Stracc'
L/Bdr	Surredge P.L.	1 HAA HKS	Died 26 Oct 43 – 60 km Camp
*Pte	Sutton A.	RAOC	
Pte	Swalwell J.	RASC	Died 13 Nov 43 – 55 km Camp
Cpl	Synnot A.E.	Royal Air Force	Died 18 Dec 43 – 105 km Camp
Lt	Tallent D.	Gen Service	
*Bdr	Tate H.	30 HAA	
L/Cpl	Taylor J.	1 Manch	Died 27 Dec 43 – Tamarkan James
Cpl	Taylor R.	1 Manch	
Bdr	Telford N.	30 HAA	
AB	Thomas D.G.	Royal Navy	
*L/Bdr	Thomas D.R.	9th Coast RA	
*Bdr	Thomas L.	30 HAA	
Gnr	Thomas T.D.	30 HAA	Died 6 Dec 43 – 114 km Camp
W/Man	Thompson J.H.	Royal Navy	
L/Cpl	Thompson J.S.	RAOC	Died 24 Jan 44 – Kanchanburi (John)
Gnr	Thomson T.	7th Coast RA	Died 14 Dec 43 – 55 km Camp
*Pte	Thomson W.	2 A & S H	
Bdr	Thorpe T.	30 HAA	Jack
Sgt	Todd L.	80 A/Tk Regt RA	
L/Bdr	Tomlinson P.	30 HAA	
Cpl	Toms P.E.	Royal Air Force	
*Pte	Toone D.	1 Leics	
*Stok	Tracey P.	Royal Navy	*Repulse* & *Dragonfly*

Rank	Name	Unit	Deaths/*Other Information*	
Pte	Tredrea S.	2 E Surrey Regt		
Sgt	Tribe F.C.	RAOC	Died 2 Mar 44 – 114 km Camp	'Pinkie'
*PO	Tucker W.H.	Royal Navy	*Repulse & Jarak*	'Jan'
*Stok	Ulrick D.	Royal Navy	*Repulse*	
AC1	Vaisey A.S.	Royal Air Force		
Cpl	Verrells D.	Royal Air Force		
Lt	Villiers R.	Gen Service		Roger
*Gnr	Waddingham J.K.	30 HAA		
L/Bdr	Wadlow S.A.	30 HAA		
*Stew	Walker P.J.	Royal Navy		
Gnr	Walsh J.	9th Coast RA		
Gnr	Walsh T.	9th Coast RA		
*Gnr	Ward C.	30 HAA		Charlie
*LAC	Wardell M.T.H.	Royal Air Force		
AB	Warner W.R.	Royal Navy	Died 14 Sep 42 – Tavoy	
Gnr	Warwick C.	30 HAA		
Gnr	Waters A.L.	30 HAA	Died 5 Jan 43 – Thanbyuzayat	
AB	Watson D.	Royal Navy	*Believed died 1944*	
Lt	Watson R.	1 HAA		
Bdr	Watson W.G.K.	7th Coast RA		
AB	Watts I.L.A.	Royal Navy		
OS	Weaver J.	Royal Navy	Died 12 Jul 42 – Mergui	
Pte	Webber F.S.	FMSVF		
Sgt	Wesley M.	30 HAA		
L/Bdr	Weston W.T.	7th Coast RA	Died 9 Nov 42 – Thanbyuzayat	
*AB	White A.E.	Royal Navy		
LAC	White J.G.	Royal Air Force		Joe
Sgm	Whittaker A.	R C Signals		
LAC	Whittey W.J.	Royal Air Force		Jim
Gnr	Wightman R.	1 HAA	Died 11 Oct 43 – 60 km Camp	
AB	Wignall F.	Royal Navy	Died 9 Dec 43 – 114 km Camp	
AC1	Wild S.S.	Royal Air Force		
*Pte	Wilding D.E.	2 Cambs		
Sgn	Wiley G.C.	R C Signals		
Gnr	Wilkinson F.A.	7th Coast RA	Died 20 Feb 44 – Kanchanburi	Frederick
AC1	Williams J.	Royal Air Force		
Gnr	Williams T.J.	30 HAA		
Gnr	Willis R.R.	30 HAA	Died 24 Jun 42 – Mergui	
Lt	Wilson A.T.	1/5 Sherwood	Died 11 Nov 43 – 114 km Camp	
*L/Cpl	Wind S.	18 Div Recce Corp		
*Sgt	Winson G.	H K S		
*AB	Witherlly H.W.	Royal Navy		
Gnr	Woods S.E.	30 HAA		

Rank	Name	Unit	Deaths/*Other Information*
*Gnr	Woodley E.L.	85 A/Tk Regt RA	
R/M	Wooton F.J.	Royal Marines	
L/Cpl	Wooton J.	4 R/Norfolk	Died 9 Aug 42 – Mergui
Gnr	Wright E.T.	9th Coast RA	
Sgt	Wringe E.	Indian Army Corps Clerks	
Gnr	Yarwood S.A.R.	30 HAA	Died 3 Dec 43 – 55 km Camp

Note: This Nominal Roll is of 501 names, inclusive of Lt/Col Coates (Australian Surgeon) who left our Battalion when we arrived in Thanbyuzayat.

Attached to the British Sumatra Battalion in Saigon on 22 March 1944

*Cpl	Bingham J.H	RAAF
*Pte	Bolton A.	A & SH
*Pte	Burns N.F.M.	STADS
*Pte	Cobley R.A.C.	STADS
*Gnr	Fixter	British Army
*Sgt	Kerr R.	A & SH
*Pte	Mendllson J.	STADS
*Pte	Park H.G.	STADS
*Pte	Rowe W.E.	AIF
*Pte	Wallace R.J.	STADS
*Pte	Williamson M.	STADS
Pte	Worley L.R.	STADS
*Pte	Varley R.	STADS
*Pte	Yates J.D.F.	STADS

Notes: Men shown as STADS were British civilians enlisted in the Dutch Army.

A note from the author about the above:

Inaccuracies do exist and particularly among initials when compared with lists derived from this roll; but which – if any – is correct? The roll was compiled from the historical original hidden and later salvaged by our CO and, as such, no corrections have, or should have been, attempted by me other than a few alphabetical rearrangements of surnames and – in Appendix II – the addition of recently acquired monumental inscriptions.

Owing to the destruction of certain records by the Japanese, some of the details given in this nominal roll may be inaccurate.

* Members of the Battalion plus the above 13 additions who were all designated '51 Kumi' and were lucky to escape being embarked with the 2,218 men who left Singapore on the ill-fated Japan-bound convoy on 4 September 1944 in which only 119 men survived.

(See Appendix IV Vessels (Allied Submarine Attacks))

APPENDIX I(B)

UNIT ANALYSIS

	Men	Officers (& Names)
Royal Navy		
Navy	79	
Marines	3	
(Merchant Navy)	1	
Royal Air Force	79	
Royal Army Artillery		
1st Light Ack Ack	1	
1st Heavy Ack Ack	5	2 Lt Oliver E.B.
		Lt Watson R.
3rd Heavy Ack Ack	1	
30th Heavy Ack Ack	110	1 Lt Dicker H.G.
7th Coast Regiment	20	
9th Coast Regiment	32	1 Lt Pocock E.I.
11th Coast Regiment	1	
5th Field Regiment	2	
88th Field Regiment	2	
122nd Field Regiment		1 Lt Power R.C.
137th Field Regiment	2	
88th Anti-Tank Regiment	1	
Searchlight Regiment	2	
Royal Corps		
RAOC	6	
RASC	16	1 Capt Storr E.
R C Signals	21	
Royal Engineers		
41 Fortress	4	
(Others)	8	
'SHIRES' & Others		
Argyll & Sutherland	8	
Beds & Herts	1	1 2/Lt Spriggs E
Cambs	17	
Federated Malay States Volunteers	4	2 Capt Davies D.J.
		Capt Graham A
Gordon Highlanders	1	
Hong Kong & Shanghai Volunteers	6	1 2/Lt Harrison J.H.

	Men	Officers (& Names)
'SHIRES' & Others *(continued)*		
Indian Army Corps of Clerks	1	
Indian Army Service Corps	1	
Leics	5	
Loyals	2	
Manchester (1st)	3	
Norfolks (4th & 6th)	9	1 Capt Apthorp D.P.
Northumberlands	1	
Sherwood Foresters (1st & 5th)	2	2 Lt Wilson A.T.
		2/Lt Stephens H.T.T.
Surrey (East) (2nd)	8	
18th Division Recce	15	
General Service (Officers)		
Civilian Appointed		1 Lt Brockman G.
		1 2/Lt Browne G.G.
		1 2/Lt Cummings J.
		1 2/Lt McGlashan F.
		1 2/Lt Tallant D.
		1 2/Lt Villiers R.
Australian Medical Officer		
Attached May – Nov 1942		1 Lt/Col Coates A.
	480	20

APPENDIX II

DEATH ROLL – CAMP ANALYSIS

Medan Sumatra (1)

Gnr Kerr, 9th Coast   Too ill to sail

Mergui Lower Burma (12)

Pte T. Blockwell 6 R/Norfolk
Sgt K.J. Chippendale RAF
Gnr F.J. D'Arcy 137 Field RA
Gnr R.G. Davies 9th Coast
Gnr R.N. Foster 30 HAA RA
Pte T. Gillett 18 Div Recce Corp
LAC E. Haynes RAF
Cpl W.R. Hill RAF
ACL B. Scott RAF
OS J. Weaver RN
Gnr R.R. Willis 30 HAA RA
L/Cpl J.Wooton 4 R/Norfolk

Tavoy Lower Burma (5)

Gnr A. Acock 9th Coast RA
Gnr C. Daines 30 HAA RA
Bdr B.Hughes 1st HAA
Pte E. Quarterly FMSVF
AB W.R. Warner RN

Railway Camps

Thanbyuzayat (14) (BASE)

L/Cpl V. Agan R C Signals
2nd/Lt G. Brockman Gen Service
LAC F.H. Dobson RAF
Gnr L. Graham 9th Coast RA
AB R.C. McCaffery RN
Sgm W. Morley R C Signals
Gnr R.F. Parker 30 HAA RA
L/Bdr H.G. Richardson 1st HAA RA
Bdr F.C. Roberts 1 HKS
Gnr A. Roger 30 HAA RA   Killed by Allied aircraft
Gnr J.E. Shaw 30 HAA RA   Killed by Allied aircraft
Gnr F. Stimson 30 HAA RA

Thanbyuzayat (14) (BASE) *(continued)*

Gnr A.L. Waters 30 HAA RA
L/Bdr W.T. Weston 7th Coast RA

18 Kilometre Camp (1) HLEPAUK

W/Man A.C. Rassmussen RN

30 Kilometre Camp (6) REJPU

MSM A.T. Ackland RASC
LAC R.A. Charlotte RAF
AC1 G.C. Green RAF
Cpl N.E. Hart RAF
L/Cpl G. Oldfield RASC
Pte F. Quale 5 S/L Regt RA

55 Kilometre Camp (20) KHONKLAN

Pte H. Arnold 4 R/Norfolk
Gnr W.C. Bachl 30 HAA RA
Pte N.C. Bailey 4 R/Norfolk
Gnr S. Bicknell 30 HAA RA
Pte J. Bland 2 Cambs
Cpl D. Bostock 1 Man Regt
Gnr R.W. Bradley 30 HAA RA
Cpl J.E. Davey RAF
OS S.A. Foster RN
Gnr F.W. Gough 30 HAA RA
L/S R.H. Hopkins RN
Gnr N. Hutchinson 7th Coast RA
L/Bdr G. Laird 30 HAA RA
AB E.J.R. McLachlan RN
Gnr F. Russell 30 HAA RA
Ck H.C. Simcock RN
Gnr W. Smith 30 HAA RA
Pte J. Swalwell RASC
Gnr T.H. Thomson 7th Coast RA
Gnr S.A.R. Yarwood 30 HAA RA

60 Kilometre Camp (16) – TAUNGZAN

AB J.W. Attersoll RN
Bdr W. Clement 7th Coast RA
Pte F. Collins RAOC
L/S N. Copping RN
Gnr H. Gill 30 HAA RA
Gnr R.B. Gray 30 HAA RA

403

60 Kilometre Camp (16) – TAUNGZAN *(continued)*

Gnr T.F. Hardy 14 S/L Regt RA
Gnr W.C. Hatton 9th Coast RA
Gnr H.J. Humphreys 30 HAA RA
LAC N. Kelly RAF
Gnr G. Lavin 7th Coast RA
Sgt J.A. Maney 1st LAA RA Burma Captive Attached
Gnr L. Marsden 30 HAA RA
AC1 H. Miller RAF
L/Bdr P.L. Surredge 1 HAA HKS RA
Gnr R. Wightman 1 HAA HKS RA

84 Kilometre Camp (1) – APALON

AC1 C. Coffrey RAF

105 Kilometre Camp (1) – AUNGANANG II

Cpl M.E. Synnott RAF

114 Kilometre Camp (39) – CHAUNGARA also CHAUNGALA-YA

Gnr C.T. Adams 30 HAA RA
Sgm. D. Bennett R C Signals
Pte J.W. Bolam RASC
Gnr H.G. Brookes 30 HAA RA
Cpl H.A. Chadwick R C Signals
L/Cpl J.E. Clarke 6 R/Norfolk
Fus N.A. Cree Northbld Fus
Bdr L.S. Faulkner 1 HKS
Gnr R.C.G. Foden 30 HAA RA
Sgm P. Garnet R C Signals
Gnr F. Harris 30 HAA RA
Pte S. Hewitt 18 Div Recce
Pte J. Hinks 5 Beds & Herts
Sgm W.J. Hughes R C Signals
Pte C. Jarvis 4 R/Norfolk
Gnr S. Kelly 30 HAA RA
L/S C. Livermore RN
Gnr C.W. Maddison 30 HAA RA
Gnr J.G.E. Mason 9th Coast RA
Bdr W. Milburn 30 HAA RA
Pte W.C.T. Morris 18 Div Recce
Pte A.S. Page 18 Div Recce
Gnr C. Payton 30 HAA RA
Gnr R.J. Pickford 9th Coast RA
Gnr R.E. Reast 30 HAA RA
Sgt G. Reed RASC

114 Kilometre Camp (39) – CHAUNGARA also CHAUNGALA-YA
(continued)

L/S S. Rodgers RN
Pte L.G. Rundle RASC
Stok F.G. Scott RN
Gnr I. Scriven 30 HAA RA
Gnr H.R. Sigsworth 30 HAA RA
Gnr H. Sills 7th Coast RA
Gnr E.J. Smith 30 HAA RA
Gnr H.W. Smith 5 Field Regt RA
Gnr T.H. Smith 9th Coast RA
Gnr T.D. Thomas 30 HAA RA
Sgt F.C. Tribe RASC
AB F. Wignall RN
Lt A.T. Wilson 1/5 Sherwood

(END OF RAILWAY CAMPS)

Tamarkan (Thailand) (8)

Sgt A.C.R. Ellis R C Signals	Alexander Claude Richard	2568715
Spr E.A. Noble RE	Eric Arthur	1871124
Pte F.J. Ockleford R C Signals	Frederick Jacques	2342179
Gnr A.J. Philpott 9th Coast RA	Arthur John	1427312
Gnr J.A. Prendergast 9th Coast RA	John	3547380
Gnr C. Roberts 85 A/T Regt RA	Caradoc	1459400
Pte J.H. Robinson 4 R/Norfolk	James Henry	5773208
L/C J. Taylor 1 Manch	James	3527543

Saigon (1)

AB T.H. Ryan RN

Believed Died 1944 – Camp Unknown (1)

AB D. Watson RN

Kanchanburi (Thailand) (26)

L/Cpl H.K. Armstrong 41 Fortress RE	Kenneth John Francis	1870413
L/Bdr G.R. Bedworth 30 HAA RA	George	3187900
Gnr W. Benton 9th Coast RA	William Thomas	
Pte J.W. Brandon 1/5 Sherwood	John William	4756039
*Stok R.W. Burbridge RN	Robert William D/Kx	113261
AC1 R.T. Bussey RAF	Reginald Thomas	434864
Bdr G. Chambers 7th Coast RA	George Alexander	835246
*AB A. Chatfield RN	Alfred Charles P/JK	276477

Kanchanburi (Thailand) (26) (continued)

Bdr T. Davies 30 HAA RA		
*AB C.J. Duthie RN	Charles John D/J	169296
Gnr R.T. Harris 30 HAA RA	Thomas Henry	1603436
Gnr L.C. Hill 30 HAA RA	Leonard Cooper	1811457
Cpl D.C. Hodgkinson RAF	Donald Christie	942162
Gnr H. Hughes 30 HAA RA	Harold Henry	1810546
AB R. Hull RN	Richard D/JK	1467666
L/Bdr R.T. Jones 30 HAA RA	Richard Treharne	1605217
LAC W. Jones RAF		
*Stok J.G. McAffee RN	James George D/KX	138902
Cpl J. McCall 2 A & S Highlanders	James	2985491
Gnr A. Moore 30 HAA RA	Arthur	1811487
Cpl B. Pleavin RAF	Basil	968522
Gnr J.G. Pratt 30 HAA RA	John	1603102
Sgt J.K. Robinson 30 HAA RA	John Kenneth	791870
Gnr G.O. Shelton 30 HAA RA	Gerald Owen	1811531
L/Cpl J.S. Thompson RAOC	John Sherloff	7626702
Gnr F. Wilkinson 7th Coast RA	Frederick Albert	1810546

Nakom Pathon (Thailand) (1)

Pte D. Enmott 18 Div Recce

Notes

(i) *see VESSELS Appendix IV HMS *Royal Sultan* for further details about these men.

(ii) Re the Thailand listings, those shown 'of 30 HAA RA' will be found in cemetery records under '3 Heavy AA', which was its parent unit.

(iii) Re Gnr R.T. Harris, 30 HAA RA, the Battalion diary records suggest that he must have died on the evacuation train (114 km Camp, Burma, to Kanchanaburi, Thailand).

APPENDIX III (A)

THE BRITISH SUMATRA BATTALION

Officers	Employment & Deaths
Lt/Col A. Coates	Medical Officer May – Nov 1942
Capt D.P. Apthorp	OC Party May 1942 – May 1943, March 1944 – March 1945
Capt D.J. Davies	OC Party May 1943 – July 1944
Capt A. Graham	
Capt W.G. Storr	
Lt H.G. Dicker	Adjt May 1942 – May 1943 (Pay)
Lt E.I. Pocock	QM May 1942 – May 1943
Lt R.G. Power	QM (Canteen) May 1943 – Dec 1943
Lt A.T. Wilson	Died 11 Nov 1943
Lt E.B. Oliver	Attached HQ Thanbyuzayat
2/Lt G. Brockman	Died 23 Feb 1943
2/Lt G.G. Browne	
2/Lt J. Cummings	QM May 1943 – Aug 1943
2/Lt J.H. Harrison	
2/Lt F. McGlashen	
2/Lt E. Spriggs	
2/Lt M.T.T. Stephens	
2/Lt D. Tallent	QM Aug 1943 – Nov 1943
2/Lt R. Villiers	Adjt May 1943 – Mar 1944 (Pay)
2/Lt Watson	

Other Ranks	Employment & Deaths
CPO F.G. Ambrose	Pay
Sgt R.S. Anderson	Ordy/Sgt
L/Bdr Bedworth	HQ. Died 26 Jul 44 – Kanchanaburi
Sgt T.W. Bousfield	Ordy/Sgt
LAC L.S. Bowler	Hospital
Sgt L.W. Bullock	Canteen & Special Duty, clandestine radio
Sgt W.W.J. Burge	Cook Sgt
Sgt E.G.V. Burgoyne	BSM
Pte W. Ducket	HQ
AC1 C. Eccleston	Hospital
L/S D.W. Edwards	Ordy/Sgt
Pte S.J. Fitzpatrick	Hospital
Cpl C. Flannaghan	Cook Sgt
Gnr F.W. Gough	Office. Died 14 Nov 43 – 55 km Camp

407

Other Ranks	Employment & Deaths
L/Bdr F.J. Guppy	HQ
Sgt W.W.H. Healy	ORQMS
Sgt D.F. James	CSM Saigon – 51 *Kumi*
*Sgt R. Kerr	CQMS Saigon – 51 *Kumi* only
Gnr L. Marsden	Office. Died 20 Oct 43 – 60 km Camp
LAC F.C.A. McBain	Hospital
CPO. W.G. Mill	CQMS
Pte A.J. Page	HQ. Died 8 Dec 43 – 144km Camp
Sgt H.P. Pearce	Ordy/Sgt
LAC R.E. Ridett	HQ Saigon – 51 *Kumi*
Sgt J.K. Robinson	CSM. Died 27 Jan 44 – Canchaubura
Sgt G. Strachino	BSM
Sgt F.G. Tribe	CQMS. Died 2 Jan 44 – 114km Camp
CPO. W.H. Tucker	Canteen & Special Duty, clandestine radio
Sgt N. Wesley	CQMS
Sgt G. Winsom	CQMS
Gnr S.A.R. Yarwood	Att. Hospital. Died 3 Dec 43 – 55km Camp

Notes
(i)   *Attached to Battalion April 1944 onwards.
(ii)   For unit details of the officers see Appendix I (b) – Unit Analysis.

APPENDIX III (B)

RECOMMENDATIONS FOR MERITORIOUS SERVICE

BOUSFIELD T.W. 851940. Sgt. RA

From May 1943 to March 1944 Sgt. Bousfield acted as Battalion Orderly Sgt. This work entailed parading all working parties, a most unpleasant task. These parties contained the minimum number of men required to satisfy the Japanese and so prevent them from turning the really sick out to work. Sgt. Bousfield did what was necessary with cheerfulness and tact despite opposition from some men who did not realise the true situation. He showed strength of character and carried out the responsibilities of his rank under most difficult conditions. It was in part due to his work that the seriously sick enjoyed immunity from work.

Recommendation: That his name be brought to the notice of authority for his excellent work.

Signed: D.P. Apthorp, Capt., The Royal Norfolk Regiment
                                   30th November 1945

BULLOCK L.W. 915503. Sgt. RAF

Sgt. Bullock volunteered to operate a hidden wireless set whilst a POW in Thanbyuzayat Camp, Lower Burma. The news received buoyed up the morale and spirit of approximately 10,000 POWs employed by the Japanese Army on the Burma-Siam Railway construction between Thanbyuzayat and the Siam Border at the Three Pagoda Pass. Sgt. Bullock carried this out with the full knowledge of the risk he was running, British POWs in Siam having been beaten to death for this very action. He operated the set from December 1942 until January 1944. Previous to the operation of the set he was given the acting rank of WOII whilst acting as Sgt. Major to a company of POWs composed of RAF personnel.

Recommendations: 1.   That his promotion to WOII be confirmed and back-dated to 1 June 1942.
                            2.   That he be awarded an RAF decoration suitable for the action performed.

The above recommendations are a copy of AFW 3121 dated 25.9.45 submitted at Rangoon and signed by Capt. D.P. Apthorp, The Royal Norfolk Regiment and Capt. D.J. Davis, FMSVF.

BURGOYNE E.G.V. 2333345. Sgt. Royal Corps of Signals

Sgt. Burgoyne acted as Sgt. Major to the labour Battalion of 499 British POWs employed on the Burma-Siam railway construction under the Japanese Army. Conditions were appallingly bad, 151 men out of 499 dying of disease and starvation in the period referred to below:

Sgt. Burgoyne carried on in the above capacity from May 1942 until August 1944 when this Battalion was merged into other POW groups. In the face of all difficulties inherent in a force in which almost all men were physically weak and full of disease Sgt. Burgoyne showed outstanding character, zeal, perseverance and a real devotion to duty.

Recommendation: That his promotion to acting WOII be confirmed and backdated to June 1st 1942.

The above recommendation is a copy of AFW 3121 dated 25.9.45 submitted at Rangoon and signed by Capt. D.P. Apthorp, Royal Norfolk Regiment, and Capt. D.J. Davis, FMSVF.

EDWARDS D.W. D/J 111512. L/Sea. RN

Leading Seaman Edwards acted as temporary 'Orderly Sergeant' to a force of 499 British POWs. He carried out the duty at various times more especially during November and December 1943 when conditions in his POW camp were at their worst. The sick rate was so high that organisation all but broke down. It was due to L/S Edwards and a few other NCOs and officers that the essential services of burying the dead, and the provision of drinking water and food were maintained. Despite the fact that he himself was ill L/Seaman Edwards willingly organised these tasks. He showed exceptional perseverance and willingness to undertake responsibility. His work was most valuable.

Recommendation: That his name be brought to the notice of authority for his excellent work.

Signed: D.P. Apthorp, Capt., The Royal Norfolk Regiment, 30th November 1945

KERR, Sgt. A & SH Not listed with Sumatra Battalion

In April 1944 Sgt. Kerr joined a party of POWs who were sent from Siam to Saigon. He immediately showed himself to be an NCO of outstanding conscientiousness and ability. He was employed as pay sergeant, second-in-command of his party of 132 men, and took charge of work outside the camp. He received only a small remuneration for these additional duties and responsibilities, undertaking them as he felt it was his duty to do so. His bearing and sense of discipline remained unaltered throughout the period he was a prisoner, and he set a standard which few NCOs under the circumstances could reach. His assistance was of the utmost value.

Recommendation: That his name be brought to the notice of authority for his excellent work.

Signed: D.P. Apthorp, Capt., The Royal Norfolk Regiment, 30th November 1945

PEARCE H.P. 4344259. Sgt. RA

Sgt. Pearce acted as temporary RSM to a force of 499 POWs during the period of May 1943 – December 1943. During the absence of the NCO who normally carried out this duty it was his unpleasant task to persuade men who were least sick to carry rations from the Japanese Supply Dump, to cut wood and draw water. The Japanese held him responsible for all misdemeanours, real or imaginary. He undertook this work willingly, often performing his normal twelve hours work on the railway line as well. His work was of great assistance to the camp organisation.

Recommendation: That his name be brought to the notice of authority for his excellent work.

Signed: D.P. Apthorp, Capt., The Royal Norfolk Regiment, 30th November 1945

TUCKER W.H. D/J 107882 PO. RN

As a POW WO Tucker was employed first as QM to a Company of Naval Ratings, he then assisted in operating a concealed Wireless Set and latterly at Saigon POW Camp as NCO-in-command Hospital. This petty officer proved himself to be a man of strong character and set the highest example to his fellow prisoners. As quarter master he carried out his duties well, in the operation of the wireless set he ran a considerable risk of which he was well aware. It was however in November 1943, the peak of sickness and deaths, that his work was most valuable. Owing to apathy and disease few men could work. For two months he carried out almost single-handed much of the essential camp work. He dug graves, carved crosses and took charge of funerals, often two or three per day, and by his example, bearing and sense of discipline inspired others, and rendered most valuable assistance to his officers.

Recommendation: That his name be brought to the notice of the appropriate authorities for his most valuable work and assistance given to the officers of his party and his fellow prisoners.

Signed: D.P. Apthorp, Capt., The Royal Norfolk Regiment, 30th November 1945

FITZPATRICK S.J. 3127635. Pte. 2 A and SH

Pte. Fitzpatrick acted as a Medical Orderly to a force of 499 British POWs employed by the Japanese army on the Burma-Siam Railway construction. In April 1943 three cases of smallpox occurred in a camp 26 kilometres south of Thanbyuzayat, Lower Burma. Despite the absence of drugs and safe-guarding disinfectants Pte. Fitzpatrick volunteered to go into isolation to nurse these cases. One case, that of Able Seaman D.G. Thomas RN was extremely severe, and it was largely due to the devoted and careful nursing of Pte. Fitzpatrick, at risk to himself, that A.B. Thomas's life was saved.
During the period from March 1942 till November 1943 that I had knowledge of Pte. Fitzpatrick's work, his zeal and character were of the highest.

Recommendation: Such honour or award as is considered suitable.

The above recommendation is a copy of AFW 3121 dated 25.9.45 submitted at Rangoon and signed by Capt. D.P. Apthorp, Royal Norfolk Regiment, and Capt. D.J. Davis, FMSVF.

FLANAGAN C. 3248492. Cpl. 18 Div RC

Cpl. Flanagan was promoted acting Sergeant while carrying out the duties of CQMS to a company of prisoners at Mergui in June 1942. He was later employed as NCO-in-command Cookhouse for a party of 499 POWs working on the Burma Railway. He carried out his duties conscientiously and well. He showed willingness for work which was not general among the prisoners and materially contributed to the efficient running of the camp.

Recommendation: That his name be brought to the notice of authority for his good work whilst a POW.
Signed: D.P. Apthorp, Capt., The Royal Norfolk Regiment, 30th November 1945

HEALY W.W.H. S/6140668. Sgt. RASC

From May 1942 to March 1944 Sgt. Healy acted as 'Orderly Room Sergeant' to a force of 499 POWs. It was due to his conscientious work that records of casualties, nominal rolls, Death certificates, and grave plans were prepared and retained. Though often in ill health this NCO consistently did work well in excess of his normal duties. He materially contributed to the efficient running of the force and the existence at the present time of casualty reports and grave plans is largely due to him.

Recommendation: That his name be brought to the notice of authority for his excellent work.

412

JAMES D.F. 802968. Sgt. RA 9th Coast Artillery

From April 1944 to March 1945 Sgt. James acted as Company Sergeant Major to a force of 132 British POWs at Saigon. This camp was highly organised by the Japanese. More than twenty-five working parties left the camp each morning. Night work was frequent. It was essential to see that all took their fair share of bad parties and night work. In the face of considerable difficulties Sgt. James made his arrangements fairly and equitably. He was also responsible for fatigue parties, mess orderlies and roll call figures. He displayed strength of character and a sense of duty which was lacking in a number of NCOs, although by virtue of his position he was liable to punishment by the Japanese for the faults of others. In June 1942, while employed in a similar capacity, he was promoted to acting WO Class II.

Recommendations: 1.   That his name be brought to the notice of authority for his excellent work.
2.   That his promotion to WO Class II be confirmed and backdated to June 1st, 1942.

Signed: D.P. Apthorp, Capt., The Royal Norfolk Regiment,
30th November 1945

APPENDIX IV

VESSELS

British Navy (FORCE 'Z') – Show of strength off east Malayan coast; *no air cover* 10 Dec 1941

HM Ships:
>
> *Prince of Wales (battleship):*   sunk 10 Dec 1941
>> Survivors within the British Sumatra Battalion
>>
>> | | | | |
>> |---|---|---|---|
>> | *V.P. Barnes* | *Tom* | *Royal Marines* | see also *Trang* |
>> | *Edwards* | *D.W. 'Bungy'* | *L/Seaman* | |
>> | *Hull* | *Richard* | *AB* | |
>> | *Sedgbeer* | *Ashley* | *Stoker* | see also *Hung Jao* |
>
> *Repulse (cruiser):*   sunk 10 Dec 1941
>> Survivors within the British Sumatra Battalion
>>
>> | | | | |
>> |---|---|---|---|
>> | *Keast* | *Reg* | *Stoker* | see also *Hung Jao* |
>> | *Tracy* | *Percy* | *Stoker* | see also *Dragonfly* |
>> | *Tucker* | *W.H. 'Jan'* | *Petty Officer* | seel also *Jarak* |
>> | *Ulrick* | *D.* | *Stoker* | |
>
> | | |
> |---|---|
> | *Electra (destroyer)* | sunk 27 Feb 1942 (Battle of the Java Sea) |
> | *Express (destroyer)* | sunk 27 Feb 1942 (Battle of the Java Sea) |
> | *Tenedos (destroyer)* | sunk 27 Feb 1942 (Battle of the Java Sea) |

HMAS (Australia)
> *Vampire (destroyer)*   sunk 27 Feb 1942 (Battle of the Java Sea)

Allied Navies (BATTLE of the JAVA SEA) – 26/28 Feb 1942 under command of Rear-Admiral Doorman, Netherlands Navy, *De Tuyter, flagship, light cruisers.*

Dutch	*De Ruyter*	sunk 28 Feb
	Java	sunk 28 Feb
	Witte de With	*(destroyer)* retired to Surabayo, damaged
Australian	*Perth*	*(cruiser)* retired to Batavia; sunk 1 Mar 1942; Sunda strait; 353 drowned; 329 rescued; 100 died at various POW camps
British	*Exeter*	*(light cruiser)* retired to Surabayo
	Electra	*(destroyer)* sunk 27 Feb
	Encounter	*(destroyer)* rescued 113 seamen of Dutch destroyer *Kortenoer* took them ashore then retired to Surabayo
	Jupiter	*(destroyer)* hit mine; sank 28 Feb; 78 crew rescued

414

| American *Houston* | *(heavy cruiser)* plus 4 destroyers, retired to Batavia; sunk 1 Mar Sunda strait; survivors put in Java POW camps of which some were sent up within American 'FitzSimmons Force' to 'join' the British Sumatra Battalion (Mar 1943) |

Evacuation & escape vessels – Allied Civilians & Services Personnel up to night of surrender of Singapore (15 Feb 1942) – relevant to POW camps Burma Railway & Sumatra (Padang)

British Navy

'*Yangtse*' *gunboats*   withdrawn from Hong Kong pre-surrender

Dragonfly   *(paddle-boat)* 585 tons; 197' x 33'. Rescued troops from behind enemy lines in Johore; 13/14 Feb joined evacuation fleet at Singapore; embarked 77 passengers; left in company with sister ship *Grasshopper*; bombed and sunk in Berhala strait; approx 45 survivors evacuated across 'Organisation' route Sumatra to Padang. Original passengers included 2 officers and 26 other ranks of the 1st Manchester Regt.**

Survivors who stayed in Padang:

Long W.J.   *'Taff'*   *Able Seaman (Dragonfly), plus 13 others of which 5 survived*

Survivors within the British Sumatra Battalion

** *Taylor J.*   *L/Cpl.*   *1st Manchester Regt.*
** *Taylor R.*   *Cpl.*   *1st Manchester Regt.*
Tracy, Percy   *Stoker*   see also *Repulse*

Grasshopper   *(paddle-boat)* sister ship to *Dragonfly*; bombed as above; complement of 74 men; Royal Marines, Allied civilians and Japanese prisoners aboard. Sunk while trying to reach the vessel. Survivors evacuated as above.

Survivors within the British Sumatra Battalion

Barnes, Harry   *Ord/Smn*
Cleaver F.   *Ord/Smn*

Scorpion	*(gunboat)* 'Yangtse flotilla'; 700 tons; 208'; 2×4" guns, 1×3,7", 2× three pounders. Sailed 10 Feb; 150 on board including 58 passengers of which 38 naval ratings. Sunk, Berhala strait 14 Feb. 101 lost; *remainder believed POWs.*
Hung Jao	*(HMM launch)* sailed from Singapore 13 Feb; arrived mouth of AndiriGiri river loaded with survivors and escapers. Then worked for the 'Organisation' searching back up the straits for further survivors. Brought in another 100 stranded men. Engines failed; scuttled in the AndiriGiri river; survivors went across Sumatra to Padang.

Among crew and ultimately of the British Sumatra Battalion

Keast, Reg   Stoker   see also Repulse
Sedgbeer, Ashley Stoker see also Prince of Wales

Jarak	*(minesweeper)* 209 tons; taken over in 1939 from Straits Steamship Company. Rescue work with *Dragonfly* and *Scorpion* of 1,000 stranded troops cut off in Malaya. Friday 13 Feb embarked 34 service specialists. Sailed south through straits to Lingga, where bombed and abandoned to drift. Later reboarded and repaired it. Headed to Dabo to await evacuation down to the AndiriGiri river.

Among crew and ultimately of the British Sumatra Battalion

Tucker W.H. 'Jan' Petty Officer see also Repulse

Joan	*(launch)* left on an organised evacuation convoy with a junk (the *Hock Siew*), the latter carrying 120 men of 30 HAA battery evacuating Kallang 'drome area Singapore, which ran aground just south of Singapore on St Johns Is. The *Joan* proceeded independently with a complement of 36 soldiers, picking up on the 'Organisation' route into Priggi Rajah with the aid of the junk the *Sir Hugh Fraser*.

Among crew and ultimately in command; and
of British Sumatra Battalion
Pearce H.P. 'Harry' Sergeant 30 HAA

Other vessels (mostly oriental) with British Sumatra Battalion connections

Sir Hugh Fraser (als Sir Theodore Fraser)	(Small flat barge-like palm oil trader) under command of MSM McLaren RASC. Used by the Army as a ferry for supplying units stationed on nearby islands. Following the surrender it evacuated some 200 escapers to Rengat, Sumatra. *McLaren J. MSM RASC*
Hiap Hin	*(130 ton native junk)* On the night of surrender she was anchored in the roads. Captain Apthorp (6 R/Norfolk) swam out to secure a sampan and then took a party out to board it. Sampan then used to ferry out 250 escapees. Made for Sumatra and rescued 100 more from Pulau Moro where directed to Priggi Rajah 'Organisation' route. Ran on up the AndiriGiri to Rengat.
	Apthorp, Dudley Captain 6 Royal Norfolk Regiment Clarke J.E. 'Nobby' L/Cpl 6 Royal Norfolk Regiment Healy W. 'Tim' Sergeant RASC North R. 'Bob' Cpl RASC (Healy and North were rescued from a rowing boat)
Hock Siew (renamed Castle-Conway)	*(junk)* Commandeered with the launch *Joan* in planned evacuation of the whole (250 men) of 30 HAA R by Battery Commander Major Geoffrey Rowley-Conway. At ceasefire 15 Feb only 120 men were available to be evacuated. Left and then grounded on St Johns Is.; launch *Joan* travelled on to IndiriGiri river independently. The Commander, several gunners and NCOs, a sergeant-major and 2 subalterns went ashore in a small boat or swam ashore, of which the Commander was taken on independently to Sumatra and finally onward from Padang on the *Sederhana Johanis* to Ceylon. The rest (108 men approx) were joined by two others who

417

came alongside in a small boat (Sgt Wringe & Cpl Daunt) to assist with refloating the *Hock Siew*, which eventually got to Sumatra, where it grounded within the estuary of the river Kampar. Eventually it was worked up river over seven days before being abandoned after trading it off for three crewed sampans. They progressed up-river for a few days and then left the boats and went mainly on foot to join the 'Organisation' route.

Other than *the Commander* (who got to Ceylon) *and some of those who went overboard at St Johns Is., who included a Gunner Brewer 30 HAA, all others survived as POWs as follows:*

British Sumatra Battalion; 1 officer (Lt H. Dicker) plus 109 other ranks, which included L/Bdr A.W.F. 'Bob' Grafton and Gnr F.W. Parrot, both 30 HAA, who got from St Johns Is to the AndiriGiri by means of a relay of small boats in company with Gunner 'Ginger' Sussex, 30 HAA, who elected to stay in Padang with Captain Morley, Captain Purvis and a few others. The fate of *Gunner Brewer* is not known. He had to be left in the care of natives after becoming delirious with a fever contracted while escaping with Bob Grafton's party. The other two who came aboard the *Hock Siew* at St Johns Is. *also became POWs within the British Sumatra Battalion:*

Wringe E.	Sergeant	E Indian Army Corps Clerks, see also Bintang Dua
Daunt H.	Corporal	Royal Engineers

(? HMS) Royal Sultan

(class unknown) this vessel has so far not been identified. However, four men of the British Sumatra Battalion are said to have crewed her. They all died in Kanchanaburi POW camp, Thailand within a period of 6 weeks. Presumably they were 'buddies' and thus (*perhaps*) died due to some form of contamination or food poisoning.

			Service No.	*Died*
Burbridge, Robert Wm.	Stoker 1st Class		D/KX 113261	11 Mar 44
Chatfield, Alfred Chas.	AB		P/JX 276477	16 Mar 44
Duthie, Charles John	AB		D/J 169296	17 Mar 44
McAffee, James George	Stoker 1st Class		D/KX 138902	24 Jan 44

Tien Kuang

(*flat-bottomed river boat*) sunk during the pre-surrender evacuation of civilians and over 3,000 RAF servicemen – ground staff – including its Air Ministry Experimental (Radar) Station personnel (AMES). Many of the 79 RAF subsequently incorporated into the British Sumatra Battalion were rescued from this vessel. They had been given very short notice to leave Singapore and in consequence of that the Army was given the task of sabotaging the aerodrome installations and HQ buildings.

Note: *Our Brigade happened to be stationed near Sembawang 'drome so I was 'volunteered in' to take a ten man detail to 'wreck-out' their HQ. On arrival we entered through a window of the office/administration suite in preference to doorways which might have been booby-trapped. We found all the office machinery (typewriters and the like) intact, and filing cabinets stacked with papers many of which were marked 'secret'! We smashed up the former and burnt the papers outside. Then we went further into the building and discovered the Officers' Mess, in which there was a large refectory table immaculately laid out with snow-white napery, about 20 place settings, 'salts', platters and etceteras – all silver – as were the vases and tureens on the sideboards and trolleys near the entrance door to the kitchen area beyond. I couldn't bear to contemplate the fact that the mess room might soon be occupied by Japanese officers with the tables laid ready for them; so I had all the cutlery etc. bundled up into the table-cloths. When we left, the whole lot was carted*

419

off to the perimeter and then stuffed out of sight up a 'monsoon' culvert – where it may yet remain!

Arse End Charlie Mk1	*(author's sampan, self-named)* approx 23.00 hrs 15 Feb 1942 departed Singapore harbour with 2 officers of the Army Pay Corps and 11 other ranks. Approx 03.00 hrs 19 Feb picked up 2 stranded RAF(?) lads. Approx 08.30 hrs 22 Feb had landed on Benku (?) Is for reprovisioning when attacked by approaching landing barges and a Japanese plane. Ran for cover with 4 others. The other 10 decided to stay and surrender under the Dutch flag, but all believed to have been shot the following morning. Procured another sampan (a.m. 24 Feb) after hiding up.
MkII	proceeded through chain of islands south to Lingga and Posik (?) Is to the AndiriGiri river, E. Sumatra, picking up 6 stranded men (26 Feb) en route. Arrived Priggi Rajah Sunday, 1 March, having covered about 200 miles mostly rowing, since leaving Singapore two weeks previously. Left *Arse End Charlie II* at Priggi Rajah 2 March and went up-river on the *Joan* before staging over to Padang.

Only known survivor within the British Sumatra Battalion was the author:

Burgoyne Eric G.V. Sergeant 2333545 Royal Corps Signals 18 Division (appointed Battalion Sergeant-Major 8 May 1942)

Other 10 survivors (names unknown) presumed to have stayed in Sumatra and worked on the Pekanbaroe Railway. (see Appendix V – Correspondence)

Following the surrender and with Padang declared an 'open town', those POWs who had refused to sign the nominal roll of men to be handed over to the Japanese as part of the Dutch–Japanese surrender terms made second bids for freedom. Very few succeeded. There were just six vessels that were in any way connected with the *British Sumatra Battalion*. Brief details are given below.

Sederhana Djohannis	*(prahu)* moored north of Padang 15 March. A party fully organised and provisioned from the 'Organisation' funds and with the assistance of the Dutch authorities. Colonel Warren, having bravely decided to stay and negotiate the smooth transfer of the POWs left in Padang, had selected 18 officers for the escape venture, among whom was Major Geoffrey Rowley-Conway, Battery Commander 30 HAA (see the *Hock Siew* details). They left moorings on 16 March and got safely over to India, arriving 19 April.
(name and class unknown)	departed Padang 16 March. *Sergeant-Major Roadnight* – with companions – walked north up the coast from Padang and secured a small vessel, which they sailed into the Indian Ocean. They were picked up by a British Naval vessel en route for Australia.
Venture	*(self-named prahu)* departed Padang 16 March. *Sergeant D. Gavin of the E. Surrey Regt* and 10 companions went 5 miles south of Padang to Sungei Penang to pick up the *Venture*, a vessel 27 ft 6 in long with 8 ft stabilising outriggers on each side. A difficult vessel to manage, it reached Siberoet and met up with the crew of the *Bintang Dua* (20 March). Sailed up north via the Nicobar and Andaman island groups. Captured after many losses 26 April. Full story in *Quiet Jungle, Cruel Sea* by D. Gavin.
(unnamed vessel)	*(log-boat outrigger, kolek)* approx 14 ft long, 2 ft wide, 8 men aboard including the author, paddled out from a fishing kampong approx 3 miles north of Padang 23.00 hrs 16 March *(see main story)*.

Crew*:	Adrian H.D.G.	'Harry'	Sapper	41 Fortress RE
	Armstrong H.K.		L/Cpl	41 Fortress RE
	Burgoyne E.G.V.	'Eric'	Sergeant	18 Div Signals
	Ingham W.		Private	RASC
	McCaffery R.C.		*AB	Royal Navy
	Pearce H.P.	'Harry'	Sergeant	30 HAA
	Puncheon ?		*L/S	Royal Navy
	Stracchino G.	'Stracc'	Sergeant	41 Fortress RE

*There has been some debate as to whether both of the above Royal Navy men who came down from the AndiriGiri river-boat work with *Harry Pearce* also came with him on the log-boat. I think not and that *L/S Puncheon* – who may have been on the *Bintang Dua* anyway – then stayed in Padang as a POW. He does not appear on the Battalion roll! (see sketch of *kolek* and story, PART ONE).

Bintang Dua 'Two Stars'

(small coastal trading vessel 'in sail' – also described as a Malay prahu) approx 28 ft x 10 ft; left Padang 16 March.

Crew*:	as above			
	Apthorp D.P.	'Appy'	Captain	6 R/Norfolk
	Beattie A.		L/S	(merchant navy)
	Dicker H.G.		Lieutenant	30 HAA
	Purvis ?		Captain	30 HAA
	Tranter ?	stowaway,		self-styled Australian Lieutenant
	Wringe E.		Sergeant	Indian Army Corps of Clerks

*And 7 'mutineers' names unknown, who went their own way. Other than those 7 all the above were ultimately members of the *British Sumatra Battalion* except *Puncheon, Purvis* and *Tranter* (see sketch of the *Bintang Dua* and story, PART ONE).

Banggai

(steamship) a Dutch-owned passenger/cargo vessel of 660 tons built in Selby, Yorks. Crew: Netherlands Koninglijke Marine acompanied by Police Commissioner Willem van Dyl with armed escort captured the crew of the *Bintang Dua* 30 March to the NE of the Siberut Is and on 1 April 1942 returned to Emmerhaven, where they were handed over to the Japanese to start their $3\frac{1}{2}$ years of POW life.

422

ALLIED SUBMARINE ATTACKS ON JAPANESE MERCHANT SHIPPING CARRYING POWs

British Submarines

HMS Tradewind	The greatest shipping disaster in the Pacific war! 18 Sept 1944 at 16.15 hours off Bengkulu 220 miles SE of Padang, Sumatra, the *Junyo Maru* (5,015-ton freighter) torpedoed while carrying 2,300 POWs and 4,200 *romushas* (civilian slave labourers) and Japanese guards. 300 Japanese rescued but few of the 6,500 prisoners.
HMS Truculent	Convoy of 6 ships en route from Belawin Delhi, NE Sumatra, to Singapore sails at 11.30 hours 25 June 1944. One of these vessels is the *Harikiki Maru* (formerly *KPM steamer van Waerwijck*) 3,800 tons, with 724 POWs on board. Attacked 26 June at 14.00 hours, 3 vessels including the *Harikiki Maru* sunk, from which *only 546 of the 724 POWs were saved.* Those saved were taken over to Singapore docks, where they were herded almost naked and ill fed for one month before being taken back for work on the Pekanbaroe Railway.

American Submarines (Pacific)

Barb, Bonita, Cachalot, Drum, Finback, Grayling, Growler, Hake, Hardhead, Herring, Pampanita, Picuda, Queenfish, Sailfish, Sealion II, Spadefish, Stingray, Tarpon, Triton, Trout.
On 19 Apr 1944 *Kumis* 49, 50 and 51 arrived in Saigon for dock work – *51 Kumi being 150 men of the now fragmented British Sumatra Battalion.* On 27 Mar *Kumis* 35–40 (900 men) all Aussies, left Tamarkan (see Appendix Speeches) Thailand, designated the 'Japan Party'. They had expected to be sent from Bangkok but were taken to join 49–51 *Kumis* in Saigon, whence all had been expected to be despatched. In the event – due to submarine activity in that area – it was decided to single out the Aussies (27 Jun) and take them by train down to Singapore to await embarkation from there when a convoy could be assembled. When the time came for embarkation 10 British *Kumis* (1,500 men) had been added *but 51 Kumi had*

fortunately been left behind in Saigon; and of the 900 Australians mentioned above, 40 *Kumi* plus 32 men from the other Aussie *kumis* were left behind; and the remaining 718 embarked.

The convoy embarked and departed for Japan as follows:

Embarked 4 Sept 1944

Kachidoki Maru (passenger/cargo)	*Rakuyo Maru (passenger/cargo)*
524 ft displacing 10,500 tons	477 ft displacing 9,500 tons
6 British *kumis*, 900 men	4 British *kumis*, 600 men
(in cargo hold)	(in cargo hold)
	5 Aussie *kumis*, 718 men
	(in cargo hold)

The convoy inclusive of many other merchant ships and a considerable Japanese navy escort departed from Singapore on 6 Sept. From 11 Sept the convoy was detected and chased by the American *submarines Barb, Growler, Pampanito, Queenfish, and Sealion II*, which systematically picked off and sank cargo and escort vessels and the two 'POW' vessels.

The survivors of the 2,218 POWs totalled 119 only:

Kachidoki Maru 20 British	*Rakuyo Maru* 36 British, 63 Australian

While it is almost certain that no *British* from the *British Sumatra Battalion* were aboard either of the vessels, there were some *Australians* who had been with us on the Burma side of the railway construction i.e. – *Brigadier Arthur Varley (senior Allied officer Thanbyuzayat POW camp) and his son John A. Varley were victims of the attack; and the Japanese officer in charge of the* Rakuyo Maru *guards was none other than 'Little Napoleon' (Tanaka), by then a lieutenant – long may he rest without peace.*

German submarine	*(name unknown)* moored in the coaling wharf area of Singapore docks to which the author daily led a British POW *Kumi* from the nearby River Valley POW camp.
Submarine (presumed USS)	that torpedoed a subsequent Japan-bound convoy carrying *the above British 'River Valley' Kumi* sinking a merchant vessel, and causing the convoy to be diverted into Saigon for discharge of the POWs to various camps in N Indochina and Cambodia.

AUTHOR'S other journeys

Troopships	British:	*Orcades* and *Orduna*
	Polish:	*Sobieski*
	American:	*Mount Vernon* and *West Point*

| Battleships | British: | *Barham* and *Resolution* |
| (1940) | French: | *Richelieu* |

VESSELS USED TO TRANSPORT POWs UP ONTO THE BURMA SIDE OF THE RAILWAY 1942/1943

Joint convoy of British and Australian POWs assembled at Belawin Delhi, Sumatra (1 to 3).

1. *England Maru* *(freighter)* about 6,000 tons; built Selby, Yorks 1898; sailed 18/19 May *carrying 499 men of the British Sumatra Battalion* and a few Dutch officers; ultimate destination Mergui, Burma; disembarked 24 May.

2. *name unknown* carrying 2,000 Australian of ex-'A-Force' Singapore discharged 1,000 at Victoria Point, Burma (Black Force) 22 May, while convoy halted. Arrived Mergui, Burma 24 May discharged all remaining POWs from vessels 1 and 2. This combined group of 1,500 POWs was designated Ramsay Force.

3. *name unknown* sailed on and presumably within two days anchored off Tavoy and left other Aussies of 'A Force' there.

4. *Tatu Maru* *(motor vessel)* approx 800 tons; anchored off Mergui 10 Aug. Above 1,500 men of Ramsay Force taken out on lighters to join other POWs (Aussies) already aboard. Two-day journey 11/12 Aug with approx 400 men (standing room only, deck and hold) up to Tavoy. Taken ashore by lighters to join the Aussies already there.

5. *Kenzu Maru* *(steamer)* approx 1,000 tons. 21 Oct British Sumatra Battalion (500) embarked from lighters for two-day journey up to Moulmein. A larger but unknown number of Aussies accompanied us. The other vessel – the *Tatu Maru* (?) – had no POWs on board.

6. *Tatu Maru (?)* 22/23 Oct disembarked and moved up to the 'Railway' base camp Thanbyuzayat to join Aussies already installed under the command of Brigadier Arthur Varley.

Note: The 114 kilometre 'Burma' section of the Burma–Siam construction was under the command of the Japanese 5th Railway Regiment. The 10,000 Allied POWs intended for employment on the section came under the jurisdiction of Lt/Col Y. Nagatomo, Chief of 3 Branch (Thailand) Nippon Expeditionary Force. The actual POW force (after partial depletion in advance of deployment) was comprised of:

American 190; Australian approx. 4,000; Dutch approx. 5,000; *British 481 (British Sumatra Battalion)*

Note: The following tell the full story of the 'Organisation', the evacuations from Singapore and the heroic (and ghastly) fate of so many vessels and people involved:

(i) The book (and film) *Return from the River Kwai* – Joan and Clair Blair (Penguin Books) tells the whole story of the USS (Pacific submarines) mentioned.

(ii) The two books *Singapore's Dunkirk* – Geoffrey Brooke (Leo Cooper) and *The Escape from Singapore* – Richard Gough (William Kimber).

APPENDIX V

SPEECHES, DOCUMENTATION AND CORRESPONDENCE

Wm H. ('Taff') Long's letter of c.1992/3 is an account of the Allied POWs left in Padang, W. Sumatra after The British Sumatra Battalion (500 men) departed for Burma on 9 May 1942. In fact, the rest of 'The Tattered Remnants'.

On June 12 1942 with the exception of a few small working parties, the main body left in Padang set out in lorries up the coastal road through Fort-de-Kok, Sibolga, up into the mountains past Lake Toba, a most beautiful expanse of water vanishing in the distance between pine-clad mountains on which the Dutch had built bungalows dotted at various intervals and which were used as holiday accommodation for fishing parties, recreation etc. We arrived at Medan on June 17.

Medan was regarded as the capital of Sumatra and although on the coast, it had no port but was supplied through Belawan which lay some twenty kilometres down the coast. I found myself attached to the Australian party who moved on down the coast to Belawan while the remainder stayed in Medan.

We stayed in Belawan for nine or ten days clearing up what the Dutch had demolished. One job in particular was rather frustrating. The Dutch had set fire to one building which contained masses of raw rubber which had melted and flowed everywhere: – along the roads, railway tracks, concrete jetty, etc., and then, solidified into one goocy mass. We were given picks and shovels to clear it up. Just use your imagination! Sixty or seventy hitting at six, ten, eighteen inches and more of rubber with picks and shovels! We bounced all over the place! In the end they sent us back to join the main party in Medan within a native jail called Gloe Goed. This consisted of a large square area of ground surrounded by twelve-foot high walls on top of which had been embedded broken glass and barbed wire.

July 18. Whole camp required to sign 'No escape' document – informed if anyone escaped or tried to escape forty men would be shot. Everyone refused to sign either singly or en-masse. The Japs then herded all of us into 2 buildings – doors locked and windows boarded, no food for 3 days and very little water given, no facilities, toilets and latrines; conditions became abysmal and then, the officers* said that we could sign under duress. We signed individually (I signed as David Lloyd George). During these three days things were very dodgy and dicey with talk of 'having a go' but common-sense prevailed.

---

*The British officer in Medan was a Major 'C', Indian Army, about whom the least said the better!

During our period in Medan we did various work, i.e., built a large Japanese shrine which involved moving large areas of earth. We also cleared a large area of jungle and burnt where we cut to enable the Japs to build a race-course (of all things); – all this, outside the boundaries of Medan! Various parties were sent to the docks, to the oil storage yards etc., etc. In the period until we left Medan – (considering our future experiences) – we were treated and fed better than any other period of our imprisonment although that left a lot to be desired. From the day of our capture they gave us nothing, – no eating utensils, no boots, no clothes, no medical supplies, quinine, bandages etc., etc. *(But why am I wasting time? You know what it was all about, Eric!)*

Towards the end of 1942, conditions began to deteriorate i.e. malaria, dysentery began to become an everyday occurrence but nothing to what we were to experience in the future. Our clothing was now in rags and a lot of us were in bare feet.

On the 7th of March we were told that all fit POWs would be going into the mountains of N. Sumatra.

This area – the Dutch informed us – was the most unpleasant part of Sumatra, the valleys being covered in thick jungle and the mountains, scrub and large tall timber. It was populated by a tribe called Achinese who for years and years had been quite a thorn in the flesh of the Dutch adminis-tration. They had the reputation of being fierce jungle fighters armed with swords and spears and no one wandered into 'Atjeh' country without arms.

On the 8th of March fifty so-called fit Australians and fifteen of us Royal Navy from the same building, fell in ready to move out. There were also about sixty British RAF and Army men from another building and possibly 120 Dutch and Eurasians with us. The remainder were left behind in Medan and little did we know that many of them we would never see again.

On the 25th of June 1944 the majority of the party we left at Medan were taken to Belawan and boarded a ship called the *van Waerwijck** destined for Singapore across the Malacca Strait.

[Taff's letter then picks up from the point when the survivors came back to Belawan with the information that Australians were also among the 724 aboard and that they lost 15 of the total 178 drowned. No specific numbers of the British aboard were given.]

In March *1945* we met some of these mates of ours in camp 2 near Pakan Bahree and exchanged experiences.

On the morning of 8th of March *1944* we set out for the mountains of N.Sumatra in trucks staying here and there overnight in various native villages the names of which if I ever had known I cannot remember now. The roads – (as we progressed further north) – narrowed and then became unsuitable for lorries so we halted for two days. We then set out to walk 90

---

*The *van Waerwijck* was an old Dutch vessel renamed and, in fact, the same *Harikiki Maru* of 3,800 tons torpedoed and written about in Chapter 36.

miles, carrying tools, cooking utensils etc. The country became more unfriendly. High timbers covered mountains. We followed jungle paths washing and drinking at streams. The natives we passed were not helpful at all and made gestures which assured us that if we fell into their hands we could expect no mercy. The British and only officer with us at that time was a Lt. Henman of the Malayan RNVR. He had been in Malaya for some time before the war. He was an excellent type of man and gained our respect for his attitude to us. For his efforts to better our treatment he was beaten up and humbled but he continued with all his power to make our conditions easier. I regret that the same cannot be said for many other British officers that we came into contact with. Lt. Henman survived the war and on returning to England found that his wife was not available. He eventually returned to Malaya a broken man and ended his life by shooting himself. Many men during 1939–1945 proved themselves by the decorations they were awarded. Lt. Henman only received beatings up, humiliation and frustration. May I say 'God bless him, and may he rest in peace!'

So we started off on our march into 'Atjeh' country and thanks be to God that we couldn't foresee the future and what it would bring. We completed the march in 5 days being forced, beaten and treated like animals every inch of the way. Those who had no footwear suffered terribly. We were in rags, I resorted to the 'Jap Happy' loin-cloth, rations were cut; – and all this in some of the most inhospitable country in the world. Every yard was sheer murder and the Korean guards made it quite plain what would happen if a man collapsed and couldn't go on, – it was the bayonet!

We finally arrived at our destination which was a bare area of earth on top of a plateau. There, we first tossed everything down – tools, cooking utensils and ourselves and slept until the following morning. That first day we spent gathering and cutting bamboo to make ourselves some shelter. We worked until dark, light being supplied by some torches cut from old pine wood from the mountain side. The next morning we were put to work on the road, some men being left in camp to complete our shelters and build huts for the guards and Jap officers.

The Dutch and Eurasians were separated from us and then marched on to where they would start working back towards us. Some way ahead of us lay a fairly large mountain. The Dutch party was sent to the far side with about twenty miles between us. Conditions deteriorated rapidly. Supplies could only be brought up by pack ponies and often with great difficulty. It rained frequently in the mountains with the result that on parts of the road ponies with loads on their backs sank in the mud up to their bellies. We then had to carry, pull, shove and cajole those ponies towards their objectives. It was while at this camp that we buried our first Australian named Ted Hopson. His was a bad case of dysentery and malaria. We buried him on the mountainside about a hundred yards from the camp. His death was the first of many to come in the next few months.

After a few weeks we moved on to Tenal Gajoe four miles away. There was no village, just a pile of rocks against which we built our own huts and then carried on with the road building.

429

The monsoon season was now upon us. We worked in the rain and slept in the rain. Our camp being at the bottom of the mountain was frequently flooded. We existed in misery with rations often failing to come up the road and we were continually hungry. Dysentery, malaria and beriberi were prevalent and burials more regular by now. The work continued until we met up with the Dutch and then – on Oct 6th 1944 we started back on our return march of ninety miles taking six days including one night march.

We were then put into trucks and taken to a so-called rest camp in Medan arriving there on October the 24th.

It appeared to have been occupied by Japanese soldiers and consisted of three large huts, two of which had been living quarters and the third the guardhouse. Other than these there was just a small cookhouse. Everything within them had been stripped bare of furnishings. We slept on the floors and spent the first week there clearing up, rebuilding sleeping platforms and repairing the roofs.

We were then put to work, the job being to build a trellis bridge across a deep gorge with steep sides. Furnished with picks, shovels, chisels, sledgehammers and crowbars we started to hack out the foundations for the abutments from the rocky bottom of the gorge. Christmas 1944 came and went. No celebrations! Work was the order of the day. During the monsoon torrential rain fell every day. Our camp was washed away twice and things were very miserable. Rations were at a minimum. We ate everything that we could catch and kill, snakes, monkeys, etc., – some men even ate rats. We also ate tree leaves and grass. Things continued like this for some time, our ranks being reduced by malaria, dysentery, scrub typhus and so on.

In March 1944 – with our bridge completed – we were moved to a camp along the line (see footnote) called No. 8 camp which was the main 'rail camp'. There we joined up with hundreds of Australians, Dutch and Eurasians – and other odds and bods – RAF, British army etc. It was here that we met up with the survivors from those we had left in Medan in March 1943.

Of our party of 50 Australians, 15 Royal Navy and 60 Army and RAF (total 125) only 92 of us had survived.

Having rejoined the others we were soon moved out from camp 8, on to camp 10 and then back again to camp 2. All the time work on the railway went on seven days a week from early dawn to dusk excavating, carrying, bridging streams and laying track. Rations were now at a minimum and our treatment was inhuman – beatings a daily happening, no news, no letters and no hope! We lost track of time until eventually one day the Japs said 'No work today!' Our officer was sent for and later came to us and said 'the war is over!' It was the 19th of August. I had received a good bashing up the day before and couldn't even stand to sing 'God Save the King'.

The Aussies were taken down to the airfield and flown home. We remained in camp 8 for another 2 weeks. Lady Mountbatten parachuted down among us and arranged for supplies to be dropped to us by Canadian RAF 'Dakotas'. Later a lorry that had been commandeered by a Paratroop major started us off on our way home by taking us to Pakan Baroe

[Pekanbaroe] the new rail extension terminus by the Siak river. From there a British infantry landing craft took us on a two day journey to Singapore. I was lodged in Alexandria hospital suffering from – among other things – tuberculosis. After that I was shipped to Madras, then went to Poona and finally arrived in England on the 23rd of December 1945 having left there on the 27th December 1939.

Footnote to Taff Long's account

Anyone who may have an interest in pursuing the saga of the conditions of POW life in Sumatra is advised to secure a copy of the following very detailed and illustrated publications written by survivors from the Pekanbaroe–Moearo Railway extension construction camps:

a) *Pekanbaroe Spoorweg* – a documentary of facts compiled immediately after the war by H. Neumann and E. van Witsen in co-operation with a great many others. (This is written in Dutch.) Or, preferably,

b) *The Sumatra Railway* – a translated copy made by S.D ten Brink. (This English edition is the sole responsibility of the author and has been realised without any financial assistance whatsoever and is no doubt subject to the laws of copyright. The only 'source' reference that I have for the publishers is: Studio Peter Mulier, Middelie.)

JAPANESE SPEECHES DELIVERED TO MEMBERS OF THE BRITISH SUMATRA BATTALION (1942 – 1945)

(1)   16 April 1942 at Fort-de-Kok, Sumatra, to the officers and men captured en-route to India from Padang on the Javanese junk the *Bintang Dua*.

You men are the tattered remnants of a degenerate nation! The Japanese Emperor has seen fit to spare your lives for work on the noble project of railway building! Thousands of you will die and leave your bones to bleach the lines!

(2)   28 October 1942 at Thanbyuzayat, Burma by Lt/Col Nagatomo on arrival there the day before the Battalion was despatched up the track to commence its work on the above 'Noble Project'.

(The full text of this speech is given in Chapter 22)

(3)   The 260 miles of track was connected through at Kon Kuta (Thailand border) in October 1943, and in November Lt/Col Nagatomo decreed two days of ceremonies and speeches held at the point where the last rivet – a golden one – was alleged to have been inserted. Wreaths were laid at the various

431

camps up near the Three Pagodas Pass and hypocritical praise directed at the souls of men who he had so systematically destroyed at the behest of his emperor 18 months previously and which ended with the words 'Please accept my deepest sympathy and regards and may you sleep peacefully and eternally!'

(4)   April (19th year of Showa) 1944 Saigon. Captain Apthorp by then reduced to chargeship of a *kumi* of 150 men designated part of a party destined for Japan *was stood down* at the wharfside after the following speech had been delivered:

You are to be transferred from jurisdiction of POW camp Thailand to that of in Japan* where you are to assume labour duties. Since the opening of this Thai camp you have been employed on enforced labour duties for more than twenty months, especially you were employed on railway construction in which your discharge of duty attained amid objective as scheduled for which we appreciate warmly. On completion of above mentioned you are to be transferred to Holy Land of Rising Sun where scenery is simply superb.

The greater Empire of Japan proper appellation being 'O'Yesma Di Nippon Tokeron' is populated with national of apprichousness, acts on morality brave yet curtous, humanious yet strictly severe on vices – Proverb is in most common use there of 'Even hunter himself will not slay astrayed bird seek refuge in his lap' will perfectly explain the attitude and habitude of Japanese sentiment.

The country is of four distinct seasons. Spring with abundance of blossoms, when birds chirp peacefully everywhere. Evergreen summer with coolest breezes easing the universe. Transparent autumn sky with clearest moon and winter in which snow-white washes the countryside purifying the inhabitants.

These are nothing but the image and reflection of his august Imperial Majesties greatest virtues to which whole nationals are led to follow in loyalty towards the Imperial family, filial piety toward parents creation of benevolency, etc, etc to eternal effect.

Therefore I say to you officers and men go to Japan with ease of mind and do your imposed duty to perfection then I verily tell you that our billion inhabitants will welcome you to share the Imperial favours with you.

On the other hand should any of you still harbour conscience of enemy nationals and proceed anything up against the interests of Japan consequential result must be born on own shoulders however severe or regrettable to all concerned. I reiterate believe in Japanese chivalry and go forward in the right way not astraying on proper and mature consideration.

---

*Appendix IV (Vessels – Allied Submarine Attacks) reveals the fate of the 2,218 men who eventually made that journey (from Singapore instead) on 6 September 1944.

I should like to call your attention to take good care of your health for the sudden change in climatic conditions and wishing you a happy journey.

With all my blessings for your 'Bon Voyage'

Col. Nackimura

POW MAIL

The author is indebted to Graham Reynolds, POW mail historian, for allowing him to present these illustrations of his research not only on items which I submitted for inclusion in his collection but also of his 'How the Mail Goes' and other items. For preserving anonymity I have made deletions from the latter.

To the best of my knowledge Graham still resides in Chesham, Buckinghamshire, and has lodged a copy of his whole collection with the Imperial War Museum.

Document 1

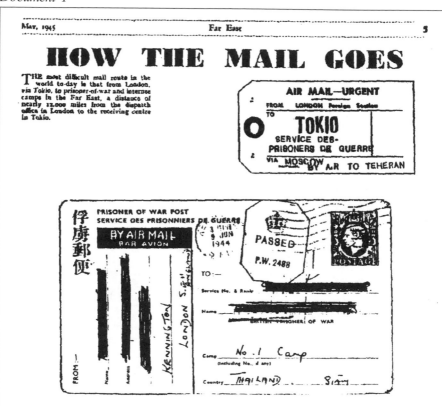

434

Document 2

SERVICE DES PRISONNIERS DE GUERRE,

IMPERIAL JAPANESE ARMY.

Our present place, quarters, and work is unchanged since last card sent to you. The rains have finished, it is now beautiful weather. I am working healthily (well). We receive newspapers printed in English which reveal world events.

We have joyfully received a present of some milk, tea, margarine, sugar and cigarettes from the Japanese Authorities.

We are very anxious to hear from home, but some prisoners have received letters or cables.

Everyone is hopeful of a speedy end to the war and with faith in the future we look forward to a happy reunion soon.

With best wishes for a cheerful Christmas.

FEELING FIT. LOVE TO YOU ~~~~~~~~~~~~~~
AND ALL. HAPPY BIRTHDAY TO ~~~~~~~ .CHEERIO SWEETHEART

From...... *JIM*

Postcard sent from "Camp 3" based at NIKE (NIkkI), Thailand during early 1944. Sent 1st February 1944 It was received In Australia on 6th January 1945 (being the propaganda text on reverse as passed by Col. Nagatomo - Jap C.O. No. 3 Camp)

Document 3 This is the full story about the item mentioned and illustrated in Chapter 46.

Charred remains of first postcard sent home by British prisoner from Moulmein in Burma.
C.S.M. Eric Burgoyne was one of an elite few who attempted escape from the Japanese In Singapore after capitulation in February 1942. He was recaptured In Indian Ocean in April 1942 and became one of the BRITISH (SUMATRA) BATTALION - the only British group sent to Moulmein to work on the "Railway" from the Burma end.

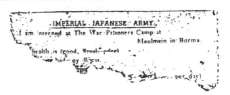

"DAMAGED BY FIRE IN TRANSIT", this card was salvaged from the Sunderland Flying Boat crash on Mount Brandon, Eire on 28th July 1943. The postcard was sent from Moulmein on 27th January 1943 (6 months transit). Army records office forwarded this "card" to wife in an "Ambulance" envelope.

Details of crash :-	
Location :-	Slievaglass, Cloghane, Mount Brandon, Dingle Pen'la, Co. Kerry, Eire.
Aircraft :-	British Overseas Passenger "Sunderland Flying Boat" (Short S25).
Complement :-	18 passengers & 7 crew. Eleven died.
Journey :-	Scheduled flight; departed Lisbon 2215 hrs on 27/7/43 for Foynes, Eire.
Crashed :-	on 28/7/43 at 0450 hrs.

Document 4

Document 5

And finally, item 5 showing *how the mail did not arrive* for many of us during the first year of our captivity. This item is a typical example. I was in Almadnaga, India, when it was posted (November 1941) and in 'limbo' by the time it reached there.

What with that and the fact that the only mail to reach the Battalion while in Burma was burnt in front of us (see Chapter 26), it is not surprising perhaps that my only delivery from home came after my release.

APPENDIX VI

STATISTICS (GENERAL AND RAILWAY), HEALTH

CHRONOLOGY OF RELATED EVENTS AND STATISTICS

mid 1930s   Japanese already had further invasion and expansion plans in mind to develop a 'Greater Far-East Asia Co-Prosperity Sphere'. Plans for a Burma–Siam railway link being formulated.

1937   Bloody wars in Manchuria followed by the 'Rape of Nanking'. 200,000 massacred.

3 Sept 1939   Outbreak of WW2. Singapore garrison comprised of 20,000 men. Five 15-inch naval guns deployed against invasion by sea.

Jan 1940   *(author conscripted into Royal Corps of Signals)*

4 Jun   Dunkirk evacuation completed. Vichy-French in Indochina sign agreement with Japan which allows them to land and assemble there to launch their conquests.

18 Aug   Highest number of German planes shot down in the 'Battle of Britain'.

Sept   *(author in Sierra Leone attached to Royal Marines and with British Army and Free-French commandos training for an attack on the Vichy-French in Dakar, Senegal.)*

Feb 1941   *(Back home. Married in March then promoted and assigned to 18 Div Signals in June)*

13 Apr   Russo–Japan Neutrality Act signed (not ended until April 1945).

autumn & winter   *(author with 18 Div and put on US troop transports* Mount Vernon *and* West Point *off Newfoundland and then, en route to the Middle East via Trinidad and Cape Town. From Cape Town diverted to Bombay first, and ultimately, to Singapore by 1942.)*

7 Dec   Attack on Pearl Harbor.

10 Dec   Japanese invade N. Malaya, bomb Singapore and Hong Kong and, sink the battleship *Prince of Wales* and cruiser *Repulse* during a sustained aerial torpedo and bombing attack off Kuantan, E. Malaya. No RAF air support given!

16 Dec 1941   Kualar Lumpur abandoned. Allied forces withdraw to defence lines in Johore.

to Jan 1942 (early)	Japanese 5th, 18th and Imperial Guard Divisions continue their advance by means of 'by-passing and infiltration' jungle tactics. By then about 50,000 troops opposing on each side. Allied forces mainly of British, Australian and Indian origin. RAF already depleted, 16 Hurricanes and little else is gradually being withdrawn to operate from Sumatra, the Palembang oilfield being the main target for conquest in the Japanese campaign. Naval Base and docks abandoned.
by mid Jan	More Allied reinforcements arriving under-trained and with loss of much of their heavy equipment due to bombing en route and while unloading at the docks and, moreover, despite General Wavell's warning to Churchill that he considered Singapore to be indefensible.
end of Jan	Floating dock off N. Singapore scuttled. Crated Hurricanes still arriving (another 16, of which few serviceable) and despite the total abandonment of the Seletar 'drome and Air Base. RAF ground and admin staff already being evacuated.
1 Feb	Causeway though mined remains little damaged.
Early Feb	Japanese 'pattern bombing' stepped up to virtually unopposed flights of 27, 54 – and once – 81 planes in the air at the same time. Massive civilian casualties.
7 Feb onwards	Imperial Guard lands to north-east of Pulau Ubin overlooking Seletar. Remainder of Japanese invasion forces cross the Johore Strait on the 8th.

(author sent with a demolition party to destroy papers and equipment in the buildings of Sembawang aerodrome HQ as the British 18 Div starts a withdrawal to the final 'city' defence line enclosing Bikit Timah, McRitchie reservoir, the city and Keppell Harbour)

During the intensified bombing and the hand-to-hand fighting that ensued, more non-committed 'specialist' forces, civilians and nursing staff were slowly being evacuated. Thousands who set out at night from Keppell were on the 42 of the 46 larger vessels that were destroyed either by bombing or by the Japanese navy between Singapore and the Java Strait. About 100 more smaller vessels – many under sail – were also got out before the city fell, in authorised and mixed groups similar to the above, which included nearly all the remaining RAF personnel such as the AMES (radar group) that left on the *Tien Kuang*.

15 Feb (7.50 p.m.)	Singapore surrendered at the final defence line, by which time General Percival had been in command of 56,000 British and Australian and, 60,000 Indian troops, some of which had been earlier either overrun in Malaya, evacuated or posted to Java.

438

(Immediate aftermath)	*(author's 'sampan party' of 13 and, just a few other groups on small vessels, managed to leave before the Japanese came in to occupy the city on the 16th)*

About 20,000 Chinese were soon being shot or beheaded and many of their wives – carrying their children – waded into the sea to commit suicide. The Allied prisoners were marched out to Changi gaol and, later, assembled on the Selerang barracks square for two days during their protest against signing a 'no escape' pact. Meanwhile, about one third of the troops of Indian origin had defected to fight for the 'Co-Prosperity' cause.

Altogether about 7,000 evacuees, escapers – and a few deserters – were either directed, or chanced their way, onto the 'Organisation' escape route set up by Colonel Warren's group, and of those, about 2,000 had to be abandoned at Padang, W. Sumatra when the Japanese overran the area on 16 March.

(the author's party and just a few others arrived in Padang only two days before the Dutch surrendered to find that the last evacuation boat – the Chilka *– had already left and had then been torpedoed by the Japanese submarine 'I'2, on 10 March)*

Of those evacuated from Padang earlier – some 5,000 – 2,000 were troops and the rest were mainly the wives, children and nurses who had been attacked and had survived the mayhem while trying to get down to Java and subsequently declared fit enough to travel on from Padang to India.

16 Mar 1942	*(at this point PART II of* The Tattered Remnants *takes over, as the author and a very few others attempted escapes on a variety of small sailing vessels)*

In order to complete this assemblage of events and statistics the following has been compiled to show as much as is known by the author about the Japanese deployments of their various groups of POWs. Of those Allied POWs deployed in Sumatra, most worked on the 'Pekanbaroe' railway extension and included in their numbers the British and Australians left in Padang after the British Sumatra Battalion moved out in May 1942. Full details of losses due to torpedo attacks are shown in Appendix IV (Vessels).

Sumatra	Native labourers – mostly press-ganged youths – slave-driven to the point of death then abandoned unfed without shelter.

	Many were then buried alive.	100,000
	Known survivors	5,000
	Allied POWs (mostly Dutch) deployed	5,000
	deaths	700
Java	Dutch – apart from those who came up to Sumatra and Burma railways.	(unknown)
	British/Australian Commonwealth garrison (and later supplemented by wounded	8,000
	and survivors from the cruisers *Houston* (US), *Perth* (Aust)	(unknown)
	Dutch/Australian/Americans sent to join 'A Force' on the Burma–Siam railway	6,500
Malay Peninsula	ERTs taken direct up to Saigon to work on the aerodrome, of which about 100 were detached for a time to work on the Hanoi aerodrome	1,000
Singapore	British/Australian – Changi complex – remained throughout as RTs (Resident Troops)	6,000

Deployments (Forces A – J) from Changi

May 1942	(A) Australian No 3 Group destined for the Burma section of the Burma–Siam railway. Used on 'drome work at Ye, Mergui and Tavoy en route – at Thanbyuzayat (Sep).	3,000
	Augmented to a total of nearly 10,000 by the addition of British, Sumatra Battalion from Padang via Mergui & Tavoy	500
	American, from those mentioned above captured in Java	200
	Dutch – 5,000 reduced by torpedo/bombing attacks – from Java	4,200
	Australian, also from Java (Williams Force)	2,000
Jul 1942	(B) British and Australian to Borneo	*1,496
Mar 1943	(E) British and Australian to Borneo	*1,000
Aug 1942	(C) The content of these (+) three forces would have been	+2,000
Apr 1943	(G) largely made up of British and Australian groups	+1,000
May 1943	(J) *taken to Japan* for work in mines and factories.	+ 900
	Quite independent of these, other groups of unknown content and numbers, were taken to Japan earlier and	

*of these 2,496 men *only 6 survived by escaping from a death march*

440

	then (in Sept 1944) the British and Australian survivors picked up by the Japanese after the sinking of the *Kachidoki Maru* and *Rakuyo Maru*	(unknown)
Mar 1943	(D) Half British and half Australian to Siam to work on the difficult cuttings, embankments and bridges.	5,800
Apr 1943	(F) So-called 'fit men' marched through the 'D' activities and ever onwards up to the Siam border at Nikki. Those who fell out were shot or battered to death. Those who arrived ran into a cholera epidemic. Of these 7,000 men, about 3,100 (44%) were dead by December.	7,000
May 1943	(H) Reinforcements – again British & Australian (relative strengths unknown), 3,000 (27%) dead by December.	3,000

With the 'Speedo' over and the railway completed groups of A, D, F and H began to disperse.

Oct 1943 to Dec	Most of the dead arising from the above had been counted by December, albeit the worst hit (D, F and H) were only able to estimate, their leaders having been too ill to maintain proper records at any time since leaving Changi, to which place thousands of their *dire sick* were returned eventually. Many never 'made it' during those dreadful train journeys or, indeed, most of those *critically ill* who were abandoned in the 'border' camps where the attrition was greatest. Those sent to the so-called hospital camps, although doing better, were rarely able to rejoin their groups or make their survival known.
Dec 1943 to May 1944	The British Sumatra Battalion survivors still in the 114 km 'border' camp go down to Kanchanaburi group of camps in January, where their dead are added to those hundreds from the Australian and Dutch who had preceded them, all of them directly attributable to the 'Speedo'. By May the fittest among them had already been either sent back to the jungle camps
Sep 1944 to war end	to do maintenance work or, sent off first to Saigon and then, on to Singapore bound for the mines and factories in Japan. (see Appendix IV – Vessels – Allied submarine attacks.) It was within those last-mentioned groups that statistics became even more blurred. The most horrific losses were once again among what the Japanese called *romushas*, i.e. the native labour – captured and conned alike – who over the whole period of their employment lost more than 100,000 of their estimated total of 200,000.

10 years later   By about 1955, after RAPWI, the Imperial War Graves Commission and the deponents at the War Crimes Tribunals had completed their input, the British records *indicated* that 52,000 POWs worked on the railway and that 18,000 (35%) died.

Perhaps remarkably, that matches a post-war estimate for the British Sumatra Battalion since their total deprivation commenced from day one of their captivity in 1942 as they arrived kitless on the east shores of Sumatra.

The railway itself: Between Thanbyuzayat (Burma) and Non Pladuk (Siam)   260 miles

One metre gauge track laid – taken from existing Burma and Malay networks. Japanese pre-planning envisaged construction would take   5 years

The actuality was that it started in June 1942 and was completed in October 1943   1½ years

So-named wooden 'Bridge over the River Kwai' was only serviceable for a few months from 1943 and it was replaced by 11 steel 'span' sections brought up from Java by the Japanese army – total length being about   300 yards

Planned to carry 3,000 tons of supplies daily, it only rarely succeeded in carrying more than 500 tons, largely due to bomb damage and the requirement to transport at night time.

The health of a survivor: My pension assessment, made nine years after the war, gives *some indication* of the residual effect on the health of an ex-Far East POW. However, it takes no account either of the many other untreated complaints that I suffered – scabies, ringworm, pleurisy, pellagra and ulcers – or of anaemia, which when diagnosed later was attributed to my three and a half years of untreated malaria attacks.

However, unlike at least two-thirds of our Battalion, I landed on East Sumatra fully clothed and with a few essential possessions. There should be little wonder therefore that so many of my peers stayed pensionable throughout lives which were both short and full of suffering.

Because of their exceptional deprivation compared with almost all other groups of men when captured, an unduly large proportion of them were assailed by strongyloidiasis

442

– an intestinal disease caused by the infestation of a parasitic threadworm. Without any footwear, soap, bandages or medicaments, they were vulnerable from the outset of their POW life.

Harry Adrian was one of the few of us who, though pensioned, reached old age (see Chapter 28). His widow Freda has been denied her portion of his pension *because he smoked!* So, once again, 'No cheer for you, lads, F—— you all!' etc.

MINISTRY OF PENSIONS

239 (ID)

Any reply should be addressed to
The Secretary, Ministry of Pensions,
and the following reference quoted:
5/14993

NORCROSS,
BLACKPOOL,
LANCS.

−6 JAN 1955 19

Dear Sir/Madam,

The report of your recent medical examination has been carefully considered and the degree of your disablement arising from *amoebiasis, ankylostomiasis, malaria, infective hepatitis, malnutrition & starvation and residual neurosis (anxiety) and hypercholesydema.*

has been assessed at _____ 6–14 _____ per cent. indeterminate duration.

Compensation for this degree of disablement takes the form of a weekly allowance for _____ four _____ weeks with a gratuity of £ 49 – 0 – 0, _____ payable at the end of that period. The award is subject to the conditions of payment which you will find set out in your Pension Order Book.

Rate of weekly allowance	Weekly addition for Wife & 1 Children	Total weekly rate	From	To
12/4	5/-	17/4	1/9/54	25/1/55
11/6	3/-	14/6	26/1/55	22/1/56

THE MINISTER HAS DECIDED THAT THE CIRCUMSTANCES OF YOUR CASE PERMIT A FINAL SETTLEMENT OF THE DEGREE OF YOUR DISABLEMENT DUE TO SERVICE AND ACCORDINGLY THE ASSESSMENT MADE IS A FINAL ONE.

You have a right of appeal to a Pensions Appeal Tribunal constituted under the Pensions Appeal Tribunals Acts, 1943 and 1949, and you should therefore read carefully form MPB 348 which is enclosed.

You will also find in MPB 348 a Notice of the Minister's decision in the form required by those Acts.

Yours faithfully,

E. G. T. Burgoyne. Esq.

for Secretary

443

INDEX AND GLOSSARY OF TERMS

Legend:

Am	American	Du	Dutch	Ja	Japanese
Au	Australian	SM	Sumatra Bn	lf	lingua franca
Br	British	Fr	French	Ma	Malay
Bu	Burman	Hi	Hindi	sl	slang
Ch	Chinese	In	Indian	Th	Thai

ABDA Au/Br/Du/Am		Defence plan
Achinese		fierce N. Sumatra tribe
Aeroplanes – main		Dakotas, Am
		Fortresses, Am
		Hurricanes, Br
		Liberators, Am
		Lockheed Lightning, Am
		various (Fleet Air Arm)
		Zeros & do. Ja
Apthorp, Dudley P		Capt (later, Major OBE) commander,
		Sumatra Bn
arbalest		mediaeval crossbow
arigato	Ja	thank you
atap	Ma	palm leaf thatch
baka-na	Ja	silly fool
benjo	Ja (sl?)	lavatory
beriberi (weakness)		vitamin deficiency
'Blue Danube'	lf	lily bulb/brinjal soup
bollocking	sl	verbal abuse
Bombayduck	In	bummalo fish recipe
brinjal		egg plant
Bukit Timah		final Singapore defence line
Bukit Timah's	Au, sl	diarrhoea
Bushido	Ja	feudal Samurai code
byoin	Ja	hospital
byoki	Ja	sick, vomiting
Camps		see chapter headings & maps
changkul		digging tool
chaung	Bu	'flash' river bed
Cheese-eater	sl	Dutchman (derogatory)
Chosenese	Ja	Korean (derogatory)
clompers	sl	wooden clogs
comfort girls	sl	prostitutes for Ja army
dammy-dammy	Ja (sl)	bad/awful
also	Ja (sl)	no-goodka

dengue fever		acute tropical epidemic
doko	Ja	where?
doover	Au (sl)	rissole, savoury cake
dung-punch	Au (sl)	anal inspection aid
also	Br (sl)	shufti scope, ditto
enijiinia	Ja	engineer
ERTs	Br	English Resident Troops
FEPOW		Far East Prisoner of War

FORCES

Sumatra Bn personnel – Appendices I, II, III

POWs (Forces A to J) – Appendix VI, deployments

flaming arsehole	sl	Japanese national flag
furphy	Au (sl)	rumour
gharry	Hi	hire carriage
ghee		buffalo milk butter
go-aheads	Au (sl)	wooden clogs
godong (go-down)	Ma	an eastern warehouse
gohan	Ja	rice
gooli	In	castration knife
goula Malacca	Ma	malacca-cane sweetener
G-string		loincloth
also 'Jap Happy'	sl	Japanese underpants
Graviou, Marcel	Fr	friend/internee, Saigon
Greater Asia	Ja	controlled paper
gunso	Ja	sergeant
Gurkhas		see ch. 35-36
hai	Ja	yes
han/hancho	Ja	commander of 100 men
hara-kiri	Ja	ceremonial suicide
hashi	Bu	bridge
Heguchi, Dr	Ja	alleged vet. for POWs
Hiro Hito		Japanese emperor/deity
also Showa Tenno		
imasu-ka	Ja	what are you doing?

INTERPRETERS   for Br Sumatra Battn.

Fort-de-Kok, Sumatra – a German

Medan, Sumatra/Burma – Menheer Hess (Du)

18 km to 114 km Burma – Drower, capt. W. (Br)

Kanchanaburi, Siam – a Dutchman

jamban	Ma	thunderbox/commode

Japanese (numbering)

rei	zero	*ichi*	one	*ni (nee)*	two
san	three	*shi (shee)*	four	*goa*	five
roku	six	*shichi*	seven	*hachi*	eight
kyu (kew)	nine	*ju*	ten	*ju-ichi*	11
				ju-ni	12 etc

joss	Ch	good luck

K (rations)		emergency food
kamikaze	Ja	(Divine Wind) 'suiciders'
kampong	Ma	cleared land/settlement
kara/kurrah	Ja	come here/desist
Karens	Bu	hill tribe loyal to Br WWII
kashira hidari	Ja	salute to the left
kashira migi	Ja	salute to the right
Kempei tai	Ja	military police
kiotski	Ja	come to attention
kolek (dugout)		native, 'outrigged'
komodo dragon	Ma	ferocious monitor lizard
krait	Bu/In	small deadly snake
kukri		Gurkhas' knife/shortsword
kumi/kumicho	Ja	work-squad/commander of,
kunero	Ja	explicit expletive
Kurisamusu	Ja	Christmas
kwai	Bu/Th	river
kwali	? Ch	very large cooking wok
laigi (leggy)	Ma (sl)	extras/second helping
lathi	Hi	heavy stick
MacArthur, Douglas, Am Gen. Supreme Commander Allied Forces		
		at Ja surrender in Tokyo Bay
meshi	Ja	food/drink
meshu	Ja	rain
Mountbatten (admiral) Lord Louis, Supreme Commander Commonwealth Forces		
nai	Ja	no
nani	Ja	no
nanji desuka	Ja	what time is it?
nasi goreng	Ma	rice-based recipe
NAVAL and other, VESSELS – see Appendix IV		
Sumatra Battalion, personnel on, ditto		
'Organisation', the		alias for escape route
palm cabbage		edible palm tree bud
pellagra		vit. def. disease (often fatal)
Percival, Gen Arthur, Commander Singapore		
pissaphone	sl	urinal (sketch Ch 23)
prahu	Ma	vessel (*Venture* Appendix IV)
Pekanbaroe Rlwy		see corresp, Appendix V
Pulau	Ma	island
rattan cane		basketwork/cladding
romushas	Ja	natives (derogatory)
sampan	Ch	'three planks' vessel
shintegar		candied sugar blocks
shoko	Ja	officer/squad leader
shoot through	Au (sl)	'like a Bondi tram'
		or, as a defector
short arm	sl	penis

shredded gascape	sl	seaweed soup
smoko/resto	lf	a short break, *yasume*
Speedo	Ja (sl)	tyrannical work on rlwy
strongaloides		liver infection via feet
sukoshi, beeoki	Ja	small/light sickness
sukoshi, yasume	Ja	short rest
suttee	In	self-immolation
takusan	Ja	plenty
Temps de Saigon	Fr	local newspaper
tenko	Ja	roll call/parade
Teruchi, Count	Ja	Supremo at Saigon HQ
Thomas, Sir Shenton		Governor of Singapore
tidak apa	Ma	so what?/another day!
Tojo	Ja	Prime Minister
tonkan		junk-like vessel
towgay/tungay		bean shoot
tunkah		soil carrier
two-up	Au	gambling game
tycho	Ja	commander
Varley, (Brig) A	Au	Commander 'A Force' Bu
verlikker	Du	crawler/quisling
Warren, (Col) Alan, Ferguson CBE, DSO Royal Marines		instigator of the Organisation escape route
Wavell, (Gen) Sir Archibald		Supreme Commander ABDA 1941/1942
Yamashita, Tomayuki	Ja	Commander in Malaya
Yoshimitso, Lt	Ja	engineer/designer of Burma–Siam Railway